Some people have a unique ability to bring out the worst in people. E. Stanley Jones had a unique ability to bring out the best in people from anywhere in the world. There are some books that have the power to change your mind. E. Stanley Jones wrote books that have the power to change your life. In gripping fashion, Bob Tuttle has given us the back-story and behind-the-scenes unveilings that created one of the greatest followers of Jesus who ever lived. I could not stop reading.

- Leonard Sweet
Best-selling author (Bad Habits of Jesus), professor (Drew University, Tabor College, George Fox University), and founder of preachthestory.com

E. Stanley Jones was one of the most important figures in twentieth century Christianity. His writings and insights inspired millions (including me). Bob Tuttle's biography captures the fascinating story of his life, while allowing the reader to hear just how relevant Jones' message is for our time. This is a terrific book!

- Adam Hamilton
Senior Pastor, United Methodist Church of the Resurrection Leawood, Kansas

Along the way, through God's providence, a subject and an author come together as a perfect match. E. Stanley Jones was and is one of God's great gifts to the world. We are only now beginning to grasp how significant his witness was and is – deeply Christ-centered and yet profoundly open to the world; I love his words, "anchored and free." Bob Tuttle is an evangelist and scholar of the highest order. His attention to and affection for Brother Stanley, and retrieval of his legacy for us is also an extraordinarily significant witness, and a gift at precisely the right moment for the people.

- Ken Carter
President, Council of Bishops, United Methodist Church and Resident Bishop Florida Conference

To appreciate the transforming power of God, we need to know the whole story of the person including their family of origin, their spiritual journey, their marriage, their mission and the fruit of their ministry. No other book about E. Stanley Jones has these unique qualities. This book will inspire, motivate and empower you with a deeper understanding of Jesus, a more passionate love for God, and a greater surrender to the power of the Holy Spirit. It is an investment of time and money that will result in your spiritual growth and a deeper engagement in God's mission to the world. Please do not miss it.

- Tom Albin
Director of Spiritual Formation for The Upper Room
and Executive Director of the United Christian Ashrams International

The life and ministry of E. Stanley Jones is one that can shine much needed light on us today. His example and insights are timeless. Bob Tuttle brings them to life in this excellent biography.

- Dr. Steve Harper
Retired Seminary Professor

Bob Tuttle knew E. Stanley Jones personally, as a mentor and a friend. How many still alive could write a biography of Jones from such an intimate perspective. Tuttle is one of the last who could. His latest work, presents Jones as a world-changer. This book radically applies Jones's life and legacy, as a life and legacy that must not be forgotten. What a book for our times!

- Dr. Robert (Bob) Stamps
Retired Professor and past Dean of the Chapel
Asbury Theological Seminary

IN
OUR
TIME

The Life and Ministry of
E. STANLEY JONES

ROBERT G. TUTTLE, JR.

IN OUR TIME: THE LIFE AND MINISTRY OF E. STANLEY JONES
By Robert G. Tuttle, Jr.

Copyright © 2019 by The E. Stanley Jones Foundation

Published by
The E. Stanley Jones Foundation
Email: anne@estanleyjonesfoundation.com
Website: www.estanleyjonesfoundation.com

Cover and Interior Design: Shivraj K. Mahendra
www.shivrajmahendra.com

ISBN: 978-1793813237

MANUFACTURED IN THE USA

DEDICATION

To the Rev. Donald and Pat Saylor
whose lifetimes of faithfulness continue to illumine
the path for others to find and experience
new life in Christ Jesus.

And

To The Foundation for Evangelism,
in appreciation for their endowed E. Stanley Jones Chairs of Evangelism strategically placed in seminaries around the world. These chairs
have extended the powerful legacy of Brother Stanley
for generations to come.

CONTENTS

Foreword

by Anne Mathews-Younes

Bob Tuttle and I met at a Christian Ashram in Minnesota in 2015 where I had the privilege of hearing his riveting presentation of his many experiences with my grandfather, E. Stanley Jones and the transforming impact of this relationship on Bob's life. We talked about Bob writing a new biography of Jones. I was delighted that he considered that idea and believed that Bob would offer a fresh word about Jones and would brilliantly convey the substance of Jones' ministry in a contemporary manner to new audiences. He has done just that and more. The family of E. Stanley Jones was delighted to share with Bob dozens of pictures of Stanley, Mabel and their daughter, Eunice, photos that have never been previously seen publicly and which now grace this biography.

I so appreciate Dr. Tuttle's lively presentation of the life and ministry of E. Stanley Jones and importantly Bob has not left my grandmother (or mother for that matter) out of this picture for Mabel Lossing Jones was an exceptional person in her own right and never lived in her husband's shadow. The same goes for my mother, Eunice Jones Mathews, who was not defined by either her well-known father or her husband, a United Methodist Bishop. At her 90th birthday

IN OUR TIME

celebration she stated that she was free to be herself in the freedom that we all have in Jesus Christ. Bob Tuttle powerfully conveys the impact of that freedom in his outstanding biography of E. Stanley Jones.

The E. Stanley Jones Foundation, in cooperation with the Methodist Publishing House, is dedicated to reprinting all of Jones' 27 books as well as publishing new commentary on Jones, such as Dr. Tuttle's book, along with a compendium of Jones' sermons which have never been compiled and shared. The Foundation has a wealth of new material from E. Stanley Jones and Mabel Lossing Jones that deserves to be in the marketplace and available to readers who wish to discover life-changing insights from E. Stanley Jones.

I am grateful to everyone who is working with the E. Stanley Jones Foundation on these publishing efforts, especially to Bob Tuttle for this remarkable book and for Shivraj Mahendra, Jennifer Tyler, Veronica Henry and Nick Younes who each play critical roles in these endeavors.

ANNE MATHEWS-YOUNES, ED.D., D. MIN.
President, The E. Stanley Jones Foundation

E. Stanley Jones

E. Stanley Jones at his birthplace in Clarksville, Maryland

Introduction

Those who know the Old Testament book of Esther realize that Mordecai's comment to Esther (Esther 4:14), that she was born for a "time such as this," make that story forever relevant—eternal. Such it is with the life of E. Stanley Jones. Arguably the greatest missionary/evangelist of the last century, his passion, his humility, his total commitment to Jesus Christ and His Kingdom comprise a story that is forever relevant—eternal.

I feel about the life of Stanley Jones the way he felt about Mahatma Gandhi when writing his, *Mahatma Gandhi – An Interpretation*. "It is like trying to interpret Mount Everest. It is many-sided. It rises in simple grandeur, and yet there are subsidiary peaks, crevices, depths, plateaus, all contributing to the sum total of the character…"[1]

About sixteen months ago my Bishop here in Florida, Ken Carter, suggested that I write a biography of E. Stanley Jones. Since Stephen Graham's biography, *Ordinary Man, Extraordinary Mission* ('05) was so well researched and some of his prose is brilliant, I was hesitant. Doug Ruffle had also written a book through Discipleship Resources entitled, *The Missionary Mindset*, featuring Stanley Jones.

Then in the summer of 2015 I attended an Ashram at St. John's University in MN where I met Stanley's granddaughter, Anne Mathews-Younes, the President of the E. Stanley Jones Foundation that is extending the legacy of Stanley Jones worldwide. She also asked me to consider writing a new biography of Stanley Jones. Along with the previous request by Ken Carter, this gave me pause.

At that point I said, let me pray about it and began to read Graham's book again, carefully. It soon became apparent to me that although Dr. Graham's research is solid and I liked much of his prose, his handling of dates and events was frequently confusing for me. Furthermore, apart from one chapter early on he makes very little reference to Mabel or Eunice (Stanley's wife and daughter).

Then, when I read Ruffle's book, although I liked his thesis, I soon realized that his focus on mission tends to omit some of the other theological emphases that were so important to Stanley's life and ministry.

So, as I continued to read and pray it became apparent that a new biography of Stanley Jones was needed.

Furthermore, a Doctor of Ministry dissertation by Luke Pederson, "Preacher-as-Witness," made the point convincingly that Stanley communicated most effectively out of his own experience, simply describing what God had done in his life. Suddenly it occurred to me that a biographer as well would need to include some personal experience related to Brother Stanley in order to be true to the life and spirit of the man. Admittedly, others could do this far better than I but it seemed that God was calling me to take on the task.

As if to illustrate the point above, now for a personal word: I met Brother Stanley at an Ashram back in the summer of 1969. He would always insist that we address each other at his Ashrams as "Brother" or "Sister," then our first names only without titles (Brother Stanley must have received close to 20 honorary doctorates over a lifetime of ministry so it was difficult not to call him Dr. Jones, but he insisted). I had returned to the rural south from England with a Ph.D. in historical theology, wire rimmed glasses and hair over my ears. I had been struggling with the KKK in a small church for two years. They literally beat me with hands and fists. I despised them. I shall never forget that when I shared some of this with Brother Stanley he replied with a knowing smile, "Brother Bob, you had about half of that coming. You apparently went in with the answers before you under-stood the questions." In an instant I was healed! Suddenly the deep seated resentment was gone. Brother Stanley took me under his wing and for much of that summer nursed me back to health. He changed my life forever.

I OWE THE MAN

Furthermore, I was the first full time E. Stanley Jones Professor of Evangelism beginning back in 1985 (at Garrett-Evangelical Theologi-cal Seminary). I then taught at Asbury's E. Stanley Jones School of World Mission and Evangelism for 5 years before moving to Florida to assist in opening the Asbury's Dunam Campus in 2000 where I was Professor of World Christianity (now Emeritus). By that time I had read all of Stanley's books, several of them more than once. How many times had I preached thinking that I was saying something for first time only to realize that Stanley Jones had said it before?

I KNEW THE MAN

I continued, however, to pray and struggle with just how to write this book. I knew that if the reader is to meet the mind and spirit of Brother Stanley it would be important to describe his life in sequence. That would be the only way to give the reader a feel for just how Stanley's life was *in process* throughout the whole of his ministry.

At the age of 83 Stanley speaks of being a Christian in the mak-ing, not yet made. Stanley struggled with his own urges. He speaks quite candidly about the self-urge, the sex-urge and the herd-urge. He once confessed to me his continuing struggle along these lines well into his eighties. I nearly fainted. He insisted that any process (or progress) must continue or fade. For Stanley people who had "arrived" — who thought they "were always right were always wrong by their very attitude of being always right. If there is no amendment, there is no attainment."[2]

It then occurred to me that I personally expect to be "converted" about once a week. Oh, I'm not going back to the Cross and getting saved all over again; I'm simply having a fresh encounter with the Spirit of the Living God on a weekly basis. Suddenly, I knew where I got that!

Stanley's own spiritual autobiography, *A Song of Ascents* (Hereafter, *Song*), is a description of becoming. He believed that heaven itself is a place of growth. To be in God's will is not a struggle but a song, a song of ascents. Stanley would sing chorus after chorus of that song for the whole of his life.

Furthermore, for Stanley to sing was to sing about something and for Stanley that something was always Someone — Jesus Christ! He apologized for some things Christian because they were only partly Christian and some terribly western in their perspective. On occasion he would apologize for the Church because she was frequently disappointing him. When it came to Jesus, however, *there were no apologies.*

As a seminary professor I swallow deeply as I say to you that Stanley rarely had anything good to say about seminary professors — the teachers of the law. He describes one seminary professor who had dismissed Jesus cavalierly. Stanley thought to himself, "Did you know this Jesus by surrender and faith and obedience? If you had, you would not then dismiss him cavalierly, but fall at his feet."[3]

I personally have always been humbled by Jesus' reaction to the "seminary professors" of his day — the scribes and Pharisees. (Dante's level seven of hell was perhaps reserved for such as these). They were always picking, always plotting, always doubting. Stanley was always praying, always praising, always believing.

I HONOR THE MAN

When preparing the proposal for our publisher I was asked to address two important questions, is it true and will it help? Let me give you some of my response.

Is it true that this book can renew your spirit and better prepare you for all of life and its trials? Absolutely! I've had my own life renewed day in and day out simply by doing the research and writing about Stanley Jones. In addition, I must say that not only is the story of Jones' life depicted here true to the facts — and the sources abound — Stanley Jones' life itself carried with it the ring of truth. The same is true for his wife, Mabel, and daughter Eunice.

Then, will it help? My prayer is that this book will help laypeople, pastors, and group leaders understand that their power base is not in themselves but in God. Read through from Genesis to Revelation; two of the greatest sins in the Bible are self-reliance and oppressing the poor. Some of my brightest students burned out after only two to five years attempting to do ministry out of their own steam, without God and without the necessary community to sustain them. As for oppressing the poor, Stanley's understanding of the Kingdom of God as present and not yet is important for our own personal expectations and development of a ministry that embraces the balance between theory and praxis — harnessing the power of the Holy Spirit to feed the hungry, clothe the naked, visit the sick and imprisoned. For Stanley that is what the oldest Christian creed — "Jesus is Lord" — is all about.

Furthermore, it is my prayer that reading about the life of Stanley Jones will help the Church understand her connection with a worldwide community of believers. That was part of his genius.

It will also help peoples of different religions and cultures find new hope for coming to a kind of understanding that could well prevent the kind of tensions that carry us all to the brink of violence and frustration.

17

It will help Christians bear witness to their faith among these same peoples of different religions and cultures.

All this is to say that it is my prayer that a better understanding of Stanley's life will help Christians of all denominations understand and communicate the Gospel of Jesus Christ more winsomely, more intelligently and more effectively.

May I say to you that most people, even in the U.S., have never really heard an intelligent/believable presentation of the Gospel. Most of my neighbors have no Christian memory. Except for the occasional wedding or funeral, they have not set foot in a church for over 30 years. Statistics show that sixty percent of Americans cannot name the four Gospels. I'm not sure I could before my senior year at Duke University and I'm the son of a Godly gifted minister. Oh, I was not an atheist. It would never have occurred to me not to believe in God. I simply had not put much thought into it one way or the other. I'm embarrassed to say that I was simply a harmless "Joe College" and a lot of good preaching had gone right by me.

Furthermore, many Christians, who think of themselves as "evangelicals," are confused. The political scene has managed to associate our understanding of personal faith in Jesus Christ with everything from gun control to the kinds of injustices that embarrass us to tears. Stanley Jones understood evangelicals as those captured by the mind and heart of Jesus Christ. I tell my students, "I don't care how you vote as long as you vote the mind of Jesus Christ."

If Christians worldwide are to envision a common voice, especially abroad, Stanley's understanding of Church Union (as a Federation) could be critical. In the same breath, Stanley also challenges the Church universal to understand our relationship with the other religions of the world, especially our Muslim friends. Stanley's Round Table Conference is an ideal setting. We will learn a good bit about that as we read.

Along these same lines we can learn so much from Gandhi's advice to Stanley. In one of their earliest encounters Gandhi challenged

Stanley in four areas: 1. Live more like Jesus; 2. Emphasize love, making love the driving force of your life; 3. Study other non-Christian religions more sympathetically to find the good in them; 4. But never ever adulterate or attempt to tone down your own religion. Those four principles from Gandhi became Truth for Stanley Jones and for me as well.

It also occurs to me that Christians for the first 40 years of the last century were divided between modernists and fundamentalists—it was the Scopes Trial mentality with Clarence Darrow on one side and William Jennings Bryant on the other. There was little in between. I was taught in seminary that the two extremes finally began to communicate when the works of Karl Barth, in particular his *Dogmatics*, were translated into English during the early 1940s by my former colleague and friend, Geoffrey Bromiley. While that may be true to an extent, there is an earlier story. Stanley Jones was engaging the two extremes in 1925 with his first book, *The Christ of the Indian Road*. There he demonstrated how understanding the Christian faith from another perspective can enrich our own understanding. I've always told my students that if you want to be convinced of the truths of Christianity, learn about other religions. Stanley's first book sold over a million copies and launched him on to the international stage where he would play to countless thousands over the next 48 years.

Jones exhibited incredible theological balance. Over 50 years in India will do that for you. This first book (and 28 others to follow) makes it abundantly clear that evangelism is not some kind of self-righteous harangue, but simply tells the story of Jesus Christ as the Word become flesh, showing a troubled world who God really is. If God is like Jesus, Stanley wanted to fall at his feet. If God is not like Jesus Stanley would look for a more honorable trade.

Many years ago my reading of Stanley's *The Christ at the Roundtable* gave me life-changing perspective (physically, emotionally and spiritually). Please notice in Chapter 5, Stanley's understanding of the moral universe—the fact that God has so created the universe that we can function effectively and be at peace with ourselves and others only as we obey the ordained principles of a moral universe. If we jump off a high building, we do not break the law of gravity; it breaks us. That made sense. If sin is a good thing Stanley believed that it would be stated as such on every page of the Bible. The reason it is not is that sin is the great deceiver. It is always promising what it can never produce.

Stanley insisted that no one can force Christianity upon people. Forced goodness is not goodness. He waited patiently for self-inflicted suffering, brought on by our own self-will, to drive us to the Suffering of Jesus Christ for relief and release. His *Song* encourages others to live according to the Way, so they can be set free from the kinds of bondage that entangles them. Stanley was fond of saying that Christians know and understand the moral law of the universe. They know better than to bark their shins on a system of things that if properly understood could save from self-inflicted pain and change their lives forever.

In the midst of doing this research I realized that I'm not into Christianity for the pain. I tell my non-Christian friends that if they have something doing it better than Jesus to let me in on their secret. They may have a convert. I never insist that I'm right and the rest of the world is wrong. I simply believe that I'm right but that does not make me right. Truth has never changed to accommodate what I believe truth to be. Truth is truth regardless of what I think it is. Brother Stanley helped me realize years ago that I'm into Jesus Christ for one reason and one reason alone. Faith in him is the only way I know how to access the power of the Holy Spirit that enables me to overcome the things of this world that would attempt to swallow me whole.

For over 60 years Stanley Jones and his wife Mabel had contacts with significant men and women of history. To mention just a few: in India he visited and corresponded regularly with Gandhi (as did Mabel), Nehru and the Indian poet, Tagore. In the U.S. he had access to the oval office during the administrations of FDR, Truman, Eisenhower and Nixon. In China Stanley Jones visited with Generalissimo and Madame Chiang Kai Shek on any number of occasions. In Japan he had audiences with Emperor Hirohito and his staff for over a span of 20 years and worked with the outstanding Christian spokesman, Kagawa. Even today, all of this still has relevance in the rapidly expanding cultures of India, China, and Japan.

Stanley communicated with thousands of students worldwide. He preached in churches and conducted missions frequently speaking three and four times a day for six, seven days a week. How can we account for such tireless energy? His books have influenced worldwide leaders including Martin Luther King Jr., who told his daughter, Eunice and her husband, Bishop James Mathews, that Stanley's book on Gandhi (*Gandhi: Portrayal of a Friend*) gave him his first vision for non-violent, non-cooperation during the Civil Rights Movement. The book is open and underlined in a case in the Martin Luther King Jr. Library.

A copy of E. Stanley Jones' book
on Mahatma Gandhi as seen in the Martin Luther King
Library. The book contains a handwritten note by King that says, "This is it!
This is the way to achieve freedom for the Negro in America."

IN OUR TIME

In 1964, Bishop James K. and Eunice Mathews met with Dr. Martin Luther King, Jr., during a reception held at Boston University in Dr. King's honor. While on the receiving line, Mrs. Mathews was identified as the daughter of Dr. E. Stanley Jones, a well-known missionary to India and long-time friend of Mahatma Gandhi. Dr. Jones had written a book entitled, "Gandhi, Portrayal of a Friend," which Dr. King had read.

He informed Bishop and Mrs. Mathews that it was Dr. Jones' book which triggered his decision to use Gandhian non-violent methods in the struggle for human rights in the United States.

I ADMIRE THE MAN

The unique features of this biography are in the telling of E. Stanley Jones' life in such a way as to see how Brother Stanley himself overcame obstacles and then embraced a vision for global impact that would change the hearts and lives of people forever.

Stanley Jones was a missionary/evangelist in that he preached the Gospel of Jesus Christ on every major continent. He demonstrated ways of communicating with people of other religions in such a way as to bring them to the place where they could fully appreciate the relevance of the Christian faith for their own lives. He was a pacifist

speaking out for peace around the world. He was an ecumenist arguing for the common voice of Christians throughout the world. He
was a staunch opponent of segregation (he would not attend meetings unless all races were welcomed and appreciated).

All that is to say that Stanley Jones is far more than a talking head.
His ministry touches the body, mind and spirit. It reached both the
individual and the Church. It spoke to nations both socially and politically. He and Mabel founded schools, Ashrams, Round Table Conferences and even the only Christian psychiatric hospital in India at
the time, and all are still going strong today. His granddaughter, Anne
Mathews-Younes (President of the E. Stanley Jones Foundation) is
recently back from India saying that Stanley Jones is still a household
name among countless Christians and non-Christians alike.

Recently, I was in a small-town restaurant in the mountains
of North Carolina heading for Lake Junaluska. I needed directions
and asked a distinguished looking gentleman just leaving the restaurant if he could help me. He said of course. When I asked about
his accent he said that he was born in India. When I told him that I
was recently in India finishing up research for a biography of a man
named E. Stanley Jones he took my arm and explained through tears
that E. Stanley Jones had led him and his entire family to Jesus Christ
while they were attending an Ashram in Sat Tal, India when he was
a child. We now correspond regularly.

I have already had various study groups ask when the book will
be published. These groups meet in local churches and in homes as
well. I believe that Stanley was such an eclectic that this book will
also attract the attention of special interest groups such as Christian
Ashrams (worldwide) and the Emmaus Walk.

If curious about contemporary issues ask Stanley Jones if black
lives matter. Ask Stanley about gun control. Ask Stanley about issues relevant to immigration. Ask Stanley about how to live a Christian life in a Hindu or Muslim community. Ask Stanley about the
devastation of war and how to prevent it (it is said that he
singlehandedly nearly prevented the bombing of Pearl Harbor). Ask

Stanley if his principles of inclusion can be useful in assisting the Church regarding the issues confronting gays and lesbians. Ask Stanley about communicating effectively with high school and college students. Ask Stanley about the importance of time apart as embraced by the Worldwide Christian Ashram Movement.

Stanley's absolute confidence in God led some to accuse him of being superficial, naïve, self-righteous and cocksure. May I say, there is not a whisper of any of that in Stanley Jones. Stanley lived all his life under opposition. He had a way of singing, frequently not on account of but in spite of...[4]

In his own Introduction to his *A Song of Ascents* Stanley writes that biography is far more than events. Stanley would never approve of that. To be faithful to Stanley, his life is not simply about events; it is about the Event. He would never let me forget that nor forgive me if I should omit his one all consuming passion—total surrender to Jesus Christ and the gift of his Spirit. Jesus was God become flesh. Again, if God is like Jesus, Stanley loved God. If God is not like Jesus, then Stanley would just as soon look elsewhere for the answers to life's greatest needs.[5]

So, the value of a biography "contributing to the body of mission and holiness literature" (and one might add to the body of evangelistic literature) is to know the mind of Jesus and to have proven him over time. Stanley Jones had 89 years to prove him throughout his own life and experience.

Furthermore, Stanley's emphases have stood the test of time and are perhaps more relevant now than they were in his own day. Stanley Jones was a man of the Word but his passion was centered in Jesus Christ as the Word become flesh.

Stanley was a man of boundless hope. His son-in-law, Bishop James Mathews, summarizes Stanley's passions and the eventual results of his vision with the following:

• Stanley left India, not with Christianity relevant only to "outcastes" but as relevant to all the castes, including leaders and intellectuals.

- Stanley left the Christian movement in India, not scattered among its doctrines and denominations but with Jesus Christ as the core central issue.

- Stanley left the Ashram movement, not on the edges of remote outposts, but international and universal.

- Stanley left evangelism, not simply appealing to the emotions but as the central issue of life of all churches — respectable and necessary.

- Stanley left evangelism not largely emotional, but as appealing to the total person — body, mind and spirit.

- Stanley left evangelism personal and social — a total way of life — not just personal.

- Stanley left Christianity not as alien to human nature but as supernaturally natural, and sin as the unnatural and alien.

- Stanley left the Kingdom of God not simply inward and mystical/futuristic, but the one issue supplanting all alternative totalitarianisms (including Communism, Fascism/Nazism and humanism, etc.) — the Kingdom of God on earth now was the issue.

- Stanley left the nonviolent/noncooperation movement not as Indian or simply the genius of Mahatma Gandhi, but as the method of finding freedom for Black Americans throughout the U.S.

- Stanley left church union, not as an alternative between church councils and mergers but placed between them his concept of federal union as a practical plan for national (if not worldwide) union NOW.

- Stanley left his concept of the Round Table not simply as a place for idle chatter, or even plotting future strategy, but as a way of allowing different perspectives to find common ground — to know and appreciate each other.[6]

I AM IN AWE OF THE MAN

In brief, *I love the man* and want to write about his ever-growing relationship with Jesus Christ because one cannot write a biography of E. Stanley Jones (or, I believe, read about such a man) without being utterly changed! I challenge you to test that thesis. May I bear witness to being utterly changed as a result of this encounter with a lifelong mentor — his sermons, his writings, his persona? Read on and be encouraged. Expect to be transformed.

So, now that I've passed my prime (and am cramming for finals), humbled by time and the haunting memories of good years gone by, dare I embrace again the monumental task of yet another biography. I wrote a biography of John Wesley many years ago and still think of it as one of my best. Yet, E. Stanley Jones! I mean he led my own dear mother to Jesus Christ after she had been a pastor's wife for many years. Can I do this? Turn the pages and see.

We begin with the Prologue in the middle of Stanley's ministry. Stanley's longtime friend and mentor, Mahatma Gandhi, was tragically assassinated in the prime of Stanley's life. Let's begin there to give you a feel for the spirit and voice of the biography as a whole.

Then in the chapters that follow we will move through the lives of Stanley Jones and his wife, Mabel, in sequence. This is to give you a sense for how Brother Stanley's and his wife Mabel's ministries evolved over the years culminating in lifelong stories of what it means to be unashamedly followers of Jesus Christ.

CHAPTER ONE

GANDHI DIED TODAY

The Need for Closure

It might seem strange to begin a biography of E. Stanley Jones with the assassination of Mahatma Gandhi. Let me explain my reasoning. This tragic event marked Stanley for the rest of his life.

Stanley was a missionary/evangelist. His entire ministry had been (and would continue to be) consumed with countless attempts to win India (and the West) to Jesus Christ. Stanley's time with Gandhi was just one of those attempts. The correspondence between these two men alone represents Stanley at his core in his attempts to reach Gandhi for Christ. In light of the fact that Gandhi never became a Christian makes his assassination (for Stanley) all the more significant and Stanley's need for closure at the end of an era. These letters reveal the minds and hearts of both men. Let me share just one from Brother Stanley and then Gandhi's response:

Monghyr, Jan. 9, 1926

Mahatma Gandhi

Dear Mahatmaji,

I desire greatly to come to your Ashram and spend at least six months. You know of my respect and affection for you. I have tried to interpret you and your message to the Western world and have been somewhat responsible for the interest that the West has in you and what you are doing. I therefore write what I wanted to talk with you about. It is unsatisfactory I know to put on paper what one would like to say face to face in the intimacies of personal communion. We of the West have been interested in you particularly because we have seen you exemplify certain things that lie at the heart of the Gospel. I find it difficult for me to hold that view now. As I have studied your writing and watched your work, especially in these last few years, I have come to the conclusion that you really have missed the heart of the Gospel. I think the ideas that underlie the Sermon on the Mount have gripped you and have, in a great measure, molded you, but the Gospel lies in His Person. He himself is the good news.

Now, if the principles of Jesus, especially those underlying the Sermon on the Mount, were all or even the greater part of Christianity I would find it difficult to be as devoted to it as I find myself at present. You suggested in Calcutta that you did not turn to the Sermon on the Mount for consolation; nor do I. I turn to the Person. He embodies the Sermon on the Mount but He is much more. In Him I find principles looking out at me from sad eyes touching me with strong hands and loving me with entire self-giving. But if the principles had not come to me clothed in flesh and blood they would leave me cold. Only life can lift life.

Now, Mahatmaji, I may be wrong; I hope I am. But I cannot help feeling that it is just here that you are weakest in your grasp. You have caught the principles but missed the Person. Again I say I hope I am wrong. I hope to hear from you saying that it is not so. But, if I am right, may I offer a suggestion? You are taking this year off to be more or less at the Ashram. I personally feel it to be providential. God has great things yet for you to do, and in this year it may be that you go over the ground again, that you penetrate through the principles to the Person, that you then come back to us and tell us what you have found.

I say these thing to you not in the spirit of a mere Christian propagandist, but the fact is that we need you. We who are Christians need you. We need the interpretation and illustration that we feel you could give if you grasp this radiant Person of Jesus. The West needs you. As India seems at the present hesitant in following your lead, appreciation of you is growing in the West. But I am frank to say to you that it is almost entirely because they have seen in you a phase of Christianity largely neglected in our Western Christianity. Their disappointment will come, as I am frank to say it has come to me, when they see that you have grasped a phase instead of an inward center.

You will forgive me, I am sure, for my open frankness. Your open frankness has been one the things I have loved and honored in you. "Like begets like," hence this letter. I trust you will treat it just as a private note of a friend to a friend.

With my warm greeting and assurances of my deep gratitude for you,

Stanley Jones.[1]

Gandhi wrote back on Jan. 18, 1926:

Friend,

I hasten to reply to your kind letter by return post. I appreciate the love underlying the letter and kind thought for my welfare. But my difficulty is of long standing. The matter has been presented to me before now by many other friends. I cannot grasp the position through the intellect. It is purely a matter of the heart. Saul became Paul not by an intellectual effort but by something touching his heart. I can only say that my heart is absolutely open. I have no axes to grind. I want to find truth — to see God face to face. But there I stop —

It will be a mistake to suppose that my people — the masses — have missed my message. But if they have I should be unconcerned. If the whole world accepted my message that would be no proof of its truth if it is intrinsically untrue. I early understood the truth that peace and light came from within and were independent of the world's verdict.

Do please come whenever you get the time.

Yours sincerely,

M.K. Gandhi

M.K. Gandhi, 18.1.26

Mahatma Gandhi
(Mohandas Karamchand Gandhi)

In subsequent chapters we will observe Stanley attending Gandhi's ashram and spending hours with the man over weeks of exposure.

Mahatma Gandhi, died virtually in the middle of Stanley Jones' life and ministry. Stanley (and Mabel) were friends with Gandhi. They admired each other. Stanley was within half an hour of meeting with Gandhi the evening he was assassinated. Stanley, wanting to attend Gandhi's prayer meeting, became distracted by the necessity of preparing to speak at an evening meeting of his own, then planning a mission and flying off to the south of India the following day.

This chapter will focus briefly on Mahatma Gandhi and on the assassin and then, as a way of introducing you to his mind and spirit, on Brother Stanley.

JANUARY 30, 1948

At the time of Indian independence, Aug. 15, 1947, the *Amrit Bazar Patrika* magazine in Calcutta published a cartoon entitled, "Great Expectations," featuring a child as an infant India casting a shadow, but the shadow the child is casting is that of Mahatma Gandhi.

Mahatma Gandhi, was assassinated at the Birla House (now Gandhi Smriti) in New Delhi on January 30, 1948. Gandhi was outside on the path leading from the steps where a prayer meeting was going to take place, surrounded by a part of his family and some followers, when Nathuram Godse, a Hindu nationalist and prominent member of Hindu Mahasabha, approached. At precisely 5:17 pm. Godse bowed before Gandhi. One of the girls flanking and supporting Gandhi (actually his granddaughters), said to Godse, "Brother, Bapu is already late" and tried to put him off, but he pushed her aside and shot Gandhi in the chest three times at point-blank range. Raghu Nayak, who worked as a gardener at the Birla House, was the first to chase Godse down and overpower him.

Gandhi died shortly after. It is said that as he was assassinated Gandhi invoked God saying, "Hare Ram" ("praise God").

Nathuram Godse, the assassin, an advocate of Hindu nationalism from Pune, Maharashtra, believed that Gandhi favored the political demands of India's Muslims during the partition of India between a Hindu/Sikh India and a Muslim Pakistan. He plotted the assassination with Narayan Apte and six others.

Godse believed that the pain and suffering of Hindus during the partition could have been avoided had the Indian government lodged strong protests against the treatment of Minorities—Hindus and Sikhs—by the majority Muslims in Pakistan. "Being under the thumb of Gandhi," however, they resorted to more feeble ways. He also felt that Gandhi had not protested against these atrocities being suffered in Pakistan and instead resorted to fasts. In his court deposition, Godse said, *"I thought to myself and foresaw I shall be totally ruined, and the only thing I could expect from the people would be nothing but hatred ... if I were to kill Gandhiji. But at the same time I felt that the Indian politics in the absence of Gandhiji would surely be proved practical, able to retaliate, and would be powerful with armed forces."*

After a trial that lasted for over eight months, Godse was sentenced to death on November 8, 1949. Although pleas for commutation were made by Gandhi's two sons, Manilal Gandhi and Ramdas Gandhi, they were turned down by India's prime minister Jawaharlal Nehru and Godse was hanged in the Ambala Jail on November 15, 1949.

E. Stanley Jones, had now been in India as a missionary/evangelist for forty-one years and since the end of WWII had been rotating between the U.S. and India, roughly every six months. He was 64 but claimed that his health was as good as when he was 24. In January, 1948, Stanley was in India working on a devotional book, *The Way to Power and Poise*. This was interrupted with the tragic assassination of Mahatma Gandhi, delaying the publication of that book until 1949.[2]

India had been longing for independence from British colonialism for well over 30 years. Stanley, after being in India for 12 years, had met Gandhi toward the end of 1919.

In 1948 Stanley's long time friend, Mahatma Gandhi, had just ended another extended fast. Gandhi's life had been threatened on five different occasions.[3] It was January 30.

Stanley's lifelong friend, Bishop J. Waskom Pickett, had visited Nehru and Gandhi on Wednesday, January 28, just two days prior, and for three quarters of an hour attempted to persuade Gandhi to move to safer lodging.

Gandhi replied, "Why should I be afraid to die. All my hopes for a better India are being destroyed [the Muslim Pakistani issues seemed to be running wild]. Perhaps Gandhi dead will be more respected than Gandhi alive."[4]

Just days before, Gandhi had spoken even more to the point: "If I am to die by the bullet of a madman, I must do so smiling. There must be no anger within me. God must be in my heart and on my lips. And you promise me one thing. Should such a thing happen, you are not to shed one tear." Stanley writes, "Here was supreme poise awaiting calmly for anything that might happen. He was never nobler than in this utterance."[5]

A heavy hearted Methodist Bishop Waskom Pickett then reported, "I failed completely!" [in his attempt to get Gandhi to move to safer lodgings].[6]

It was now Friday and Stanley himself, arriving from Agra at 4:20 pm., had just had an important series of meetings where the interest, attention and response the night before was especially gratifying. The large venue was amazingly almost full. Students were eager to talk over their problems (religious and political), not combative, but wistful, wanting light and encouragement. Stanley comments that the moral collapse in the lower brackets of Government is bad (he would complain to Nehru regarding such corruption on several occasions) but the integrity of the higher ups (where Stanley had most of his influence) was magnificent.

Stanley then comments that "I was in Delhi only 14 hours, and yet those 14 hours were the most tragic-packed and hope-inspiring I have ever experienced. I had asked a friend to arrange an interview with Mahatma Gandhi but I found on arrival that the only chance I had to see him would be to go to his daily prayer meeting. If I could get a taxi I could just make it, but owing to a supper address I was to give later, I decided against it." [Stanley comments that the taxi fare was too expensive].

"I came near witnessing a tragedy second only to the crucifixion of the Son of God. I was grateful I was spared that, but I am more deeply grateful for what I saw as I looked into the soul of a grief-stricken nation. Never have I seen anything so spontaneous as the grief and sorrow that seized the soul of India."[7] Stanley would compare it to the dropping of an atomic bomb. The universal comment seemed to be, "He came to a Christ-like end."

Stanley's own initial reaction, "My heart is broken. I can only compare his sacrifice with the sacrifice of Jesus."

Let me now fast-forward just a bit to the next morning to give you bits of Stanley's own response to this incredible tragedy (from a letter to his family).

On the plane, Delhi to Madras to Colombo, January 31

Dear Ken [Jim Mathews] and all:-

I have just gone through 15 harrowing hours. I have seen a nation convulsed with grief over the tragic death of Mahatma Gandhi.

I think the motive for the assassination was resentment that Gandhi was making peace with the Muslims. All of the seven [actually eight] *points of his fast were in favor of the Muslims....*

Stanley's book, *Mahatma Gandhi: An Interpretation*, attempts to explain this in the chapter, "The Meaning of His Death."[8] Gandhi was on a fast to protest the disunity and dishonesty in Indian policy. "It was a great fast with great objectives. But all the objectives were seemingly in favor of the Muslims. He had laid down eight conditions, one of which was the restoration of the 117 mosques in Delhi that the Hindus and Sikhs had turned into dwellings or temples after the mass slayings. All of Gandhi's conditions were in favor of the Muslims. Some Hindus laid bare their feelings to me about the matter: 'Why didn't he fast against Pakistan, for Pakistan is the guilty party? Ours was retaliation. They began it all and are therefore responsible for what happened.'"Stanley's immediate reply was simple, "The Mahatma's strategy is correct. Suppose he had fasted against Pakistan. They would possibly have shrugged their shoulders and said: 'Let him die. What is that to us?'"[9]

Muslims had for some years been eager for an independent Pakistan (Pak "holy," stan "place" or a holy place of Islam). It had become the passion of the Muslim leader, Muhammad Ali Jinnah. Jinnah was originally an Indian nationalist who supported the Indian National Congress and its goal of Indian independence. In the late 1930s, however, he became "a bitter Muslim communalist" whose goal was the creation of a separate Muslim state independent of both Britain and Hindu India.

Jones had actually corresponded with Jinnah praying for a resolution and Gandhi had asked Stanley to publish this correspondence but Stanley could not bring himself to do it. Stanley could scarcely believe that Muslims would want to divide the newly independent India and Jinnah had reneged on a promise to Stanley (in private conversation) to reconcile. Stanley (and Gandhi and Nehru for that matter) felt betrayed.

The end result was that Pakistan for Muslims would hurt the 40 million Muslims remaining in India more than it would hurt India. The remaining Muslims were unwilling to be a peaceful minority. They remembered how, before British rule, they were the proud inheritors of Islamic destiny. The ruling Hindus were unsympathetic and persecution now ruled the day on both sides of the "border."

So Gandhi had fasted for peace.

Eventually (after 6 days) Gandhi became so weak that both sides signed an agreement conceding his points so the fast was called off. The fast wrought a miracle of the first order. People were parading the streets crying, "Save the Mahatma. Down with communal strife. Hindus and Muslims are brothers."[10]

Immediately the Muslims saw Gandhi as their friend. This fast proved it. Their doubts were over.

Not all were relieved, however. This aroused fanatical Hindus who felt that Muslims should be severely dealt with because of the August to October massacres and migrations in Punjab just months before.

The assassin was from Poona, the section of India from which Shivaji, the Hindu hero god, who conquered the Muslims, originated. The local cry was, "Shivaji makes the Maratha's blood flow faster as he thinks of Hindu ascendancy over the Muslim invaders." Maratha, the sworn enemy of Hindus, was ripped apart by a "tiger claw" concealed in the hand of Shivaji as he extended his hand to Maratha in mock friendship. The tiger claw was now a gun that Godse drew as he extended his hands to Gandhi in apparent salute.[11]

In Stanley's own words, he believed that there were really two reasons behind the killing of the Mahatma: his wanting an India for all — Muslims included — and his nonviolence. The group that Godse represented felt that in advocating nonviolence the Mahatma was emasculating Hindus. So Godse would attempt to stop nonviolence by violence. The result? The opposite of what he had expected or hoped. He succeeded in making the power of nonviolence a global issue that would affect movements worldwide.

Stanley concludes, "I think that Gandhi will be greater in death for now he is a martyr for the cause of peace." Had Gandhi lived to a ripe old age the country would have lovingly put him on the shelf in his decaying years, and would have honored him, but would not have

36

followed him. Now he dies at the height of his powers, and at the pinnacle of his influence, for he never stood higher and more triumphant than after his last two fasts, one in Calcutta and the other in Delhi. Gandhi was loved but almost as many were won to an allegiance to him by his death as by his life.[12]

The delay in Jones' writing *The Way to Power and Poise* was not simply the death of Gandhi, however, but a telegram from Abingdon Press, his publisher. "How quickly can you produce a manuscript for Mahatma Gandhi…"? *Mahatma Gandhi, an Interpretation* would be the only book that Stanley wrote on request and he initially rejected the publisher's offer. After thinking and praying about it, however, he decided that he could lay an honest tribute at the feet of the great little man and in two months he had finished the manuscript.[13]

Stanley initially thought the book a failure until Martin Luther King, Jr. sent him word that this was the book that gave him his vision for his own civil rights movement (in fact, a marked copy of the book is on display in the MLK Library in Atlanta opened to the page marked by MLK stating that this where he caught the vision).[14] Stanley later wrote to his son-in-law, Jim Mathews, "I'm glad they asked me to write it.[15] Stanley's letter to his family, written the day after Gandhi was killed, continues:

> I am now on a plane consumed with thoughts that need to be remembered; so I write. After my arrival from Agra, I was walking up and down in meditation when the play stopped on an athletic field next to us. One of the players came over to me and told me that Mahatma Gandhi had been shot and had died. People turned pale as the news was dispersed. Would chaos ensue with Gandhi's influence for peace being removed? Little groups stood and discussed the happening in awed tones.
>
> My friend and I went over to the Congress headquarters. They had all gone to the Birla House where Gandhi's body was being prepared. A broadcast was given by Jawaharlal Nehru and Vallabhbhai Patel at 8:20 pm. Jawaharlal Nehru could scarcely help from breaking

with emotion. As we sat around the radio a group of 50-60 at the Y.M.C.A., people broke and wept, in uniform, no exception. They asked me to read a passage of Scripture and pray. It wasn't easy to do without breaking.

After the broadcast we walked 2 miles or more to the Birla house. I called Dr. John Matthai on phone and he said he had tried to get to the house, but there was such a crowd that he couldn't get near and advised me not to try. But we went on foot and got there at 10:30 pm, managed to get through the gates, soldiers allowing a white face in, got up to the house, but the secretary came out and said that he was sorry no one was being allowed in, the door was shut. We paid our respects. The Viceroy had been there and all of the national leaders.

We picked up a Tonga and got back towards midnight. I couldn't sleep – got only about 2 hrs., thinking on the events of the day. We are not sure yet what the motive of the shooting was. He is a man from Poona, a Hindu, fired at a distance of about 2 yards three shots, in the middle of Gandhi's breast. He was on his way to the prayer period, leaning on two of his grandchildren (girls), when the man in Khaki fired. Gandhi collapsed and was dead in half an hour. There was no news of whether he was conscious or said anything before he died.

I have suggested that Gandhi would be greater in his death than in life. As we went to the airport in the dark this morning people were winding their way to Birla house. The funeral will take place in an hour from now beginning at 11:20 am. (Sat. January 31) and going in procession to the burning ghat on the Jamma River. The funeral pyre will be lighted about 3 pm.

Kisses to the kiddies.

Lovingly, Daddy[16]

Gandhi was not only Stanley's inspiration; he was his friend.

Nehru requested that Bishop Pickett speak for Christians at the memorial service. Pickett also conducted a memorial service for students at the Isabella Thoburn College, saying "Gandhi was not of an age, but was for all time," The congregation sang a favorite hymn of Gandhi's, "Lead Kindly Light" by John Henry Newman.[17]

LEAD, KINDLY LIGHT

Lead, Kindly Light, amidst th'encircling gloom,
Lead Thou me on!
The night is dark, and I am far from home,
Lead Thou me on!
Keep Thou my feet; I do not ask to see
The distant scene; one step enough for me.

I was not ever thus, nor prayed that Thou
Shouldst lead me on;
I loved to choose and see my path; but now
Lead Thou me on!
I loved the garish day, and, spite of fears,
Pride ruled my will. Remember not past years!

So long Thy power hath blest me, sure it still
Will lead me on.
O'er moor and fen, o'er crag and torrent, till
The night is gone,
And with the morn those angel faces smile,
Which I have loved long since, and lost awhile!

Meantime, along the narrow rugged path,
Thyself hast trod,
Lead, Saviour, lead me home in childlike faith
Home to my God.
To rest forever after earthly strife
In the calm light of everlasting life. Amen.

E. Stanley Jones

Mabel Losing Jones

E. Stanley Jones, Eunice, and Mabel Lossing Jones, 1916

E. Stanley Jones and Mabel Lossing Jones, c. 1913

CHAPTER TWO

MABEL AND STANLEY ARE LAUNCHED INTO MISSION

The Need for Meaningful and Purposeful Lives

I like Mabel Lossing! Stanley Jones was married to her for 62 years. Most biographers make little mention of Mabel. She was a fascinating woman and the driving force behind the home front while Stanley was consumed with his preaching/teaching schedule around the world. They were a remarkable couple, both called of God and each determined to follow their own inner voice. Let's watch them develop.

MABEL LOSSING

Just at the end of her time in India Mabel, having returned to her childhood home in Clayton, Iowa, wrote a 358 page book on education that was just as close to Mahatma Gandhi's understanding of *satyagraha* (the theory of education emphasizing peace, non-violence and truth) as Stanley's own understanding of *satyagraha* as related to evangelism and mission.[1] Mabel and Gandhi actually became friends and corresponded for twenty-five years.

Mabel was born in the small town of Clayton, Iowa on the Mississippi River, April 3, 1878. Her mother and grandmother were Methodists with strong Quaker ties inherited from paternal grandparents. We know little of Mabel's father, Charles. He has been portrayed as a struggling farmer who apparently left the farm in 1885 and moved his family to Dubuque.

Mabel's Conversion: Mabel speaks of a Christian conversion in a local church at age 12. We know little else until she graduated with honors from Dubuque High School at 17 (1896). This is remarkable in that just the year before, tragically Mabel's 5 year-old-sister, J. May, died from a cerebral disease. Then, just two months later, her mother, Carrie Freeman Lossing, died of tuberculosis.[2]

Following high school, Mabel, with her two sisters, moved back to Clayton to take care of her grandfather. Her grandfather, John Lossing, was a carpenter, builder and contractor who had migrated from Canada. He was the son of John and Hannah Treffry, a family of nobility from England. Mabel loved her grandfather dearly and would laughingly tell him that his prayer for guidance was answered because if he had not gone to Clayton he would have not been poor and she was sure the he was much happier poor than if he had been rich.[3] So go the Quaker roots. She would research the history of her noble English ancestry well into her later years.

Remarkably, Mabel soon was made principal of a small rural school in Clayton, no doubt in preparation for her later work in India. As soon as other members of the family could share responsibilities at home, Mabel attended a small college nearby, eventually moving on to Upper Iowa University (UIU) in Fayette in 1899. While at UIU, after a "complete surrender to the Lord Jesus Christ," two years later (1901) Mabel became involved with the Student Volunteer Movement.[4]

IN OUR TIME

Upon graduation from UIU in 1903, Mabel again became a principal, this time of the high school in Fayette. Mabel's home Methodist church in Fayette was noted for its missionary minded congregation. Just the previous year Mabel heard a missionary, Dr. Mary Stone, speak at a branch meeting of the Women's Foreign Missionary Society of the Methodist Episcopal Church. Dr. Stone, then serving in India, made quite an impression with her appeal for teachers. Mabel spoke to her after the meeting and Dr. Stone gave her this challenge: "There are many to take your place here, but there are twenty schools in India that need you more."[5]

Mabel had been awarded a scholarship from Iowa State University to work on her Master's Degree but she turned it down sensing the call to the mission field.

Known for her discipline and gift for speaking Mabel soon became a regular subject of the local newspaper, *The Post Card.* Interestingly, in one of the last *Post Card* articles regarding Mabel, she announces her decision to become a missionary soon to be commissioned by the Methodist Episcopal Church and sent to India.

On Nov. 12, 1904, Mabel sailed out of New York Harbor with four hundred pounds of books. She took little else with her except for a reputation as a serious minded Christian, a successful teacher and linguist. She arrived in Bombay December 9, 1904. She was 26.[6]

E. STANLEY JONES

Eli Stanley Jones was born in Clarksville, Maryland, January 3, 1884, but grew up in nearby Baltimore. His childhood was not a happy time and on occasion he would purposefully refuse to talk about it. There is rarely mention of these formative years in any of his books or even in his spiritual autobiography, *A Song of Ascents.* Once, a former pastor asked Stanley to write about his childhood and he replied, "I do not know what I would say for there does not seem anything to be particularly interesting or inspiring in my boyhood. My life really began with my conversion so I am afraid I will have to ask you to forgive me for not complying."[7]

We believe that Stanley's father, Albin Davis Jones, had challenges with alcohol and as a result was prone to economic disasters while his mother, Sarah Evans Jones, held the family together. She supposedly lost an eye by (according to her doctor) refusing to cry.

Stanley's father was a toll collector on U.S. Highway 40, "the National Road." Unfortunately Jones family lost nearly everything on a number of occasions, probably related to Albin's alcoholism. Stanley would later favor prohibition as a result of his father's "illness."

Stanley was close to his mother. She would lay hands on him from her deathbed and pray that he would become an evangelist and preach the good news. Stanley claims that this was "the greatest ordination I ever had."

Stanley's Conversion: Stanley describes his own conversion at some length in his *A Song of Ascents*. His first memory of any contact with religion was as a five year-old boy at the Frederick Avenue Methodist Church in Baltimore. He recalls rather humbly that he was allowed to pass the collection plate among the grown-ups, not so much expecting to receive money as to collect compliments on the new suit he was wearing. It was "here that he ran unwittingly into the central problem with religion—as such—the self-assertive self."[8] Not a good beginning.

Then, ten years later, as a fifteen year-old seated with his "chums" in the gallery of the Memorial Methodist Church, Stanley asked one of these chums to go forward with him as the invitation was given but his friend said, "No. I'm going to see life first." Stanley went forward on his own but "took church membership as a substitute" for what he really wanted—the Kingdom of God.

Again, rather humbly, Stanley states that from that moment on his mother thought he was a Christian "but I wasn't." He "felt" religious for a few weeks but then the experience faded. He "was converted horizontally but not vertically, outwardly but not inwardly." His "half–conversion" was a total failure.[9]

Then it happened. Two years later (1901) Stanley would experience the "real thing." Robert J. Bateman (who would die on the Titanic leading the Chorus, "Nearer My God to Thee") was preaching a week long revival at Memorial Church, in Baltimore. The first two nights Stanley went to the "altar," both times. Miss Nellie (his first grade teacher, long time friend and correspondent) knelt alongside him and on at least one occasion quoted John 3:16 saying, "God so loved Stanley Jones…"

The third night Stanley prayed before the service, "O Jesus, save me tonight." And, he did! He describes himself running to the church, sitting on the first row waiting for the service to begin and the sermon to end. With the invitation he went quickly forward grabbing the man next to him exclaiming, "I've got Him."

Stanley, in his *Song* eagerly explains what he meant. He did not have an it, but a Him. He had Jesus and Jesus had him. They had each other! At that moment he went from self-preoccupied to Christ-preoccupied. He did not have to give up his sins as if by an act of the will; they were gone! He looked into the face of Jesus and was forever spoiled for anything unlike him. This was his birthday — the birthday of his soul. It was in February 1901.

Stanley's mother's strictness had been a schoolmaster to lead him to Christ. This strictness held him to a degree of decency until Jesus took over. Jesus took him, and then his mother a bit later. He recalls in the *Song* that his mother went forward and he knelt beside her, "Mother, what do you want?" She replied, "I don't know, but I want what you have." In that moment she was given what he had.

What had really happened? Stanley describes his conversion as if all of his senses, like colors, like the strings on a three stringed lyre were being blended, harmonized.

First, there was a sense of forgiveness and reconciliation with God, self and others. He recalls that before his conversion he had stolen some pigeons, but after his conversion he made restitution. He then writes that like the homing pigeon he went through a period of circling before he found his true direction. He was now converted, born again, the past had been blotted out

Related to this was a sense of being at home in the universe, the universe was now his native land. This at "home-ness" in his own person—body, mind, and spirit—would, for Stanley Jones, become the central characteristic of the Christian life.[10] There was a sense of being a whole person, his entire being was awakened, including his mind! There was a sense of grace, of divine adequacy, freely given!

Then, there was a new sense of purpose that delivered Stanley from being tossed like a raft on a sea of meaningless emotions. Now he had the power to move toward a goal, a sense of direction. He had a sense of not being alone. He knew God personally! He was so overwhelmed that he felt undeserving/unworthy but he found himself going off alone to read the New Testament and pray. When a verse spoke of Jesus he would frequently press that verse to his lips. Jesus (to use the words of Rufus Moseley) was his everything. He had Another who knew and understood him perfectly, and was always with him. In spite of knowing Stanley, with all his quirks and faults, he knew that Jesus loved him. Stanley was no longer self-absorbed and with that came a sense of caring about others that would only increase over the years! In short, he now wanted to share what he had found with others. His life really did not exist before his conversion.[11]

The day after his conversion Stanley went to the barbershop. He did not play cards as usual but read his New Testament. His chums asked him to read to them as well. He tells of leading a notorious gambler named Jim to faith in Christ. When Stanley was asked, what kind of hand he played when he won Jim away from poker. His response, "the pierced hand of Jesus." This was Stanley's "break from the herd."

FINDING HIS LIFEWORK

We know Stanley was a good student. Following his conversion he worked for a while in the law library at the Courthouse in Baltimore hoping to save enough money for college. He writes that his boss "tried to knock Christianity out of him." He did not succeed. Persecution simply drives the nail deeper. A power not Stanley's own was reinforcing him. Like a plane rising against the wind he learned not to fight it but to use it.[12] When things were intended to harm or destroy, they became grist for the holiness mill.

Stanley had soon saved enough money to go to college for one year on his $2.75 a week pay at the law library. He would walk 5 miles to save 5 cents on carfare.

Then calamity struck his family. We know little of this. His father, probably due to his alcoholism, lost his political job and court cases swept away house and home. Apparently the door to college had been shut.

By 1902 — he was eighteen — Stanley was selling insurance and helped hold the family together. He came out of this calamitous experience toughened. He now understood poverty first hand. This would prepare him later for India (then the most poverty-stricken land in the world). Stanley then writes that after his being filled with the Holy Spirit he was driven into the wilderness of tough, tangled relationships for one year to be tempted. He came out this not only *toughened* but *tendered*.[13]

Parenthetically, another aftermath of Stanley's conversion was an unexpected incident. It happened in this same year. He led his eighty-two year old grandmother to Jesus. While visiting her she suddenly confessed that she feared she was not ready to die. Stanley said, "Let us go on our knees and talk to God about it." In moments she clapped her hands and kept saying over and over: "He has come to me." For some time following Stanley would go into her room and they would pray together.[14]

Stanley was still feeling the need to go to college. He told his mother; but she said, who will pay the rent? He said he would send back enough money to pay the rent each month. He left and managed to send back money until his brother graduated from medical school and took over an existing practice so that he could now pay the family's rent, enabling Stanley to pursue his education. Stanley writes, if God guides, God provides. Now free to pursue his studies Stanley was making enough money during the summers preaching in evangelistic meetings to pay for the coming year so that he finished college without debt.

ASBURY COLLEGE, 1903-1907

Stanley enrolled in Asbury College nestled in the blue grass of rural Kentucky, in the small town of Wilmore. He was an exceptional student and, like Mabel before him, had another awakening where he not only surrendered his life completely to God but sensed his call to the mission field. The "*Song of Ascents*" was on....

Watch this unfold. Stanley was grateful to be led to Asbury. He was influenced first by H. C. Morrison (one of the last old southern holiness preachers who was soon to be President of Asbury College). Morrison was holding meetings in a Methodist Church in Baltimore. Stanley was deeply impressed. If Asbury could teach him to preach like that he wanted to go to Asbury. When Stanley told his pastor, Rev. C. T. House of Memorial Church, that he had been called to preach, House said, then you will preach your first sermon on Sunday night three weeks hence.

Stanley prepared well. Since he had started out studying law (he wanted to be God's lawyer), this first sermon would be a brief for God. He would plead God's case. He would be lawyer/minister blended. He wrote to Robert Bateman, asking advice. Bateman wrote back that the world needs Christian lawyers but to do nothing until he had heard from heaven.[15]

When Stanley got up to preach that first sermon, the words that he had prepared left him. He remembered using the term "indifferentism" and a young girl laughed. He immediately got unnerved and lost his train of thought. He drew an absolute blank. All he could do was apologize and as he was about to take his seat, *God spoke*, "Haven't I done anything for you?" Stanley said, "Yes, of course." God said, "Then tell them about it."[16] So, he gave a witness from the front of the church and a young man, Stanley Warfield, was converted and would become a minister while his sister would become a missionary to Africa.

From that moment on Stanley writes that while he did not hear from heaven with specific guidance but his interest in law began to drop away to the margins and ministry moved more and more to the center—"It gripped me."

Stanley had discovered, somewhat painfully, that as a would-be lawyer putting up God's case, he was a failure, but as a witness, telling what God had done for him, he was a success. He would not be God's lawyer but God's witness to the grace of God revealed in Jesus Christ. Eventually Stanley would witness to what God had done for an unworthy sinner before princes and peasants, Brahmins and outcastes, the mighty and the miserable. Stanley writes that he found what people wanted to hear—a testimony about what had already happened and what was happening to him now.

When Stanley told his mother that he had been called to the ministry she exclaimed, "What! A poor Methodist preacher?" He was licensed to preach February 12, 1903.

While at Asbury, Jones established a lasting friendship with J. Waskom Pickett, whom we met briefly in Chapter One. While a student, Stanley lived in the Pickett home. Waskom would later follow Stanley to India where he became a Bishop.

On September 11, 1903 a long correspondence with Miss Nellie Logan began (we met her briefly at Stanley's conversion). She was his prayer warrior, confident and friend. This continued up until the

1940s. Stanley's mother is now trusting Miss Nellie to stand next to Stanley after she was gone. When she was dying, she called Miss Nellie and said: "These years I have prayed for Stanley. Now I am going. I'm turning him over to you, for you to take up my vigil of prayer for him." Miss Nellie stated years later that she "had been true to that entrustment."[17]

Stanley writes that it was now time for a fourth string to be added to his three stringed lyre. We mentioned the first three strings earlier when describing what really happened at his conversion. The first was *reconciliation and forgiveness*. He was converted, born again, the past had been blotted out. The second was *adequacy*, he had been cleansed by the Holy Spirit and invaded by his love to witness for his Lord. He is quick to note that God had taken the initiative; all he did was gratefully receive. The third was *knowing God personally*. God was no longer a name. He was a fact, within, around, and above. With these three strings he set out a happy pilgrim. Yet something was still missing.

The fourth string would be *witnessing*. Stanley was convinced that all great literature is autobiography and that all great preaching is testimony. While philosophy reasons; moralism demands; music and art please; witnessing shares at the depths — deep speaking to deep. The keynote for his ministry would now be witnessing![18]

Another experience from his college days was opposite to his first sermon failure. Stanley felt that he was given his license to preach by the District Superintendent too easily. When questioned about church polity he drew another blank, but was given grace and approved. Then his second sermon, his first as a licensed preacher was at a women's prison. The women were so moved that they began to shout and the guards needed to quiet them down. Note the contrast. His first sermon was a failure. His second was too successful. One was too low, the other too high. *He needed a moderating* fifth *string for his lyre*. No more mountaintops, no more valleys, but simply to be on the Way, an Ascent. This Way would later be a gentle incline but now it was abrupt with sharp ups and downs.

Interestingly, for the next several years Stanley would hold seven revival meetings and then camp meetings in Virginia and Baltimore for the three months during the summers.

Fortunately for Stanley, Asbury College had an emphasis on both experience and expression. Asbury picked out of the Methodist movement and the Eighteenth century evangelical revival two things as a focus: the warm heart and the world parish—again, experience and expression.

As to the warm heart, although Asbury was in the conservative theological mold, it was not a cantankerous conservatism. Common experience was more important than rigid creed agreement. As John Wesley was fond of saying, "If your heart is as my heart then give me your hand. Outside essentials, we think and let think." If you were born again and filled with the Holy Spirit you were accepted and leeway was given as to how you got there. Asbury graduates went into mainline churches as evangelical leaven in various denominations. This would serve Stanley well on the mission field.

Speaking of the mission field, the world is my parish insisted that the experience and expressions of the faith were universal, applicable for every culture. Furthermore, responses were not to be looked for (conjured or manipulated), they were the gift of the Holy Spirit, they just happened—spontaneously, unexpectedly. Let's allow Stanley to give a witness....

Probably in 1903, but perhaps as late as 1905, the first Asbury Revival struck the college campus and then the entire town of Wilmore, Kentucky. This was the time when Stanley experienced the filling of the Holy Spirit and became a self-proclaimed "holiness preacher."

Stanley writes that he and four or five of his classmates were praying in one of their rooms (Jim Ballinger's). Suddenly it happened, seemingly out of the blue, without provocation. As they prayed, at around 10 PM (Stanley was almost asleep) they were swept off their feet by a visitation of the Holy Spirit. All were filled with the Spirit—

flooded by the Spirit. It was a new Pentecost and would become one of the most sacred and formative gifts of his life. "We appeared drunk with God for three or four days." At first all they could do was to walk the floor. L.L. Pickett (Waskom's dad) came up to the room and said, "Stanley, the Lord giveth his beloved sleep," but sleep was out of the question. By morning the effects of this unexpected "outpouring" went through the entire college campus and then into the town in a flash.[19]

There was no chapel service in the ordinary sense. People were in prayer. No one led it. It was led by the Spirit. There were no classes for three days. Every classroom became a prayer meeting among both students and faculty alike, all experiencing the Spirit and then witnessing. This soon spread beyond the college and town to the countryside. People flocked in but before they could get to the assembly hall they were stricken to the ground with conviction. They would fall to their knees crying for God's pardon and release.

On one occasion Stanley was called out to minister among those on the ground when a strange thing happened! He was "suddenly taken possession of by an infinite quiet, a holy calm within, as the calm at the center of a cyclone. It became easy to help people and until the movement of the Holy Spirit subsided he had nothing but holy calm within."[20]

There were shades of Pentecost and Azusa Street—the entire student body was transformed. Again, townspeople and many from the countryside were also converted and transformed. As for Stanley the lasting effects were at least three.

First, during his three days of ecstasy he was released from the fear of emotional enthusiasm. He was drunk with God. Yet, these were the clearest-headed, soberest moments he would ever know. He writes, "there was joy, joy, joy and love, love, love." Second, at the moment of the highest emotion and ecstasy he was suddenly released from his emotions and a calm took possession. It was as if he was weaned from the highest emotion in a moment, so much so that he did not desire a repeat of that experience. Third, all the marks of the first Pentecost were there except speaking in tongues. Tongues were not resisted, the emphasis was simply on the Giver, not the gifts. There was no division between tongue talkers and non-tongue talkers to leave them divided. The Holy Spirit was evident, by the Spirit's presence and power. They were united around the fruit of the Holy Spirit, which is love.[21]

Significantly, at this point Stanley would connect with other emotions that would affect the choice of his life's work as a missionary, especially for India.

Stanley needed to be freed from the inner fetters of an unmentioned sense of superiority over the more emotional Kentuckians. Stanley had struggled with the influence of the more reserved culture of his youth. These fetters were now burned away by the fires of the Spirit. During the revival he had been more emotional than any of them. He had become a fool for God, for the Holy Spirit. He was free from the herd instinct with its superiorities and inferiorities. He had now a careless indifference.

Now the Holy Spirit would talk with Stanley and he was disposed to listen. He could work in the power of the Holy Spirit, or better yet, the Holy Spirit could work through him heightening all his limited powers. Importantly, these experiences did not unfit him for the details of life around him. Life itself became sacramental. He was suddenly a better student. He could read "secular" books on his knees. Suddenly everything was sacred.

The biggest thing, however, was his preparation and call to the mission field. The Student Volunteer Movement invited him to speak on Africa. In preparing, he became so burdened he prayed, "Now, Lord, I don't want to go into that room to give a missionary address. I want you to give me a missionary. God said, 'According to your faith, be it unto you.'" When Stanley spoke he began by saying that someone is going to the mission field from this place. Little did he know that he would be the one.[22]

Stanley at this point thought Africa. At the time Africa was grim and going there was like signing your own death warrant. He wrote to his mother who seemed averse. Then his brother called to say that their mother was dying. Stanley, on the way to visit his mother, heard the voice of the Tempter saying; "You've killed your mother."[23] When he arrived he found her barely alive (she had been pronounced dead twice). .... No one, including his doctor brother, actually understood her illness. She was simply dying. Stanley was consumed. "What do I do?" It was the prayers of his mother that had been holding the family together.

At that moment, as Stanley would be prone to do for the rest of his life, he threw the whole matter back into the lap of God. He said, "Father, I can't be responsible for the results of my call. I can only be responsible for answering my call. You'll have to take care of the results. I'm following the call no matter what happens to me or my mother." At that moment, to the surprise of everyone present, God raised up his mother, not only physically but spiritually as well. She became radiant. Suddenly, she was proud to send Stanley to the mission field, no matter where. He was to go with her blessing. When she later died triumphantly, Stanley left utterly released.[24]

The stage for his future seemed set but there were still some unanswered questions, again, "What do I do?" Stanley was such a good student that upon graduation he had several options. There was an invitation to teach at Asbury (which he did during the fall while waiting on his approval for the mission field). There was also a letter from a trusted friend to consider being an evangelist in America. Then there was a letter from the Methodist Mission Board offering to send him to India.

Stanley knew that this decision could not be the will of anyone but God's. At this point he prayed and the unmistakable VOICE spoke to him. It's India. From that moment the matter was settled, closed, no question.

On November 3, 1907, Stanley left on the S. S. Victoria bound for Southhampton, England. There was no fanfare. He left without any seminary training and little money. From England he sailed on to India via Port Said, arriving in Bombay and then up to Lucknow in December, 1907.[25] Stanley was 23.

Even in route Stanley was always learning, studying a Hindustani grammar on board ship, and always in ministry among his fellow passengers. He arrived fully alert and challenged, determined never to mistake God's ability for his own native ability, a lesson he would have to return to time and again. The next eight years would test his strength, both physically and emotionally.

MABEL JONES

We left Mabel arriving in Bombay on Friday, December 9, 1904, just three years before Stanley. She was met by missionaries and taken to the Thoburn Deaconess Home for the night but early the next morning she was driven five hundred miles north to Jabbulpore. Upon arrival they discovered that the orphanage was horribly overcrowded so Mabel thankfully accepted an invitation to stay with a Dr. Johnson until her appointment was made at Conference within the next two to three weeks. It seems the Conference had been delayed due to the plague that was killing fifty to sixty people a day. Dr. Johnson's table servant had just died.

In spite of it all Mabel never lost her ability to observe the beauty of what God had placed before her.

> We saw a very blessed sight yesterday. Dr. Johnson took about fifty of the Orphanage girls into the church. The whole body, about two hundred and fifty marched in and as I looked from them in their clean white Chuddars, with their pure happy faces to the dirty naked or half-clad, repulsive looking children thronging the streets outside, I could not keep back the tears. Later most of the girls and about thirty native men and women knelt at the altar for the Lord's Supper. It was a sight worth coming from America to see.[26]

Mabel was soon appointed to the Khandwa Orphanage, about three hundred miles east of Bombay. She was given charge of educational work among one hundred and twenty-two girls between the ages of three and eighteen. She was one of only two teachers

Mabel writes that she was as happy as could be and still be in the body. Yet within weeks of her arrival at Khandwa a famine swept India and people were dying of hunger in the streets. She was small and slight but with amazing endurance. Struggling with languages and culture Mabel was soon making her way up and down the streets with horse and cart rescuing babies and small children off the dead bodies of their parents and bringing them back to the orphanage.[27] Within a year the missionary in charge, Mrs. Lee, had a nervous breakdown and Mabel (along with her teaching) was given full responsibility as principal of the school.

It is interesting that during this time, Mabel, admittedly worried about Mrs. Lee, wrote a poem in the night that would be included in one of her earliest newsletters, *The India Witness.*

Rest a While Apart

"Thou seest, Lord, the harvest fields are white
The drooping heads are ready for the blade.
My sickle's sharp; I fain would rush to reap.
Give answer, Lord, why am I staid?"
"Patience; though fields await," the voice was mild,
"Still come apart and rest a while, my child."

"Oh, Lord, Thy sheep upon the mountain stray.
The nights are dark and snares on every side;
No shepherd, they, and no one nigh to save:
Release me, Lord. Why must I bide?"
"Alas my sheep! Would they were on my breast;
But thou, my child, come thou apart and rest."

"Oh Lord, while souls are dying, daylight flees;
The shadows, gathering, lengthening, do not stay;
The dark comes on, the many have not heard.

Oh, let me labour while 'tis day"
"The work is mine, and precious to my heart,
Fret not, my child, but rest awhile, apart."

This was an amazing woman. In the meantime, Mabel, along with all of her other duties, was struggling four hours a day to learn Hindi (some labeled her a workaholic, forever taking on more than she could handle) but she nonetheless rejoices in a revival that spread throughout India in early 1906. She comments that the Spirit was not "worked up but prayed down."[28] Stanley would approve! These two would be exchanging and reinforcing each other out of their own histories for the rest of their lives.

During all of this Mabel managed to complete the work for her Masters' Degree at UIU in 1907 (in absentia). It must be noted that at this time the people of India believed that women could not be taught even to read because of their "defective intellectual powers." Boys could not be taught by women and there were few schools for girls. We will watch Mabel change all of that.

MABEL AND STANLEY

Upon arrival in Lucknow Stanley was soon ordained and then, at the same Northern India Annual Conference, appointed him to the English speaking Lal Bagh Methodist Church in Lucknow. For the next 8 years (1907 to 1915) he would be consumed by "self-striving, self-effort and eventual collapse from wearing too many hats."

India had seven annual conferences and Stanley's was numerically the largest (from the Ganges to the borders of Tibet and Nepal). Bishop James M. Thoburn (bishop 1888 to 1908) was known as an "imperialist" in that he expected his missionaries to become expansionists. He espoused mass movement evangelism that "began with the individual but then relied on the family and social networks (usually of the caste system) to extend the scope of missionary activity."[29]

Contrast this with a more person centered evangelism where the convert is frequently led away from his or her natural environment. Stanley was forever weighing the pros and cons of both of these approaches.

Mabel remained at the large orphanage in Khandwa until **1908.** During this time she made every effort to learn about the history and culture of India. Although she was never trained in medicine she also took on the responsibility of helping thousands in times of epidemics and emergencies. There was only one government doctor for a town of 40,000 people and the surrounding villages. Mabel rarely took a vacation.

Then, at the end of 1908, Mabel was sent to the Isabella Thoburn College in Lucknow to fill in for a missionary teacher who, like the missionary in Khandwa, had suffered a nervous breakdown. Mabel began attending the Lal Bagh Methodist Church and soon met the young American pastor, Stanley Jones. She became the organist and Stanley was smitten saying that she was the "sweetest girl in the world."[30] The well-known evangelist, James Robb, writes that Stanley was able to lead Mabel into the experience of "entire sanctification" the year they met.

MARRIAGE AND MISSION

Stanley, uncertain as to how to manage his romance with Mabel, one Sunday met her in the aisle as she was leaving church and blurted out a proposal asking Mabel to be his wife. Mabel accepted but then soon left India on furlough in February 1910. While in the U.S. she would apply to the Methodist Board of Missions in preparation for her return to India and her marriage to Stanley. They would now be serving under the same board. Her application indicated that she had studied Greek, Latin, German, Hindi and Sanskrit. Stanley never really mastered a sophisticated facility with Hindustani but had managed to pass his exam just before Mabel left on furlough.

It is interesting that Stanley and Mabel had a pre-marital agreement that both their calls were legitimate. The two entered marriage with the understanding they would pursue their own callings. Mabel had been commissioned and serving in India for 7 years before marriage. Both esteemed her call just as valid as Stanley's. Both had the need for meaningful and purposeful lives.

Stanley and Mabel were married in Bombay upon her return from furlough in February 1911 and immediately moved to Sitapur where there was no electricity and no running water. The caste system strictly delegated duties to specific persons within each of their castes — for life. No single Indian could perform all of the household duties so several helpers had to be employed.[31]

Furthermore, Mabel was a very private person, humble and "other oriented." Stanley, by his own admission, struggled with vanity and pride and was constantly laying this matter at the feet of Jesus.[32] We really don't know what the relationship between Mabel and Stanley was really like. There are no details in their papers. James Mathews once wrote that Mabel had told him that she would rather have Stanley for two weeks than any other man she had met for fifty-two. They were both willing to stand and support the other for the sake of the Kingdom.

We know that Stanley empowered Mabel in the early years of their marriage. Stanley worked tirelessly alongside her getting the school for boys up and running. Then, while Stanley was away she would keep things on an even keel.

Stanley originally planned to spend six months helping Mabel establish her boys school and then serve as a traveling evangelist for six months. Unfortunately, he was given so much responsibility by the Board of Missions and the Methodist Conference that much of this evangelistic work had to be put on hold. This lead to frustration on both of their parts.

Then, during that first summer in the Sitapur District cholera broke out and 10,000 people died within 6 weeks. Stanley was forced to sit at his desk writing letters, appealing for funds, something he did not enjoy doing.[33]

Mabel envisioned a primary school for boys run completely by women (again, it was unheard of for women to teach boys in the Indian society but Mabel did not think that the men took the task seriously enough). Mabel made the change and women teachers taught the boys and the school was a huge success. Bishop Warne stated that the school "far exceeded expectations."[34]

By the end of the year Stanley was also boasting about Mabel's exemplary school. Even Mohandas (Mahatma) Gandhi, who carried on a lively correspondence with Mabel as well as Stanley, would commend the success of her school.[35] Nonetheless, by the **end of 1911,** Stanley is preaching more regularly and beginning to see significant results. His Indian friends say that out of 330,000,000 Hindu gods not one is mentioned as loving.[36] Stanley's message was that of a God of love!

At one point in 1912 Stanley writes Miss Nellie that the entire lower caste was at the point of becoming Christian. Then he senses the "inner voice" calling him to the upper castes as well, especially among the educated middle-class seekers. His publication, *The Indian Witness,* along with his letters to Miss Nellie, tells the story. Christianity is not merely an intellectual proposition to be won by clever argument. Christianity is true because it reveals the truth of God's love for everyone in the person of Jesus Christ. It was not always a simple message to proclaim. Frequently he was forced to demonstrate "loving one's enemies" as many were eager to test that conviction.[37]

In May, 1912 when the school closed for the summer, Stanley and Mabel were finally able to get away to Kashmir for a bit of rest. Nonetheless, Stanley's frustration with not being able to go out and preach his evangelistic services as often as he liked grew throughout 1912 and 1913 as more and more pressure from the Methodist Conference kept piling up. He was now made superintendent of the much larger Lucknow District.[38]

IN OUR TIME

Eventually his responsibilities with the Conference, his preaching throughout India and neighboring countries, including warding off diseases, snakes, scorpions and the summer heat began to take its toll. He actually believed that he could do it all out of his own strength. This would lead to a spiritual, emotional and physical collapse in 1917.

Dedication Stones of
Mabel's School (Above)
and the Chapel (Right)

E. Stanley Jones & Family at Sitapur Home

Mabel's School at Sitapur

CHAPTER THREE

CRISIS AND RECOVERY: LEARNING TO TRUST GOD ALONE

The Need for Healing: Body, Mind and Spirit

B rother Stanley's ministry will now begin to take shape in the midst of personal crises and a World War.

PERIOD OF ADJUSTMENT: LUCKNOW, 1907-1911

Even before he reached India Stanley had "stumbled" into an understanding of the Gospel that was universal, both in scope and content. With regard to *scope*, India, by and large, would by and large be his physical setting but the "world would be his parish." With regard to *content*, Stanley now asks, would his understanding of a universal Gospel change his fundamental understanding of the Gospel? No! He would never be a "universalist" believing that all peoples were saved and destined for eternal salvation regardless of their beliefs or the way they conducted their lives. That would destroy the integrity of his evangelistic call. Yet, Stanley was always quick to say that he never wanted to be the Judge. That was God's job, not his (regardless of what Mabel might have thought on occasion). Stanley would do the preaching; God would do the judging.

Stanley also knew that his call was to all persons, not just to Hindus or Muslims or Sikhs, not just to people from the West or people from the East. Most Indians appreciated this in that they saw an unbiased focus in his missionary/evangelist ministry. *"We do not want to be the only ones in need of conversion."*[1] Stanley preached that all people needed conversion, as people, at their core. India was on the brink of revolution. Stanley prayed that the Gospel he preached would turn out to be a revolution—and not just a self-government revolution, but the revolution of all revolutions?

During the four years Stanley was in Lucknow (1907-1911), learning the languages and being a pastor, he realized that he was not in the real India. He was at the edge of Indian life, not at the center. He became more and more aware, even at this early date, that India's life revolved around the movement for self-government.[2] Although the British had contributed much to India it was time now for India to take over and assume her own responsibilities for a new and better life for all Indians. Stanley wrote an article to that effect, the gist appearing in the national papers. There he made an appeal to all Anglo-Indian peoples to throw themselves into the growing national movement toward independence: "No movement in India will succeed that cuts across the growing movement for national independence." Many of the Anglo-Indians looked on this askance, some even as treason. Stanley was uncertain how to respond. The Anglo side had privileges and they thought— deservedly so! The Viceroy, Lord Mayo, was heard to say, "We are British gentlemen engaged in the magnificent work of governing an inferior race."[3] Then, as these privileges began to disappear, many Anglo-Indians were leaving India.

Stanley's confidence (self-assurance) was eroding to the place where he was beginning to feel woefully inadequate. As an aside in his autobiography, *A Song of Ascents* he tells the story of Asa Jennings, a disabled YMCA secretary who single-handedly managed the rescue of 200,000 Greeks when the Greek army was fleeing the advancing Turks. Stanley writes that Jennings had no knowledge, and hence no inhibitions.[4] Stanley could relate to that. He writes *that the most valuable thing about me in those days was my colossal ignorance."* All he knew was evangelism — people needed to be converted, to be changed. So, he began to act on that faith. His favorite text was, "Thou shalt call his name Jesus: for he shall save his people from their sins" (Mt. 1:21).

Knowing that Jesus had accepted him with all his imperfections enabled Stanley to see and love others in spite their imperfections. This saved him from a rigid sort of perfectionism that was always too quick to judge. Jesus did that for him and as Jesus Christ had done for him, he would do for others. Stanley felt that perfectionists could not get along with others — even themselves. Stanley found that faith in others is founded on a faith in God. It believes out of the need for believing. It has faith out of the need for faith. It loves out of the longing for love. Christian faith produces faith, hope produces hope and love produces love.[5]

You might recall that Stanley came into the Kingdom back at Asbury crying "MORE!, more gratification. Such "pleasures" all have upon them the doom of an *unquenchable thirst.* You get them only to realize that they are not what you really want. This realization would later lead to Jones' understanding of a moral universe referred to in our Introduction. "What you really want is more of Jesus. Conversion is once for all yet ever expanding to larger areas of life."[6] Stanley insisted that we are forever Christians in the making. We need that Word from on high, a first-hand personal assurance.

Jones learned never to put his full weight on any one person, such as Miss Nellie, as important as she was, but only on ONE PERSON. Stanley learned to glance at women like Miss Nellie and at men like Robert Bateman but to *gaze* at Jesus. Matthew 6:22 told him to let his eye be single. "Saints" like Miss Nellie and Bateman could take him only so far. They took him to the threshold of the Holy of Holies but only the Redeemer could take him to his heavenly Father. Jesus was his one Mediator. It was Jesus who mediated God to him. In Jesus God was available. To know Jesus was to know God.[7]

Stanley notes that on the Mount of Transfiguration the disciples wanted to put Moses (the Law) and Elijah (the Prophets) on a par with Jesus. Stanley insisted that Bible is not equally authoritative. The Old Testament is an ascending preparation, pre-Christian, perhaps even sub-Christian. Christianity is Jesus Christ reinterpreting the Old Testament! "Ye have heard it said, but I say to you…" Stanley may not have been a fundamentalist but he loved the word that was forever taking him to the Word![8]

A ROUTINE ESTABLISHED

During Jones' four years in Lucknow, he would preach on Sunday morning for the regular congregation on the deeper life and on the cleansing of the Holy Spirit. In the evenings members of the community would come and he would speak on conversion by a Savior, for he shall save his people not *in* their sins, but *from* their sins. He gave an invitation to accept Jesus Christ at each of these evening services and for four years there were conversions every Sunday — except for two Sundays when it was too hot for anyone to decide anything. He soon learned that in Lucknow there were two seasons — Paradise and Purgatory.

Although not all these "converts" were soundly converted, Stanley speaks repeatedly of significant conversions. He quickly learned the lesson of the four soils. Some of the seed fell on the path, some on rocky ground, some among thorns, and some on good soil.[9]

In the *Song* Stanley tells of a Hindu jockey who seemed sincere in his conversion. He asked Stanley for money to buy a horse and tonga (a two-wheeled carriage) so he could manage a more respectable trade. Stanley thought it a good idea until he realized that the man used the money to buy a racehorse and entered it, in Stanley's name, at the Lucknow track. Stanley was amused to hear that the horse won and but never heard from the man again. He marked it off to "profit and loss."[10] So, there was need for accountability.

Following the Asbury Revival, class meetings had formed on the Asbury campus. These class meetings met weekly so that members could tell of their experiences, their successes, failures, joys, problems. Stanley's own first testimony at a class meeting was that there is only one thing better than religion, more religion. Thankfully, in time, he would change the emphasis here as religion, as such, was always disappointing him. Religion was a philosophy of life whereas a relationship with Jesus was a way of life. In fact, I do not recall Stanley using the word "religion" to refer to Christianity or to the Kingdom of God beyond this point. He spoke of religion as our search for God but refers to the Gospel as God's search for us. It is significant that at one point Stanley says that he almost fell back into sin. He then went to a class meeting and was healed.[11]

Understandably, class meetings were also introduced to the church at Lucknow. In subsequent chapters you will see these early class meetings become the germ (seed) blossoming into a worldwide Christian Ashram movement.

At the end of Stanley's ministry in Lucknow (1911), Stanley and Mabel Lossing now married and moved to Sitapur, fifty miles away. For the next 40 years Sitapur would be their headquarters and home.

THE CRISIS: SITAPUR, 1911-1915

During the earlier years in Sitapur Stanley was not traveling in evangelistic campaigns as much as he did later (especially in the 1920s, 1930s and beyond). He took more personal responsibility for the operation and administration of the boys' school as well as for the supervision of Christian workers and preachers in the Sitapur District.

He and Mabel often wrote joint "duplicate letters" to their friends and financial supporters in the U. S.

In August 1911 Stanley and Mabel embarked on a building project that would continue for nearly four years. Stanley complains in a letter to Miss Nellie sharply revealing his humanity.

> Well, I've had to be what I wasn't intended to be — a house builder & contractor and labor extractor and a beater down of wages and setter of prices and settler of disputes & punisher of boys and a preacher of the gospel and comforter to the persecuted new Christians and so on ad tiredom! I always hated figures and here I am from dawn til sunset keeping three buildings going & then til midnight figuring out how much I had been beaten out of during the day! I have been trying to get a plant suitable for my wife's place of labor so I could go out free to preach but there seems no end of this.[12]

In Sitapur, however, Stanley soon took up a ministry mostly among outcastes. Here he felt he was closer to the real India. Seventy million outcastes had no standing within the four castes — Brahmin (priestly), Kshatriya (warrior), Vaisya (trading caste), and the Shudra (the serving caste). Below these were the outcastes. Merely to touch an outcaste was to become unclean. It was thought that these unfortunates suffered as a result of their misdeeds in a previous life. One of Stanley's emphases as Christian missionary was to show that this was profoundly false.

Stanley was loved and even revered by the lower castes. He tells of an encounter in the home of an outcaste. "*Sahib walk through my compound and everything will be purified.*" Stanley told him that only Jesus could do that.

While at Sitapur, Stanley also implemented a campaign to take the gospel to every home. Suddenly people stopped talking about the raging cholera and plague and began talking about Jesus Christ. Jones was no longer simply a foreign missionary, he was "the Jesus man."[13] Unfortunately these important ministries would take more and more from his inner resources and would now keep him from home weeks at a time.

1914 was a momentous year. Stanley's *Song* speaks fondly of Mabel's inner (Quaker) resources that enabled her to endure his long absences. "Few women would have been equipped for such an adjustment and sacrifice."[14] Eunice (their only child) was born on Apr. 29, 1914. Stanley missed her actual birth but arrived soon after. When Mabel was age 100 she was asked by a friend about her happiest memory. With a quiet murmur she said, "The day Stanley came home after Eunice's birth and held me in his arms."[15]

Increasingly for Stanley there would be times apart from Mabel and now from daughter Eunice.

World War I broke out in June 1914 and by August Great Britain had declared war on Germany. Though reasonably content, Stanley, like his childhood homing pigeons, was still circling. With the war there were food shortages and soaring prices. Then in October 1914 Stanley was taken to a Lucknow hospital with a ruptured appendix — it was life threatening — but Stanley had no notion of dying. When Bishop Warne came to relieve Jones of his duties Stanley objected. Eventually he recovered and was given responsibility for the large Sitapur District with a million people. Since international travel was disrupted missionary replacement was delayed and several posts had to be abandoned. Therefore, following his recovery (though he was still having difficulty with tetanus infections) even more responsibility was added to him the following year (1915). These added responsibilities included the Lucknow District, then the Hardoi and Rae Bareilly Districts as well. In addition he was also made the Agent of the Methodist Publishing House. He was a first term missionary (ten year term) but many of the missionaries' health broke before the 10 years were completed — Stanley was one of them. Using his own words, after 8 and half years he began to have nervous collapses, just short of a complete breakdown.[16]

In the meantime, while Stanley struggled, Mabel had established a reputation of her own, "famous and highly respected for her educational pioneering success." The Methodist Bishop John W. Robinson wrote in one of his own letters back home that:

> The prejudice and custom of the country had practically compelled the old missionaries to employ "school fathers" to look after the dormitory life of the little fellows and men teachers to instruct them. It has all along been sadly evident that boys taught and cared for in this way in our primary school did not make the intellectual progress nor develop the Christian character of the girls, who were not only looked after by my matrons, but had Christian teachers living in the school with them day and night. Some time ago we decided to defy custom and ignore prejudice and make the experiment at Sitapur of a boys' primary school taught by Christian women and looked after by a matron.... There was a remarkable improvement in morals and character.[17]

Mabel, was of course, at the very center of all this. The Bishop adds "that with the help of Mrs. Mabel Lossing Jones, we have at last been able to inaugurate a long cherished plan." Then in February 1915, all the hard work seemed to have paid off. The new building that Stanley and Mabel had begun during their first year in Sitapur now included their school for boys. Robinson writes that:

> The boys are learning respect for women. At first there was a great inclination for even the small boys to say wrong and silly things about girls and women. ... Now if a boy forgets himself enough to make a wrong remark he is reported at once by the other boys and they seem horrified that such a thing might be possible. So while we are providing a better system of education for our young men, at the same time we are raising the status of women. These boys who are the men of the future will remember that their first teachers were women and will respect womankind accordingly.

> The boys are having their moral life quickened. A boy recently came in from another school and tried to corrupt the other boys. He was reported by the boys and punished. When he repeated the offense he was expelled on the unanimous vote of the whole school... But one of the best results of the new regime is that the boys are be-

ginning to love school. When the morning bell rings, the pell-mell rush for the doors is indicative of their joy in their work.[18]

Even as Stanley and Mabel adjusted to parenthood, with Stanley's recovery from his ruptured appendix and tetanus and the opening and successes of Mabel's school God was at work in other ways as well.

Stanley was weary. His growing ministry among the outcastes was taking its toll. God, however, apparently had a plan. It would not come to fruition until the Jones returned from Stanley's furlough but the seeds were being sown.

Stanley would often play tennis at the club of the Indian officials and lawyers and after the matches, they would get together for conversation. These were important encounters. Early on a Hindu judge asked, "Why do you go to the outcastes? Why don't you come to us?" Stanley had assumed that they did not want him as a missionary. He had taken the line of least resistance by going to the outcastes.

Stanley was then told by the judge that the upper castes did indeed want him, provided he came "the right way." That phrase, "the right way," remained in his heart and mind from that moment on. He would spend his life trying to find and apply that "right way." There would be complications. When he asked, "Who is a Hindu?" The judge replied, "Any good man is a Hindu—you are a Hindu." Stanley asked, "Where does the Hindu end and the non-Hindu begin?" He replied, "You can believe anything and still be a Hindu." Stanley asked, "Anything from atheism to pantheism?" The judge, "You can believe anything and still be a Hindu provided you don't reject the rest." Stanley realized that Hinduism is syncretic. It takes in everything provided it doesn't "reject the rest." Stanley, however, belonged to a Person who presented himself as the Way, the Truth and the Life. How could there be a "right way" under these circumstances—a right way in the eyes of the Hindu judge? Strangely enough, Stanley was fascinated by this problem and its possibilities. He began to feel pressure from within (his *inner voice*) and a call from without to enter this world of India's intelligentsia—to present Christ there. Jones knew that the intelligentsia would determine the future of the new India.[19]

This 'call', however, brought on a spiritual crisis. A call to the upper castes seemed right but how to do this with all of his other responsibilities seemed unreachable. While he passed his exams in Urdu and Hindi he was confined to preach superficially as his linguistic skills did not permit him nuanced communication. He found that he was only speaking of surface things and his spiritual life became surface-like as well. This "physical sag brought spiritual sag." His body was no longer throwing off disease (his tetanus infection was affecting him like never before) and his anxiety and stress-induced "collapses continued." Even in the midst of preaching his mind would often go blank and he would have to sit down, embarrassed and perplexed.

Eventually he was ordered to go to America on an early furlough. He had not finished his first ten-year term but he was finished. His new call came with an embarrassing collapse. He knew he was called to put Christ into the minds, souls and purposes of the intellectual and political leaders of this new awakening India but when he looked at his resources, they seemed to be not at all available. That Jones should respond to this call was clear. Just how, was far from clear.[20]

FURLOUGH: MARCH, 1916 - JANUARY 1917

So, Stanley took the doctor's advice (and that of the Mission Board) and began the long trip back to the U.S. Early in March 1916 Stanley, Mabel and Eunice left on an early furlough after only eight and a half years (missionaries were expected to wait 10 years between furloughs). Due to the war in Europe the family headed east stopping on the island of Penang (now a part of Malaysia) and Singapore. Whey they reached Hong Kong they were able to catch a steamer for San Francisco by way of Japan and Honolulu. The trip took three months.

Stanley relates a rather harrowing experience in the *Indian Witness* (June 1, 1916),"Notes Along the Way" that perhaps reflected his own inward spiritual turmoil.

> In the Inland Sea of Japan there was a scare on board when, at dinner time, our ship smashed into a large fishing junk and sank it. The heavy mast of the sinking ship tore off part of our side-railing. In trying to get out of the way of this one, our ship ran into another one and smashed it up as well.[21]

Although Stanley does not mention his spiritual turmoil in that article, in his *Song* he recalled his state of mind at the time. On board ship he took the Sunday morning services. His sermon title was *"I Know Both"* and his text was from Phil. 4:12,13: "I know what it is to be in need, and I know what it is to have plenty...," *"Paul could say that he had such an inner steadiness that he knew both how to be abased and how to abound, 'I have been very thoroughly initiated into the human lot with all its ups and downs — fullness and hunger, plenty and want. I have strength for anything through him who gives me power'"* (NEB). Stanley then adds, "I was preaching beyond my experience. There was a time when I could have preached on this text with a glow, but the years in India had worn that experience thin, so in the midst of my address everything left me. I had to sit down — a very humiliating experience. The outer collapse took place because the inner experience could not sustain it. I had taken it as a life motto that I would not preach what I was not experiencing, so the outer and the inner came together — in collapse."[22]

Nonetheless, Stanley, even while on furlough, maintained a heavy speaking schedule while Mabel (with two year old Eunice) "rested" in Clayton keeping up her communications and writing mutual friends. In July 1916 Mabel writes to Miss Nellie regarding Stanley. "Miss Nellie, he has the 'wander lust' so much developed that it is difficult to hold him."

We know that Stanley spent the furlough year doing deputation work and making missionary addresses. Forever feeling as if he lacked the necessary training to fulfill his missionary calling and forever feeling the need for more education Stanley spent some months in Princeton Seminary where he met a fellow student, Toyohiko Kagawa. Kagawa, in time, would become perhaps the brightest light in Japanese Christendom but at this point neither particularly impressed the other. Twenty-five years later they would form a deep and lasting friendship that nearly averted the war with Japan.

Mabel during this time must have missed her husband and felt the weight of caring for Eunice alone. She would not have any more children. The birth of Eunice had been very complicated. Years later Eunice would write that at times (perhaps during her early years when she was away at boarding school up in the Himalayas) she and her mother were not particularly close but Mabel, although not particularly demonstrative, certainly made the attempts.

We know that during this time Mabel wrote children's stories,perhaps, in part, to entertain Eunice. Publishing them in the *Junior Missionary Friend,* her tales were always about life in India among the boys and girls of her own mission. Simply reading these gives us significant insight into Mabel's ways of teaching.

One of her stories, "The Quarrel" tells of two little boys, a Hindu and a Christian, at odds, fighting. The Hindu boy throws a stick and breaks the other's arm. The Christian's father comes and the Hindu boy tries to buy him off. The father says, "We are Christians, our Book teaches us to love those who hate us and do good to those who despitefully use us. We don't want your money. We will pray for you."[23] Speak of "going high." This is a tremendous example from an earlier era!

JANUARY 1917: BACK TO INDIA

Then, the Missionary Board Secretary sent Stanley a letter asking him to return to India. In early January, 1917 the Jones headed back to India via the Philippines and Singapore. The trip again took three months. Stanley felt he was not yet ready to reengage with his former mission but got on the boat. In the Philippines Stanley attempted to get some rest but insisted on meeting among students and had another collapse. His yearlong furlough had apparently done nothing for him. *Later he would be grateful that the change that would ultimately reignite his ministry for the rest of his life would happen in India where God had called him to be in ministry.*

The Jones' arrived early April. Stanley was still not ready to take full responsibility for his work and immediately went to the mountains to recuperate. He was at the end of his rope.

Mabel, however, "kept on keeping on." E. Stanley Jones scholar David Bundy remarked in an address at Asbury Seminary, 2001, that "Mabel's importance to her husband's ministry has been almost always underestimated. Except for her, Jones probably would have been sent home as a 'missionary failure.' At this point Stanley was ill at ease and did not want to be in India, when he could not find God's way." Mabel offered a more discerning evaluation, similar to what she had previously expressed to Miss Nellie. In his own words Stanley comments, "My wife says I am a chased rabbit."[24]

Mabel was without question an extraordinarily successful administrator and some think, such as Bundy, that she was the reason the Board allowed Stanley to "stick it out."

In July 1916, Mabel reopened her school for the new-year with eighty boys on the roll.

All of these boys, with the exception of eight, are under twelve years of age but do their own upkeep—cooking, mending, sweeping, etc., and still find time to earn money for Church and Red Cross by doing "extras." This month they have pulled weeds and gathered up dry leaves and carried bricks for twenty-five cents an hour to earn money for the Red Cross in Mesopotamia. At the beginning of the month the teachers volunteered to do the matron's work and the boys promised to help, so that the money saved might go towards buying bedding for the cold days that are almost upon us.

Only three boys seem hopelessly dull and as soon as they are able to read their Bibles they will be put where they can learn a trade. We have a number of boys who but for the school would have been homeless.

The Sitapur Inspector of Schools who visited each class said: "I know of no school in North India as well taught or where the boys are doing as well." As this is the only boys school in North India taught by women we believe this explains its unusual success.[25]

It should be no surprise that this school would eventually be named for Mabel Lossing Jones.

In August Stanley, still no better, went back to the mountains to recuperate again. He writes to Miss Nellie, on August. 20, *"My head is troubling me and I must go off tomorrow for a rest in the hills again, though I just came down a little over a month ago. This weather seems too much for my thinking apparatus. So I will go off for two more weeks & not look at a book or give an address."*

After the second time he felt the game was up. He could not go on.... He had reached the end. There was a need for healing—body, mind and spirit.

THEN IT HAPPENED!

In this dark hour Stanley was led by the Spirit of God to the Central Methodist Church in Lucknow. The Rev. Tamil David was in charge of several evangelistic services. Stanley was in the back of the church kneeling in prayer, not for himself, but for others, when God said to him: "Are you yourself ready for the work to which I have called you?" He replied, "No, Lord, I'm done for. I've reached the end of my resources and I can't go on." The Lord replied, *"If you'll turn that problem over to me and not worry about it, I'll take care of it."* Stanley's eager reply, "Lord, I close the bargain right here!" Stanley arose from his knees knowing that he was well.

Stanley walked home with a group of missionaries along the Cantonment Road. They knew nothing of what was happening within him but he was scarcely touching the earth as he walked along. He was possessed with life and health and peace. For days after that He wondered why he should ever go to bed when bedtime came. He scarcely knew that he had a body.

Then, for a moment, Stanley wondered if he should tell others about this experience. If he did, it would be sink or swim before the world.

Happily he never hesitated to share his experience. He knew this was reality so he announced it before a large audience in Lucknow. Years later a marble tablet was put up in the wall of this church with this inscription: "Near this spot Stanley Jones knelt a physically broken man and arose a physically well man." In fact it was far more than physical healing; he was made whole — body, mind and spirit.

Jones at the place of his healing

He was flooded with a sense of energy, peace, power and adequacy. He was taken possession of by the Holy Spirit — the "Spirit of Truth" — and he had an assurance that this would "abide with him forever."[26]

In Stanley's own words he had moved from "weakness to strength; from confusion to certainty; from inner conflict to unity; from 'myself to his Self.'" Before, he doubted he would have had the nerve to carry on. The task was too demanding for mere human resources. Now he would rely on the Spirit's resources. He had started with so little that he needed so much. If he had had adequate resources (degrees, etc.) he would have been tempted to rely on those but he honestly believed that he had nothing.

Significantly, Stanley was truly healed. His own testimony is that now he no longer relied on his own resources but was now exclusively reliant upon the Holy Spirit.[27] Stanley's testimony was that the Spirit of Truth within makes us alive to everything and everybody. God educates us in the School of the Spirit where we never graduate. Again, Stanley was aware — deeply conscious — that he would be forever a Christian in the making.

At this point Stanley speaks of a threefold assurance, a threefold cord that could not be easily broken. This assurance involved physical resources, spiritual resources, and intellectual resources — that the right answers would be supplied for every objection. The verse, "Do not be anxious regarding what to say… " (Mark 13:11), would become the basis of his confidence among the intellectuals of India. Stanley went from nothing to everything, from so little to so much. Stanley would now put his faith in the faithfulness of a Triune God — the trustworthy Father who loved him, the obedient Son who redeemed him, and the ever-present Holy Spirit who empowered him. It was not that he was invulnerable. He was still a very human instrument. He would continue to learn much by trial and error, corrected by his own mistakes. Yet, the God who raised Jesus Christ had given new life to the new Stanley (Rom. 8:11).[28]

Mabel must have been deeply grateful and deeply relieved.

THE MESSAGE

What about the message? How would Brother Stanley now share this new experience? Since Stanley had been raised conservatively should he now be out to defend everything he had been taught? If so, he would be forever on the defensive. Not that his theology was changing, but now he felt that he should adventure out and follow truth, found anywhere and to whatever end. He inwardly turned pale as he let go of the securities of a blocked-off faith to follow truth to unknown destinations. He now had the inner strength to launch out in the face of the storm. Small wonder Stanley has been typed in some circles as having the mind of a rigid fundamentalist with the heart and soul of a flaming liberal.

So, in the fall of 1917, Stanley took stock. He had offered the securities of his faith on the altar, no longer nervously held for now this faith held him. He was free to explore and appropriate any good, any truth, found anywhere, for he belonged to The Truth, Jesus Christ. There was only one point on the compass — it was Jesus. He was both anchored and free — again, a fundamentalist mind with a modernist soul. With Jesus Christ as Lord, Him crucified and raised from the dead at the center of his message, his task was simplified.

Stanley would forever honor the Bible. We mentioned earlier that the Old Testament would become God's preparation for Christianity, but the Old Testament was not Christianity. Jesus made his own word final, "*You have heard it said, but I say unto you…*". Stanley once had a Hindu lawyer challenge him with pages of questions from the Old Testament but Stanley refused to answer them. The Hindu went wild. "Who gave you the right? What council?" Stanley simply said, "No council." He did not preach church councils, he preached Jesus Christ. He was following Christ. Jesus Christ was the climax of history, a new beginning. Questions regarding creation were not the point. Jesus Christ is the point. In him dialog became decision. Jesus is the point of decision. He is the judgment day. We judge ourselves when we look into his face. In him we see what we are and what we might become. He is judgment and possibility, condemnation and confidence. Again, He was now the Word become Flesh that secured his message and held him to the task.[29]

Stanley took his stand at Jesus, "from verbal to vital," from "inconclusive to conclusive." He would no longer defend western civilization or western forms of Christianity. These were only partially Christian. He would not even try to defend the Church as an organization as the Church as an organization was always disappointing him. His focus, for the rest of his life was Jesus. Jesus would never disappoint him.[30]

To say this a bit differently, Stanley believed that true Christianity is the father of all that is good in the West and Stanley was grateful for that. He was not, however, about replacing cultures. He was always challenging Indians (and others) to keep what was good in their own religion and culture. Indians could contribute to the West, especially with their emphasis on nonviolence and noncooperation. Jesus Christ was the only "thing" exportable. When others would challenge Stanley's Jesus his response was always that Jesus was not a way but THE way. Jesus was not merely the founder of Christianity; he is the Foundation of Christianity.[31]

Stanley was now free to learn from other cultures and even religions. He could learn from them emotionally but there was a limit. He would cooperate with any group who was working for the good of India, but he would insist that all religions did not lead to the top, nor should they be viewed as equally true. His faith was not simply in the teachings of Jesus but in the person of Jesus. His two key verses were John 1:14 (the Word became flesh...) and Acts 4:12 (no other name...).

"This Jesus," said Peter – "alive, available, at work now, healing sick men, redeeming from fear men like me who denied him because I was afraid; and now I preach him because I am not afraid."

Stanley adds, "*This Jesus* is the most alive issue in the world and the one hope of our humanity. It is all breathtaking, for it is life-changing now."[32] Note: It is this Jesus, not that Jesus. Jesus is present. The Holy Spirit was not given to compensate for the absence of Jesus but to guarantee his presence.

This was the message and the challenge to communicate but it was not always convincing. Some would respond that there was nothing new in the New Testament. They could find things in Hinduism, for example, that paralleled the Sermon on the Mount. They had three main objections: *It isn't new; it isn't you* (you Christians do not live it); and *it isn't true.*

Stanley responded, first to it isn't new. There were apparent parallels in Hinduism where the word became word but the Gospel presents the Word become flesh. This was the decisive difference between Christianity and all other religions — the difference between the word becoming word and the word becoming flesh. Jesus did not bring good news; he was good news. The Gospel lies in his person. That difference was profound. Whereas moralism points to the way, Christ was the Way. Whereas philosophy points to the truth, Christ was the Truth. Whereas religion points to life, Christ was the Life. Jesus points to himself as the Word become flesh. When Stanley thinks of goodness he thinks not of virtue but of Jesus. When he thinks of God he thinks of Jesus.[33]

Stanley goes on to say, (and you might want to read this paragraph twice) *"Scripture says that Jesus is the word. Words express hidden thoughts so that the thoughts are bigger than the word. All expressions of word limit thought. The word is the thought available. God, the eternal Spirit is a hidden thought. He reveals himself in the Word, Jesus. The thought and the word are one but the thought is greater than the word. Yet, he who takes hold of Jesus takes hold of God. Again, the Father is greater as thought is bigger than word. The unexpressed God is greater than the expressed Word — Son. Yet the Father and the Son are one."*[34] OK, I confess. I like that.

Stanley believed that in Jesus the divine quality is not imposed upon human nature but exposed through human nature. The human framework and the divine imposition were one and produced the God-Man Jesus. History is replete with some who would impose divine qualities upon man and these inevitably create monstrosities or absurdities. Jesus is the only guru. Where do we find him you ask? You find him in the heart of the New Testament.[35]

As for "It isn't you," Stanley admits that some Christians are not living the life they profess. Like the Scribes, the Pharisees, the Teachers of the Law in Jesus' day, they are always finding fault with true Christians and missing the point. Interestingly Stanley rarely has a good word for the modern equivalent—theologians and seminary professors. He mentions a theologian (we met him in the Introduction) who cavalierly dismisses Jesus. "We know little about Jesus, so I can dismiss him cavalierly." Stanley replied, "Then I can dismiss you cavalierly as a witness who does in reality know little or nothing about Jesus. But some of the rest of us do know a lot about him; and, moreover, we do know him and hence fall at his feet in complete allegiance." He has us, and that having us is producing the deepest satisfaction and joy and certainty that life can know. It works![36]

As for "It isn't true," Stanley simply invites his objectors to, "Try it." I shall always remember Brother Stanley challenging a skeptic, "One might ask that if Jesus never lived who invented him. How could so much good come from a lie? How could a lie produce such honesty?" Jesus said he was Savior and when people accepted him as such they found themselves saved, not from hell but from what they had been, to what they wanted to be, and ought to be—from guilt, frustration and emptiness. At one of his meetings chaired by a non-Christian, the man said, "If this isn't true it doesn't matter, but if it is true, nothing else matters."

Stanley challenges anyone anywhere to expose his or her inner life to Jesus Christ in repentance, faith and obedience. He virtually guarantees the outcome. Such persons are inevitably changed, profoundly changed in every fiber of their being so that the *objective and subjective* become one reality of verified experience.

Let's allow the Brother to explain these two realities: *objective and subjective* (history and experience as it were). One by itself is not enough. Objective reality is the reality of history but doubts remain (as with the theologian Rudolph Bultmann and so many others in the last century who insisted that history by itself is never reliable—it cannot carry the weight of absolute truth). Similarly, subjective reality can be found in experience but doubts remain there as well. It is essential for the objective and the subjective to come together and corroborate each other. Christian faith does that so that the objective life and teachings of Jesus in history are corroborated by our experience of Jesus as we respond by faith and unconditional surrender. Bultmann writes that if there were no Jesus it would make no difference in his faith. He was left with only the word become word but not with the word become flesh. He was left with his teachings but not with his Person. As Stanley would say, Bultmann's faith was verbal but not vital.[37] Christianity was not tried and found wanting. It was gently nudged, found difficult, and not really tried at all.

Through the centuries Stanley writes that Christians have fastened on three infallibilities. Perhaps today he would choose a different word for infallibilities but we will allow Stanley to speak for himself. He is referring to the infallible Bible, the infallible Christian experience, and the infallible church. Here is the key, however. None of these can be taken alone and none is infallible on their own. So, where does our authority lie? It is at the junction of these three when all three say the same thing. The objective reality (the infallible Bible) becomes the subjective reality (the infallible Christian experience) and is corrected and corroborated by the collective witness (the infallible church).

All through the ages people have tried and found that Jesus is giving them what only God can give them—forgiveness of sins, power over evil, reconciliation with God, with themselves and those around them. Here is an adequacy to meet life and conquer it. Jesus as Lord fills them with hope and joy—he gives them eternal life now. That collective witness to Jesus Christ as Savior and Lord, all saying the same thing in different languages and in different ways, is one of the most impressive things on this planet.[38] Again, this is not the precarious certainty of dogmatism or even of experience. This is the confirmation of the *Word* — of the objective word in the Bible, of the incarnate Word in Jesus, and of the collective word in the church.

All of this leads Stanley beyond a kind of existentialism that focuses only on the present — what has bearing on my present existence — disregarding history. Jesus is past, present and future (Revelation 1:4; Hebrews 6:5). As a result of this Stanley believes that he has the universe at his back, a sense of cosmic approval. We will return to this thought in subsequent chapters when Stanley begins to develop his thinking on a *moral universe* where God has so arranged created matter so that living according to the innate principles of the universe brings fulfillment. I like this. Know the Truth and the Truth will set you free from "passing fads." When Stanley would introduce the Round Table Conferences in the 1920s, he did not have to defend Jesus, Jesus is his own defense. People would argue with dogma but not with the person of Jesus. Stanley says you can fling mud at the sun but sunshine itself is its own defense.[39]

Let's conclude this section predictably, with Jesus. Jesus appeals to the soul as light appeals to the eye, as love to the heart. Paul was not so successful in Athens as he spoke more of *good views* than *good news*. He then went on to Corinth determined to know nothing but Jesus Christ and him crucified. Stanley too would preach nothing but Jesus Christ and him crucified. That was his message.

THE SETTING AND THE AUDIENCE

Now, having discussed Jones' message at some length, we turn to the stage, the setting, to his audience. Before his emotional breakdown and ultimate 'breakthrough' Stanley had been focusing on the outcastes. He now realized that his call as an evangelist was to the educated middle and upper caste Indians. He believed that only the upper caste Indians (who had been neglected by Christian missionaries) could ultimately influence India as a whole. The social, political and religious life of India was built around ideas and these ideas came primarily from the thinking "upper" castes. These ideas should then percolate down and hopefully find expression and reality in the daily lives of the masses.[40]

Almost immediately, while Mabel was busy with the school, Stanley began his evangelistic ministry. Before the end of 1917 he speaks of filling the Town Hall in the city of Hardoi where he preached the gospel of Jesus Christ in a series of meetings. On the third night he gave the opportunity of asking questions. For three hours he underwent a cross-examination from about twenty lawyers before the whole crowd. When he got through he felt like a rag; but he was a very happy rag.[41]

To prevent another breakdown, Stanley then developed a routine for the next several years. During the summer rainy season travel was virtually impossible so he would take three months off for intensive study in the Himalayas, usually at the now Sat Tal Christian Ashram. He would carefully compose five addresses to be delivered in public halls in most Indian cities with a population of over 50,000 (imagine). He would stay in each city for one week. The five addresses were delivered Monday through Friday, each took an hour and a half to deliver (when an interpreter was needed, twice as long). His message was clear. He would speak of a *disentangled Christ.* Then he would answer questions from the audience. His responses frequently took another hour. On Saturday he spoke to non-Christians and on Sunday in churches. Finally, on Sunday night he would board a train to the next destination.

Early on in 1918 Stanley's routine included a 4,500-mile trip by rail to Allahabad, Calcutta, Madura, Palamcottah, Travendrum, Coimbatore, Vellore, Bombay, and Ahmednagar. Trains were crowded with military and others. He frequently slept on the train floor. At each city he held meetings for Christians in the morning and for the educated non-Christians in the evenings. Note, these were public meeting halls, not churches. In fact, the chairmen and audiences, were mostly non-Christian. Stanley described these meetings as "intensely evangelistic." They were non-denominational meetings chaired by the most eminent men in the city, again principals of law colleges, professors, judges, army officers… Among the chairmen were Parsees, Hindus, Muslims and Christians.[42]

Then, significantly, in same year, the YMCA offered Stanley a platform inviting him to speak at interdenominational evangelistic meetings to educated non-Christian audiences. The YMCA would arrange the meetings throughout India. At first Stanley's Methodist Board of Missions said no to Stanley identifying solely with the YMCA but then quickly followed up by saying that if the door was open, in principle, Stanley could work with all the various denominational missions in India. Stanley said this was one of the first steps toward ecumenicity. The Methodist Mission Board would support Stanley but then commissioned him to work with and for all missionary work throughout the subcontinent of India. This would remain true for the next 50+ years. Stanley would work with all missions, including the Mar Thoma Syrian Church of South India (for 45+ years). These Mar Thoma Christians would take Stanley in as one of their own.

All this served a two-fold objective: first to strengthen Christians within the Church (including converting "unchristian" Christians within the Church), and secondly to convert the non-Christian educated Indians among the upper castes. The Methodist Mission Board would pay Stanley's salary but Stanley would pay for his own travel expenses.

The routine, under this scenario with the YMCA, was to preach to "Christians" in the churches but at nights to the non-Christians in public halls, theaters, school halls and at out-of-door compounds. Non-Christians could not go in large numbers to churches so Stanley found neutral places to deliver what he called "lectures." The crowds gathered. This was better than the BBC, Al Jazeera, FOX News or MSNBC. Stanley had a way of understanding the issues from many different perspectives.

Early in the week he would lecture on world affairs but then later in the week switch to preaching about the Cross. As noted earlier, Jones frequently asked non-Christians to chair these meetings. There were usually anywhere from 20 to 200 lawyers in attendance. Again, Stanley quickly adopted Matthew 10:19-21 as his rule ("Take no thought about what you shall say for it shall be given to you by my Spirit..."). As always these verses would sustain him across the years. They never let him down.[43]

So, Stanley was now committed to evangelism among the intellectuals of India, the leaders of this new resurgent India. He knew his message was sound and needed but were his methods of approach to India the right ones. He proceeded carefully.

Remembering the advice of the Hindu judge, "You must come to us in 'the right way,'" Stanley immediately rejected some of the old methods such as attacking the non-Christian faiths or presenting the Christian faith as the fulfillment of the non-Christian faiths. He refused to put Christian against non-Christian but he succeeded in putting Christianity against all that was contrary to a *moral universe*. As there was much in the old faiths that was consistent with the moral universe he soon realized that the old methods would not be tolerated in the new sensitive, resurgent India fighting for independence. Stanley would rarely mention non-Christian religions. *He was determined not to speak to Hindus or Muslims but to persons in spiritual need.* Jesus Christ had met his needs and he could meet theirs as well. This message would be person to person, not preacher to audience.

Stanley studied their thinking—especially that of Hindus and Muslims. They would know that he knew their thinking without mentioning their religions. Stanley's Christ was *disentangled* from western culture and western forms of Christianity. He spoke directly to the needs of persons as persons without any cumbersome entanglements.

As we observed Stanley being delivered from his bouts with depression and anxiety it is understandable that he would be especially drawn to those Scriptures that emphasized God's love and love as the fruit of the Holy Spirit. Once when I was meeting with him one on one at one of his ashrams we studied the "love" passages in 1 Corinthians 13. As we began our study I shall never forget Brother Stanley leaning toward me with a sparkle in his eye and saying, Brother Bob, "Paul dipped his pen in the blood of his broken heart and set pain to music." That was Brother Stanley's *Song of Ascents* and as we slip a bit further into the year 1918 in the next chapter, this song was about to carry him into the hearts and minds of millions.

E. Stanley Jones & Family at Bhimtal, 1918

CHAPTER FOUR

STANLEY MEETS GANDHI AND ENGAGES THE INDIAN INDEPENDENCE MOVEMENT WHILE BEGINNING THE ROUND TABLE CONFERENCES

Mabel Struggles with a Breakdown of Her Own

Let's embrace the years 1918 to 1925. That takes us from the end of WWI through a period of near exhaustion for Mabel and on to the publication of Stanley's first book, *The Christ of the Indian Road*. It would eventually sell over a million copies and would launch Stanley onto the worldwide stage.

Stanley was now speaking before Christians, Hindus, Muslims and Sikhs in many different venues. God had a way of always showing up — often surprisingly! In his *Song* Stanley gives several examples of how the Spirit strengthened and sustained him, sometimes even bailing him out of difficult situations.

Christians were sometimes heckled, even pommeled with old fruits and vegetables, as they sought to address the peoples of India. Stanley tells the story of speaking in a wrestling pit, a popular sports venue at the time. He claims to have "wrestled" for the souls of men as there was no way out of the pit and Stanley's host was concerned that the crowd seemed restless. "What if they should suddenly turn violent?" After just a few minutes, however, you could hear a pin drop.[1]

A significant breakthrough for Christians came through the Indian National Congress strong man Vallabhbhai Patel. It had been customary for centuries for small princes to rule their own states. Sensing that the split between India and Pakistan seemed inevitable Patel gave these princes an opportunity to choose India over Pakistan. There was no compulsion. They could opt for either when the division took place; but if they opted for Pakistan he felt that they would have to suffer the consequences. They opted for India and within one year the power systems built through the generations collapsed like a house of cards before the rising tide of democracy.

Relevant to this is that much of the earlier abuses of Christians now ceased. People, sensing an ally (at least in Stanley) in their struggle for independence, listened more carefully. What had happened? In part, because of generations of loving and devoted service by Christian missionaries, both Indian and foreign, trust began to build. Stanley does not mention this but it was also due in part to his own understanding approach to these sensitive issues.[2]

Hindu leaders would, (under the new constitution) give Christian missionaries (and others) the right to propagate their religion. This was terribly significant. Over the years three Indian Presidents would attend and actually chair Stanley's meetings, (Chakravarti Rajagopalacharia, Dr. Rajendra Prasad and Dr. Radhakrishnan).

Stanley's *Song* tells the story of Hyderabad (a Muslim state) with 16 million Hindus. Stanley spoke to the prime minister of the state saying that he would need to do two things immediately to save his dynasty—first, opt for India and second, give responsible government to the people. Stanley quoted to him the Scripture regarding making peace quickly with your adversary lest he take you to court and you end up in jail (Matthew 5:25).[3] The prime minister waited too long and went to jail.

At this point there is an interesting turn that highlights Stanley's influence even more. We have mentioned that he was grateful for the centuries old influence of Christian missionaries. After World War I, however, he was one of the first to realize that Western Christianity generally and Western Christian missionaries in particular, were now consciously or unconsciously often co-opted into becoming agents of Western Imperialism. The numbers of Christian baptisms had been declining so conversions became their focus. This would not set well with most Indians, due in some part to the Arya Samaj movement (founded in 1875) by a Sanskrit scholar from Gujarat to reestablish Hinduism in its pure and original form. Then, as British imperialism continued to loom, more secular Indians were quickly becoming increasingly suspect of Christian motives and methods.[4]

With great diplomacy Stanley would spend the next 30 years trying to dodge the accusations of imperialism as India was about to become obsessed with her own struggle for independence.

It was here that Stanley realized that he needed to listen more carefully to his *inner voice*. This would provide his "life assurance." The only way he could account for the certainty of this inner voice was the Holy Spirit. His leading was from a power not his own.[5] Little wonder the entire Bible interprets "self-reliance" — trusting anyone or anything other than God as one's only hope for salvation and strength to survive — as perhaps the greatest sin of the people. The Spirit would be the working force in Stanley's life. He simply did what he did because of the leading of the Holy Spirit.

Stanley Jones believed that he went farther — accomplished more, with fewer natural resources and with less academic education — than anyone he knew. He was always a surprise to himself. Again, the only way he could account for it was the Holy Spirit. A Power not his own was working through him and doing things he was incapable of doing on his own. Stanley writes, "*AND, the good news is that all of this is available to anyone who has the sense, to take it.*" This "unexpected and undeserved" giving of the Holy Spirit would persist for the next 50+ years with unabated and unfailing power—available through faith in Jesus Christ—"the Life of my life, the Joy of my joy, the Power of my power—my All." Without him he would not step over the smallest threshold; with him, he would go to the ends of the earth.[6]

A FRESH APPROACH TO EVANGELISM

In 1918 F. B. Fisher, a former missionary to India (who frequently traveled with Stanley), proposed raising $1 million for mass movement evangelism but before he could launch the initiative another special commission among the Methodists was launched called the Centenary Commission. This was set to commemorate the centennial of the Women's Foreign Missions Society in 1919. Stanley was skeptical. The lofty goals of the commission were 200,000 conversions from non-Christians and 100,000 baptisms among the unconverted Christian communities. Stanley was appointed chairman, but nonetheless, he had his doubts. "Can our mass movements be run by a committee? A committee might well prove to be a hindrance."[7]

We said in the last chapter that in his *Song*, Stanley writes that early on in his ministry he would not accept the old approaches to evangelism, primarily attacking the non-Christian faiths as lacking in truth or even presenting Christianity as the fulfillment of these non-Christian faiths. Christianity on the attack could not be appreciated in public debates any more than "sweet music in a dog fight." In a newly sensitive, resurgent India, fighting for her independence, this method cancelled the message. Again, neither could Stanley accept the method of "fulfillment"—Christianity fulfills the best in Hinduism. Hindus invariably objected to any interpretation of Hindu doctrines, especially when you brought them up to say that "Christianity was the perfect fulfillment of an imperfect faith."[8]

Stanley would insist that it was far better not to mention non-Christian religions, at least by name. As noted earlier, he would not speak to others as Hindus or Muslims, but as persons — persons in spiritual need. Jesus Christ had met his need, and he could meet theirs as well.

As if to illustrate all this we find the important story of C.T. Venugopal (Stanley referred to him as Venu), an outstanding Christian layman of India. He was a mathematician. His brother invited him to one of Stanley's meetings and Venu said, "If that isn't true, it ought to be true." He was converted, and later became the head of the railroad for all of India and Pakistan. The conflict between India and Pakistan would be brutal; thousands would die. Once, when trying to get the two countries to cooperate and share train schedules so that their lines would not be cut, the Muslims had refused to share their records. Indians were hoping to trade one record for one record. Venu, not wanting to give up his vision, went the second mile and gave them all of his records unconditionally. The Muslims reciprocated saying that they would not be outdone by a Christian (former Hindu) and yielded all of their records as well.

Venu would say to his employees, "I'm a Christian; help me to become a better one." He was not a gifted speaker — the same was said of Kagawa in Japan — who, like Venu, rarely said much but when he did it was straight from the heart and mind of Jesus. They both made significant sacrifices. Someone once added about Kagawa, "when you are hanging on a cross you don't have to say a great deal." Venu's own mother said, "I want the faith my son has." His brother, also a mathematician, was not so committed, so much so that Stanley said of him, "He applied math to pure math so that the math became word." Venu applied math to the mind of Jesus so that his math became flesh. Stanley insisted that Venu's example created a quiet and dynamic revolution.[9]

On November 11, 1918 the war was over. This would be an important year in transition for both Stanley and Mabel!

THE GROWING INDIAN INDEPENDENCE MOVEMENT: *SATYAGRAHA*

As India was about to be consumed by the emergence of Indian Nationalism Mahatma Gandhi quickly surfaced as its leader. Gandhi, had returned from South Africa with his vision of *satyagraha* – a way of life based on love, compassion and peace – a *Truth*-force as an outgrowth theory of education emphasizing non-violent/non-cooperation.

Stanley's book on Gandhi states that Gandhi was a combination of East and West. He understood the West but his soul was intensely Eastern. Born in the native state of Porbandar, where his father was the prime minister, Gandhi early embraced the ideas of independence. He was Indian to the core, and yet he was deeply influenced by the West. Stanley comments, "Had Mahatma Gandhi not been educated in large measure in the West, he would never have had the world-wide influence that he had." He stepped out of India for 26 years, exposing himself to the West. He studied law in Britain before moving to South Africa to establish his practice in the midst of Apartheid – white minority rule.

Gandhi, in his attempt to embrace the West was never at ease, however. He honestly tried to absorb the civilization of the West – including dinner clothes, spats, meat eating, and all. He soon saw that this was not for him. It was like Saul's armor on David. It did not fit. Gandhi's inner reservations would never allow him inwardly to surrender to Western civilization so the "clothes" were discarded. India was ready for a man who could voice her "incoherent cry, embody her aspirations and lead her out of her bondage."

Gandhi, out of the fire of the struggle for the rights of Indians in South Africa would hear a "voice," his own: "Now you must go and deliver the people of India from their bondage." South Africa being the nerve center of Apartheid, the discrimination experienced there provided him with motive and understanding. Gandhi's call would not only influence India but the world (eventually including South Africa).

It is significant that God was also preparing Britain for this hour as well. There came into power a group of men who essentially agreed with Gandhi, who believed in what he was fighting for, namely, freedom for people everywhere.[10]

By 1919 Gandhi was established in his Ashram in Gujurat and was becoming the new leader throughout the country launching his *satyagraha,* again a soul-force campaign expressed through nonviolent civil disobedience and noncooperation. As if to illustrate, he called for *hartal* — the closing of shops and businesses as a symbol of opposition to the oppressive British rule. Stanley was at first against this kind of protest and wrote to Gandhi begging him not to begin it. Eventually, however, his thinking was changed by the heart and soul of the movement.

The heart and soul of *satyagraha* was this: When you wrong me, I won't hate you but I won't obey you. Do what you like to me. I will match my capacity to suffer against your capacity to inflict suffering. It will be my soul force against your physical force. I will wear you down with good will. Gandhi had first tried this successfully in South Africa and then brought it to the 400 million souls in India. Do not submit to a wrong or an evil system and do not to go to war! Stanley was impressed!

As if to prove the point, Gandhi was arrested April 8, 1919. The next day Hindus and Muslims marched peacefully through the streets in support of Gandhi. On April 11, the British declared martial law. The Indian nationalists had planned a public meeting on April 13 in Jallianwala Bagh but the British General Dyer was eager to show force and a massacre occurred killing officially 379 persons (but unofficially closer to a thousand). Eventually, Jallianwala Bagh would cost the British the "moral right to rule the country.[11]

Nonviolent noncooperation included the surrender of titles and honors bestowed by the British, resignation from government offices, withdrawal from government-affiliated schools and colleges, and boycotting elections, law courts, and foreign goods. Civil disobedience went a step further by calling for noncompliance with many British laws (for example, by not paying taxes), or even the breaking of discriminatory British civil laws.

Noncooperation also tried to abolish the "untouchable" status of the lower castes. Gandhi often stayed with low caste persons to the scandal of the "holy" Brahmin.[12]

It is significant that although Stanley would become more and more sympathetic to the Indian nationalists he was not a revolutionary. For example, he reacted against Annie Besant's "home rule movement." Besant was a radical social activist and theosophist, controversial both in her home country of England as well as in India. Importantly, his reaction against the extremes would continue to give him some leverage within the British regime.

BROTHER STANLEY IS LAUNCHED INTO EVER WIDENING INFLUENCES

It is critical that in mid 1919 Stanley's Board of Foreign Missions received a follow-up request from the year before to allow Jones to preach and teach at meetings arranged by the trusted YMCA. Dr. Sherwood Eddy (1871-1963), who recruited Stanley, was the first YMCA Secretary to Asia, remaining so from 1911 to 1926. Eddy would arrange the venues for his meetings. This would free Stanley up; **but**, the Missions Board was already committed to the Centenary Commission and dare not release him as they were pressing for more baptisms.[13]

Further evidence of the strength of Stanley's call and his ability to see both sides of an issue would lead to his willingness to compromise. He continued his evangelistic work among educated non-Christians as arranged by the YMCA but committed himself to the Centenary Campaign as well.

In August 1919 Stanley wrote in the *Indian Witness*, "Notes on the

Eddy Campaigns." He and Eddy had just completed a six-month tour in forty-three different locations with significant results. In his *Duplicate Letter* dated August 6, 1919, Stanley writes that these campaigns "included both Christian and non-Christians and were ecumenical in that all denominations took part from the highly ritualistic Syrian churches and the high church Anglicans, all the way to the Salvation Army." The goal was personal evangelism; that is, it was the responsibility of each Christian to be an evangelist. For the meetings that included non-Christians this resulted in a new approach. At a strategic point in the meetings, the speaker would announce a break in the proceedings for personal conversation. For about fifteen minutes "each Christian" would turn to his non-Christian friend and give a simple witness. This format was well received by both Hindus and Muslims as it took the "nervousness" out of the atmosphere, established points of contact while "introducing timid workers to their task." In one place there were 123 baptisms on a Sunday morning among sixteen different castes.[14]

During this tour Jones and Eddy also visited the Malabar Coast (the southwestern coast of India along the Arabian Sea). There, German Christians from Basel had established a successful Mission that before the war had built industries to hire Indian workers. They had been wonderfully successful. Unfortunately the War had taken its toll. Perhaps affected by this, as the War was winding down in Europe, Stanley became more and more of a pacifist. He believed that pacifism reflected the bedrock Christian principle of love. War, by and large, the result of the male ego, sought only revenge.[15]

Toward the end of 1919 Indian nationalism began to fuel the drive for independence even stronger. It was not enough to be free; they wanted dignity. Christians, especially evangelists, were confronted by a new India. Feeling more and more pressure to present a Christianity that had become naturalized in India, Stanley was attempting to put himself more and more in positions of understanding potential converts. He wrote from Jubbalopore to the corresponding secretary of the Missions Board, Dr. Frank Mason North, that his non-

Christian meetings had been arranged by both Hindus and Muslims. He would announce in advance his lecture topics: 1. Jesus and Democracy. 2. Can Christianity be proved? 3. Is Jesus fitted to be universal. 4. Who was Jesus Christ, a conscious pretender, one unconsciously deluded, a good man or the Son of God?[16] The question and answer sessions following would sometimes go on for hours.

STANLEY MEETS GANDHI FOR THE FIRST TIME

It was also toward the end of 1919 that Stanley first personally met Mahatma Gandhi. Stanley writes that this contact with Gandhi was the one that "brought him the most unalloyed joy of all the contacts through the years." It was soon after Gandhi's return from South Africa when he was just beginning to take up the threads of his work in India. Their relationship had not been clouded by any controversy. Neither was on the defensive, and neither was on the offensive. The exchange was simple, natural and unstrained.

Stanley was giving addresses in St. Stephen's College, Delhi, and Principal Rudra said rather casually: "Mr. Gandhi [this was before he became Mahatma, "The Great-souled"] is upstairs. Would you like to see him?" In contrast with later years, the house would have been surrounded night and day with a curious crowd. Simply to get an interview with him would not have been easy, for people from all over the world would have been pressing him for an audience. But here "I was being asked if I would like to see him! He was seated on a bed surrounded by papers, and he greeted me with an engaging and contagious smile." Stanley, at his best without preliminary, went straight to his question: "How can we make Christianity naturalized in India, not a foreign thing, identified with a foreign government and a foreign people, but a part of the national life of India and contributing its power to India's uplift? What would you, as one of the Hindu leaders of India, tell me, a Christian, to do in order to make this possible?"

Gandhi responded with great clarity and directness: He suggested four things.

1. Talk more about Jesus and live more like Jesus.
2. Emphasize the love side of Christianity more; make it your working force, for love is central in Christianity.
3. Learn about other religions and study them more sympathetically to find out the good that is within them.
4. But never adulterate your own religion; don't tone it down.[17]

In his book on *Gandhi*, Stanley writes that these four suggestions were genius. He had put his finger unerringly on the four weak spots in our individual and collective lives.[18] Stanley then goes on to explain why these suggestions were critical.

First, "talk more about Jesus was Stanley's peculiar genius." Stanley got to the place where he would rarely attempt to defend Christianity as such. Christianity had frequently come across as far too Western. Similarly, he would never attempt to defend the Church as such. Although he loved the church and understood her importance, she was all too often disappointing him. So, Stanley talked about Jesus — what Jesus had done for him and what Jesus could do for others. Jesus, as the Son of the Living God, was not Western, he was God's revelation to all people that they might know who God is, a God of love, mercy, justice, faithfulness and long-suffering — the Word become flesh. John 1:1ff.

Slain before the foundation, Jesus was sent to planet earth at just the right moment. Stanley, understanding history, realized that the time of Jesus' appearing was right — at the height of the Roman Empire. The stage was set. This was the window of opportunity. The spread of Christianity even fifty years earlier would have been inconceivable. The roads had not been built. Pirates still ruled the seas. There was no common language that could embrace the realm. As all this was changing a light dawned in the small Judean town of Bethlehem.[19] John writes in the prologue of his Gospel that "Through him all things were made; without him nothing was made that has been made. In him was life, and that life was the light of men. The light shines in the darkness, but the darkness has not understood it…. Though the world was made through him, the world did not recognize him…"[20] Stanley's call was to make Jesus known.

Secondly, "emphasize the love side of Christianity more, make it your working force, for love is central in Christianity." Stanley believed that far too many Christians, even among themselves, did not demonstrate the love manifested in the life and teachings of Jesus. Again, this was absolutely critical. Since love is the fruit of the Spirit (Galatians 5:22 names love as the singular fruit followed by the fruits of the fruit — joy, peace, forbearance, kindness, goodness…), Stanley would emphasize again and again how important it was for Christians to love each other and their neighbors as themselves. It follows that this would later become the foundation for his Christian pacifism. Even among gifted "Christians," gifts without the fruit of the Spirit were not the gifts of the Spirit. "Dear friends, do not believe every spirit, but test the spirits to see whether they are from God…. let us love one another, for love comes from God. Everyone who loves has been born of God and knows God. Whoever does not love does not know God because God is love." Galatians 4: 1-8. Period!

Thirdly, "learn about other religions and study them more sympathetically to find out the good that is within them." Stanley believed that if you truly wanted to be convinced of the truths of Christianity, learn about other religions. Although he rarely spoke of other religions as such, his witness would be a head-on presentation of Christ, combined with the witness that Christ had met his needs so he could meet their needs as well. It was person to person and not preacher to audience. "But in speaking to their needs, mental and spiritual, I would have to know their needs; so I gave myself to a thorough study of the background of their thinking in Hinduism and Islam. They would know that I knew their thinking, though I would not mention their faiths by name."

One Hindu asked Stanley after a meeting, "Would you please

speak about the better phases of Hinduism tomorrow night, so we can see what you mean?" Stanley replied. "Yes, but I do not speak about Hinduism as such; the Christ I present is the disentangled Christ—disentangled from being bound up with Western culture and Western forms of Christianity. Jesus must stand on his own, speaking directly to the needs of persons as persons without any cancelling entanglements." Such was Stanley's genius.[21]

Finally, "never adulterate your own religion; don't tone it down."Imagine a Hindu giving such advice. Gandhi believed that the only way for Stanley to be accepted as a Christian in India was to be forthright and honest—to speak his own understanding of the truth without apology. Gandhi also believed that Stanley sometimes took that advice to a fault. He was once asked, "What do you think of Stanley Jones?" The Mahatma replied: " He is a very earnest man, and a very sincere man, but he is too certain about religion and therefore lacks humility." Total reliance upon God and the unwavering awareness of his presence in one's life can sometimes come across that way. To illustrate the point further, Stanley then writes that Gandhi was missing the heart of revelation because he had not come into vital contact with the Person of Christ—his understanding was second hand, embracing the principles but not the Person.[22]

Soon afterwards, Stanley wrote from Sitapur that Gandhi was outwardly Hindu but had been Christianized in his conceptions. The *Gita* was the center of his loyalty and his devotion. He was a Hindu by allegiance and a Christian by affinity. Again, he was a Hindu who was deeply Christianized—more Christianized than most Christians. Gandhi stated that when Kali Charan Banerjee, a great Indian Christian, attempted to lead him to Jesus Christ that he (Gandhi) came "away not sorry, not dejected, not disappointed, but I felt sad that even Mr. Banerjee could not convince me."[23]

In Chapter One we observed Stanley himself, making an attempt to lead the great man to Christ. Gandhi responded writing, "All I can say is that my heart is absolutely open. I have no axes to grind; I want to find the truth, to see God face to face. But there I stop. Do please come to the Ashram when you have the time."[24] Stanley would do just that.

THE ROUND TABLE CONFERENCES

It was during the 1920s (up until the Great Depression) that foreign missions reached its zenith. It might help to know that early in the 1800s there were less than 300 Catholic Priests in Missions and only 100 Protestant missionaries worldwide (no women). By the 1920s there were thousands. In 1928 alone $60 million were spent by Mission agencies, a staggering amount in that day. Although officially neutral towards British rule and Indian independence, things would begin to change. Many of the more traditional approaches to evangelism were no longer as effective in many countries around the world. Increasingly American missionaries in particular would be facing this problem, especially in light of rising Indian nationalism.

Perhaps understanding these issues more than others, in the 1920s Stanley began organizing his "Round Table Conferences" that for the rest of his life would become one of his most effective tools for influencing both Christians and non-Christians alike. At one point he felt that his style of lectures mentioned previously were "too public and professional and not sufficiently personal to be an authentic instrument of Christian evangelism." Then, using the same group of local Indian leaders and officials who organized and chaired his lectures, he asked them to invite about forty or so of the "leading men" of the city to participate in a Round Table Conference. At these Round Tables (usually 2/3 non-Christian and 1/3 Christian) no one sat at the head of the table. Each person was asked to share their own experience as to what their religion had done for them. Stanley would go last and talk about Jesus.

Stanley insisted, "know the Truth and the Truth will set you free from passing fads." As stated earlier, at the Round Table he did not have to defend Jesus. Jesus was his own defense. People would argue with their images of Christianity, even dogma, but not with the person of Jesus. Stanley frequently says: "You can fling mud at the sun but that sunshine is its defense. Jesus appeals to the soul as light appeals to the eye, as love to the heart. Paul was not so successful in Athens as he spoke more of good views than good news. So he went on to Corinth determined to know nothing but Jesus Christ and him crucified." Stanley's aim as well would be to preach nothing but Jesus Christ and him crucified.[25]

The Round Table was never a place for idle chatter or even for plotting future strategy. It was a way of allowing different perspectives to find common ground, to know and appreciate each other. Many of the participants were then drawn to Stanley's larger meetings and were soundly converted.[26] This was even more evidence of Stanley's genius.

At one point Stanley wrote regarding one of his Round Table conferences, "Christ was upon us to the point of tears." He returned to his room thanking God for the way Christ is capturing the heart of India.[27]

As the years progressed, Stanley would hold more and more Round Table Conferences for his inter-religious discussion groups in conjunction with his evangelistic meetings. These were always the best venues for including the various religious leaders in the area.[28]

THE CRISIS

Early in 1920 Mabel and Stanley were in Sitapur. They built a new house close enough to the school for Mabel to supervise her teachers and other workers.

Stanley then had to leave for an extended preaching mission. Eunice was ill with typhoid and Mabel—in the midst of tending to Eunice—had her office work to do as she prepared for the opening of another school term. She was understandably stressed. She comments that Stanley seemed to be away more than at home of late. Then, in the midst of her angst, the school was nearly overrun by snakes, scorpions and infectious diseases. Remarkably, Mabel still managed to raise enough money from her friends in the U.S. ($700) to build a separate hospital building. In May of 1920 she wrote in her *Circular Letter* that, "Last week when I discovered two more cases of measles, I was so thankful for a place to take them."[29]

Then, the following summer of 1921 Mabel would experience the most serious crisis of all. Again, Stanley was off for two months doing evangelistic work. On July 20, with both Mabel and Eunice not feeling well, her school opened for the new-year. It was boiling hot, yet boys and teachers returned in good spirits and began their work in earnest. "Little did I dream of the sad story I would have to write."

The following Monday I walked through the school and noticed little Gyan was absent. I then found him playing in the hostel. He said laughingly that he had a headache and could not go to school. I sent him to bed and he ran off smiling.

An hour later Miss George came running to me saying, "Gyan has just now vomited twice and is unconscious. I started at once for the hostel and found him dead. I tried to get a doctor but all were out. I finally decided that it must have been a heat stroke. I telegraphed to the boy's parents, who are our workers and we prepared the body for burial."

As we worked, Miss Rosaline came running and said, "Victor has vomited and is turning cold." I hurried to him and found our lovely, plump faced, fourth class boy as cold as death, his eyes and face sunk in, his finger nails blue and with no pulse.

I finally succeeded in getting an Indian doctor from the jail. Before he got there two more boys were taken. He gave a glance at the boys, said briefly, "Black cholera," and went to work. He opened a vein in the arm, injected a tube and gave each boy about a quart of saline injection. It was like watching a miracle to see warmth return to the body, the face fill out and consciousness return. That night, however, little Chunnie died before we knew he was really ill, and several others were taken down.

My teachers, mere girls most of them, worked day and night with no thought of their own danger. Rev. Albert Gulab and Christ Chand worked with them as well. I sent telegrams to parents and tried to get the well boys off to their homes and segregated the orphans. The next day reports began to come in from the boys who had gone home. James Sunder Lall who ran so happily to his train reached home safely but died at midnight. Noble Briscoe and Solomon Har Dayal, splendid sons of our preachers, and dear little Chotte Lass, who had left in seemingly the best of health were all dead the next day.

Each day brought more cases and more deaths until I felt I could bear no more. My splendid boys, bright, clean, healthy, happy, promising little lads, who had been with me until they seemed like my own sons, snatched away while we stood helpless. I had nursed the boys through 42 cases of influenza. 36 cases of small-pox; measles, mumps, malaria and all sorts of complaints, and we had saved them all, but this was a foe more terrible than any that had ever come our way." Then, finally, it was over. We had used permanganate pills by the score. The wells were purple with permanganate water. The hostel was disinfected. The boys returned. We had saved 22 of our orphans, but some of the boys who had been sent home had not escaped.

Thirty-two of Mabel's boys died. They "would never again attend school, unless in the Great Beyond there is provision for such as these. One learns not to walk in fear in India. But I never really recovered from the horror of that experience."[30]

The stress and anxiety of this tragedy were simply too much for Mabel. Now, with the need of ten-fold strength and endurance, she, like several of her missionary friends before her, was diagnosed with a nervous collapse.[31] Two new missionaries, Dr. and Mrs. Rockey, temporarily took over the boys' school as well as Mabel's other responsibilities. Mabel telegraphed Stanley to return from Calcutta, and Miss McCartney, who was with the nearby girls' school, took Mabel and Eunice to Landour into the Himalayas. Mabel, like Stanley be-fore her, was seriously ill and was ordered complete rest for a month. After her experience nursing Eunice just the year before, this new strain "put on the finishing touches." The doctor told her that her time in India was "up" as her heart would not take it. He was wrong.

The last couple of paragraphs of the little book that Mabel wrote about *Education in India* are interesting in this light.

> There is fascination in a task that calls for every bit of wisdom and ability that one possesses. But a foreigner can stay too long in India. To live in a climate that drains one's physical vitality, to be constantly in an environment that makes exhaustive demands upon one's sympa-thies, may result ultimately in not only physical deterioration but an unhealthy feeling of inadequacy and frustration. Fortunately, it was only the physical that sent me home.

> Among the Arabs there is a saying that whoever drinks of the Nile, forever wants to return to drink again. Not because the water is clear and sparkling and desirable. It is not. But something calls. It is equally true that one who has worked in India, even while home on brief fur-loughs among loved ones, has that restless urge to return, not because of the fascination of a land so different from our own, not because of the beauty of the country – although there is much breath-taking love-liness; not even because of dear friends, Hindu, Mohammedan, and Christian.

> An American dentist who had once lived in India, remarked on his return to live in America: "India makes it hard for one to be content anywhere. When I was there I kept thinking of the life in America. But here I am constantly thinking of India. Especially do I remember the buckets of teeth I took out on Saturdays for the poor devils who could not afford to go to a dentist. I wonder who they can go to now." Some-one has said, "A call is the perception of a need that I have the power to meet." The perception of that need, the realization that there is a work that may not be done if you do not do it, is something that per-petually haunts one.

As if in proof Mabel at the time testified to the depth of her own commitment to the mission work in Sitapur. "I am planning to go down the first of September and gather together the scattered rem-nants of my flock and begin again."

Imagine! Mabel, like Stanley before her, would recover from her collapse, but not so surprisingly her workload, like Stanley's, would increase as her school continued to improve and impress.

Some years later Mabel in one of her routine letters gave us a window into her life as a tireless worker during these early years.

Dear Friends,

I do want to thank you for the way you have been upholding us by your prayers and financial help this year.

There have been times when I felt that physically, I could not carry on. And then there would come an influx of strength that would carry me through the day and I know someone had been praying.

There have been times when it seemed that money was an absolute necessity for His work's sake and the box was empty. Not only that, but there were bills unpaid and obligations that could not be met. And then the home mail would come with a check and I knew that He had put the burden on someone's heart even before I prayed!

What a reservoir of power there is in earnest prayer!

Someone wrote me recently, 'I wonder what you do all day. Could you outline a "typical" day at work?

Well, days differ; but as far as I can remember, today has been rather typical and it has been like this.

5 am. to 6 am. Awoke on the roof, looked up at the sky and asked the Lord for help and guidance for the day. Had my bath and a cup of tea and a slice of toast and read a little from the Word as I ate. Made some boric lotion for a village woman who brought me her baby with sore eyes. Showed her how to use it. Took some onion seed to the garden and told the man in charge where to plant it.

6 am. Took prayers with the boys in the sick room and investigated the cause and gave each a dose of castor oil. Went into classrooms to see who was absent and why.

7 am. Returned to the bungalow as the health officer was waiting to see if we wanted cholera inoculations. Mail came and I answered

two business letters. Village man: "My baby has had fever for five days. What shall we do." This reminds the blind man who pulls the pankah to keep me cool, or perhaps I should say cooler, when I have time to sit under it! He complained, "My toe pains me very much." I look and find the nail gone and a festering sore. Clerk, "Will you please take these fees from day pupils and sign the receipts?:

8 am. A woman who was baptized recently, threw her arms around my feet and begged me to let her come to school long enough to learn to read. A Mohammedan official calls and asks if I have anything as good to read as "The Imitation of Christ" which he has just finished.[32]

9 am. Investigated a bad odor from a school drain. Took a sick woman to the hospital. Started to write out a new time table for school as we will soon change from morning school to day school. Matron came with complaints against a teacher.

10 am. Took the carburetor off the car to clean it. Had breakfast.

11 am. An English lady who was in great trouble called for sympathy and advice.

Noon. Hot and tired. Laid down. Got up three times and decided to stay up. The cook wanted money for butter. The sweeper wanted a new broom. The mail man brought a C.O.D. parcel.

1 pm. A note from the doctor saying that he would examine all the boys at 4 pm. A teacher reports that the chalk is all gone. A father who wants to put his boy in school but fears Christian influence came to talk it over.

2 pm. The pastor came to ask about some affairs connected with the church. A Hindu called to borrow a book. He is a well educated man and getting interested in Christianity. He said, "After I read the gospel a while, I want to go out and help some one. I want to tell them of this good God. When I read the Vedas or the Puranas I never feel this way. Only the story of Christ effects [sic] me like this."

3 pm. Cut out a dozen pair of pajamas and sent them to Class four for their sewing period. Had lunch.

4 pm. The Indian doctor came and we went over the physical condition of each boy. Found one case of itch and various other minor ailments. Wrote out his recommendations and ordered medicine.

5 pm. Boy Scouts Commissioner called to see when I would have time to attend a meeting of the executive committee. He said the boys from the Mission school were the very brightest of all the boys who were enrolled as Scouts. He said, "What does your religion do to the boys? They have no business to be so superior, considering the fact that they are from our lowest classes."

An Indian Official called. He said, "I feel very discouraged over my country. Things change slowly."

Discovered an Indian "holy man" going into the hostel. Ran after him and got him out and headed for the gate. He was dressed in a patch of cloth about the size of my hand, tied on with a string and his body was smeared with ashes.

6 pm. A boy was brought to me for discipline for swimming in the river without permission. A man came to borrow 30 cents. A woman to beg for work. Grain merchant delivers rice and wants his pay. I make out his bill and get his signature and file the voucher.

7 pm. An early dinner because I am alone and I want to get at the pile of unanswered letters on my desk and sent a note to the little daughter [Eunice] away in Boarding School. And now I shall soon climb the stairs and look up at the stars and commit the day to Him. Of course I have not got down everything that happened today but this is a rather brief outline of a day that is not unusual.

Someone asked me what U.P. meant in our address. It stands for the United Provinces (of Agra and Oudh.)

Several want to know what to send for Christmas. I really think a gift of money, no matter how small, is best. It is easy and cheap to send and the boy can get what he likes best. It is pathetic, but it is true, that the average Indian child leads such a poverty stricken existence that articles of utility appeal most to him. I once gave some little boys scrap books made in folder form on red calico. I was amazed a little later to find them wearing the calico for loin cloths, having carefully taken off the pictures and put them away in boxes.

And now my evening is gone. As I fold these letters and put them in the envelopes it will be with a little prayer for each individual to whom they go. May his blessing be yours! In his glad Service,

Mabel Jones.[33]

As an aside it is significant that the caricature of missionaries — depicted in stovepipe hats and black frocks, sweating beneath palm trees, grimly corralling thousands of natives like captive birds of paradise, replacing their simple pleasures with the Victorian sense of sin — is grossly unfair. Although mistakes were made, most like Mabel and Stanley, were noble beyond belief.

Even apart from Mabel and her struggles 1921 was an incredibly busy year for both Mabel and Stanley. The Methodist Episcopal Church appointed N.L. Rockey to replace Stanley as the District Superintendent of the Sitapur District. This freed Stanley up for his everexpanding evangelistic campaigns.

STANLEY'S MINISTRY OF EVANGELISM EXPANDS THROUGHOUT INDIA

Now the dye was cast! After years of prayer, learning and struggling the Holy Spirit was in control of both Stanley and Mabel and history would bear this out time and again. Watch it happen, first with Stanley's ministry.

By far the most Christian part of India at the time was in the south, in particular the southwest coast, where the Syrian Christians comprised about a fourth of the total population. Stanley and Sherwood Eddy visited the Syrian church bringing a message of spiritual renewal in hopes of motivating them for evangelism. According to tradition a mission was founded by St. Thomas the Apostle in the first century on the east coast of India. Most of these Syrian Christians had then migrated in the fifth century further west and were granted status given only to high castes.[34] Unfortunately, as the centuries rolled by these Syrians tended to become comfortable and accommodating so that they tended to vegetate. Stanley claims that some of the churches had not taken a convert in 1500 years.[35]

For Stanley, raised in the Wesleyan holiness tradition, for him to engage the high church tradition of the Syrian Christians was a challenge almost beyond belief. Fortunately, in the mid-nineteenth century a Syrian "Christian priest" was converted to a more personal understanding of the Christian faith in a transplanted Wesleyan revival and as a result of his reforms the Mar Thoma Church was born. By the time Stanley visited, the area this reformed branch of the Syrian Church numbered over 100,000. "There were swinging censers and chanting priests and the sign of the cross being constantly made in the service, but there was a deep devotion amidst it all."[36]

Significantly, a week long Syrian Church convention was held every year at Marramannu (Maramon) in Travancore, India. Between twenty-five and thirty thousand people attended. Stanley comments that this was probably the "world's largest Christian Convention." He was first invited to speak to the Maramon Convention in 1919 but could not accept the invitation until the following year (the Spring, **1920**). Then he spoke to the largest crowd he had ever addressed. The people sat on the sand (ten thousand women all dressed in white on one side and twenty thousand men on the other. Remarkably the acoustics enhanced by the nearby riverbank enabled him to be heard by all. There was absolute silence from nine in the morning until one in the afternoon. "The two Bishops in their long purple robes, complete with head dresses and golden girdles, sat on the platform. Below them were about fifty priests in flowing garments. The tide of power rose day by day." The meetings began on Sunday and by Friday morning Stanley realized that the decisive hour had come. "When I gave the invitation for those who would surrender to Christ to stand they began to rise by the thousands, and there they stood in the presence of God while His power shook them. Practically the whole audience arose amidst muffled, but reverent cries of Hallelujah!.... Some of the priests broke down and wept over their people surrendering to God. "Moments like these in the Convention were great—unforgettable!"[37]

At one point, even though his meetings with such Christians were "the best I have ever had in India," Stanley seemed frustrated that he was not getting out more among non-Christians (probably due to the changing political climate). Then, as a result of the thorough preparations by the YMCA, doors seemed to open among non-Christians as well. Stanley describes a meeting in Hyderabad where he spoke in the Cinema Hall to a "splendid audience" of educated non-Christians, primarily Muslims. Quite a few signed cards stating that they would study the Bible with an open mind and heart. He received a similar response in Belgaum where among those responding to the Gospel, nearly half symbolized their allegiance to Gandhi and to the cause of Indian nationalism by wearing clothes made of *khaddar cloth*, a homespun Indian fabric manufactured by hand on crude wooden spinning wheels or *charkas*. This was to dramatize Indian economic self-reliance and the Indian boycott of imported British fabrics.[38]

During this same period (the fall of 1921), Stanley writes about time in Jaffna, Ceylon (Sri Lanka) where he "had the finest gathering of Indian Christians I have seen anywhere in the East." He also held equally successful meetings for non-Christians. "Here I received the most intelligent and searching questions I have received anywhere in the East. The lawyers must have sat up all night making up lists of questions. The meetings went on about three hours each night, with intense and sympathetic interest. There were a number of Hindus who declared their purpose to take their stand for Christ."[39]

Then there was Coimbatore where Stanley held meetings for Hindu women in the Cinema for three days. He asked Christian women to share their testimonies with the non-Christian women and they did so with "telling effect." In an after-meeting Stanley (forever seizing the moment) asked those who would like to surrender and find a new life to hold up their hands for prayer. The large majority did so and did so sincerely.

In terms of spiritual impact, however, the most successful meetings of the entire tour were held in Victoria Hall in Madras. Here the Central Committee of Christian churches had prepared well for Stanley's visit.

"The crowds grew until, on the fifth and sixth nights, it was crowded to the doors. The last night, after speaking on the new birth, I asked the nominal Christians and the non-Christians who would like to find the new birth to stay for an after-meeting. There were about three hundred who stayed, of whom about one-third were Hindus. As I explained how to surrender and trust, they repeated a prayer of confession and self-committal." Stanley then received word that some had decided to begin their witness for Jesus Christ immediately.[40]

Ironically, at the end of the 1921 campaign many were fearful that the political unrest throughout India would affect the reception of the Christian gospel but, in fact, such conversions simply exposed the nation's deep spiritual hunger. India was increasingly open to the Gospel.

AT THIS POINT STANLEY BEGAN TO TRAVEL OUTSIDE INDIA

1922 would mark yet another significant turning point in Stanley's life and ministry on many different fronts. As his ministry expanded geographically it also expanded his intellectual and spiritual scope as well, moving away from some of the narrow orthodoxy of his Wesleyan Holiness Tradition. He never backed off his belief in the uniqueness of Jesus in order to make it more palatable but he did envision a more universal Christ. He now believed that foreign national expressions of Christianity were just as valid as his western one. He was now convinced that the human heart was the same around the world (he has a growing awareness that we all live in a moral universe). Quoting Augustine, Jones writes: "We are [all] made by God and we rest not until we rest in Him." We will return to the relevancy of this in other areas of Stanley's ministry in later chapters. For now, this developing attitude (the validity of cultural expressions of Jesus) made some of his colleagues and friends a bit nervous. Miss Nellie did not write to him for seven years.[41]

In March, Stanley visited Mesopotamia (Iraq). Bishop Warne asked him to take the trip because of his contacts with the Syrian Church in South India. He describes meetings with Assyrian refugees. These were Christian refugees before WWI living in Iran (converted by a Presbyterian mission descended from the Nestorians). Eighty-five thousand of these Nestorians, abandoned by their Russian allies, fled to Baghdad only to be attacked by the Kurds and the Turks. Thirty-five thousand died in route.[42]

Understandably, Stanley had mixed emotions regarding Iraq. In 1922, an *Indian Witness* included an article, "Evangelizing in the Land of King Feisul" where he wrote that although Mesopotamia was often called "the cradle of the human race" … degeneracy is written over everything." He believed that the problem was religion.

"The trouble with Mesopotamia is Mohammedanism. The 'will of God' is everywhere and over everything, and there seems little place for the will of man; so, the fine qualities of the Arab go to waste, either in a surge of fanaticism fighting for the cause of Allah, or are corroded by lethargy and kismet [fate]. Lift that incubus from his soul and there is not finer material in the world."[43]

As if to offer proof of this potential Stanley speaks of meetings in Baghdad on the day he arrived. Although only a few Europeans attended, Asians flocked in droves, including several hundred Indians. These Indians were members of the Indian Christian Band organized by Bishop Warne in 1920. It is significant that as many non-Christians attended as Christians. There were twelve meetings a week where forty-nine persons were baptized. As if imitating the New Testament, the members all lived together voluntarily in the same houses, eating the same food. Stanley visited one house that included Buddhists, Hindus, Indian Christians, Burmese, and Anglo-Indians, all living joyously together.

In spite of Stanley's glowing reports, however, the Methodist Episcopal Church did not establish a mission in Mesopotamia—a missed opportunity.

From Mesopotamia Jones and Sherwood Eddy went to **China** for three months—October through December, 1922. Stanley felt as if he was getting into a rut and increasingly felt the need for the added prospective gained from traveling to still another culture. In Peking (Beijing) he met the leaders of the Renaissance Movement (actually an Anti-Christian Movement at the time). It was less than a year old. After having lunch with the leaders, in true Stanley fashion he announced that their movement was dead for want of a soul. Wanting their attention he admitted that the government they were resisting was indeed paralyzed through graft. He also felt that such political and social turmoil made Christianity even more attractive, especially to students.

Stanley also managed to spend time with General Feng, the Christian General and Governor. Twenty years earlier Feng was anti-Christian but was impressed with how Christians died during the Boxer Rebellion and was converted in a meeting held by the legendary missionary, John R. Mott. He was baptized in a Methodist Church. Stanley writes that he is now one of the "most outstanding Christians in China."[44]

If in search of another example of how Christians dying, captured the attention of those watching, consider the story of Madagascar. In 1849, Queen Ranavalona ordered her soldiers to seize every Christian, bind them hand and foot, dig a pit on the spot, then pour boiling water on them and bury them. Eighteen Christians were killed, fourteen hurled over cliffs and the others buried alive. An eyewitness reported, "They prayed as long as they had life. Then they died, but softly. Indeed, gentle was the going forth of their life, and astonished were all the people around them that beheld the burning of them."[45] After the Queen's death, Christians "reappeared as if they had risen from the dead," singing the pilgrim song, "When the Lord turned against the captivity of Zion, we were like them that dream." (Psalm 126:1).

Stanley then describes the sobering experience of approaching the remnants of war in Foochow. He spoke at Amoy University to students that were mostly atheists but seemed open to the Gospel. All of this would become more and more grist for his ever-expanding holiness mill.

BACK IN INDIA: INDIAN CULTURE AND HERITAGE
AND THE IMPORTANCE OF THE ASHRAM

The Methodists had in times past sworn loyalty to British rule but in 1923 the Central Conference adopted a report, submitted by its committee on the State of the Church, that Methodists support and encourage non-Christian groups in India "in such national movements as reflect legitimate aspirations." This report even identified one of these legitimate aspirations as the "movement to obtain *Swaraj* (meaning self-rule or independence) as the ultimate goal." In later years, as the Indian nationalists, led by Gandhi and galvanized by his tactics of nonviolent civil disobedience, became more outspoken and more insistent in their demands for the immediate and complete independence of India from Great Britain, *Swaraj* would acquire more and more radical connotations.

As a result, although Methodism was still officially neutral, freedom would be given to individual Methodists to participate in the political parties of their choice. Later the Methodist Church would contradict its former impression of neutrality by looking for ways to make "Dominion Status" successful. Dominion Status was not full independence but, like Canada and Australia, would give India a greater degree of self-government within the British Empire. This was apparently not enough, however. Although the British were willing to move toward Dominion Status the Indian National Congress, actually a political party and the largest nationalist organization in the country, rejected the more moderate position and insisted on full independence. Gandhi began his second campaign of civil disobedience and noncooperation. Although the British convened a round table conference in London, the Indian National Congress refused to participate.[46]

Even though Methodist Bishops did not officially support full independence, Stanley did. Since his first meeting with Gandhi in 1919 Stanley had been becoming more and more of a universal Christian, teaching a universal Christ as standing in the gap of all oppression in whatever form.

Later in 1923, Stanley was back with the Syrian Christians at the Maramon Convention asking them to accept outcastes as full and equal members of their churches. The church voted overwhelming to include them, baptizing outcastes in large numbers.

Then surprisingly, in his *Indian Witness* (August 1, 1923) Stanley asks the question: "Has the time come for missionaries to pack up and go home? NO! It is time to pack up and go forward." Stanley wants to send Indian missionaries to America but this was totally unacceptable to most American Christians, even though Indian Christians like, Sundar Singh (the Saint Paul of India), were already influencing and enriching Western Missionaries. Besides, the message of religious imperialism was no longer acceptable in India. Unfortunately, too many western missionaries still seemed to be pressing for baptisms (the numbers of baptisms was thought to be the best indicator of spiritual growth and vitality). Stanley wanted heartfelt decisions for Christ, emphasizing Christ, his forgiveness and salvation.

In 1923 Stanley wrote a tract for non-Christians for his upcoming crusades. He discusses several reasons why Indians should find Christianity attractive. For example, leaders like Gandhi were drawing moral strength, politically, from his (Gandhi's) understanding of Jesus Christ. Stanley preached that Jesus could also fulfill India's spiritual heritage.

In Stanley's meetings in May in Nadiad, non-cooperators were in charge with audiences of 1000 in attendance. He was realizing more and more that the local church (especially the laity) should do evangelism. Indians were increasingly realizing that you could have Christ without Western civilization. Christ needed to be expressed through India's own national genius and thought, intellectually and spiritually.

Consequently, 1923 was also the year that Stanley began to immerse himself in the Indian Ashrams. *It would be difficult to exaggerate the impact these would have on Stanley's ministry going forward.* Even as Indians were becoming increasingly aware of the importance of their own history and culture, Stanley would as well. India could make its own unique contribution to world civilization. Stanley was the first to realize the potential here for the Christian witness in his adopted land. What was left was to experience this for himself. What better way to immerse himself in the ethos of India than to visit Indian Ashrams.[47]

Stanley then spent two months at the Santiniketan Ashram of world famous poet Rabindranath Tagore. Like Samuel Beckett, John Steinbeck, and Hermann Hess, Rabindranath Tagore won the Nobel Prize for Literature. Stanley claims, without exaggeration that this Ashram experience changed the course of his life and ministry.

Santiniketan (meaning Home of Peace) was in West Bengal, about forty miles north of Calcutta. The Ashram sat in beautiful natural surroundings. The motives for the ashram were clearly religious as Tagore was Brahma Samaj, a reform sect of Hinduism. Predictably Tagore's Ashram was organized around his own spirit. The guru makes the Ashram — for good or for ill. There was to be no idol worship, no caste distinctions and no discrimination against women. Stanley wrote there was also no speaking of any religion with disrespect. In addition to its religious and spiritual emphasis there were also three educational institutions, one for boys up to university age, then the Vishvabharati or International University (where Stanley was asked to teach) and then an agricultural section of the university teaching scientific methods of farming. No question, Santiniketan would influence Stanley's understanding of the Indian expression of Christianity — a mixture of Christianity and of "orthodox and liberal streams of Indian thought." It was here that Stanley was to see what Indian Christianity might become.

The Ashram spirit breathed the loving friendliness of everyone, communion with nature, the simplicity of life and dress, and the spirituality of it all. Stanley would now become a serious student of just how Indian heritage could influence his own presentation of the Gospel.

It was stated earlier that it was during this same period that Mabel heard Gandhi speak in Sitapur and was so impressed she wrote to him asking for a copy of his powerful address. He wrote back beginning a 25 year correspondence (1923-1948). Since Mabel's correspondence with Gandhi would focus on education and disciplinary matters, it is significant that Mabel's philosophy of education was far closer to Gandhi's Satyagraha than it was to the West. Both Stanley and Mabel remained close friends with Gandhi. Once when Stanley was visiting Gandhi the Mahatma received a beautifully woven tea cloth from Kamala Nehru (the wife of Jawaharlal Nehru). Although Gandhi was grateful he had no need for the gift and gave it to Stanley saying, "Give it to Mrs. Jones with my love."[48]

By this time Mabel is already writing more than 20 letters a day. During some years she accomplished the remarkable marathon of raising enough money through her letters to keep her boys (eventually over a thousand) in school per year.[49]

Then late in the summer of 1923 Stanley and Pickett met in Arrah for a meeting and, like Elijah on Mt. Carmel, stayed to pray with the people for much needed rain. The rains came with a vengeance.

Similar trials for Mabel, however, were just beginning. One rain seemed to follow another until water was five feet over the floor of the bungalow and three feet over the school. Fortunately no lives were lost and eight-year old Eunice now sported a living room full of fish. A year's supply of rice was soaked and apparently ruined along with all her medicines, school-books, papers, clothes and bedding. She was absolutely dismayed at the loss but not to be undone, Mabel had a plan. The soaked rice had cooked in the heat so she sent out word among the starving villagers that she had cooked rice for them and invited them to bring their bowls, their buckets or whatever vessels they could find. Long lines showed up for a shovel full of the precious steaming commodity.[50] Her quick and creative thinking surely saved many lives.

1924-25: ANOTHER TIMELY FURLOUGH

On February 21, 1924 Stanley, Mabel and Eunice left for the U.S. on their second furlough, traveling via the Holy Land, France and England. They would not return to their home in Sitapur until October 1925. Arriving in early May, they traveled immediately to a home in Dubuque, Iowa. Mabel, anticipating family time together with a wonderful change of scenery, was happy. Eunice was now 10 and was about to experience American life for the first time. Stanley, however, was forced to leave within three days, holding his meetings night and day. While Mabel continued the correspondence Stanley traveled and worked on his first book, *The Christ of the Indian Road.*

We have already noted that after WWI Stanley was one of the first to realize that Western Christianity generally and Western Christian missionaries in particular, were often consciously or unconsciously co-opted into becoming agents of Western Imperialism. Stanley's inner voice led him to be one of the first to realize that, especially in Asia, Africa, and Latin America, the Christian gospel was all too often enmeshed with images of the economic and political self-aggrandizement of the Western nations. This was not an easy revelation. He came to this conclusion only after much prayer, study and reflection on his own experiences as an evangelist in his attempts to reach the educated classes of India. He was, in effect, declaring his moral and intellectual independence from the political and religious imperialism of the West.

Now we begin to see in Stanley's first book, *The Christ of the Indian Road,* the way his mind was turning in his presentation of the Gospel.[51] Written primarily from the addresses delivered while on furlough in the U.S. (revised and enlarged) the book describes a whole new approach to the Gospel. Many Western Christians found it provocative and controversial, a deadly frontal assault on the cultural prejudices of most European and American Christian missionaries in the late nineteenth and early twentieth centuries. Curiously, even

Bishop Thoburn was accused of being an unwitting religious imperialist. This might have further turned off Miss Nellie who was still not writing (although Stanley continued to write to her for a while).[52]

Although Indian thought tended to focus in pantheism — everything **is** God (Stanley believed that this was totally inconsistent with Christian thought), Stanley spoke of "Panentheism" — everything is **in** God. We are not God but a counterpart of God. He then called for the church to renounce its presumption of religious and cultural superiority in India. He also confesses his own complicity. Going through painful self-examination, Stanley wanted to explore any hidden Christian truth, even in Hindu theology.

So, *The Christ of the Indian Road* (1925) would challenge the religious and cultural imperialism of Western Christianity. He was forever looking for transferrable concepts, transcultural images, even redemptive analogies in other cultures that could communicate the Gospel more intelligently. At the end of Chapter One Stanley tells the story of a Hindu Brahmin saying to a Christian friend, "I don't like the Christ of your creeds and the Christ of your churches." His friend replied quickly, "Then how would you like the Christ of the Indian Road?" The Hindu thought for a moment envisioning the Christ of the Indian Road "dressed in Sadhus garments, seated by the wayside with the crowds about him, healing blind men who felt their way to him, putting his hands upon the heads of the poor, unclean lepers who fell at his feet, announcing the good tidings of the Kingdom to stricken folks, then staggering up a lone hill with a broken heart and dying upon a wayside cross for men, but rising triumphantly and walking on that road again." He suddenly turned to the friend and earnestly said, "I could love and follow the Christ of the Indian Road."[53]

Then in the summer of 1925, Jones took part in an American Seminar organized and coordinated by his old friend, Sherwood Eddy. Eddy brought together religious and social leaders to study the problems of preaching the Gospel in Great Britain and continental Europe. Stanley leaves the U.S. as the group sailed together for England.

There were lectures and discussions every morning on board ship, arriving in England where they were greeted by the Archbishop of Canterbury. Stanley is then off to Holland and Berlin. He visited Professor Adolf von Harnack (arguably one of the world's greatest theologians at the time) and was even received by President Hindenburg.

Stanley then journeys on to Turkey where he writes about Kemal Ataturk and the overthrow of the rule of the caliphs just two years earlier (1923) and the westernization of Turkey. In Constantinople (Istanbul) he goes to the museum to see the block of stone taken from the Temple in Jerusalem: " Let no Gentile pass this point upon pain of death." This, Stanley believed, was fundamentally inconsistent with the mind of Jesus. Stanley is becoming more and more sensitive to racial prejudices.

From Constantinople Jones and Eddy traveled to Ankara (the new Turkish Capital), then on his own, he traveled to Jerusalem where he met Mabel and Eunice who had just arrived from the U.S. The family then spent a month together in Palestine and in Egypt. They did some sightseeing, perhaps to assist Stanley in writing a commentary on Nazareth, Jacob's Well and Garden Tomb in Jerusalem. These were the places where Jesus had opened himself up to the work of the Holy Spirit that he might become the Word become flesh.

Back in India, Stanley completes and publishes, *The Christ of the Indian Road*. This book made Stanley famous, worldwide. It would become an international phenomena. Although Stanley would go on to publish nearly 30 other books, it should become increasingly obvious that there was far more to Brother Stanley than his books and there was far more to Stanley and Mabel than their countless letters and articles in Christian periodicals. As we anticipate the next important chapter of their lives, watch both Stanley and Mabel embrace even greater opportunities for service and ministry.

E. Stanley Jones, James Mathews, Eunice Jones and Mabel Lossing Jones
(Jim & Eunice' Wedding, June 1940)

Rufus Mosley, E. Stanley Jones, Eunice Jones and others

Mary Webster, E. Stanley Jones, Anne Mathews, and others at the Maramon
Convention in Kerala, India, 1968

CHAPTER FIVE

THE JONES' RETURN AFTER THEIR SECOND FURLOUGH TO EMBRACE AN EVER WIDENING UNDERSTANDING OF MINISTRY, INCLUDING THE CHRISTIAN ASHRAM MOVEMENT

The Need to Create an Environment Where Seekers Can Experience the Living God

We left Stanley, Mabel and Eunice as they returned to India in October, 1925. They had been away from Sitapur for more than a year and a half. Then Mabel's father died November 24, less than two months after their return. She hardly had time to mourn. Stanley would be gone again in three days for several months teaching and preaching while Mabel was busy managing over four hundred scholarships raised while on sabbatical. Graciously Mabel would share this bounty with other impoverished schools leaving Mabel running her school with a monthly deficit, "we have not kept enough for ourselves. But we expect God to see us through."[1]

Although Stanley gave the commencement address at Asbury College earlier in the year (he had also been given an honorary Doctor of Divinity degree there in 1920), he is again harboring feelings of inadequacy. Fortunately these times drove him to his knees. This is the "forever key" that opens him to the Holy Spirit. He had no doubt learned from the Apostle Paul that our greatest strengths are anointed weaknesses (2 Corinthians 12:9-11). He is bold to proclaim a gospel of *redemption*, not just "a great ethic or a beautiful character."[2]

India had now changed even more. The noncooperation movement had gained greater and greater momentum. Consequently Stanley would now hold more and more Round Table Conferences. Many of the traditional approaches to evangelism were no longer as effective in India, or for that matter in many countries around the world.

Stanley writes: "The first three months in 1926 have been the finest since I've been in India." Watch it happen.

In January Stanley receives news from corresponding secretary for the Board of Foreign Missions, Ralph E. Diffendorfer, that *The Christ of the Indian Road* is a phenomenal success. In an attempt to avoid the splits that many churches had been experiencing, Stanley writes to Diffendorfer that his book was an attempt to hold together both modernists and fundamentalists. The tension seemed to revolve around the lingering 1925 Scopes Trial mentality. Lines had been drawn between Clarence Darrow defending creationism on one side and John Scopes defining evolution on the other. After Fundamentalism was established at the Niagara Conference in 1895 the Wesleyan holiness movement split 25 different ways over the next 12 years with Fundamentalism on one side and Modernism on the other. There was very little happening in between. Significantly, Stanley's book was one of the few works being read by both sides with any great interest and enthusiasm.[3]

We noted in Chapter One that Stanley wrote to Gandhi on January 9, 1926 "a private note to a friend." He was quite candid calling for caution regarding non-cooperation. Stanley admits that he has been trying to interpret Gandhi's message to the western world. Then he reminds Gandhi again that he had missed the heart of the Gospel that lies in the Person of Jesus Christ. Jesus Himself is the good news. Gandhi had caught the principles but missed the Person. Jones then asked for permission to attend his Ashram.

Gandhi replies January 18 thanking him for his kind letter. He appreciated the love and understanding but he could not grasp the position through the intellect. "It is purely a matter of the heart." He says he is open with no axes to grind. He wants to find truth—to see God face to face. Gandhi then invites Stanley to his Ashram.

Stanley is now visiting Ashrams more frequently. Tagore's whetted his appetite. There were even a few Ashrams among Christians. In April he visited a Christian Ashram at Puri where a "notable Christian leader" set up an Ashram to make Christianity more indigenous. Stanley was impressed as seeds were sown for his own Ashrams soon to follow. Although the Round Table Conferences made a significant contribution to communicating the Gospel (his book, *Christ at the Round Table* would be published in 1928), it would be the Ashram that had the greatest impact worldwide.[4]

Also in January Mabel had written that Stanley was a stranger in his own home. She was alone again but stayed on top of the family and mission financial transactions (virtually for 80 years).[5] In June, however, Stanley and Mabel managed to take a month off to rest in Naini Tal. Eunice joined them. Stanley even took time to spend a week of fishing at a lodge close by.[6] This was much needed time away from the routine as Stanley feared that a sense of hopelessness had crept over the soul of India in the past two years and he was feeling the need to regroup. Somehow, he needed to find a venue for healing. One answer would serve him well for a lifetime—the Ashram.

We have already established that Brother Stanley's lifelong passion for the dynamics of the Ashram experience began with

Rabindranath Tagore's Ashram in 1923. In July 1926 Stanley makes his first visit to Gandhi's Ashram at Sabarmati. These ashrams (Tagore's and Gandhi's) influenced his life in several different ways. First, there was simplicity in the disciplined corporate living where the 'chelas,' or disciples, would seek for 'moksha,' or salvation. Then each ashram had a "guru" (which literally means a "dispeller of darkness") where a teacher would provide spiritual enlightenment to those who came to learn. Brother Stanley began to understand the value of the ashram as an authentic and indigenous means to bring the truth of Jesus Christ to the people. Jesus Christ, the Word become flesh, the Light of the world, would be the guru, the teacher. In his book, *Along the Indian Road,* Stanley would describe the Indian context.

> The Indian spirit is difficult to define, but anyone who has come in contact with it knows what I mean — there is an inner poise, a spiritual sensitivity, a love of simplicity, an emphasis on the gentler virtues, and a spirit of devotion with an ascetic tinge. Just as the human spirit is touched and redeemed by the Spirit of Christ, the adventure of putting them together was a glorious one and I believe that the Ashram was a magnificent vehicle.[7]

While at Gandhi's Ashram at Sabarmati, Stanley writes that Gandhi looked on salvation as an attainment through disciplined effort. The two of us "would go aside at the end of the prayer period which began at 4 am. He would tell me what religion meant to him and I would tell him what it meant to me.[8] For ten days we looked into each other's hearts. One day he said to me,

> If one is to find salvation, he must have as much patience as a man who sits by the seaside and with a straw picks up a single drop of water, transfers it, and thus empties the ocean. Salvation comes through one's strict, disciplined efforts, a rigid self-mastery. If one believes that salvation comes through one's own disciplined efforts, then of course he dares not speak of it. To speak of it would be indelicate and would lack humility, for it is his own.[9]

Stanley then responded: "But I looked on salvation, not as an *attainment* through one's efforts, but as an *obtainment* through grace. I came to Christ morally and spiritually bankrupt with nothing to offer except my bankruptcy. To my astonishment he took me, forgave me, and sent my happy soul singing its way down through the years." At the end of his Chapter on "Gandhi and the Christian Faith," in his book on Gandhi, Stanley writes: "So one of the most Christian men in history was not called a Christian at all. And the man who fought Christian civilization, so called, furthered the real thing. God uses many instruments, and he has used Mahatma Gandhi to help Christianize unchristian Christianity."[10]

Early in 1927 Diffendorfer advertises that Stanley Jones (by now a world-renown missionary/evangelist) would write personal letters from time to time (*Circular Letters*) to all who were interested if they would pay $1 to the Mission Board (300 had sent in their dollar immediately).[11]

In March Stanley was holding evangelistic meetings in Rangoon, Burma. It was a very cosmopolitan crowd of over 2000 including Burmese, Chinese, Tamils, Telegus, Hindusatanis, Persians, Armenians, Karens, Bengalis, Europeans and Americans. He was grateful for the response to his message. We then find him in Mandalay and Moulmein before he returns to Rangoon for a final meeting for those who had signed cards with an interest in converting to Christianity during his earlier visit. He comments that he left a good bit of his heart among a "most lovable people." Ironically, Buddhism left the Burmese with a dryness of soul that he did not find among the Hindus. He felt that Burma, for the most part, was spiritually dead.[12]

In Stanley's *Circular Letter* for June 20, 1927, he writes that he spent the previous two months of his vacation time (during the hottest time of the year) "in the quiet hill station of Almora" to begin his second book, *Christ at the Round Table* (a very detailed account of what was said and done at these conferences).[13]

Then, in the fall of 1927 Stanley goes to Malaya. Malaya had large Indian and Chinese populations — and for Stanley that meant a land of opportunity. In Kuala Lumpur he held Round Table Conferences in association with his evangelistic meetings. This was done to great advantage as one complimented the other.

From Malaya Stanley travels to Singapore for meetings arranged by the YMCA. The YMCA continues to have influence in Singapore even today. Stanley spoke at an Anglo-Chinese school with some success. His last stop for this trip was Siam (Thailand). He took the train from Singapore north up the peninsula through virgin forests to Bangkok. The Buddhist influence was so strong there that he did not receive as favorable a response as he had in Malaya and Singapore. Nonetheless, at the Bangkok Christian College there were fifty-two decisions for Christ and at the State University he shared his faith with the chairman of the meeting who was a member of the royal family. Finally he returns to India believing that although "our Methodist Mission" has by-and-large missed the opportunity, Malaya was "one of the ripest, if not the ripest, mission fields in the world."[14]

Stanley is now convinced even more that the human heart is the same around the world. He finds himself returning to his understanding of living in a *moral universe* where we cannot live outside the principles of God's intended purpose for his creation, especially as outlined in the Sermon on the Mount, without destroying ourselves. The theme of a moral universe would gain more and more momentum as his ministry continued to evolve.

In March 1928 Stanley was headed back to the U.S. He would leave his wife and daughter in the heat of Sitapur and an India amidst heightened sensitivity to national aspirations.

In the first week of May 1928, Mabel became ill. She was terribly lonely in Sitapur. "I shall remember May for another reason. I have never felt the heat so much. Day after day the thermometer registered 110 in the shade and sometimes 114." She came down with fever and an acute attack of inflammation of the larynx and windpipe, "Because of my throat I could not have a fan. We kept the house closed because any breeze from the outside felt like the blast of a hot furnace. One night I fought all night long for breath and sometimes I felt

I could not struggle any longer. But a good doctor and a good nurse and later on an operation on my throat all helped to bring me past the danger points and I am now hoping to give a few more years to India." She then traveled to Naini Tal to recuperate fully.[15]

Meanwhile, the Indian National Congress had made a formal declaration; if the British refused to grant full and complete dominion status to India within a year, the Congress would for the first time demand *purna swaraj*, complete independence from Great Britain. Britain dragged her feet and Gandhi would begin his first campaign of civil disobedience and the end of passive non-cooperation.[16] Stanley would not return to India until May 1929.[17]

In route to the U.S. Stanley stopped off in Baghdad, then drove across the desert to Jerusalem where he attended a Conference in the Russian Church on the Mount of Olives (staying in tents). This was an important conference for Stanley. The discussion focused upon a scathing criticism of Western civilization. The consensus was that non-Christian religions were just as valid as Christianity, an intense dislike of religious imperialism and whether or not Christian missions were obsolete. Stanley's emphatic answer was a resounding NO!

By May of 1928 Stanley was in Kansas City as a delegate to the General Conference. The Conference seemed to reach an impasse in the process of electing Bishops. Much to his surprise and chagrin Stanley was elected Bishop. When Mabel was informed she put a sheet over her head. Eunice wrote fourteen reasons why she did not want her father to be a Bishop (the first was that "she loved Sitapur" and the last was, "Daddy won't be happy"). Unbeknownst to them Stanley could not sleep a wink that night and the next evening when he took his seat amongst the Bishops his "inner voice" said, "Now is the time to resign." He took the floor, thanked the conference for the great honor but he was called to be an evangelist and missionary and resigned, much to the discomfort and even animosity of some.[18] Eunice and Mabel were greatly relieved. Yet Mabel continued to have her moments of loneliness as Stanley was gone so much of the time, even when in India. She writes that she and Eunice were unhappy that

Stanley was still in the U.S. The woman survived with the realization of the strength her own calling. She was tough.[19]

After General Conference Stanley toured the Central and Eastern U.S. conducting Round Table Conferences for pastors of different denominations in the mornings and preaching in the evenings, sometimes to as many as 7,000.[20] As his notoriety spread, Stanley was asked by Diffendorfer in January 1929 to address the Foreign Missions Conference of North America in Detroit. He was given the topic "Meeting Current Objections to Foreign Missions." He began his remarks quite frankly by acknowledging their problems. "We are ordinary people who need Divine Power." Accessing that power was the key to his ministry throughout! Diffendorfer wrote to Mabel saying that he realized that his decision to keep Stanley in the U.S. until Easter was a great disappointment to her and Eunice. He then adds rather boldly, if not audaciously, "Maybe it will be of some consolation for you to know that his remaining in America is certainly a direct leading of our Heavenly Father."[21]

Meanwhile, Mabel and Eunice were "like children counting the days" until Stanley's return. A recorded 47,000 snakes had been killed in India that year, but none of Mabel's children had been bitten. Furthermore, no child had gone hungry and all the bills were paid — another testimony to Mabel, her prayers and to her faith.[22]

On April 6, Stanley finally left the U.S. for a week in Liverpool, England (being asked almost immediately for interviews by both the religious and secular press.). He then addressed the prestigious London Missionary Society, made radio addresses and held a service in the Liverpool Cathedral. Next, he traveled to Marseilles where he boarded a ship for India leading his cabin-mate (a captain in the army) to Jesus on day two.[23]

In May, 1929, Stanley is back in India. The Great Depression hit October 1929. As a witness to this the 1930s would chronicle a legacy of entrenched global depression and a sinister quartet of totalitarian "isms" — communism, fascism, Nazism, and a relatively new version of military imperialism (Japan) — not to mention a largely demoralized, ineffective, even stupefied Christendom. Amid such a rash of brutalizing "outwardisms" (as Stanley would call them), it is telling that Stanley would maintain his inward spiritual equilibrium.[24]

By this time, although Stanley was well known, continuing to write during his time away, Mabel was not such a public figure. Yet, she was terribly important, educating hundreds of boys, teaching them literacy in their own language (Urdu) and then, after they finished primary school—as many as were capable—following them with scholarships to higher education. Boys that would not benefit from further education she helped into trade schools or whatever they could manage. Many of her boys grew up to become significant leaders in the church and in national politics.

1930 was a momentous year! Although back in India, Stanley was home in Sitapur for only ten days throughout the year. In January the Indian Congress once again pledged itself to a declaration of independence and this time decided on civil disobedience. Eunice tells the story of Mabel being caught up in a near riot.

> Mother had gone alone in the car to the bazaar to purchase materials for the school. Suddenly her car was surrounded by a multitude of people shouting, "Mahatma Gandhi ki jai" [victory to Mahatma Gandhi], a slogan for independence. She looked around for someone she knew but the crowd was mostly from out of town. They began rocking her car and shouted the slogan even louder. Mother quickly used the claxon horn on the car to keep time to the rhythm of the chant. Its loud hoarse noise in rhythm to their chant attracted the crowd's attention and amused them. Finally someone shouted, "Even a foreign car is for independence— but it has a cold." Just then one of the merchants known to her pushed through the crowd, climbed on the car and shouted that she was an American missionary from the mission station and not English. The crowd quickly parted in good humor and let her pass, laughing at her horn's chant. A crowd can be fickle but her quick thinking saved the day.[25]

While Stanley saw the Indian push for civil disobedience as a good thing, Mabel disagreed. This was not their only disagreement.

In February Stanley writes (against Mabel's better judgment) that, "we are changing Eunice from the Naini Tal school (Wellesley) to the Mussoorie school (Woodstock)." Mussoorie was a hill station in the Himalayas. Eunice, now sixteen, was delighted as Woodstock was not as austere as Wellesley. Although there were both American and Indian students, Woodstock had become a mecca for American missionary children of all denominations. It had an American curriculum. Mabel would have preferred that Eunice stay at Wellesley where the environment was better controlled.[26]

THE EMERGENCE OF THE CHRISTIAN ASHRAM

Then, early in 1930, E. Stanley Jones and Rev. Yunas Sinha, an Indian Christian missionary, wrote a preliminary statement published in the *Indian Witness* (now circulating throughout the U.S.) regarding the purpose and spirit of a Christian Ashram. It was to produce the type of Christianity more in touch with the soul of India. The actual formation was a joint effort by Brother Stanley, Yunas Sinha, and, Ethel Turner, a retired member of the London Missionary Society. "Three nationalities came together in that humble beginning — American, Indian and English. It was a humble beginning. We hadn't the slightest idea that we were beginning something that would become a worldwide movement."[27] Initially, during May and June, the two hottest months of the year, the Ashram would become a fixture at Sat Tal, situated at an elevation of 5,000 feet in the foothills of the Himalayas. Stanley, reflecting on the Sat Tal Ashram stated, "We determined to live in simplicity, wearing Indian dress and eating Indian food. We attempted to be as Indian as possible... for India and her genius will be exceeded only by our reverence for Christ, His way and His truth."[28]

The acquisition of the property is a miracle in itself. Sat Tal was ideal for an ashram located on approximately 400 acres with a number of lakes, including Panna (Emerald) Lake. Stanley and Mabel had spent several summers at Sat Tal while it was operated as a summer resort by Mr. A.C. Evans, a retired British engineer, and his wife. When the Evans became too old to maintain the property they sold it to Stanley who, using the profits from the sale of his books, paid the Evans an annuity until Mrs. Evans died in 1947.

Sat Tal (meaning seven lakes) had an interesting legend about the origin of the name. Eunice learned of the legend from Mrs. Evans and wrote about it in a magazine published on the Ashram's fiftieth anniversary, *Sat Tal Ashram Golden Anniversary, 1930-1980*. It seems a poor native woman gathering twigs happened upon an old man sitting under a tree. He appeared to be very ill and asked her for water. The nearest spring was far down the hill and she had nothing but her hands to carry the water. She made the trek seven times and as the man (reportedly a god) revived, he promised that a lake would be formed among those hills for each one of her seven kindnesses.

Again, learning from the ashrams of Tagore and Gandhi (and the few Christian Ashrams already in place), Stanley's ashram was for Christians with a bit of a twist. The spiritual character of Stanley's Ashrams was a mixture of Christianity along with orthodox and liberal streams of Indian thought. In an effort to reinterpret Christ through the Indian genius, his curriculum was not necessarily couched in forms of Christian expression. He did, however, have this disclaimer.

Some people would surmise because we have a Hindu term that therefore the Christian Ashram is an amalgamation between Christianity and Hinduism. Nothing could be further from the reality. This was no syncretistic combination of Hindu and Christian ideas or that the ashrams were eclectic, picking and choosing among Christian and non-Christian concepts. Eclecticism picks and chooses, syncretism combines, but only life assimilates. The Christian faith, being life, assimilates. Like the plant which reaches into the soil and picks out things akin to its own nature, takes them up into the purpose of its life, but transforms them according to the laws of its own being, so the Christian faith reaches into the culture of every nation and takes out things which can be assimilated into its purpose, but in so doing makes something entirely different.[29]

It is interesting that the word, *ashram* comes from two Sanskrit words, *a* meaning from, as in away from, and *shram* meaning hard work. So, an ashram was a retreat from hard work, usually in an outdoor or forest school under the guidance of a *guru* teacher whose name was usually attached to the experience. The key to the success of Stanley's ashram in India, and eventually in America and throughout the world, was that the real leader or *guru* of the Christian ashrams was Jesus Christ. This central focus on Christ meant that Stanley, just like the other members of the ashram, was accountable first of all to God and then to the others.[30]

Tom Albin, Executive Director of the North American Christian Ashrams, writes that important to the Ashram spirit was that Brother Stanley knew that "Hindus, Buddhists, Sikhs, Jains, Jews, Muslims, agnostics, and atheists all agree that Jesus is a person to be honored and emulated." Consistent with his belief that the Holy Spirit was at work in everyone, regardless of faith or tradition, and then his growing certainty of the universal appeal of the Word become flesh in the person of Jesus Christ, helped him to see that there was no need to attack or diminish any other religion or faith tradition. People did not have to be Christian to admire Jesus. What they did need was a place where everyone was welcome to come and experience Jesus — to live and learn from people who followed him. Therefore, the culture and customs of this Ashram were to reflect the teachings of Jesus, to be centered in him. The mission of the Christian Ashram was to be "the Kingdom of God in miniature."[31] Stanley writes that the center of that Center is the Word become flesh. Philosophies and religions are the Word become word, a philosophy or a moralism. In Jesus the Word has become flesh. If so, then the center of our manifestation of that Word become flesh must be that this Word must become flesh in us. If Christianity is looked on as a teaching — a philosophy or a moralism—then the group will become a discussion group where we get verbal answers to verbal questions. If the emphasis is on the Word become flesh, then the group must not find an answer, but be the answer in their corporate life. They must be the Word of the Kingdom become flesh—a Kingdom in miniature. Imperfect, of course, because it is made up of imperfect people, but in some real way the new order realized.

In typical Stanley rhetoric he adds;

> If you universalize this new order you have the answer. This sets the group on a quest, instead of on a question. The quest is vital instead of verbal. If the group is to be the Kingdom, then we must get down barriers, for the Kingdom is God's redemptive invasion of us, especially the barriers of race and class. The Kingdom is colorblind and class-blind; it sees a person as a person for whom Christ died. So we will not go where all races and all classes cannot come together on the basis of complete equality. We get down the barriers that titles bring—those who have titles are high caste and those who do not are low caste—so we leave all titles at the door. There are no more bishops, professors, doctors, judges—there is simply "Brother Stanley" or "Sister Premi." This has a psychological leveling effect for it's not easy to be high and mighty if someone is calling you by your first name. We add the "Brother" and the "Sister," for it is a family of God.[32]

THE MOVEMENT GROWS

The evangelistic witness and mission of the Christian Ashram in India is not a story of easy progress and continual success. Stanley had initially dreamed of a full-time Christian Ashram—similar to the ashrams of Tagore and Gandhi. He actually opened a full-time ashram in Lucknow but it lasted only a few years before it had to be disbanded. Stanley adds that God was at work for good in the midst of the failure. In his own words written some year later, "The disbanding of the Ashram as a full-time Ashram, while it seemed a calamity at the time, led to a new form. As a full-time Ashram it could not have been transferred to another social climate; as a part-time Ashram of about a week in length it has proved that it could be transferred — and universalized. So the calamity became opportunity."[33]

Initially, the Christian Ashram in Sat Tal was a two-month gathering during the vacation period — May and June — which would account for some of Stanley time away from Sitapur. Missionaries, British officials, and Indians would join us and have a "vacation with God."[34] These participants held very different views about religion, politics and economics. In a place where "Jesus is Lord," however, all were welcome; all were treated with respect; diversity was valued. It was in this context that Stanley learned something important for his ongoing work as an evangelist.

One of the first lessons we learned was that the human mind breaks up between conservative and radical. Never once through those years did the discussion break up between Westerners and Easterners. It was always between radicals and conservatives — the radical Indian and the radical Westerner on one side and the conservative Indian and the conservative Westerner on the other. That is a good division: if we were all conservative, we would dry up; and if we were all radical, we would burn up! However, between the pull back of the conservative and the pull ahead of the radical we make progress in a middle direction.[35]

Stanley's ashrams also had this innovation. There were not only no titles used, there was an attempt to confront and attack the barriers of distinction between manual workers and white-collar workers. Those who do not work with their hands are supposedly high caste, and those who do are supposedly low caste. So, Stanley devised a Work Period each day when everyone worked with his or her hands. We harnessed our exercise period to constructive tasks; we leave the place better than we found it.[36] So, each member of the ashram was asked to perform some kind of manual labor. Stanley actually gave the workers a holiday once a week and asked for volunteers to do their jobs, including the sweeper who cleaned the latrines. In these early days it had to be done by hand since there were no flush toilets. To do this work would humble the person who did the work of a sweeper, the lowest caste in the eyes of the Brahmin and other Hindus. The first day of vacation for the workers Stanley, along with several others, would volunteer to do the sweeper's work. Every time he looked out his window, there stood the sweeper fiddling his hands in semi-adoration, his face wreathed in smiles, without a word. That silence was eloquent. Once when a Brahmin convert was hesitant to volunteer, Stanley asked him when he was going to volunteer. He shook his head and said, "Brother Stanley, I'm converted, but I'm not converted that far."[37]

Stanley tells the story of an Indian ex-superintendent of police, decorated by the British government for sending so many of the followers of Gandhi to jail. He was converted when he and Stanley prayed together in Calcutta. He then came to the Sat Tal Ashram and volunteered to do the sweeper's work. Afterward he went to Brother Stanley and said, "Now that I have done that, I'm ready for anything." Little did he know what "anything" would mean. He would eventually resign his job, attend theological courses in India, Cambridge and Union Theological Seminary in New York City only to return to India and become the Secretary of the National Christian Council.[38]

GANDHI'S LONG WALK

By this time most (including the British) assumed that India would one day be independent. The question was would an independent India be open to the Gospel. Stanley felt he now had the answer. He believed that perhaps he could even act as a political mediator. We mentioned that the British convened a Round Table Conference in London but much to Stanley's disappointment the Indian National Congress boycotted it.

Gandhi (walking stick in hand) had begun his famous Salt March (protesting British monopoly on salt) in March 1930, vowing not to return to his ashram until India was free and independent. Now non-cooperation would move to active and deliberate disobedience of British Law. As his first act Gandhi would defy the British monopoly on salt. He informed Lord Irwin that he and his followers would march from his ashram near Ahmedabad to Dandi, a small village on the West coast of India and mine the abundant salt on the beaches there that had not been taxed or approved for sale by the British. Gandhi and seventy-eight of his followers took twenty-four days to complete their two hundred forty-one mile march. The pace was deliberately slow so that Gandhi could attract maximum public attention. The march was touted as a brilliant success.[39]

Gandhi was not arrested but the British Government ordered local officials to suppress the illegal production of salt. Within a month sixty thousand Indians were arrested in Dandi and when Gandhi announced he would lead the occupation of the salt works at Dharasana, he was arrested as well. This fueled a popular uprising throughout India. One hundred thousand more were arrested when the Viceroy declared martial law.

Stanley writes at the time that he went to the Indian National Congress at Allahabad as a visitor where he met Nehru, "a man of deep sincerity but of very radical views." Stanley was somewhat skeptical. He then vowed, "I have to speak to India and I must know what India is thinking."[40]

The longing for independence from British rule was still growing but would not come to fruition for another seventeen years. In the interim Stanley became a staunch supporter of the movement and would visit Gandhi on any number of occasions (especially the times when Gandhi was in prison).

Before it was over two hundred thousand of the leading men went to jail. Gandhi had gone to the Yervada Jail. Once when some violence crept into the movement Gandhi called the movement off and fasted in penitence and purification, and, like Jesus, took the sin of the people upon himself. On one occasion, he fasted for forty days to compel Hindus to give up the sin of untouchability toward seventy million outcastes.[41]

It should be noted that Hinduism dates back to the third millennium BC. According to those who broke away (Jainism and Buddhism) the most insidious aspects of Hinduism involved the myriad of gods and the creation of levels of human interaction—the caste system.

When Stanley visited Gandhi in jail he asked two questions: the first question was "What did Gandhi think of castes?" Stanley was against them. Gandhi was against them somewhat, but held to a modified form of caste believing that deeds from former lives did affect one's status in this life (karma). Dr. Bhimrag Ambedkar, the leader of the outcastes happened to be there listening in on the conversation. Ambedkar, after independence, would write the Bill of Rights where there could be no caste discrimination on the public scene (hotels, restaurants, temples, etc.).

The second question, "Did Gandhi not think that fasting unto death was a form of coercion?" Gandhi responded, "Yes, like the Cross."[42] Gandhi's fasting had some interesting history. For example, two men were once caught in immoral acts at his Ashram. Gandhi fasted and after 6 days the two men came to him weeping and begging him to end his fast and to forgive them. Gandhi forgave them.

At this point, Jones and Gandhi had an interesting discussion. Stanley asked could Gandhi have forgiven the men without the fast. Gandhi then replied that the fast, like the Cross, gave forgiveness integrity. Forgiveness without the fast, like forgiveness without the Cross, would cheapen both. Stanley understood this. The Cross is the power of the Gospel. Forgiveness without the atoning sacrifice of Himself is forgiveness that is shallow and incomplete.[43]

A THEOLOGY OF THE CROSS

Stanley, in his *Song*, gives us some important theology at this point. He turns to Revelation 7:17, "The Lamb who is at the heart of the throne will be their shepherd." The Lamb, slain from the foundation is God wanting to be reconciled with creation (God created wanting someone to love — the void was not enough). Then the Creator antici-pates the fall and makes provision before the foundation. The Lamb, looking as if it had been slain, standing in the midst of the Throne, speaks of power (the seven horns and seven eyes were evidence of ultimate authority).[44]

Stanley then asks the question, what is the nature of ultimate power? He gives these alternatives: "1. Among the Greeks — Zeus with his thunderbolts — spectacular power is at the heart of the throne. 2. Confucius — genteel peace. 3. Buddha — desirelessness, undisturbed peace. 4. Stoicism — detachment. 5. Judaism — almightiness. 6. Islam — an unapproachable autocratic almightiness. 7. Modern cults — peace of mind. 8. Shaivism — a cosmic dance. 9. Scientism — dependable law. 10. Semi-Christian Modernized cults — goodness and dependable law. 11. Christianity — The Lamb is at the heart of the Throne — self-giv-ing, redeeming, sacrificial love is at the center of power in the uni-verse. Sacrificial love must be at the heart of all our motives, at the heart or center of our very lives."[45]

Stanley writes that we can choose between the two great forces that have emerged in this generation: "The power of the atom, atomic power (India itself would acquire nuclear weapons), and the power of the *atma* — soul force. We can now choose atomic power and em-brace mutual destruction, or we can choose *atma* power, the power of invincible goodwill, and we can harness this atomic power to the needs of the world and start a new era." Although Gandhi was not a Christian, Stanley believed that as a Hindu he had grasped the prin-ciple of the cross and had brought it into the consciousness of a na-tion and made it work. People said of Gandhi that he was "Christlike." Stanley adds, Gandhi's noncooperation was important but it was not the cross. Gandhi did, however, grasp the principle of the cross and dared to apply it on a national scale, betting his life on the validity of that principle, and won." Stanley concluded that his own contact with non-Christian India led him more and more to the Cross.[46]

One of Stanley's most powerful lectures to college students at the time was "Karma and the Cross." The issue, in effect, was deeds against faith. Deeds meant that you reap what you sow (which of course is true); but the Cross meant that Christ is reaping what we sow. Faith in the Cross says that forgiveness of sin is the act of God on the Cross. He bore our sins in His own body. He forgives us with a forgiveness that is costly, not cheap. Stanley goes on to say that the Christian faith believes in the law of Karma — reaping what you sow — but that Christ bears the cost. Again, we live in a moral universe and to go against this moral universe is to reap the benefits of our actions. Our obedience (by the grace of God available through repentance and faith) has cosmic backing.

Karma, we reap what we sow, is a half-truth as others also reap the "benefits" of what we sow. Hindus insist that we attain to Brahma status on our own via the ladder of austerity. There is no helping hand. We must achieve on our own. The Cross on the other hand shows God's helping "nail-pierced" hand. Hindus worship their gods primarily in solitude, it has little or nothing to do with corporate worship. The Cross, however, binds us up in a bundle of caring lives; serving God produces serving people. If the Cross is absent in a "Christian" nation selfishness prevails. If our understanding of God is that God does not care, then we do not care.[47]

Predictably, Stanley's outspoken advocacy of equality was rooted in his concept of the kingdom of God. Stanley keeps returning to the laws of the moral universe as the principles of the Kingdom of God are applied to human behavior. The first law of the moral universe is equality. We are all created with equal moral dignity by God; therefore, we should all have equal moral dignity in the eyes of one another. God created human beings to live and interact in a world governed by these laws of the moral universe. When we obey these laws,

IN OUR TIME

we cooperate with God in the purposes of human creation and we reap the abundant fruit of living in harmony with both God and one another. When we knowingly disobey these laws, however, we resist God's purposes and reap the bitter fruit of living in tension and conflict with God, ourselves and with those around us. This is why Stanley insisted on racial equality for all people around the world. Racial equality was a Kingdom principle.[48]

In April 1930, twenty-five persons showed up for the first Ashram at Sat Tal, both Indians and foreigners with diverse experiences of Christianity from Quaker to High Church Anglican.[49]

As the basis for group discussions Stanley would often use his book manuscripts or his ideas for evangelistic addresses. "If the response was faint or unsatisfactory, or just not what it ought to be, the message was quietly laid aside or interred." For the rest of his life Stanley wrote prolifically. Since these early ashrams lasted for several months, much of the research and writing was done during these Ashram periods. During this first ashram he wrote and published, *The Christ of Every Road – A study in Pentecost.*[50]Then during the next year's Ashram, he wrote, *The Christ of the Mount – A Working Philosophy of Life.*

THE CENTRAL FOCUS: SELF-SURRENDER TO JESUS AS LORD

Again, the central focus of the Christian Ashram is Jesus Christ – the living Word become flesh.[51] The central problem of human kind is self-centeredness. We have already established in a previous chapter that the two biggest sins in the Bible are self-reliance and oppressing the poor. The essential response to this living Word of God is self-surrender. We surrender to the *only One* who can sustain us. We rely totally upon God. In the Christian Ashram:

> We try to put our finger on the central problem of life whether inside the institutions or outside, the problem of self-centeredness,

by insisting on self-surrender.... I cannot go down any road with anybody on any problem without running into the necessity of self-surrender. Yourself on your own hands is a problem and a pain; yourself in the hands of God is a possibility and a power. Not who you are, but whose you are, is the central question in any person's life." ... So self-surrender is the theme song of the Ashram. Apart from self-surrender all our surrenders to God are marginal and unimportant. This is it, and it carries all the lesser surrenders with it. . . . Only when the self is surrendered can you cultivate your spiritual life around the new Center—Christ, and Christ in control. Then everything falls into its place.[52]

This movement born in the heart of India and nurtured in the heart of Brother Stanley has universal congruence with the mission of God—to call his wayward children home. The Christian Ashram is a place where "home" is experienced here and now—the Kingdom of God in miniature—on earth as it is in heaven.[53]

Stanley writes, "Of all the notes that make up my *Song of Ascents*, one of the most important is the Ashram note. Without it I would have lacked a disciplined fellowship.... [where I could] live out my life in a close-knit fellowship of the Spirit—they responsible to me and I responsible to them, at a very deep level, the level of experimental living. . . . their transformations have been an invitation and a spur to further transformations in me. They have helped make me."[54]

It is important to note that the earlier ashrams were called a complete success as most of the participants were spiritually transformed. They returned to their work renewed and refreshed.

EVEN IN STANLEY'S ABSENCE, MABEL'S INFLUENCE IS NEVER FAR BEHIND

Mabel also had her successes. She tells in her April 1930 *Newsletter* of a recent lunch with His Excellency, Sir Malcolm Hailey, when he spent the day in Sitapur, at the District Magistrate's home. On another occasion at a garden party Mabel had given a Muslim official a copy of the *Life of Christ* who came to thank her for it. He had almost finished the book but was sorry and disappointed that he could find nothing in it of which he disapproved. Hmmm....[55]

Even more recently a Hindu priest called. He said, "I am a Brahmin." Mabel said, "Yes I know." He apparently felt that she was not satisfactorily impressed and added, "You know people worship me." She said, "Do you think you ought to be worshiped?" He replied, "Why not? I am a part of God." When Mabel spoke to him at length from the Gospel of John to illustrate what she believed, tears came to his eyes.[56]

Snakes were again plaguing Mabel's wellbeing. She was constantly reminding her patrons of her constant need for God's protection. In September she reached into a cupboard that was always kept closed and locked to pull out an account book and found a fresh, perfect cast-off skin of the vicious Krait clinging to it. She wrote in her Newsletter for September 10, 1930 that "this little snake, whose bite could send one into eternity in fifteen minutes, is hidden in there somewhere among my books and papers and five or six times today I have carelessly reached in to get something, never dreaming that there was danger.

Our Eunice once had a narrow escape. She dropped down on the couch one afternoon and then decided that her head was too high. She sat up and lifted the top cushion and coiled on the pillow beneath was one of these small brown vipers."[57]

Mabel never liked having anything to do with medicine or disease but when folks walked miles for help and are likely to die without it, what could she do?

The boys fared well in the fall of 1930 but she had never known such suffering in the city and villages. "I have spent hours mixing magnesium sulphate and Vaseline for boils; sulphur and Vaseline for itch; quinine and water and sulphuric acid for malaria; weighing out and making protargol lotion for inflamed eyes; measuring out bismuth and salol for dysentery; pouring out castor oil and counting out cascara pills."[58]

Mabel was not just about medicine either. There is a wonderful story regarding the Magistrate. He was impressed with Mabel's understanding of the *Bhagavad-Gita* and the *Qur'an*. Mabel writes, "One could not hope to witness effectively to what she knew was sacred for Christians without a deep comprehension of what Hindus (or Muslims) regard as sacred.[59]

For the rest of 1930 Stanley was busy as usual. In October he was holding meetings in Madras speaking in schools and colleges throughout the city. At night after the lectures he met with some of the leading Brahmins of Madras. "There was utmost frankness. I had seen His Excellency the Viceroy and had talked over the situation with him and I brought his message and outlook to these men. I tried to urge on them the necessity of going to the Round Table Conference in London and not to boycott it... When they found that I was interested in their national problems they were ready to listen to anything I had to say on religion."[60]

In December Stanley was with Christian students at a camp near Delhi. Many were enthusiastic supporters of the independent movement. They put up the national flag on their school building. Some loyalists tried to bring it down but several students spent two weeks on the roof protecting it. When Stanley gave his invitation the leading nationalist stepped out and one by one the entire group (several hundred) followed to make it unanimous. "It was one of the greatest meetings I have ever conducted — a valuable lesson learned, students could be nationalists and be responsive to Christ."[61]

In January 1931 Gandhi and the other Congress leaders who had been jailed in the aftermath of the demonstrations following the Salt March were unconditionally released. During the next two months Gandhi met with Lord Irwin face to face on several occasions. As a result, Gandhi agreed to call off the civil disobedience movement and to attend the next Round Table Conference if Irwin would free all political prisoners. The British would not, saying they could not tolerate violence against British Rule. The radical Bhagat Singh and two others were hanged March 23, 1931. Yet Britain was by now considering Dominion Status (like Canada and Australia). They would no longer attempt to divide and conquer (primarily between Hindus and Muslims but also between Sikhs and Christians as well as among castes). Tragically, the second Round Table Conference late in the year failed.

To complicate matters further the issue of proselytizing came up between Stanley and Gandhi. Gandhi assumed that missionaries would proselytize (switching from one religion to another and that within the caste system that would split whole families). Remarkably, Stanley promised to disavow such proselytizing completely as it smacked too much of religious imperialism. Gandhi then backed off.[62]

Again, as in the previous year, Stanley's schedule kept him away from Sitapur for months on end. The second Ashram took place from April to July 1931. It was marked by the conversion of a famous Hindu swami or leader. This Swami had his own Ashram where about 3,000 families look to him as their guru. During the Ashram Stanley was both leader and active member during the sixteen-plus-hour days. He still found time to meet with some Asbury College students visiting for a few days on an evangelistic world tour. His comment, "They were lovely singers."

Then, in October Mabel had a hard fall. Stanley came home for Christmas but Mabel was dealing with her residual aches and pains from the fall and it was well into April before she fully recovered.[63]

Stanley and Mabel were due a furlough at the beginning of 1932 but Mabel thought it best to postpone it until the end of the year so that Eunice could finish high school in India. Diffendorfer was pleading with Stanley to come to the U.S. The General Conference was also in 1932 and this would mean that Stanley would miss it. Also, the Great Depression had taken its toll on Foreign Missions and Stanley could help in raising monies. The debate ended when Diffendorfer then wrote to say that there were no funds for sabbaticals at this time.[64]

Then, shortly after Eunice began her senior year she was having constant headaches and weight loss. Her doctor wrote to Mabel suggesting that Eunice may be on the verge of a complete nervous breakdown (another misdiagnosis for the Jones). After taking x-rays, however, he found that she had three wisdom teeth that were putting pressure on nerve centers. Mabel was at her side for ten days while she was hospitalized (Mabel had had her own recent problems with her teeth). Then Eunice was diagnosed with tuberculosis and Mabel stayed with her for two more months. She wired Stanley, "You must come and take us to Switzerland at once and put her under treatment there."[65] Understandably, Stanley prayed like a "saint" saying that he would do whatever the doctor ordered. Then, after joining Mabel and Eunice his "inner voice" assured him that Eunice would be healed. After another examination, the doctor confirmed. "There is scar tissue, but nothing active." Stanley then felt that God was saying that Eunice would be OK. Although Eunice was much improved; however, there would be relapses the next year.

After Gandhi's failure to negotiate a settlement with the British the previous year, the following January (1932) he launched another campaign of civil disobedience. Again, he and thirty thousand other important Indian Congress nationalists were jailed without trial or hearing and the Congress was "banned as an illegal organization. Stanley visited Gandhi while in jail and while there met again with Dr. Bhimrao R. Ambedkar, the champion of the depressed classes, who again happened to be visiting Gandhi at the same time. Ambedkar was, with Gandhi, trying to unify the nationalist movement. In speaking with Stanley after they had visited, Gandhi stated clearly that Ambedkar was too narrow, only interested in social equality for the depressed classes and the abolition of castes.[66]

In April of 1932 Stanley writes in the *Indian Witness* that the past year had been far and away the best year ever. He now felt that India had reached the point of critical mass with regard to her receptivity to the Gospel. He personally felt that after 25 years he was no longer on the edges of the soul of India but within it.

He was no longer lecturing to India but standing close enough to hear her heart beating.[67]

Stanley's friend Gandhi was trying desperately to keep the Harijans (the depressed castes) within Hinduism. On September 20, 1932, he would begin his fast unto death, protesting the discrimination by the caste members against the outcasts. Again, Stanley felt that Gandhi's fast "unto death" was pure coercion. Gandhi said no! His fast sprang from love. He then added that "it is the implicit and sacred belief of millions of Christians that the love of Jesus keeps them from falling... His love bends the reason and the emotion of thousands of His votaries to His love... and, if all this love could be regarded as coercion, then the love that prompted my fast was coercion, but it was that in no other sense."[68]

The success of this fast was nothing short of a miracle. For the first time ever, untouchables were admitted into Hindu Temples. Caste members and outcastes actually ate together.

Stanley is soon off preaching again. He writes of a meeting in Benares, the chairman for the first night was to be a leading nationalist but he had been jailed. There were requests to cancel the meetings but Stanley carried on with some success.

Christians were split over the issues of independence. Stanley decided not to take sides, touching political issues only indirectly. He signed the pledge given to missionaries throughout the Empire that "all due obedience and respect should be given to the lawfully constituted Government... while carefully abstaining from political affairs." Stanley rarely toed the line but it was a delicate balance. Gordon B. Halstead, a member of the staff of Lucknow Christian College sided with the nationalists and was deported.[69]

During the third Ashram at Sat Tal (1932) the "Kingdom of God" begins to emerge as Stanley's central message. For him, this is now the heart of the Gospel. Sixteen different presentations on various aspects of the Kingdom of God were made at that Ashram.

Stanley records his own personal testimony regarding a visitation by the Holy Spirit at a time of personal and family crisis. He was worried about Mabel and Eunice. He considered taking off from his regular duties for several years to nurse Eunice back to health. At that moment, the Spirit of God gave him such assurance that his heart sang.

On July15, 1932 Stanley left for a six-month tour of the Far East.

The first stop was Rangoon, Burma. Stanley held large meetings for several days. The Chief Justice of Burma "exhorted [preached the gospel] after one of my addresses." Then Stanley spent twelve days on the Malay Peninsula, including the Island of Penang (an island resort), Ipoh, KL, and then down the straits to the cities of Malacca, and Singapore. Stanley estimated that on this tour a thousand students signed commitment cards professing faith in Jesus Christ after his meetings. Then on to Hong Kong and China where Dr. Tsui of the National Christian Council was in charge of the local arrangements. He had selected ten provincial centers in various parts of China where Christian workers were invited for a series of conferences in the mornings. Then there were meetings in the afternoons and evenings for non-Christians (by ticket only).

From Hong Kong Stanley travels to Peking where he addressed an assembly of all the paid staff of the YMCA throughout China. He writes that he was "somewhat shell-shocked by the anti-Christian movement that had swept across China in the late 1920s. He needed a new courage and new power to come back again and confront the secular youth of China with a program that focused on the spiritual.[70]

Then it was on to Hankow in East Central China on the Yangtze River. Students at the college there submitted questions, one hundred and ten questions grouped in six categories—theological and philosophical; personal religious life; the Bible and science and religion; the church; social questions; and political questions. For example,

What is the use of prayer—if any? How can we make Christianity indigenous? Explain what is God, what is life and what is conscience. How are they related? Define religion. The more we try to spread religion the worse the world becomes. Why is this? Why does God not force us to be good? If He wants us to be good will He give us the right way to do so? If there is only one God why are there so many religions? What about so-called Christians whose deeds are so unchristian? How can we answer non-Christians on this matter? Can one be a Christian without joining the Church?[71]

Stanley was in his element. This would open doors that would affect many of these students forever.

Next was Mukden, the capital of Manchuria. There the primary question was, "What should the Christian response be to the naked Japanese aggression in Manchuria." In spite of tension (bullets whizzing) Stanley held his meetings. Two hundred and fifty non-Christians signed cards.

Back in Peking Stanley visited with General Feng again and met General Chiang Kai-shek. He thought communism was spreading because of a two-pronged strategy. First was ruthlessness to instill fear. Second, teaching the people (to read and write). Communists thought that Christianity was the only religious opposition that presented a serious threat to their power.[72] At the end of the China tour there were an estimated three thousand decisions for Christ. He also sold twelve thousand copies of Chinese translations of his books and twenty-four thousand of his pamphlets, *What is Christianity.*"[73]

Stanley was back with Mabel and Eunice in India in January 1933. The first few months in were spent planning for their upcoming furlough. Mabel was feeling ill. The extended time at "home" would serve her well.

On February 4, 1933 Stanley has an interview with Gandhi. Gandhi would then publish his account in his magazine, *Harijan*: "Rev. Stanley Jones paid me a visit the other day before sailing for America. He said that in America he would be asked many questions about the campaign against untouchability and had, therefore, some questions.

I was glad of the visit. One of his questions was why not do away with the caste system altogether instead of speaking out only against untouchability." Gandhi answered that for him there was a very real difference in kind, not mere difference in degree, between caste and untouchability. Untouchability for Gandhi was a "sin again God and man. On the other hand, the caste system was a social institution consisting of trade guilds that had admittedly outgrown their original purpose but unlike untouchability were not sinful and were "no bar to spiritual progress."[74]

On the brink of an upcoming furlough Stanley was now a middle-aged missionary evangelist with a rapidly growing international reputation. As his public recognition increased, so did the strength of his personal relationship with God. He relied more and more exclusively on what he called the "inner voice" or the voice of the Holy Spirit. "He began to see a world that others saw only dimly and obscurely or not at all. Even amidst the deep and widespread skepticism of the Jerusalem Conference in 1928 he saw not the tensions and frustrations and factions among Christians but a deep inner unity that would become the basis for renewed and expanded missionary evangelism."[75]

Stanley, Mabel and Eunice then left early in February 1933 for the U.S.

Eunice and Mabel Jones, 1930s

Stanley, Eunice and Mabel, 1933

CHAPTER SIX

1933-1939: MABEL AND EUNICE ARE IN THE U.S. WHILE STANLEY EMBRACES THE WORLD. THE KINGDOM OF GOD BECOMES A DOMINANT THEME

Stanley's Need to Sense the Spirit of God at Work in the World—Listening to his "Inner Voice"

S tanley, Mabel and Eunice leave India for the U.S. in February 1933 by separate routes. Mabel and Eunice continued to struggle with various illnesses—Mabel with pleurisy while Eunice has lost even more weight.

MABEL AND EUNICE IN ROUTE TO THE U.S.

In route, Mabel, Eunice and Eunice's friend, Nancy Moffat (the daughter of missionaries), sailed on the *Victoria* from Bombay to

Naples. Mabel and Eunice spent "wonderful time together" staying at the Crandon Institute, a mission school in Rome sponsored by the Women's Foreign Missionary Society. Eunice, now a high school graduate was trying to earn enough credits in French and Latin for college. She actually gained five pounds in April.

Remarkably, on several occasions Mabel and Eunice heard Pope Pius XI address the gathered thousands from his balcony in St. Peter's Square. They even heard Benito Mussolini speak from his balcony in the Piazza Venezia. They also enjoyed trying to trace the footsteps of Peter and Paul.

From Italy they traveled to a Deaconess Rest Home in Spiez, Switzerland, high in the Alps. Then, after a few days at a youth hostel in Paris they hurried on to Winchester, England before making their way down to Southampton to board a ship bound for New York.

1933: BACK IN THE UNITED STATES

As a result of her illnesses, Mabel was nearly six years in recovery and would not return to India until December 29, 1938. Once arriving in the U. S. she is under doctor's orders to do nothing until Christmas.

In August Stanley joined Mabel and Eunice for "a heavenly month of peace and quiet" in Ventnor, New Jersey. Eunice started classes at Oberlin College in Ohio in the fall. Mabel further recovers from her illnesses in a house across the street from Eunice's dormitory. However she would not receive the medical certificate required by the Board of Foreign Missions to return to India for several more years.

Stanley, while Mabel continued to recover from illnesses and stress, is soon busy conducting missions, holding meetings and speaking at conferences for both Methodists and interdenominational groups. For six weeks during the fall of 1933, he speaks in Chicago,

Milwaukee, Des Moines, Omaha, Oklahoma City, St. Louis, India-napolis, Washington, Philadelphia and many places in between.[1]

In spite of Mabel's illnesses, her schedule soon begins to rival (in some ways) Stanley's global schedule. Many believe that she is beginning to get in touch with her own voice as a bit of a feminist. No question, Mabel fully understood women's issues but as a fully liberalized woman she felt that most of the chatter about "liberation" was irrelevant to her. She writes in an open letter that she needed prayer warriors. "We cannot win India by might, nor by power, nor by money alone; it will be by His Spirit working in us — and in you."[2]

Related to this, although still not well, Mabel wrote a newsletter in November, 1933 stating that she understood Hindu and Muslim men and was at ease with them as she sat with the District Municipal Board for 20 years (the only woman, only Christian and the only American). She also (in line with Stanley's *Indian Road*) understood that Hindus are reserved and felt that "religious experience should not be shouted as that would take away from the bloom and beauty."

On December 15, 1933, Catholic Charities held a fund-raiser in Washington, D.C. charging $4 a plate. Both Stanley and Eleanor Roosevelt were in attendance and (in light of the worldwide depression), both complained about the price of the meal.

At Christmas Eunice had a bout with tuberculosis.[3]

THE ISSUE OF IMMIGRATION

If there is ever any doubt as to the relevancy of Stanley Jones' ministry for the world today, watch this happen!

Toward the end of December 1933, Stanley met with President Roosevelt (FDR) to discuss two crucial issues on relations between the U.S. and the Far East, Japan in particular. After WWI Woodrow Wilson had a vision for a League of Nations that could possibly unite the Far East (much like NATO would in the North Atlantic) but it failed miserably as the United States washed its hands of involvement in international affairs and retreated into a foreign policy of isolationism and xenophobia. This fear of foreigners (especially racial prejudice against Asians) was reflected in the restrictive immigration laws adopted by Congress in the 1920s.

As a result, Japan was excluded from the League of Nations and then the immigration quotas against Asians so offended the Japanese in particular, that these two issues would become the main source of Japanese grievances against the West and were never resolved to Japan's satisfaction. Japan responded by turning to militarism and imperialism and this would set in motion the events that would lead to WW II.

Stanley believed that his sensitivity to these issues was a part of God's call on his life. He was one of the first to perceive Japan's feelings of being victim of international prejudice, especially in light of its needs for land and natural resources (there will be more about this later). Japan was being primed to act independently.

After the visit with Stanley, Roosevelt promised to look into the matter but it is said that sometimes the President would promise to look into something and then do nothing. Unfortunately, he did nothing and the stage was set for war in less than eight years. Stanley had done his best.

Stanley is now 50 years of age. After the New Year, Stanley is traveling again in an attempt to touch as many bases as possible before setting sail for India in less than two months. As usual Mabel and Eunice were counting the days, hoping to see him before he left for India. Once again, however, it seemed that the fates were against them seeing each other. Although Stanley spoke at a banquet at St. Luke's Church in Dubuque, Iowa on February 22, 1934, Eunice was still recovering from her bouts with tuberculosis and Mabel was too sick to attend as well. Mabel's pleurisy lingered and her doctors insisted that she cancel her speaking engagements to search for the "illusive germ" causing fluctuating temperature and chronic tiredness. The only cure, according to the doctors, would be complete rest.[4]

In his absences, however, it is good to know that Stanley was faithful to keep them informed by letter, always beginning, "My Dear Mabel," and then signing, "Affectionately."[5]

STANLEY IN ROUTE BACK TO INDIA, A LIFE CHANGING EXPERIENCE

On February 28, 1934 Stanley (leaving Mabel and Eunice behind) sailed on the *S.S. Manhattan* for England. He writes that he was tired and worn from his years in India but, nonetheless, the journey back to India itself would change his life forever.[6]

In England Jones was greeted by Charles Collet, the Lord Mayor of London. As a result, he would be treated with great respect. On March 9, he addressed the Missionary Demonstration in Methodist Central Hall at Westminster. The substance was "Christian Missions, Not Domination, nor Denomination, but Christ." His notes were published by the *Methodist Times and Leader,* a British Methodist newspaper and then in the *Indian Witness.*[7]

Before leaving London, Stanley preached at a lunch hour service to an overflowing crowd at the Wesley Chapel on City Road. John Wesley's house (where he died) is next door. His grave is just behind the Chapel. Stanley admired the words on the grave, "Reader, if thou are constrained to bless the instrument, give God the glory." Wesley's mother, Susanna is buried in Bunhill Fields just across the road.[8] Stanley leaves England feeling better and far more confident. "The crowds were great and responsive. I loved them."

Stanley is then off to the Netherlands where he is entertained by Baroness Boetselaer. The Baroness had promoted Stanley's book, *The Christ of the Indian Road,* in Holland and had given Queen Wilhelmina and Princess Juliana a copy before they heard him speak in The Hague.

The Queen commented, "Any Christian of the Indian Road is dangerous!" Stanley sensed that she might have been a bit uneasy about his attitude towards the Dutch colony in South Africa. Nevertheless, Stanley found the people of Holland very responsive (especially the youth). In Utrecht, he had to hold a second youth meeting (the hall being too small for the first). Another day "400 ministers came together for the first time (fully a third of all the ministers in Holland). The Baroness, who had written a book about Stanley, had nothing but high praise.[9]

From Holland Stanley travelled on toward India through Russia (the longest leg of the journey back to Bombay.) Jones and the Methodist Bishop Raymond Wade, first spent several days in Leningrad (St. Petersburg) in European Russia, arriving on Easter Sunday. Bishop Wade commented, "the strangest Easter we have ever spent." Stanley found that the Soviet Union, an atheistic society, embodied a surprising number of Christian principles. As in China, he was taken by the appeal of communism but especially by its apparent spiritual power. He found the contradiction was not just an intellectual puzzle, it was an emotional and spiritual blow both to his understanding of Christianity and to his association of Christianity with a democratic government.[10] The Tsarist regime had been harsh and self-centered and Stanley found himself warming to the closing lines of the *Manifesto*, "Workers of the world unite. You have nothing to lose but your chains." Perhaps they knew something of a "moral universe."

When their guide asked what they would like to see, Bishop Wade suggested the nearest open museum, knowing that St. Isaac Cathedral next door was now the Anti-Religion Museum. After the tour, Stanley admitted to the guide that the museum made "a pretty thorough case against the church and particularly against the Russian Church, but not against genuine religion." The guide quickly asked, "What does your religion mean to you?" Stanley concluded that this was his opportunity to deliver an Easter sermon in a land where God's voice was heard small.

Significantly (perhaps "ironically" is the better word) Bishop Wade was visiting Russia to investigate the state of the Methodist Church in Leningrad. Before the 1917 Revolution the one church building there had been owned by the Methodist Board of Foreign Missions but had been "liquidated" by the Soviet regime. Wade was not encouraged. It seemed a total loss.

From Leningrad, Stanley took a train to the Azerbaijan city of Baku on the Caspian Sea. As he traveled through the countryside it was obvious that Russians were making every attempt to obliterate church and religion. This trek through Russia was a life changer for Stanley. He would describe the experience in his book, *Christ's Alternative to Communism,* published just over a year later (1935), as "a shock, a terrific thud." Russia and communism hit Stanley hard. The experience would change his life and ministry forever.

Many years later Stanley would write that he was stunned by the impact of this visit. On the one hand, he saw potential and even hope in the eyes of the old babushkas that would have their children secretly baptized when the government was not looking. Then, on the other hand, the American Methodist Episcopal Church was in the process of willingly withdrawing its only official presence in the Soviet Union. This would be still another missed opportunity that would not find significant root for another 50 years.

STANLEY IS BACK IN INDIA WITH RUSSIA STILL ON HIS MIND, THE KINGDOM OF GOD BEGINS TO DOMINATE HIS THINKING

From Russia Stanley journeyed on to Bombay via Teheran and Baghdad. Once back in India (the early summer of 1934), he immediately attended the fifth Ashram at Sat Tal. While there, and during the non-stop evangelistic meetings to follow, he is meditating and reflecting on his impressions from Russia, no doubt working on his book, *Christ's Alternative to Communism.* His reflections were most interesting....

What I saw in Russia so deeply impressed me that I felt as never before, that this was the problem we would have to face in the future. I know there are two sides to the question of Russia. There is the poverty, the lack of liberty, the drive against religion. But there is another side: The enthusiasm of the people who believe that they have the truth that will hold the future: the self-sacrifice of all classes to make a new Russia in which all have a share in the good life, the sheer drive of the whole thing, all this and more, makes one feel that this is an issue that will have to be faced. We must choose, on a world scale, whether we shall make the future after the pattern of Marx or after the pattern of Jesus and the Kingdom of God. I am not fair in setting them in such bold opposition, for in many places they coincide; in many things we must sit and learn from Marx. However, in the end, the Kingdom of God offers something that we must take, or be compelled by the force of the pressure of circumstances to take the Russian brand of communism.[11]

Was Stanley's contrast of Christianity and Marxism losing some of its edge? He is now increasingly identifying the central message of the New Testament Gospels as the Kingdom of God.[12] The question is, what is the content of the Kingdom of God on earth. Does it have anything in common with Marxism? This question would consume him for decades.

The Russians were enthusiastically building a new civilization without God! Youth were heard singing, "We are making a new world." Russia was not yet a menace seeking world domination. A bit naively, Stanley thought she was conducting an interesting social and economic experiment.

Again, Russia led him to a deeper insight as to the nature of the Kingdom of God, this time, the Kingdom as realism. It was on the train to Azerbaijan when it happened. Quite innocently, a Russian actress, sitting across from him in the same compartment said to him as he read his Bible: "I suppose you are a religious man?" He replied that he was. She replied: "You are religious because you are weak.

You turn to God for comfort. Do you want someone to hold your hand?" She then took his hand. Stanley said, "I'm afraid that you are wrong. I do not turn to God for comfort, but for adequacy. I do not want God to hold my hand; I want Him to strengthen my arm so that I can lift a helping hand to others. I do not want him to wipe my tears; I want him to give me a handkerchief so that I might wipe the tears of others. I repeat—I turn to God not for comfort, but for adequacy to meet whatever comes." Then she accused him of being an idealist. Stanley responded, "Yes, I suppose I am." She dismissed him with a wave. "I am a realist," she said. She thought that communism was realism and Christianity was idealism.

All of this set Stanley thinking. Was he an idealist or a realist? He would spend the next two years searching the New Testament to find out if he was a realist or an idealist. He would conclude that if he was to be a Christian he must be a realist. His book, "*Is the Kingdom of God Realism?*" (1940) was written out of the impact of that experience. From that point on the concept of the Kingdom as realism would run through his preaching and writing as a refrain. It took possession of him.[13] Pay close attention to the next few paragraphs, these insights could change your life forever.

In his *Song*, Stanley writes that first of all, the center of our faith, Jesus Christ, is the Word become flesh, not the Word become idea. Had it been the Word become idea, it would be a philosophy, a moralism. But, the Christian faith is not a philosophy, but a fact—the fact of Jesus Christ. In him all the ideas have taken shoes and walked. The message is the Man, for the Man is the message—incarnate. The message is not "among," but apart from, different, unique. "Never a man spoke like this man, for never a man lived like this Man." You never tell where words end and deeds begin, nor where deeds end and words begin, for his deeds were words and his words were deeds.

If, however, the life and teaching of Jesus Christ make the Christian faith realism, there is something else even more startlingly realistic. It is that God created everything through Christ. The passages that explicitly say so are these: "Through him [Jesus] all things came to be; no single thing was created without him. He was in the world but the world, though it owed its being to him, did not recognize him" (John 1:3, 10; cf. Colossians 1:15-16, Hebrews 1:2 and Revelation 3:14).

These passages say nothing less than God created through Jesus Christ. If they mean anything they mean that everything has the touch of Christ upon it, everything (physical, emotional, spiritual) has been structured to work in his way; and if it works in his way, it works well, and if it works in some other way it works its own ruin. The Christian way is written, not only in Christ as a person and in the New Testament as a record, but it is written into the constitution of things.

Unfortunately, the Church has not taken these passages seriously, perhaps because they seem incredible. "Modern theologians think they are the work of the early church — a reflection, not a revelation." The issue, however, is not so much who wrote these words but are they true. What does life say about the Christian way being written into us — into our nerves, our tissues, our organs, our relationships?

Luke's account in Acts describes Christianity as the *Way*. "It is the way of salvation, but much more than that, it is the way, unqualified. It is the way to do everything, to think, to act, to feel, to be in every circumstance, in the individual and in the collective, for God and for humanity." There are just two things, the Way and not the way. The Christian Way is always the Way and the unchristian way is always not the way. For Stanley there were no exceptions, anywhere.

Stanley believed that we are destined by our very makeup to be Christian — we live in a *moral universe*! We were predestined to be conformed to the image of Christ. (Romans 8:29). Our destiny is not found merely in the inscrutable will of God, but it is written into our physical and spiritual makeup as well.

An African chief says, "I'm doomed [destined] to be a saint. Coming to Christ is a homecoming. Going away from Christ is the feeling of estrangement, of going away from home. Is it hard to be a Christian? No! It is hard not to be a Christian. It is hard to live life against life. It is hard for the lungs not to breathe, for the heart not to beat, and to love. "My yoke is easy and my burden is light." The Russian, Solomon Richter, wrote that, "Christianity is a set of scruples, imposed on human nature, to keep it from functioning naturally and normally. Stanley says, "Nothing, absolutely nothing is more false than thinking that the Christian way is a 'set of scruples imposed — foreign laws.' The Christian way is the natural way to live — it is supernaturally natural. To find Christ is to find ourselves." Stanley adds, "Here is a Methodist preaching like a Presbyterian…" (perhaps, but Stanley would rarely meet a Presbyterian that did not at some point preach like a Methodist).[14]

Stanley writes of two great approaches to life — the Christian and the scientific. Christians work from revelation down (Plato). The scientific works from the facts up (Aristotle). Stanley believes that as the Christian approach becomes more Christian and as the scientific approach more scientific, they come out at the same place — at the feet of Jesus. Stanley speaks of the surgeon who discovered the Kingdom of God at the end of his scalpel. It is in the tissues. The moral thing is always the healthy thing physically. "The Christian way is written in us, as if making a scientific discovery." A leading economist then adds that the Christian way is always the healthy thing economically. Similarly, the Christian thing is always the healthy thing sociologically. Love your neighbor as you love yourself. Therefore, down the whole gamut of life the right thing morally, the Christian thing, is always the healthy thing.[15]

People don't break God's laws written into the nature of reality; they break themselves upon them. The surgeon was right: "the right thing morally, the Christian thing is always the healthy thing physically and conversely the wrong thing is the unhealthy thing. The Christian way is even written in our glands — if they are upset it changes the moral character of a person. Morality is in the glands. If glands are normal and if we live truly as Christians our glands function perfectly. We have Christian glands. This is true psychologically as well. Ask Menninger, who after experimentation wrote: "Love is the medicine for the sickness of the world."[16]

Again, if you work from Christ down (Plato) and then from the facts up (Aristotle) both come out at the feet of Jesus. Stanley believed that to revolt against Christ was to revolt against yourself. This gives new meaning to "Cutting off your nose to spite your face." If you will not live with Christ, you cannot live with yourself. God has us hooked. Mary Webster (a long time friend later in Stanley's life) was always saying, "Life is a laboratory in which the Christian way is verifying itself as the Way."[17]

Most of the world tries everything else except Christianity and nothing works. In the struggle for survival on planet earth, Stanley's call was to convince the world that the Christian Way is the best way to happy, useful and contributive survival.

Call the roll of emotions, thinking, attitudes, actions that upset or produce disruptive living, what do you have — "fear, resentment, guilt, self-preoccupation, sense of inferiority, refusal to accept responsibility, dishonesty, quarrelsomeness, negativism, pessimism, hopelessness, retreat from life, refusal to cooperate, sexual impurity, anger, jealousy, envy, pride, mammon, criticism, backbiting, hate, lack of love — all unchristian (Galatians 5:19-21)? Now call the roll of emotions, thinking, attitudes that produce harmonious, well-adjusted, creative personalities and what do you have — "love, joy, peace, forbearance, kindness, goodness, faithfulness, gentleness and self-control — all Christian, the fruit of the Spirit (Galatians 5:22)?

Stanley quotes Jesus: "That my joy might remain in you, and that your joy might be full (John 15:11). Jesus is apparently saying that his joy and our joy are not alien. To have more of him is to have more of me. The surgeon says, "If you don't come to Christ for salvation you will probably have to come to me for surgery." Stanley speaks of a psychiatrist who circled the globe looking for attitudes of mind and spirit that make for mental health. He came back with the Beatitudes.[18]

The modern theologian, Reinhold Niebuhr, said that the soul is naturally pagan. The ancient theologian, Tertullian, said that the soul is naturally Christian. Stanley sided with Tertullian. That would be the message of "original righteousness." The Gospel is good news, bad news, good news. The original good news is that we were created in the image of God. The bad news is that we blow it. The ultimate good news is that God is in Jesus Christ reconciling us to Himself, restoring us to our original righteousness.

The truly natural is Christian and the truly Christian is the natural but it is not impersonal as the "death of God" theologians, J. A. T. Robinson and Thomas J. J. Altizer would argue. Christ keeps it personal—all things being made by Him and for Him and if we revolt against him we revolt against ourselves. Live in Him and you are alive, body, mind and spirit—including relationships. Stanley's refrain is "He lives—I live." True! The philosophically minded East and the scientifically minded West have challenged and tested Stanley and Stanley is forever coming out at the feet of Jesus.

Stanley was speaking at Columbia University on "My Personal Religious Experience." He was fearful until he realized that he was not on trial but that his faith was on trial. If they can break his faith let them do it. He could not rest this side of reality. He won the day (or God won the day). The Christian way is the Way—and that Way is realism.[19]

So, Stanley would ask, "Are you a realist or an idealist?"

MEANWHILE, THE INDIAN NATIONALISM

On November 15, 1934 Stanley states that he had his "most important interview" with Gandhi. Significantly, Jones was one of the first to perceive the spiritual power of Gandhi's non-cooperation and civil disobedience. He perceived that ultimately Britain would have to yield to the superior moral power of Indian nationalism.

With others present, Stanley asked Gandhi about his proposal for village reconstruction throughout India. Was it to be "non-political and non-religious?" Gandhi assured them that it was. They then told Gandhi that the Christian community could be an active and enthusiastic partner in the process. Stanley then asked Gandhi if he believed in full social and religious equality and if he would do away with castes. Gandhi, hedging a bit, replied that he "would do away with inequalities in the social order or do away with anything that creates distinctions of high and low and make it occupational only." He confessed, that by retaining castes, people could fulfill *dharma* in accordance with the Hindu concept of functioning with abilities that they possess from a previous life. Most interesting! Gandhi remains sensitive to the Hindu mindset and this was essential if he was to lead the movement.[20]

Stanley then asked Gandhi about communalism — the government assessing political power on the numbers within a given religious community. Stanley was concerned that Christians were organizing to get political power. Christianity could be corrupted in the process. Stanley wanted Indian Christians to stand for India and not for Indian Christians alone. Stanley said that he was willing for the Christian community to fade out as a political entity provided Gandhi would allow Christians to stay in their homes without disability or penalty.

Stanley then tells the story of being called to meet with the British Viceroy, Lord Irwin. The British were organizing another Round Table Conference in London and the Viceroy needed Stanley's advice. He had several questions: First, "Do we invite Gandhi (when his cronies were advising against it). Stanley replied, "You don't get Gandhi, you don't get India." The next question, "How do we get Gandhi? Do I go into the jail and make him offers?" Stanley said, "The only way to get Gandhi is to offer Dominion Status (like Canada). The Viceroy said, that would be difficult and it never happened. Later Stanley thinks that if Dominion Status had been offered at that point Gandhi (and Indians) would have accepted it. The last question was, "Should we try to work on reconciliation between Hindus and Muslims" (again, Irwin's cronies were advising against it). Stanley said, "Try! And even if you fail, Indians will know that you are not pleased with the divisions." [21]

Stanley summarizes that he had been drawn (or driven) to crossing into a new and vital way of understanding political issues. The example of Gandhi showed how it was possible to secure national and social change through nonviolence and noncooperation. The Indians would not knuckle under to wrong but they would not go to war. The alternative was to match soul force against physical force. They wore down the Brits by their good will. They would love them as they left and then they would welcome them back (as visitors) in love. [22]

As Stanley relates this story in his *Song*, he calls us to remember that the Lamb, looking as if it had been slain, is at the heart of the Throne — the very center of power (Revelation 5:6). Stanley was fond of saying that self-ruled lives lead to self-ruined lives — again, it is the sin of self-reliance. Again, our greatest strengths are anointed weaknesses. Stanley had come to India to get a message that he once possessed. That message now possessed him — it was the message of the Cross.

In December 1934 Stanley makes the decision to extend the Sat Tal Ashram to Lucknow. The Sat Tal Ashram would meet in the summer (up in the hills) and Lucknow in the winter. Stanley would pay the salaries of those needed to sustain the Ashram, including the salary of an American Methodist Missionary from Belgaum, an Indian city in northwestern Karnataka, J. Holmes Smith. The detailed plans would be laid out the following year.

On December 20, 1934, Stanley writes in a *Circular Letter* that since he left the fifth Ashram (mid-July) he had been in evangelistic meetings nonstop and they were (Stanley sometimes loved the superlative) the "*finest round of meetings ever.*"[23]

1935: TWO TOTALITARIANISMS, COMMUNISM
AND THE KINGDOM OF GOD ON EARTH

Russia is still on Stanley's mind. He seems nearly obsessed by the contrasts and comparisons between communism and his growing understanding of the Kingdom of God! This year he would publish his book, *Christ's Alternative to Communism*. As we have already seen, the central message of the gospels was that the Kingdom of God is the heart of *Christ's Alternative to Communism*. The Christian reconstruction of society was the message. In fact, many of Stanley's articles in the *Indian Witness*, begin with the question, "What is the Christian program for reconstruction of society in general, and of the depressed classes in particular?" Along these lines, Stanley was taken by the work of Dr. Bhimrao R. Ambedkar. You recall that Stanley had met Ambedkar while visiting Gandhi in prison back in 1932. In the 1920s and 1930s Ambedkar, a Western educated government official and lawyer emerged as the leader of the depressed classes of *Harijans*. Gandhi would coin the term *Harijan* (meaning "children of God") to refer to the outcastes or depressed classes. Ambedkar, born an outcast became their spokesman and representative in negotiations with the British about Indian independence.

During the early part of 1935 Stanley wanted to go deeper in his understanding of the Kingdom of God. We say "deeper" only if one realizes that theology is deep when it makes us deep. Obscure theology makes us obscure. Many of the theologians attempting to engage Stanley were seemingly arguing, "If you want to impress them; confuse them." Well, they confused them all right. Stanley was looking for simplicity and he had to leave the U.S. to make the major discovery that was now consuming him — true simplicity can be found only in the Kingdom of God. He had made this discovery in Russia, of all places. Stanley would be called by some a communist after reading his books, *Christ's Alternative to Communism*, and *The Choice Before Us*. Although he would readily admit that he said a few things in those books that he would not say later on, the simple truth was there.

Like today, Chinese communism, Russia, and other autocratic regimes (even the Islamic State), can be formidable on the military side but on the side of producing better order, the fleeing refugees are voting with their feet — those who have experienced it firsthand. The Achilles' heel is that although some of those autocratic regimes produced a stronger order, Stanley believed that they did not produce a better place to live. The eventual collapse of the Soviet Union would prove it. Again, Stanley believed that human totalitarianisms will collapse if we can show that God's totalitarianism, the Kingdom of God on earth, works better, meets the needs of the individual better and the collective better — it is just that simple.

In the immediate case, the decision was then and (to a degree still is) between materialistic atheistic communism and the Kingdom of God — the choice between earthborn totalitarianism — communism — and God's heaven-born totalitarianism — the Kingdom of God on earth. This remains the same, if we are to meet any alternative, we cannot do it by verbal blasts or lethal weapons. We have to produce a better order and that order is the Kingdom of God.[24]

When Stanley was prompted to focus on the Kingdom of God while in Russia he realized that this was something he had always known, it was there, but it had not become vital and all compelling. It now possessed him. In his quiet time in Moscow a verse came to him, "Therefore let us be grateful for receiving a kingdom that cannot be shaken" (Hebrews 12:28). Stanley saw in a flash that all human-made kingdoms are shakable. They must be held together by purges, by force, they cannot relax that force or they will fall apart. The kingdom of capitalism is shakable. The kingdom of self is shakable, but the Kingdom of God is unshakable.

During these days, Stanley was living on that verse from Hebrews, "Jesus Christ, the same yesterday, and today and forever" (13:8). Death cuts us all down to size except for Jesus. His death enhanced him, universalized him. We put the symbol of his death on the crosses of our churches, around our necks and in our hearts.

Stanley came out of Russia with two things in his mind and heart:

the truths of an unshakable Kingdom and an unchanging Person—the absolute order and the absolute Person. With these two strings in his harp he could sing those truths in the face of everything. He now saw that the unshakable Kingdom is embodied in the unchangeable Person. He was the Kingdom! Jesus Christ is not only absolute good; he is absolute power.

This wiped out the distinction between the individual and the social—they were two sides of the same coin. To have a relationship with Christ is to have a relationship with an order that embraces the whole of life, individual and collective. The clash between the individual gospel and the social gospel had always left him cold. The Gospel embraces both body and spirit, or else it becomes ghost or corpse. The message to the individual is repent; and the message to the social is repent.

Stanley believed that psychology teaches us that we have three basic needs: to belong, to find significance and to have reasonable security. The first need is not personal liberty but the need to belong. The first thing in life is to obey, to find something, or rather someone, to whom you can give your final and absolute allegiance. Where do we bend our knees is the absolute question.[25]

Stanley was asking the questions, we do have a need for freedom but what kind of freedom and then, how do we get free? It is obviously not freedom to drive on the wrong side of the road or to ignore the principles of flight while flying an airplane. The answer is, we have freedom through obedience. Total freedom is total obedience to a total order—the Kingdom of God. Again, it is just that simple. So, why do we make it so difficult? Stanley would respond that the Kingdom of God is certainly a moral and spiritual order, but it is also a total life order. Jesus came saying, "May thy Kingdom come and may thy will be done on earth as it is in heaven." So, how is the Kingdom of God done on earth as it is in heaven? It is a completely totalitarian order demanding a total obedience in all of life—God's totalitarianism. Do not object: "Aren't you trying to get us out of one totalitarianism and into another?" Stanley says, YES, and more! Human totalitarianism is content with outer conformity—fit in; you survive. The Kingdom of God demands our thoughts as well. You cannot have a thought without the approval or disapproval of the Kingdom. Read Matthew 21:43: "The Kingdom... shall be taken from you, and given to a nation bringing forth the fruits thereof." Some argue, this would be total bondage. NO! The Kingdom is a totalitarianism that when totally obeyed, gives total freedom! Stanley does not argue with the reality. He knows that the more he belongs to Christ and his Kingdom, the more he belongs to himself. Bound to Him is to walk freely on earth—we find freedom through surrender—complete surrender to Jesus Christ!

Stanley was accused of being obsessed by the Kingdom of God. He easily replied, "Oh that it were true." Jesus was obsessed with the Kingdom of God. "Seek first the Kingdom...". The Kingdom was the only thing he called good news. He sends out his disciples—preach the gospel of the Kingdom. Seek to replace this present unworkable world order, based on greed and selfishness, with God's order. That is radicalism—beneficent, blessed radicalism. H.G. Wells comments, "The Kingdom of God is the most radical idea ever... It means nothing less than replacing some human order with God's order."

So what happened with the disciples of Jesus and this Kingdom preaching? Stanley implies that it was apparently too great for their small hearts. In the post resurrection what does Jesus talk about—the Kingdom. The disciples tended, not to reject but to reduce the Kingdom to some nationalistic goal, like the American way of life. By the time the creeds were written the Kingdom of God had slipped from star on stage to the supporting casts.

The Creeds mention only marginally what Jesus mentioned 100 times. A vacuum slipped in that was dedicated to alien philosophies of life—a toned down Christianity. The world was saying, "We will give you (the Church), an inner mystical experience now and your collective experience hereafter, but we will take over the rest—the economic, social, political and international—and we will run them according to our ideas... So, why are we shocked that things have gone so poorly!

Stanley was not afraid to test his understanding of the Kingdom against the "ways of the world," for he knew that we could produce a better order out of those that are free than out of those that are semi-slaves. Ironically, and this is only one of the reasons that Stanley is incredibly relevant, Christianity is not necessarily an antidote to communism (or ISIS for that matter) because much of the so-called Christian West is also in crisis!The Kingdom of God is needed by both the East and the West. Moral decay threatens us all. Stanley says that the "new morality" is nothing more than the old immorality demanding acceptance and public approval.

It is uncanny how few things ever change (read the Book of Judges). As far I can tell, today's Christians have no master plan of their own. What do we do to bring life together? All of our so-called political answers seem tawdry and cheap, superficial and unworkable. Even most of our so-called religious answers seem divisive and impractical — all except one, Jesus' answer — the Kingdom of God. Perhaps God is applying shock treatment to bring us back to a reality of a true totalitarianism.

MABEL AND EUNICE ARE STILL IN THE U.S.

As Stanley is busy in India, Mabel is interacting with her boys, raising money and writing letters from the U.S. She decides to send "Duplicate Letters" as the only way to meet all of the correspondence obligations. Her schedule in some ways would become just as packed as Stanley's. Eunice is now at American Methodist University in Washington, D.C. Mabel is grateful for that as this seems to be a healthier environment. Then, however, Mabel began to have trouble with her teeth and remained sickly through much of 1935 staying with her friend, Mrs. Lum, in Washington, D.C. Mabel and Mrs. Lum had become close friends in India.[26]

By June of 1935 Mabel (at 57) was seemingly well enough to return to her old family home in Clayton. She spent much of the summer there happily gardening and hiking, trying not to pine for the 500 boys she was responsible for back in India. Late summer she ventured over to Ventnor, N.J., spending time with Eunice, relaxing a bit on the beach and studying. They missed Stanley who was busy at his Ashram in the Himalayas. Unfortunately, Mabel's teeth became infected again, affecting her health even more. She was in constant pain. She finally had them pulled.[27]

THE HARIJANS (DEPRESSED CLASSES) MOVEMENT IN INDIA

At a 1935 conference of the depressed classes in Bombay, Ambedkar called for a complete break between the Harijans and the rest of the Hindu community. He also renounced the Hindu religion because it "is not good for us," that is, not good for the Harijans. Ultimately, Ambedkar wanted to lead the Harijans out of Hinduism and into some other religion. Stanley obviously saw this as a heaven-sent opportunity for Christianity in India. Jones' letters to Diffendorfer and his "Circular Letters" between 1935 and 1938 reflected his enthusiasm about the possibility of tens of millions of outcastes becoming Christian. On November 25, 1935 he wrote to Diffendorfer that as a result of Ambedkar's announcement there had been a deep stir in India. All religions were bidding for these Harijans. Stanley called it "the most tremendous thing to have arisen in Missions in decades." In the same letter he reports that his good friend, J. Waskom Pickett "has had a most satisfactory interview with Dr. Ambedkar in Bombay."[28]

In January 1936, Stanley writes that Ambedkar's statement "is the most amazing challenge that has ever come before Christian Missions since the first missionaries came to the shores of this wonderful land." Stanley saw this as a once in a lifetime opportunity and his letters were filled with hope and anticipation. On February 28

Diffendorfer writes to Stanley, "What shall we do about the Harijan movement in India?"[29] This issue would continue to demand Stanley attention for the rest of the year.

STANLEY IS BACK IN THE U.S. PREACHING AND WRITING

Throughout much of 1936 we find Stanley participating in preaching missions across the U.S. Called National Preaching Missions, these were not organized by the Methodist Episcopal Church, but by the Federal Council of Churches, the forerunner of the National Council of Churches (NCC). It was during this time that Stanley begins to focus on unity (seemingly avoiding the term "ecumenism") as the cutting edge for his emphasis on the Kingdom of God.

During the first missions in January and February, Stanley was one of eighty missionaries who entered the fray in twenty-five cities across the country. Stanley, the only missionary to participate throughout, describes the plan.

The mission was to be three/four days in a place, two places a week, so that each place would have a Sunday either at the beginning or the end, … He goes on to say that the response to the preaching missions was "very great indeed." Christians throughout America had taken new heart and courage. Every place was packed out with loudspeakers, sometimes placing them in adjoining halls or even out in the open. He describes one experience in Madison Square Garden where he spoke to twenty thousand persons. Eight thousand remained after the meeting to make personal decisions for Jesus Christ. The impact was such that Stanley sensed a social and moral change beginning to happen in many venues. The Roman Catholic mayor of St. Louis said that if the mission would stay in his city another week, "he could dismiss the police force."[30]

It is significant that as all this was happening Mabel has recovered enough so that between February and May she is speaking extensively as well. We find her in Buffalo, Rochester, Philadelphia, Scranton, Columbus, Harrisburg and many other cities in between. When Mabel was well she was wonderfully effective as a speaker, writer, administrator and teacher, in her own indomitable way. In a letter to Stanley, Rev. Crossland, a participant, at several of her meetings wrote, "Your charming wife has doubtless already written you of the addresses she gave us this year in the Genesee Conference. She did for us a fine piece of work in bringing to our four District Conferences her enthusiasm for the great cause of India."[31]

During this same period, even as he travels, Stanley is still remembering his Russian experience, especially as it was contributing to his own understanding of the Kingdom of God. He simply could not turn it loose. In two long installments of the *Indian Witness* (February 13 and 20, 1936), Stanley writes on "The Christian Program of Reconstruction." The gist was this: The content of the Kingdom of God was best expressed by Jesus as recorded in Luke 4:18-19. There Jesus stands in the synagogue in Nazareth and reads from the scroll, "The Spirit of the Lord is on me because he has anointed me to proclaim good news to the poor. He has sent me to proclaim freedom for the prisoners and recovery of sight for the blind, to set the oppressed free, to proclaim the year of the Lord's favor." Watch what happens as Stanley allows Jesus to set the stage.

THE NAZARETH MANIFESTO

"Then he [Jesus] rolled up the scroll and gave it back to the attendant and sat down to speak, "Today this Scripture is fulfilled in your hearing....". Stanley would come to call this his "Nazareth Manifesto." This was Christ's alternative to the *Communist Manifesto* (Marx and Engels, 1848). In order to explain the full revolutionary significance of Jesus' manifesto, Stanley identified the *poor* as "the economically disinherited," the *captives* as "the socially and politically disinherited," the *blind* as the "physically disinherited," the *bruised* as "the morally and spiritually disinherited" and *the year of Jubilee* as "a fresh world beginning."

Stanley honestly believed that the Nazareth Manifesto could banish poverty and bring freedom from race, caste and even gender prejudices. The Nazareth Manifesto would establish the laws of the Kingdom to be like the natural laws of the universe — like the law of gravity — we suffer consequences if we disobey. "We are free to choose our actions but we are not free to choose the results of those actions. We do not break the laws of God. We break ourselves upon them."[32]

Perhaps the crowning point of Jesus' Nazareth Manifesto for Stanley was a response to the communist criticism of the traditional Christian philosophy attempting to save society one soul at a time. The communists insisted that this was too slow. Revolutionary results could only happen by working (trickle down as it were) from the social masses to the individual. Stanley heard that!

The key here, especially after *The Christ of the Indian Road* (1925), and then increasingly throughout the 1930s, was to recognize the contribution of each nation's cultural and social heritage to the different expressions of Christianity. It became clear to Stanley (with deeper and broader spiritual insight), that God wants His Kingdom on earth to embrace and yet transcend all the distinctive human forms of Christianity by creating and establishing a new God-inspired and Spirit-filled humanity, all of whose relationships, both personal and social, were more thoroughly and more authentically Christian.[33] The Spirit of God seemed to be feeding him thoughts on a daily basis. It is important to note that Stanley's "inner voice" would now emerge as a regular monitor and guide.

On October 1, 1936, Stanley recorded his earlier personal experience with Dr. Ambedkar in an article in the *Indian Witness*. Dr. Ambedkar had made it clear that he was going to leave Hinduism and take at least one-half of the outcastes with him. Soon after, when Stanley visited with him again in Bombay, Ambedkar repeated his intention to persuade the depressed classes to move *en masse* to another religion. This would involve some 30 million people (the most astonishing thing to happen in any religion for centuries). Then there was the question: "What if the Harijans wanted to become Christians?" This gave pause to many Christians. Would these masses paganize Christianity? Christianity might never be the same.

Nonetheless, Stanley encouraged Christians to face realistically the possibility that millions of outcastes would come into the Church. He was just as interested as getting Christ into the collective will of the people as in the individual, communism had taught him that much. Unfortunately, the Christians of the West were afraid of losing their control among so many millions of new converts unschooled in the traditions of the Church. Alas, the "conversion" of 30 million Hindus would never happen.

The year 1937 was not an easy time for Mabel. When she was not on the road addressing huge crowds at Federated Church Conferences called the "Chain of Missions," she spent much of the winter in Florida (eventually buying a home in Orlando). During the spring she spent much of her time between the dentist chair and the couch. The doctor told her that she would lose her hearing if she went back to India before the infection was healed. She laments, "So, I may be here another year — worst luck!"[34]

In the midst of his preaching mission, on April 14, 1937, Stanley published an article in the *Christian Century*, "Afterthoughts on the Preaching Mission." He concludes that the need for evangelism has not changed but the methods must change as Americans were changing. They had become suspicious of anything that smacked of manipulation. Stanley says such a climate demanded that evangelism be "sincerely and simply real."

Eunice graduated from American University in June 1937 and over her mother's objections decided to join her father as his secretary back in India. Mabel was still concerned about Eunice's health, remembering that X-rays in 1932 and 1935 both showed tuberculosis. Nonetheless, Stanley missed being with Eunice, "We've spent years separated; I've traveled and you've been in boarding school and college, so it's time we get better acquainted." Eunice takes a secretarial course in order to join him in India in the fall.

STANLEY AND EUNICE BACK IN INDIA

Early summer of 1937 Stanley returns to India (spending only a few hours with Mabel before leaving the U.S.). Eunice would follow in the early fall. Stanley would now focus more on the educated upper castes. Except for an interview with Ambedkar and a letter to Lord Halifax, he was generally more interested in Gandhi's proposals for the nationalist movement than working with the Harijans. Here is why.

THE HARIJANS ARE LOST TO THE CHURCH

While Stanley was still in the U.S., the Methodist Central Conference in India had adopted a number of resolutions with respect to the Harijans (outcastes). The overall conclusion, however, was that the Methodists were not psychologically nor spiritually prepared to rethink its concept of the purpose and methods of Christian missions. They did not make a comprehensive response to Ambedkar.[35] As with the Church of Rome when Kublai Khan asked the Pope (through Marco Polo) for 100 missionaries to come to China to lead the Chinese to Christ, he sent only two and they both lost heart in route.

By June 24, 1937, just before leaving for China, Stanley is in Bombay for another visit with Ambedkar. He writes Diffendorfer two days later that Ambedkar "said that it would be no trouble for him to decide to be a Christian if he were free to make his choice, but he is bound up with this [Harijan] movement and must move with them. He is nearer being on the Christian side than at any time I have ever known him." Within a year the issue will be decided, one way of the other.

182

Meanwhile the Lucknow Ashram has now opened as an extension of the Sat Tal Ashram. It will be at Sat Tal (where it was cooler) in the summer and Lucknow in the winter.

BACK TO CHINA, A NARROW ESCAPE

Stanley wants Eunice to come with him to China but the political situation between China and Japan was too tense.[36] In route to China Stanley wrote to Diffendorfer (July 26, 1937) that he was shocked by the blunt honesty of the Japanese justification for their intervention in China. "Poor China, if Japan would only leave her alone," but one of the Japanese on the boat said to me, 'It is our Mission to bring order into China. We have given them a hundred years to set their house in order and they have not done it. Now we must do it for them. It is our Mission."[37]

Upon arrival in Shanghai in July 1937, for the next two months Stanley became embroiled in a controversy of international politics. First regarding Shanghai—he was holding a series of meetings at Mokanshan, a mountain retreat west of Shanghai, when fighting broke out in the city between Chinese and Japanese troops. His experience in Mukden, Manchuria, several years earlier (1932) was child's play compared to what he found in Shanghai when he returned from Mokanshan. "The closer we got to Shanghai in the car the more we saw that trouble had started..."[38]

In his first real encounter with war, Stanley was acutely aware of the international political and moral implications of what was happening in Asia. He had been placed directly in the path of destruction as a Chinese bomber mistakenly rained death on over 800 people. The bomb fell in the center of a circle crowded with people. Dr. Rawlinson, a devoted missionary committed to the causes of China, stepped out of his car when the bomb exploded and sent a piece of shrapnel through his heart. He died in his wife's arms. Two days later, on August 15, 1937, Stanley managed to preach the memorial service for Dr. Rawlinson at the Community Church. In that service he quoted an Open Letter to the People of Japan entitled, "An Appeal to the Governments and People of Japan and China." This letter (and other similar letters) would cause reactions that would later shake Stanley to the core. Sadly, Stanley would then be forced to abandon his speaking schedule and flee along with hundreds of other Americans to Manila. Amid these life threatening circumstances, Stanley had Frank Cartwright of the Methodist Board of Foreign Missions, cable Mabel, "EVACUATING SHANGHAI."

On board the *President McKinley* in route to Manila, Stanley wrote to Mabel regarding the events that led to the evacuation:

We found that modern war knows no safety. As we sat in the office of the National Christian Council in Shanghai, deciding whether we should try to go on with the evangelistic campaign, we looked out of the window to see what was the reason for the uproar of guns and there before our eyes, not two hundred yards away, the Japanese flagship anchored inside the International Settlement (it had no business being there) was being attacked by the Chinese bombers. Crash! We had grandstand seats. A piece of shrapnel comes through the window and spatters glass all over the Mission Treasurer's desk. Small happening compared to what was to take place next. We went out into the street to find if we could go on with our campaign. The Travel Service said, No! A tide of a million refugees poured into the city. We stood for a moment at a place where in less than an hour a terrible tragedy was to occur. A Chinese airman about 400 yards away dropped a bomb on the Palace Hotel killing about 400 in the hotel. Later I went through the cordon of ropes and found pieces of reeking bodies still lying amid the debris. Well mother, this is the first war I have seen! Not anxious to see another.

Then in a private note to Mabel, Stanley recounted further the events of his evacuation:

A special launch took about 300 people down to the *President McKinley* on which I am at present writing [in route to the Philippines]. Everything was very tense as we to go down the river. U.S. marines stood guard on the launch... We passed Japanese battleships every hundred yards and they kept firing at the Chinese as we passed... The terrible booming of their big guns not twenty-five yards away as we passed... No one got hysterical at all. We went down the river through ten miles of this and guns boomed all the way down to the *McKinley* anchored down at the mouth of the river and they had had some experience of the booming too."[39]

During Stanley's time in the Philippines, he comments that Manila was twice as noisy as when they (he, Mabel and Eunice) were there before. "They blow their horns but there is an air of hopefulness over everything." He remained in the Philippines until October 15, spending three weeks in the Southern Islands and three weeks in the Northern Islands.

TWO CONTROVERSIES

While still in the Philippines, the first of two controversies erupted.The first involved Japan. In his September 20, 1937 *Circular Letter* from Manila Stanley included his previously mentioned, "Open Letter to the People of Japan" condemning its intervention in China. He then wrote another open letter as "an appeal to the Christians of the world for economic withdrawal from Japan..." This appeal to British and American Christians for an economic boycott was to expose the naked barbarism of Japanese aggression in China and Stanley hoped (perhaps naively) would encourage Japan to confess its international crimes and withdraw from China. The response to his letter to the people of Japan was nearly instant. Arthur Jorgensen, honorary secretary of the National Committee of the YMCA of Japan, explains the explosive nature of Stanley's appeal. Stanley had even appealed to the Japanese people to break with their military leaders. This would prompt severe reaction from the new censorship regulations. No newspaper or magazine could avoid immediate and indefinite suspension, to say nothing of the fines if they were to print his letter. Although Jorgensen felt that the letter was a fairly accurate presentation of world opinion, all he could do was to distribute discreetly approximately twenty-five copies to Christian leaders within the YMCA.[40]

Even the National Christian Council of Manila reacted to Stanley's appeal with such vigor that he was shocked and bewildered. On September 24 the Council wrote in a telegram that they were "greatly distressed by report that you plan to urge boycott of Japanese goods. Boycott there would be seen as a campaign of hate, making war easy and closing the door to goodwill."

Then, there was the reaction from the U.S. Frederick Libby, the executive secretary of the National Council for Prevention of War in Washington, D.C., elaborated on the points of the Manila telegram after placing Stanley's article in the September 27, 1937 edition of *The Indian Witness* and *Christian Century*. In his own comments he stated that the war between Japan and China should be seen in a larger international and historical context. He thought that Stanley's distinction between Japan as the "aggressor" and China as the "victim" was an oversimplification of the situation that ignored historical perspective and the economic causes of war.[41] Quite frankly, Libby's argument was compelling.

Stanley was also vigorously and widely criticized by church leaders, both in the U.S. and in the Far East. In fact, the list of those opposing the proposals in his articles, apart from Frederick Libby, included notables like Rufus Jones and others who read like a "Who's Who" of American pacifists and Christian churchmen in the present era (1930s).[42]

As to whether this criticism was justified, judge for yourselves. Stanley had first spoken of his affection for the Japanese people. He cites his personal intervention with FDR seeking to replace the blatant racial discrimination against Japan in the U.S. immigration laws. The quota system used for the Japanese was different than the one used for other nations. Then, however, he turns to the real purpose of addressing specifically Japan's policy towards China. He does not mince words condemning Japan's conquest of China as the central international crime that is being committed in the world today."

Still again, perhaps making matters worse, in an *Open Letter to the Christian People of America and Great Britain*, Stanley called on the Christians of the world, acting independently of their governments, "to institute an economic withdrawal from Japan." He rejected both military intervention and various nonmilitary options. No doubt, reflecting the influence of Gandhi, he writes that the only real choice for Christians was an "attitude that implements good will in positive action and is not punitive but redemptive [go high]." Such action was necessary because of the close economic relationship between Japan on the one hand and Great Britain and the U.S. on the other. That meant that all American citizens and British subjects were to some extent morally responsible for Japanese aggression in China. The bottom line, "Our hands that buy and sell are stained with the blood of the Chinese."

True to the character of Brother Stanley he does accept the value of valid criticism. Substances of this debate would surface in many of his letters, articles and books written after 1937. Although he never retracted his proposal for an economic withdrawal from Japan by American and British Christians, after 1937 he did put more emphasis on the historical and economic sources of Japanese imperialism in China. He then added that before they could condemn Japan, the U.S. and Britain must also repent of their sin of imperialism in the Far East.[43] Help!

As a follow-up, Stanley's message, recorded in his October 14 (1937) *Indian Witness* was that moral condemnation of Japan was only the beginning, not the end, of the Christian response to Japan's "international crime." Christians "must be open to God's guidance as to how we can implement that moral judgment and make it effective." As Christians we must use the principle of "using calamity for higher ends." This redemptive principle had become an integral part of his understanding of the Kingdom of God.

After six weeks of almost nonstop meetings in the Philippines, Stanley was able in mid-October, 1937 to return to China to resume the heavy schedule of public speaking and personal interviews that had been interrupted by the Japanese invasion of Shanghai. This tour included preaching in Hong Kong, Hankow, Changsha, Chengtu, and Chungking. Although these cities did not pose the immediate threat as in Shanghai, he did have numerous close encounters with Chinese air raids.

By early December 1937 Stanley had concluded his China tour and began his return journey to India, fearful for the Chinese people.

On board ship he wrote his *Christmas Letter,* dated December 9, apologizing for not sending a more personal letter. While other criticism of his *Open Letters* was to follow, and in spite of the physical, psychological and spiritual toll the war conditions in China had taken on the 53 year-old missionary evangelist, he did not seem discouraged.[44] He assured Diffendorfer that after a day or two on the boat to India... "I'll be alright again."

Tragically, not so China as the notorious "rape of Nanking" would happen on December 13. The Japanese killed 150,000 Chinese, raped thousands and executed soldiers. Stanley had barely escaped the carnage.

THE YEAR 1938

After Stanley's return to India he made his first official response to the critics of his proposed economic withdrawal from Japan. It was published in the *Christian Century* and entitled, "Apply Gandhi's Method To Japan!" Here he states that he wants to clarify "some points apparently confused in the minds of some." He reiterates his proposal for economic withdrawal from Japan but that this admonition was only for the individual Christians in those nations. This was a kind of "noncooperation" in the same sense as Gandhi's.

The criticism that prompted his longest response was that an economic withdrawal was ethically indiscriminate, punishing innocent Japanese women and children along with those who should be held morally responsible for Japan's war against China. The claim was that those who boycotted would be just as much at fault as Japan itself.

Stanley's response was that an economic withdrawal would be the fault of Japanese leaders, not Christians refusing to trade with Japan. Stanley felt that his relationship with Japan was like Gandhi's relationship with Britain — a redemptive friendship.[45]

At the same time Brother Stanley is still consumed by his prayers that Dr. Ambedkar would lead the Harijan people into Christianity. Unfortunately, the issue of communal representation for the outcastes arose. The Government of India Act of 1935, passed by the British Parliament after a Round Table Conference discouraged the conversion of outcastes to Christianity as the number of electorates would be given in accordance with the size of the religious communities. Stanley thought (initially) that communal representation was a bad idea. With the possible inclusion of the depressed classes as Christians, however, he believed that they would share equally any political advantage that the Christian community would be given. Stanley presented the issue to the British in a letter to Lord Halifax on February 3, 1938. The problem for Ambedkar was that the Act made no provision for any change in representation if there is any considerable change in the numbers. Stanley was now ambivalent, unsure how these matters would sort themselves out. Eventually, due to the uncertainties of Ambedkar and the hesitancy of the Christians (the Methodists in particular), the movement of outcastes to Christianity never happened.[46]

Then, a second controversy erupted. This one was the result of an attempt by Brother Stanley to reignite his vision of the Kingdom of

God as the focal point of the ministry of the church (somewhat ne-glected of late). After his return to India, still in 1938, he became (ac-cording to his own testimony) *"spiritually* on edge or even cranky, unreasonably insistent, emphatic, outspoken, or implacable, vis-à-vis the status quo church." Diffendorfer advises Stanley to take some time off. He did not! Instead, he attended a missionary conference at Tambaram, near Madras.

In 1938 the International Missionary Council (IMC) hosted a con-ference at Tambaram (also called The Madras Conference or Tambaram 1938). This was a majority world Missionary Conference that would eventually create the World Council of Churches (WCC). Interestingly, the same buildings were used again in 1988 (Tambaram 1988) to commemorate this landmark event that focused contempo-rary thought on ecumenism where Christianity would engage world religions and traditions. In the words of Bishop Stephen Neill, this event was "the most international gathering held up to that point in the entire history of the Christian Church." The famous missionary theologian, Lesslie Newbigin was there.[47]

Stanley's critique of the conference at Tambaram sparked an in-ternational debate. He honestly felt that the conference had missed its way. Acting on his understanding of the Kingdom of God that had revolutionized his life, his view was that the Kingdom of God was so totalitarian that it was not just a view of reality, it was reality itself. This connection would be vital for Stanley.

Craig Clarkson, in his dissertation, "Who Says Mission, Says Church : the Church-Mission Affirmation of Tambaram, 1938," writes that Stanley's single-minded focus on the supreme reality of the King-dom of God consumed his every thought, both spoken and written. This made it difficult for him to listen objectively.[48]

Stanley wrote an article in the midst of the conference. He was apparently put off by the apparent obsession with ecumenism (even-tually a passion of his own under another name, Federal Union). He writes,

I missed a church that started where Jesus started, the Kingdom of God, and found instead a church that started with itself.... I missed finding a church that was under the conscious discipline, correction and cleansing judgment of an order higher than itself. I missed a church that, while conscious of its mission as the chief instrument of the Kingdom of God, also was humble enough to rejoice that God was using other instruments... even Gandhi's movements to conquer by suffering and the vast movements for social and economic justice outside the church. I missed a church that said that the Kingdom of God is the hope of the church and of the world and found instead a church that said, 'I am the hope of the world'. I missed a church loyal to the Kingdom of God and found a church, by emphasis, loyal to its own fellowship.[49]

Many in the missionary hierarchy never forgave Stanley for that article. As a bit of a correction, Stanley wrote that he believed in the Ecumenical Church (his later Federal Union discussions would prove that beyond any doubt), but at the time he had simply lost confidence in the "Church's ability to affect change. He felt that the Church Universal had only a relative understanding of an absolute Kingdom. "The Church is the subject of salvation; the Kingdom of God offers salvation. The Church may contain the best of the Kingdom; but it is not the Kingdom. The impact of the modern Church upon modern totalitarianisms is faint. The Church has turned the task of dealing with totalitarianisms over to the state and the state has reacted with force so that nations have lost their moral and spiritual impact. Our security, especially in the West, is the atom instead of the *atma* — physical force for spiritual force." Think about it.

Stanley keeps reminding us that we do not say, "Repent for the ecumenical Church is at hand..."Jesus said, "Repent, for the Kingdom of God is at hand." When Stanley reminded people of that, no one laughed. Stanley insisted that if we have any spiritual susceptibilities we should feel our knees bending.[50]

Furthermore, we do not build the Kingdom—we receive it. As the author of this book, I'm not sure I fully understand that statement but I believe it. We should be grateful to receive a Kingdom that cannot be shaken. The first beatitude is, "Blessed are the poor in spirit for to them belongs the Kingdom of God." We must not capitulate to the kingdoms of self, nationalism and money — to do that is to have nothing more. If we belong to the Kingdom of God, however, body, mind and spirit, including our possessions, and relationships, then we have the significance of that Kingdom: the sum total of that reality behind us. We are unafraid and adequate.[51] Think about it.

Stanley insisted that for the individual to discover the Kingdom is like a voice crying in the wilderness but for the collective Church to make that cry, is to discover a Kingdom that would shake a world desperately in need of salvation.

Yet, there were two major objections to making the Kingdom of God our head-on and total answer to our total need. One objection comes from within the Church: "The Kingdom will not come until Jesus, the King, comes again." Certainly, there are passages of Scripture that suggest that the Kingdom will come suddenly — an apocalypse — at the return of Christ. Then another set of passages suggests that the coming would be gradual: "First the kernel, then the blade, then the full ear of corn." One keeps us waiting, expectantly (there has rarely if ever been a significant revival that did not have the expectation of the imminent return of Christ). The other gets us involved — now — as an agent. It is our task for the Kingdom of God to come through us. One gives me my hope and the other my task. We have no timetable but the last word will be victory. Jesus admonishes us in Acts. 1:7: "Our task is to witness and leave the times and the seasons to God.[52]

The other objection comes both from within and from without the Church. People complained, "We need to turn our attention to something more realistic than the Kingdom of God. Our feet must be on solid ground, we need solid facts beneath us to sustain us. This objection is widespread, pervasive and paralyzing. It must be overcome." Stanley insisted that the Kingdom of God is realism, the only realism. Anything outside or against that Kingdom is unrealistic and doomed to failure.[53]

Having said all that, Tambaram was not Stanley's finest hour. Although *Time Magazine* would call E. Stanley Jones the greatest living missionary evangelist in 1938, 1938 was not an easy year for Jones. Again, he was in the midst of controversy regarding his views on Japan's invasion of China. Then, having just returned from yet another tour of China he was not in the mood to engage any thoughts on missions at Tambaram that did not mention the Kingdom of God.

For the rest of his life Stanley would remained adamant that the Madras conference had failed. Again, his article in the *Christian Century*, "Where Madras Missed the Way" claimed that the conference had chosen the ecumenical church as its strategy and emphasis instead of the Kingdom of God. He knew that the missionary hierarchy would never forgive him for this article. He had cut across the prevailing accepted emphasis of the ecumenical Church, but he was unrepentant.

Diffendorfer reminded Stanley again that he was long overdue for a sabbatical. By not taking time off he was at risk of sacrificing his position as "a respected leader of Protestant Christianity."

All of this for Stanley (reminiscent of Madras) was still driven by an irresistible force to embrace an understanding of the Kingdom of God impressed upon him by his call to be a missionary evangelist. During a five year period (1935 to 1940) Stanley would average writing a book a year (most of them devotional) completing his book on the Kingdom of God (*Is the Kingdom of God Realism?*) in 1940.

Stephen Graham writes of Stanley at this point that "Jones lived in a different world. He saw and heard things that others did not, or saw and heard only indistinctly. The kingdom of God was not, for Jones, merely a theological concept or simply a lifestyle choice, although it embraced both theology and how he lived his Christian life. The kingdom of God, which was so utterly unrealistic to most people and even to many Christians, was, in fact, more realistic than the empirical world of sensible and tangible 'facts.' Because he wanted above all else to live in the higher reality of the kingdom of God, and because by God's grace he was privileged to be a citizen of that kingdom on Earth, he brought countless other souls into the same kingdom as fellow citizens, and achieved a degree of influence over nations and governments and over church and society, which no combination of facts and circumstances can even begin to explain."[54]

BACK IN THE U.S.

Stanley returns with Eunice to the U.S. in the early fall of 1938 to be with Mabel and to continue his preaching missions there. Eunice accompanied him. They arrived on September 21. Mabel had been eagerly awaiting them. They had not seen each other for 18 months but within two days Stanley and Eunice had gone off on a university tour.[55]

The impact of the 1936 preaching missions on the Federal Council of Churches, the YMCA, and the Student Volunteer Movement in the U.S. had been significant so that the missions two years later were taken on with great enthusiasm and anticipation. These were sponsored by the University Christian Mission Society and were led by a team of 15 missionaries—Stanley included. In the fall of 1938, they visited 12 state colleges and universities in the U.S. This was significant for several reasons. It was the first time that public colleges and universities had invited Christians to help them achieve their educational objectives. These meeting were openly evangelistic. The mission teams would challenge both students and faculty. The results were surprising.

In the mass meetings there seemed to be four categories of those responding to the messages: there were some who simply needed to go home and settle the matter with God on their own; then there were some who needed to meet with someone right away and talk it over personally (these were directed to trained team members for more in- depth counseling); then there were some who had questions and objections and who remained to receive answers from the trained staff; and finally, there were many who wanted to be instructed as to how to find God, then and there. The last two groups were asked to stay behind after the rest had been dismissed. Stanley writes that every night anywhere from one hundred to two thousand persons responded. Eunice was impressed.

Stanley confesses that this last U.S. mission squeezed out of him the last ounce of his strength. "I was dead tired, speaking six times a day with interviews in between." He was ready to return to India. In December 1938 Mabel and Eunice would return with him. They all sailed for India on December 2 and arrived in Bombay on December 29. Stanley thought that the trip over on the Queen Mary would renew his strength. It did not.

Upon arrival Mabel bought a car and immediately drove to Sitapur to see her "boys." What a reunion! She was 61.

Stanley travelled to Lucknow and lived at the Ashram. The leader of the Ashram there, J. Holmes Smith, had been struggling with the issue of British imperialism. He and Stanley talked at length.

Stanley visited Mabel every few months and Mabel would visit him at the Ashram on occasion but she was so caught up in her own work, that she was not directly involved in that part of Stanley's life.[56]

By the end of 1938, the German sabers were rattling and the war was ramping up so that travel (especially abroad) became difficult and sometimes impossible.

The beginning of 1939 was still a difficult time for Stanley. Since Mabel had returned to India he wanted to be both husband and father. He also sensed that the Holy Spirit was continuing to renew his focus on the Kingdom of God. His life, then inundated with grueling travels, intensified speaking schedules and increasing responsibilities in ministry, became more and more of a chore. Then, in addition to his usual evangelistic work (in India and abroad), his copious correspondence (along with his self-imposed writing schedule), produced not only tremendous job-related stress, it produced fatigue in body, mind and spirit. With misunderstandings, criticism and opposition from detractors and foes (including a few of his friends) he struggled in his own spirit. It would take the better part of a year to work it out. It was his "inner voice" that prepared the way. This experience of overcoming would be just as significant as the ones in earlier years. Again, watch it happen, but do not be surprised if it takes a surprising turn.

CAN YOUR *SONG* SING IN THE MIDST OF STRESS AND CONFLICT? STANLEY'S "LISTENING POST" AND HIS "INNER VOICE" PROVIDE THE ANSWER

Question: How could a faith that has a cross at its heart promise exemption when the noblest and purest heart that ever beat was not exempt from unmerited suffering? Good question; Stanley had a way with those! The answer is in the Cross. Jesus took the worst thing and turned it into the best thing—redemption. He did not bear the Cross; he used it. The cross was sin and he turned it into the healing of sin. The cross was hate and he turned it into a revelation of love.[57]

Here then is the answer. Do not bear trouble; use it! Luke 21:13-14 says that we will be dragged before kings and governors for his sake and for the sake of his Kingdom and that will be opportunity for you to bear witness. Take whatever happens—justice and injustice, pleasure and pain, compliment and criticism—take it up into the purpose of your life and make something out of it. Turn it into testimony. Do not explain evil; exploit evil and make it serve you. The lotus flower takes up the mud and becomes the flower. Reader, are you listening!

Always go high![58] Stanley then says with that key in your hand go to the New Testament and it will unlock everything. "Where did the matchless parables of the lost sheep, the lost coin and the prodigal son come from?" Out of unjust criticism from the Pharisees. Jesus could take their criticisms and turn them into revelations (a teaching moment). Jesus turned their plots into parables, took criticisms and turned them into revelation — the revelation of a redemptive God. He turned the lowest into the highest, destruction into construction. When the Pharisees (the seminary professors) threatened to kill him, he spent the night in prayer and when morning came he trusted the twelve (Luke 6:11-16), a scruffy bunch of Bedouins with the future of the Kingdom implanted deep within their minds and hearts.

Paul wrote much of the New Testament from prison, "Those death defying Epistles [though Paul was beheaded on the banks of the Tiber] have guided and blessed the world." His preaching alone would have been lost but his Epistles live on. Stanley once read I Corinthians 13 to Gandhi, "How beautiful; how beautiful." It brought tears to Gandhi's eyes. Paul whose bodily presence was weak, his speech contemptible, was accused of not being a real apostle. The Corinthians, after giving his very life to them had turned on him with such criticism. Paul then writes 1 Corinthians 13. Read it now and be blessed!

Stanley was criticized frequently, some of it just, some of it unjust. He would ignore the unjust and learn from the just. If just, he would change so that his critics made him better — *the unpaid watchmen of his soul*. Ultimately, he had no enemies because he had no enmity. The Japanese had an expression — knocked down seven, get up eight. We Christians must learn from that!

Stanley describes a blind Japanese professor who turns to Buddhism for an answer. The professor was told that his blindness was the result of sin in a previous life. He did not believe it so he went to Christianity and found the man born blind, "Who sinned, this man or his parents? Jesus replies, Neither.... " (John 9:1-3). The professor asked, "Could God be manifest through my blindness? Then the answer, "I will use this blindness." He opened his heart to the power and love of Jesus Christ and became a flaming evangelist. May I say? It served him right!

Jesus said, "The prince of this world is coming. He has no hold on me; his coming will only serve the Kingdom (John. 14:30-31). The devil would serve Jesus unwittingly. He whispered to the people, "Put Jesus on the cross." Thinking that would finish him, it only served to open the gates of heaven. Jesus did not say, "I am finished, but it is finished." He made the devil serve his purpose. No one is safe unless they can stand anything that happens, and then *use* it. "Simply standing is Stoicism; *using* it is Christianity." Make the works of God be manifest through the accidents of nature. Stanley speaks of the family in Calcutta who lost all six of their children in a landslide. Later the mother would write, after building a home for 100 children, "I've never had a sorrow…" Stanley writes, "Her sorrow became a song." It was set to music.

Stanley comments that he had made many attempts to get the Western world (especially as the world seemingly was preparing for war) to set its house in order, to be prepared to throw off Nazism, Fascism and even Communism, to produce a better order. He had his attempts turned into half-truths.[59] Some (only in the West) accused him of being a communist, who had never really read the Bible. When anyone read his book, *Christ's Alternative to Communism*, in China the communists would arrest them and force them to burn the book. Among the communists Stanley was enemy #1.[60]

Once during the Mar Thoma Convention in southern India Stanley preached to 30,000. All the communist leaders were there as many were becoming communist because Christianity gave them a social conscience but no social program. The air was electric. He spoke on "Christianity and Communism." He then answered questions for several hours. He gave the same address in several other places as well and then, two years later, he spoke again at the same Mar Thoma Convention to another 30,000 but this time the atmosphere was different. Why? Stanley asked. The people had decided that they could not have two totalitarianisms in their lives. Both Communism and Christianity demand total obedience. They decided to be Christians. The communist-oriented paper, *Blitz*, blamed the mass conversions to Christianity on Stanley.[61] The man had a way!

Stanley then concluded that he had turned as many from communism to the Christian Faith as any living person, perhaps more but when he returned to the West he was still labeled "red." He would quote from *Christ's Alternative to Communism*, "Lives there a minister with soul so dead, that his congregation has never called him 'Red'?" These lines were first published in 1935 before communism in Russia had become a worldwide menace and when capitalism was floundering in a depression. In subsequent editions he would take that line out. Stanley wanted to convert capitalism from its dog-eat-dog economy to a brother-help-brother economy. Nonetheless, although he had nothing to do with them, he would continually be unjustly associated with the American League for Peace and Democracy — a group associated with communism. He was offended by that association but continued to sing his song.

Stanley speaks of his "listening post." Both compliments and criticisms sit lightly on him. Early each morning, he would speak to God, "Lord, do you have anything to say to me — I'm listening." Sometimes, Stanley heard God say, "You had better change this or that;" but one morning he heard God say, "You are mine; life is yours." Stanley reacted, "Oh, please say that again — 'You are mine; life is yours.' If I belong to Him, then life belongs to me. I can go out and master it, conquer it, and overcome it, and make something out of it. Life belongs to me."[62]

Stanley believed that God guides in at least five ways: 1. Our general guidance is the life and character and teaching of Jesus Christ as recorded in the New Testament. God is Christ-like and we must be Christ-like. God would never guide in a way contradictory to the life of Jesus — he is our code. 2. Through the counsel of good people. This is often clear but not final. 3. Through your heightened moral intelligence. "Can you not of yourselves judge what is right? said Jesus. He expected us to judge our way to right Christian conclusions. The Hindu expected you to kill the mind and only then meditate. Christians say however, "Thou shall love the Lord thy God with all your mind — the intellectual nature — with all your heart — the emotional nature — with all your soul — the willing nature and — with all your strength—the physical nature. The total person is to love God—mind, emotion, will and strength—not just one but all four. 4. Through an opening of providence. Here is a need, your life can meet that need, therefore that need may be a call to you. Test this by the other three, however. And finally, through the "inner voice." Stanley does not mean an audible voice. The words frame themselves within the mind as when you talk to yourself. How can you distinguish? Perhaps the rough distinction is: the voice of the subconscious argues with you, tries to convince you; but the inner voice of God does not argue, does not try to convince you. It simply speaks and is self-authenticating. It has the feel of the voice of God within it. "The sheep follow him; for they know his voice" (John 10:4). Stanley then adds that he does not use the inner voice largely or exclusively as his method of guidance. The danger is that you are likely to manufacture that voice from the subconscious and call it the voice of God. Stanley is suspect of one who would say, "God said to me." That is too slick, too glib. Stanley first goes to the first four and only then turns to the inner voice.[63]

As Stanley looks back he can remember only two cases where he mistook the voice of the subconscious for the voice of God. In both instances he was too emotionally involved and projected. In most cases, however, the "inner voice" turned out right. Although the two mistakes made him wary, the many surprises led to "overwhelming and overflowing gratitude."

Stanley also describes two instances where he was spot on—one small and the other big. In the first he asked God to help him find his glasses. He found them. Stanley realized that miracles were possible in a world of moral and physical law. God worked through the laws of nature—not by whim, notion, or fancy—but not straitjacketed in them. Nature is orderly because God's mind is an orderly mind. So, Stanley believes in miracles, but not too much miracle because too much miracle would weaken us—make us too dependent upon miracle instead of our obedience to natural law. There is just enough miracle to remind us that God is present.

The second instance (for some say the first could have been coincidence) relates to their daughter Eunice. When she was diagnosed with tuberculosis Stanley was in Sat Tal while she and Mabel were in Woodstock. Mabel wired Stanley, "Come home and take us to Switzerland at once for treatment there." The next morning, while he was consumed with the thought of Eunice's illness and having to leave India, the inner voice spoke very quietly but convincingly, "She will be well." He was overcome with a sense of quiet peace. Not wanting to substitute his inner voice for the doctor's verdict he went to the school prepared to obey the doctor's verdict but inwardly knowing that they would never have to go because she would be well. The verdict — she had scar tissue but nothing active. She was well and has been ever since. She lived to be over 100.[64] Stanley had learned to trust his own spirituality.

MEET JAMES KENNETH MATHEWS

James Mathews (known as Ken while at home and college to distinguish himself from his father who had the same name) worked hard, not only to put himself through college but to help support his family. Embracing the pre-med track he fully expected to become a surgeon until he hit his head on a rock after diving into a river. Not expected to live, after lying in the hospital unconscious for several days, Ken not only survived, he experienced a genuine conversion and a call to ministry. Then in the fall of 1937 he decided to attend seminary at Boston University School of Theology. One October evening, Ken had a similar experience to Mabel's 1904 experience listening to an Indian missionary. Speaking at Trinity Church in Copley Square Boston, Bishop Samuel Azariah, from South India, impressed young Mathews. The next morning the secretary of the Board of Foreign Missions of the Methodist Episcopal Church mentioned that a pastor was needed in the English speaking Bowen Memorial Methodist church in Bombay.[65] Within three months the twenty-five year old set sail for India putting his seminary training on hold for nearly 20 years.

During 1938, Ken, now Jim, hit the ground running. Early on, he and his friend Paul Wagner travel to Sevagram on church business. Sevagram was also the home of Gandhi's ashram. Early one morning, out for a stroll, they noticed the small brown man with a walking stick emerging from the ashram gate. Gandhi cordially invited the young men to accompany him on his walk, asking them who they were. They replied that they were Methodist missionaries. Gandhi said, "I thought so," and then added, "I wonder if John Wesley were alive today, would he recognize you people?"[66]

Then in the summer of 1939, Stanley, with Eunice at his side, is expected to preach and teach for a week in Poona. He and Eunice stayed with a missionary couple there. Known as the "matchmaker" the wife then tells Eunice that she has invited a young minister from Bombay to come to the meetings and then boldly adds that she believes that he may be the one for her.

Jim had welcomed the invitation and took the first train to Poona. When he was introduced to Stanley and Eunice he "was smitten when Eunice walked into the room and into my life."[67] Although Jim did attend Stanley's lectures he and Eunice managed to carve out some time for bicycle rides and even borrowed a car to tour the countryside.

Stanley and Eunice traveled together on missions from September to December, 1939. Mabel was in Sitapur dodging cholera, snakes and scorpions but now had electricity and a fan. Eunice and Jim would begin a serious romance.

September 1939, World War II was on. The British Viceroy announced unilaterally that India was at war with Germany. Understandably, the Indian National Congress asked the British government how its "declared war aims" of protecting democracy and defeating imperialism, applied to India. The Viceroy's answer was noncommittal. Indians were conflicted but so was J. Holmes Smith, Stanley's appointed leader of the Lucknow Ashram.

J. Holmes (Jay) Smith felt that the Indian people deserved better.

The British had insisted that all foreign missionaries throughout the Empire sign a pledge that "all due obedience and respect should be given to the lawfully constituted Government... while carefully abstaining from political affairs." Although Stanley signed with his tongue in his cheek, Smith could not in good conscience sign.[68] This was no small matter. Gordon B. Halstead, a member of the staff of Lucknow Christian College, had sided with the nationalists and had been deported.

On December 3, 1939 Jay Smith resigned as leader of the Lucknow Ashram. He felt that his convictions were inconsistent with the missionary pledge, forcing his resignation. Stanley writes to Diffendorfer January 28, 1940, "We ...never asked for Jay's resignation, nor did we desire it. It was entirely his own initiative."[69]

By this time Stanley was so consumed with his evangelistic missions that he was unable to lead both the Sat Tal and the Lucknow Ashrams. The Lucknow Ashram would close within months. Stanley writes that the closing of the Ashram was an emotional and soul-wrenching event, "To see the child of one's heart die, and to see it die without a tear is an experience."[70]

On December 13 the North India Conference of the Methodist Episcopal Church met in Bareilly and honored the Joneses, particularly Mabel. "Our hearts are filled with manifold thanks and obligations that Dr. and Mrs. Jones with their daughter are amongst us.... Mrs. Jones has a sincere love for this school.... The boys have profound love for Mrs. Jones and she is also not unmindful about them."[71]

Stanley, Mabel and Eunice would then return to Sitapur to be together over Christmas.[72] The war was now raging among Germany, France, and Britain.

Eunice and Jim were engaged in January 1940 and married June 1 the same year. Stanley and Mabel gave her away. Stanley then returned to the U.S. almost immediately.

Eunice Mathews, Mabel Jones,
Jan and Anne

E. Stanley Jones and Mabel Jones, c. 1950

1940 to 1946: Another World War

The Need to Maintain Relevant Ministry in the Midst of World War II, while Stanley, Mabel and Eunice were Forced to Live Apart

By this time it should come as no surprise that Stanley Jones played a key role in some of the most significant historical and political issues of his time, events that continue to shape our world today.

With the closing of the Lucknow Ashram Stanley was particularly heartened when Mr. E. V. Moorman wrote to him in India, saying that if Stanley would transplant the Christian Ashrams into America, he would pay for setting them up and if Stanley would be willing to conduct them personally he would further enlist the administrative assistance of Dr. Jesse Bader, the executive secretary of the Department of Evangelism of the Federal Council of Churches, who would make the necessary arrangements. Stanley agreed. After ten years of Ashram experiences in India Stanley was ready to transplant them to the U.S.[1]

For the first three weeks of January, 1940 Stanley was in Sat Tal working on his soon to be published book, *Is the Kingdom of God Realism?* (1940). Sat Tal was always a place of spiritual and physical rest and refreshment for Stanley. When he confronted the unpleasant and disappointing fact that he would have to close the Lucknow Ashram, he needed the solitude of Sat Tal. For the early months of 1940 he was virtually alone and could spend weeks in prayer, study, and writing. He even had time to write about a leopard that was plaguing the villagers who begged him to kill it. He had never given himself to big game hunting but the villagers helped him to set up a blind so that he successfully shot and killed the beast.

While still at Sat Tal, Stanley continued to struggle (as always) with *church unity*. As he prayed he sensed a spiritual malaise among Christians due to a lack of unity. In India obstacles to Christian unity came from two sources, first the social, economic, political, and racial differences between Western Christians and Indian Christians, and second, the denominational differences among Christians within India. Across the years Stanley's ministry focused on both of these issues at one time or another (especially in the late 30s and early 40s). This problem had plagued him throughout his ministry. He would address it in some detail once back in America.

In May Stanley made his travel plans back to the U.S. He now realized that he needed to be in Michigan in July for the first American Ashram as promised. Because of the war in Europe his initial travel plans were canceled. He was forced to book passage on a ship from Bombay to New York via South Africa that was not scheduled to arrive in New York until ten days after the opening of the Ashram in Saugatuck Michigan. He realized that he would need God's help getting there. Then, his Inner Voice spoke to him, "It's all right; I'll get you there safely and on time." He was learning to trust the Inner Voice.[2]

Stanley left for the U.S. immediately after the wedding of Eunice and Jim Mathews, arriving in late July 1940 but because of visa and travel restrictions during the war he would not return to India until

January 10, 1946. This was another long separation between Stanley and Mabel (and Eunice as well). Eunice writes that after her marriage she and her mother developed an even deeper relationship.[3]

On board ship Stanley continued to work on *Is the Kingdom of God Realism*. In Cape Town, South Africa the captain of the ship told the passengers that the ship would have to stop in Trinidad for fresh water. Stanley looked at the map and found a Pan-American Airlines flight from Trinidad to Miami. He wired Dr. Bader, who made plane reservations for him. From Miami he took a train to Chicago and there, met by a pastor, they drove by car to Saugatuck. In spite of car trouble they miraculously arrived just as the Ashram bell was sounding.[4]

A reporter for the *Kansas City Star*, Clarence Hill, visited this Ashram. He wrote, "The ashram was held in a secluded heavily timbered camp on the edge of a resort village on the shores of Lake Michigan." Furthermore, "The camp is on a high hilly plot overlooking a wide expanse of beach and there each morning the day begins with prayer, meditation and song, with the gentle lash of the waves as a background. The Biblical images are brought vividly to mind as Dr. E. Stanley Jones, Methodist missionary to India and moving spirit of the ashram, dressed in native Indian costume, his feet covered only by the strips of sandals, plods slowly to the mound of sand upon which he sits with legs crossed in the manner of an Indian teacher, to lead the service."[5]

In these "international" ashrams Stanley adopted a different format from the manuscripts and lectures of Sat Tal.

Tom Albin, the executive director of the United Christian Ashrams, outlines the Key Elements or Pillars of the Jones' Ashram model. Albin describes the "Open Heart" at the beginning of the experience and the "Overflowing Heart" at the end. At the Open Heart, those who attend are first asked to participate in an experience of voluntary self-disclosure where each participant describes their reasons for attending the Ashram. It was during this time that the stage was set for establishing the needs of the people (symptoms as it were) to be addressed during the duration of the ashram. With Bible teacher, Church in Action teacher and Evangelist (usually Brother Stanley giving addresses that addressed the needs of the Ashram participants, the "prescription" as it were to remedy the expressed symptoms), all of these resources sought to address these needs. Again, the remedy was "not preaching, but prescription." Then, at the end the Ashram you had the "Overflowing Heart" where the people described how their needs were met.

Thus guided by the evangelist, the participants during the Open Heart answer three questions: 1) Why are you here? 2) What do you want? And, 3) What do you need from God before this event is over?[6] According to Brother Stanley,

> The last question is the really important one.… We hasten to say that you don't have to tell your needs, and you'll not be out of the fellowship if you don't tell your needs; but you'll be poorer, and we'll be poorer. From forty to four hundred people, from all walks of life and from all denominations and ages, come together for the first time and within the first few hours tell their needs straight off, without any maneuvering or urging. They will do this — *provided the leader begins by telling his own needs*. I do. It is a catharsis. To bring up your own needs and look at them fairly and honestly is halfway to the solution.[7]

Albin then adds:

> "The relevance of the Open Heart for evangelism in a pluralistic society is unmistakable. It provides insight into the spiritual needs of the participants. The evangelist and Bible teacher can focus their teaching and preaching to meet the expressed needs of the community."[8]

In his *Song*, Stanley describes a typical day at the Ashram. It begins with the Morning Watch, an hour with God before breakfast, half spent in silence with reading and reflecting on the Scripture identified by the evangelist the night before; and, the second half in sharing what they had found. All become teachers, and all become taught.

The aim is to establish a spiritual practice that the participants can continue at home.

After breakfast there is Bible Study, the Bible reveals *Jesus – the true teacher and guru of the Christian Ashram*. The Scripture study, therefore, is focused on one of the Gospels or the Book of Acts.

After the Bible Hour is the Church at Work Hour. For two hours "We step out of the Bible to talk about how we can function as a church in the world around us. Then, after those two hours we have a Work Period, where we work with our hands. This gives us recreation and re-creation – muscles attached to constructive purposes."

After the Work Period the evangelist will speak on one of the main emphases of the Ashram – usually Jesus Christ and his uniqueness, or the Kingdom of God, or self-surrender, or the Holy Spirit, evangelism, or discipleship.

Immediately after lunch we have the Family Meetings in which we ask the group to bring up any constructive suggestions for change – what can we do better? We remind them that if they do not bring up issues at the Family Meeting, they should not bring them up anywhere else, so that there will be no secret criticism. If there is no outer criticism, we know there is no inner criticism, so there is a relaxed fellowship. Each day we give opportunity to wipe the slate clean. This Family Meeting was added in America to the Ashram program – a real contribution.

After the Family Meeting there is time for rest, recreation, special interest, or a talent show until 4:30 pm. At 4:30 pm. we have Prayer and Reflection Groups. These groups are not for the discussion of prayer; that would be the Word of Prayer become word; but groups that really pray – the Word of Prayer become flesh. The leader does not discourse on prayer; he/she simply directs the praying of the group.

After supper, there is a vesper service that includes an evangelistic message and the invitation to fix publicly the decisions made during the day.[9]

A Healing Service usually takes place on the last night of the Ashram, with a message on some phase of Christianity and health and healing. Since the Christian answer is a total answer, the body must be included. "We ask three groups to come forward: first, those who want physical healing; second, those who want spiritual healing; third, those who want both. Usually the last-named is the largest. During the time Brother Stanley was alive, four leaders would lay on hands simultaneously on the four people in front of them. One prayer was offered aloud for the four people who came for healing. The evangelist explains that those praying are not 'healers,' simply disciples lending their hands to Christ for his healing to come through them. When healing comes, the recipient must praise Him, not the prayer team. Meanwhile the congregation is encouraged to pray from their seats."[10]

There are no absolutists in regard to healing. The Christian Ashram does not hold the position that all diseases must be cured in this life or else there is some lurking sin or a lack of faith. This theology leaves unnecessary shame and guilt among people who are not healed by prayer or medicine or surgery. We explain that this is a mortal world and we are not supposed to be immortal. Sometimes the body breaks down; death is a part of life. Some diseases must await the final cure at the resurrection. God will heal us now, or give us power to use the infirmity — not *bear* it but *use* it — until the final cure is manifest when we receive our immortal glorified body. "Death is but an anesthetic that God gives us while changing our bodies."[11]

On the last day, there is often a *Eucharistic service,* followed by the commissioning of the local Ashram leaders. Finally is the Overflowing Heart. Participants can now express gratitude for the work God has done in their hearts. This is a spiritual opportunity to do what one of the lepers did when, having been healed, turned back and fell at the feet of Jesus and said: "Thank you, thank you." That is psychologically, as well as spiritually, sound. Stanley would say that this is a law of the mind. "That which is not expressed dies. Impression minus expression equals depression. To express it is to impress it. It is also spiritually sound. It attaches the changed person to Jesus Christ and not to the movement through which the change came."[12]

Beginning immediately after the Open Heart and concluding just before the Overflowing Heart, the entire Christian Ashram is undergirded with prayer. Participants and leaders alike make a commitment to pray in 30 or 60 minute shifts, 24-hours a day, for the entire Ashram. Prayer was the foundation for the ministry of Jesus and it is for the Christian Ashram as well. Where there is much prayer, there is much spiritual power. Where there is little prayer, there is little spiritual power.[13]

The final event of the Christian Ashram is the Closing Circle, where the participants join hands and repeat this statement written on the wall of the Sat Tal Ashram: "*Unreservedly given to God, unbreakably given to each other.*" The fellowship is an unbreakable fellowship, for it is in Christ and not in that particular session. That session breaks up. He abides.[14] Then the evangelist says, "Jesus is LORD!" and the people respond with their final affirmation, "Jesus is LORD!"

For Stanley, who was unable to visit Mabel often, these ashrams both in India and the U.S. (and eventually worldwide) would become his virtual home for the rest of his life. Since his first Ashram at Sat Tal in 1930 until his death, nothing was closer to his heart than these spiritual retreats. On the basic principle of self-surrender, these ashrams continually transformed Brother Stanley and those who participated in them.

Although the format changed outside India, some say that these Ashrams were perhaps Stanley's most enduring contribution to the Body of Christ. Certainly his books and articles inspired millions. His public evangelistic meetings led thousands into to a personal relationship with Jesus Christ. His interviews and counseling sessions reoriented the lives of thousands more. Yet, it was the Ashrams that had the greatest global impact.

Inspired by the steadying influence of these Ashrams, Stanley learned to sing in the midst of all that was going on around him. He writes: "With WWI and then WWII, needlessly destroying lives, how can you sing? You can sing by gazing at Jesus and glancing at evil. Never gaze at evil (pessimism) and glance at Jesus (optimism). Live spelled backward is evil. Good has everything behind it so evil is weak and good is strong. If life misses the mark—misses Jesus—it becomes iniquity. This is not a doctrine. This is a demonstration, demonstrated around us daily."[15]

STANLEY STRUGGLES WITH THE PROBLEM OF EVIL

During this time away from India—while Mabel, Eunice and now Jim remained—Stanley traveled, preached and wrote. In his *Is the Kingdom of God Realism?* (1940), he began to use the word *totalitarian* in reference to the Kingdom of God (mentioned at Tambaram in 1938) in most of his published works. His use of the word was intentionally provocative, hopefully making conventional Christianity uncomfortable with its watered down views of the demands of what it means to be the body of Jesus Christ. After all, the Russians (communism), Germans (Nazism) and now radical Islam (ISIS) fully understand the implications of totalitarianism. They know that their convictions should extend to every walk of life, politically, socially, and "religiously." Christianity, as the Kingdom of God, must embrace every human characteristic of body, mind and spirit and every personal and institutional relationship. Unlike other forms of totalitarianism, however, the Kingdom of God (are you listening?) draws inspiration and strength from God and is thus able to affect total and permanent change in all of these human characteristics and relationships.

A young seminary student at one of these Ashrams asked this question, "Brother Stanley, isn't your philosophy of life too neat? Too Rosy?" Apparently he had a professor who attempted to reverse the words of the Apostle Paul to say, "Where sin abounded, grace did much more abound," into "Where grace abounded sin did much more abound." Stanley was singing his song against the grain of modern theological trends that were prevailingly pessimistic.

Stanley responded that Jesus pronounced the doom of all evil. "Every plant that my heavenly Father has not planted will be pulled up by the roots" (Matthew 15:13) — perhaps not today or tomorrow, but the 'third day,' YES!" Paul speaks about "dethroned powers..." (I Corinthians 2:6). It may take time but evil is doomed. Isaiah pronounced the doom of Assyria "by no human sword" (Isaiah 31:8). What was that "sword"? It was the Word of God proclaiming an inherent moral universe! Stanley would bet his life on the moral universe having the last word. There is Hope! Sin tries to assimilate what cannot be assimilated. Stanley is concerned about the direction the world seems to be taking — its moral decay — but NOT overly so. He knows that in the end, God prevails.[16]

There is, however, another side of evil — unmerited suffering. Stanley had his back to the wall on this issue for several years. Hindus and Buddhists simply say that suffering is not unmerited. It is the result of sin from a previous life. All suffering is just. Stanley was always suspect of a premise that came to that conclusion. What kind of a system of rewards and punishments has no memory connecting the reward and the punishment? "So, when trouble comes, 'My karma is bad.' I deserve this." This may make for a patient people but it puts a brake on repentance and faith in Jesus. A Hindu once said to Stanley: "Jesus must have been a terrible sinner in a previous life."

Nor can Stanley accept the Stoic answer. "My head might be bloody, but it will be unbowed under the bludgeoning of chance." In shutting out suffering, however, the Stoic shuts out love and pity as well. It made him hard and uncaring. Stanley concludes that if the righteous were exempt there would be chaos. A righteous person would lean too far over a tall building and the law of gravity would be suspended while the bad person experienced its natural consequences. Increasingly Stanley knows that he must obey the laws of the moral universe as the purpose of those laws are to produce character.

Nor could Stanley accept the Muslim answer that insists that all suffering is the will of Allah. Where has God gone if everything that happens is his will? Similarly, Stanley could not accept the possible Old Testament solution — the righteous will be exempt from trouble (the premise behind Job's miserable comforters). The prophets struggled with that as they saw the righteous suffer, sometimes because they were righteous. Society demands conformity. If you fall beneath its standards it will punish you. If you rise above it, it will persecute you. "Woe unto you Jesus said, when all men speak well of you."[17]

The Old Testament does, on occasion, suggest another answer, "In spite of it all, I will rejoice in the Lord, I will find joy in the God of my salvation" (Habakkuk 3:17). "Stuff happens! It rains on the just and the unjust." Habakkuk calls God a wimp for two chapters before he finally gets the point in Chapter Three. God does not exempt the followers of Jesus from trouble, God guarantees it, yet God is faithful and grace is sufficient that "You might not be tempted beyond your ability to endure" (1 Corinthians 10:13).

CHURCH UNION

During the latter part of 1940, Stanley's meditations at Sat Tal the previous year on the need for unity are now back with a rush. Perhaps with some memory of his reaction to the perceived over emphasis on ecumenism at Tambaram, Stanley now begins to focus on church union. This focus would give him fresh insight into ecumenism.

He now came to three conclusions about the church. First, "Christians are the most united body on earth — if they only knew it — united at the center but divided at the circumference." Second, God does not prefer one Christian denomination over another. God delights in any of the saints, no matter the denomination, if they surrender to Him." Thirdly, the expressions and manifestations of the faith and life that are common to all Christians are varied and diverse.

On the basis of these three conclusions Stanley proposed that all Christians in the U.S. drop their denominational labels and become members of a federal church — The Church of Christ in America. In an article in the *Christian Century*, written some years later he would conclude with words reminiscent of the *Communist Manifesto*, "We have nothing to lose except our dividing walls." He honestly believed that the Church united could speak with authority both to nations and societies. The Church failed because she did not speak with one voice. His idea of a federal church would never find traction but would eventually result in his *Christ of the American Road* (1944).

THE WAR WITH JAPAN:
ATTEMPTS FOR PEACE AND A NEW WORLD ORDER

1941 was a critical year. Early in the year, January to March, Stanley is involved in another exhausting American evangelistic tour with the National Christian Mission. He had been speaking two to five times a day for the entire tour throughout the U.S. and still managed an article for *Christian Century* on Christian mediation. He was pre-occupied with the growing tension between the U.S. and Japan. He was convinced that the U.S. could act as a mediator on the Kingdom principle of Ephesians 2:14-16: "For he himself is our peace, who has made the two groups one and has destroyed the barrier, the dividing wall of hostility by setting aside in his flesh the law with its commands and regulations. His purpose was to create in himself one new humanity out of the two, thus making peace." The purpose of Jesus' death was to "create *in himself* one new man, that the one body be reconciled. In his *Is the Kingdom of God Realism?* Stanley made it clear that the Kingdom of God was, in fact, the only ultimate reality.

At one point during this tour Stanley interrupted a series of meetings on the Pacific Coast to go to Washington, D.C. There he encountered the source of the war mentality that was engulfing the nation. He discovered that while 80-85% of Americans were opposed to war,

80-85% of the newspapers and officials at Washington felt that war was inevitable.

As an alternative to war, Stanley suggested in an undated *Circular Letter* that the U.S. "should be the mediator of a new world order based upon equality of opportunity. He actually proposed the idea to a luncheon meeting of business and professional men in Washington. He then met with a group of congressmen and proposed the same idea. The congressmen felt that the nation was in a "race against time" and action needed to be taken in the next 30 days or the decision would be made.[18]

Stanley also had a scheduled meeting with President Roosevelt but because of the President's busy schedule he had to submit his idea in writing. He did manage a meeting with an associate justice of the U.S. Supreme Court, Felix Frankfurter. Stanley had been told that Justice Frankfurter "was the brains behind the whole thing," meaning that Frankfurter had the ear of the President. The meeting with Frankfurter (arranged by FDR's secretary) began on an unexpected negative note. Stanley wrote that the Justice was angry that Stanley should think that he (Frankfurter) could have any influence in the Government (he claimed that he did not see the President for months). Stanley accepted his statement with a nod and asked if he could simply put before him his proposal of a "new world order" as an ordinary citizen with particular reference to the Pacific. The Justice assented. In the end they were not very far apart on the goal but Frankfurter insisted that first Germany had to be defeated, as only then would they listen. Stanley added that whether they listened or not, we must hold to this position, to keep it alight within our own hearts and broadcast it at every opportunity. Frankfurter agreed and "We parted friends."[19]

While still in Washington, Stanley also presented his concept of the U.S. as mediator of a new world order to various peace groups, including in a public evangelistic meeting. In all of this (his meetings with businessmen, congressmen and Frankfurter) Stanley had "the sense of God unfolding this whole thing with our simply following the gleam. It seemed as God were doing it all and we were just following the gleam."[20]

The end of February, 1941, Stanley returns to the West Coast to conclude his National Christian Mission. He had made plans to return to India from California in March but suddenly encountered unexpected problems with his intention to sail on the SS *President Hayes*. First, the ship's departure from the West Coast was delayed because of needed repairs. Stanley suddenly had a premonition that he was not to return to India at this time. He wrote to his friend Miss Nellie on March 8, "Perhaps God is in these changes, at any rate the inner assurance is very real."[21]

Then the Holy Spirit confirmed his premonition on the very morning (March 20, 1941) that his baggage was to be put aboard ship for India. "I was in Los Angeles ready to go. I was awakened in the hotel room about 4 am with the inner voice saying: "I want you here." It persisted. I struggled with it. "Lord, I can't. The National Christian Mission is over. My work is done. My wife and daughter are in India. I haven't seen them for over a year (as it turned out it was to be over six years). The boat with my trunk is leaving San Francisco today (I was to pick it up in the Philippines). I do not see how I can stay. "But the voice was persistent: I want you here. After fighting with it for two hours I succumbed, I said I would obey."[22]

Stanley immediately (the same morning, March 20, 1941) sent a wire to Diffendorfer. "Guidance postpone indefinitely return to India writing about plans Stanley Jones." The next day, March 21, Diffendorfer sent him an airmail letter writing that "we are not at all surprised at your decision." Diffendorfer's own inner voice had told him that Stanley might well stay on in America.

Perhaps Stanley was beginning to feel that his efforts for peace was unfinished business, infinitely more important than his return to India. Even though another ship, the *President Harrison*, would be leaving San Francisco on April 20 and his bags were in route to the dock, once again the "inner voice" would not release him. He had no choice but to obey. He had his bags taken off the ship and then continued his Los Angeles mission until April 24.[23]

Although Stanley was tired and longed to return to India his "inner voice" had confirmed the delay, at least until fall.[24] Then, in spite of repeated efforts to secure the necessary papers, the doors closed for another five years, as he would be denied multiple requests for visas (the British believing that his assumed sympathies for Indian independence was against their national interest). The effect was that just as they had been separated for much of the time while Mabel was recovering from her illnesses in the U.S., they would again be separated for the years during the war.

Speaking of Mabel, in June she spent time with Eunice and Jim in Kashmir. "We lived on various lakes and rivers in a houseboat about as roomy as an American trailer. But we had all out-of-doors and a cool climate and we returned refreshed and invigorated."[25]

As for Stanley, in the early summer of 1941 all the instructions from the Inner Voice were confirmed. He and his Princeton acquaintance from 25 years earlier, Dr. Toyohiko Kagawa, now a famous Japanese Christian leader, were both speakers at the same conference in Lake Geneva, Wisconsin. Kagawa told him that the Japanese ambassador in Washington, Adm. Kichisaburo Nomura, was not a member of the war party in Japan that wanted to resolve the escalating tension between Japan and the U.S. by going to war. In fact, Nomura wanted peace and Kagawa strongly urged Stanley to visit Nomura and suggest an idea that could reduce or end Japanese imperialism in the Pacific. Kagawa's idea was that New Guinea, the world's second largest island (after Greenland), which was sparsely populated but richly endowed with natural resources, be given to Japan. If Australia and the Netherlands, countries that controlled New Guinea at that time, could be persuaded to give up the island, then there would be a real basis for peace in the Far East.[26]

Stanley's inner voice would reconfirm this proposal time and again. During the rest of the summer of 1941, after the meetings with

Kagawa, while Stanley waited for Washington life to resume after the summer vacations, Stanley continued his efforts to keep the U.S out of war. His proposal for the U.S. to mediate a new world order was printed in the *Congressional Record* and read by the Secretary of State. It was then sent to approximately 100,000 Christian ministers, and spawned two grassroots movements — the Mediation Committee and the Churchman's Campaign for Peace through Mediation.[27] Stanley was weary of the clash between militarists and pacifists. His vision was for the Church to rise above them both and get the nation together in the search for peace.[28]

Stanley also completed a full schedule of evangelistic meetings throughout the U.S. In mid-July he managed to speak at the World Sunday School Convention in Mexico City. The American Ambassador, Josephus Daniels, twice came to his meetings. They had lunch. A week later Stanley wrote to the wife of Dr. O. G. Robinson, a prominent Methodist pastor from Dayton, Ohio with connections to the White House (both O. G. and his wife were significant friends), saying that Daniels was so interested in and sympathetic with Stanley's ideas for peace in the Pacific that he "sent a copy of my memorandum to the President in his diplomatic bag.[29]

Stanley then led three summer ashrams during the months of July and August, one at Occidental College in California (where he began the practice of an all-night prayer vigil), another at Blue Ridge , North Carolina (where "our negro friends were received on the basis of complete equality"), and a third back at Saugatuck, Michigan. As the fall approached he was beginning to work on a new book of one-page devotional meditations for each day of the year, *Abundant Living*. This would be published in 1942 and prove to be his single most popular devotional title.[30]

"SHUTTLE DIPLOMACY," STANLEY BACK AND FORTH TO WASHINGTON D.C., SEPTEMBER TO DECEMBER 7, 1941

Just prior to U.S. involvement in the war with Japan, Stanley became an unofficial negotiator among diplomats in Washington, D.C. representing Japan, China and the United States. He goes to Washington for three days out of each week between September and December 7 (Pearl Harbor Day) to see what he could do to head off the war. He would have evangelistic meetings in different parts of the country from Sunday to Wednesday and then go to Washington from Thursday to Saturday. O. G. Robinson, set up the interviews in Stanley's absence and sat in on all the sessions except those with the President.

While Mabel had concerns for India's inability to strike a pose for war, Stanley was clearly a pacifist. Mabel, at the time, had a very different view of political climates. Stanley was against militarism while Mabel was concerned that India has pinned her faith to non-resistance and non-cooperation for so long that it was hard for Indians to realize that "there are times when evil has to be actively resisted."[31]

Stanley wrote a *Circular Letter*, September 13, 1941, reassuring his faithful that his jaunts to D. C. would not interfere with his call to be an evangelist. He would continue to preach the Gospel. He told his friends that his book, *Abundant Living* was rooted in his previous book, *Is the Kingdom of God Realism?* (actually, *Abundant Living* puts his understanding of the Kingdom of God into principles and techniques of applied everyday living). Meanwhile the events about to be told are a compelling story of courage, determination and ultimate frustration.

Stanley was persuaded that FDR "wanted peace, at least in the Pacific." During these months, however, there was apparently no public recognition of a peace party in Japan. Diplomatic relations between the U.S. and Japan deteriorated rapidly as the U.S. put an embargo on the sale of oil to Japan, froze Japanese assets in U.S. banks and ordered American nationals living in Japan to leave. In fact, in September, his friend, Kagawa, as a prominent Japanese citizen was ordered to leave the U.S. Shortly after he returned to Japan Kagawa sent an urgent cable to Stanley, "SITUATION VERY SERIOUS HERE. SEE PRESIDENT ROOSEVELT IMMEDIATELY. GET HIM TO AVERT CATASTROPHE IN PACIFIC. AM WORKING WITH UN-FAILING FAITH AT THIS END."[32]

Stanley could not see FDR in September but in the meantime he pursued the idea, first suggested by Kagawa, that sparsely populated New Guinea be given to Japan as a place to settle some of its over-crowded population and as a source of badly needed natural re-sources. Stanley even approached Richard Gardiner Casey, the Aus-tralian minister, with the idea. Casey was "very sympathetic" and agreed that there must be an alternative living space for the densely populated Japanese islands. "If we don't do it now, we will have to do it in ten years." Casey asked Stanley to take the idea to the U.S. Department of State but also to propose that the U.S. pay both Aus-tralia and the Netherlands $100 million as compensation for those now living in New Guinea who would be displaced. Stanley did so. Although there was some support, the State Department concluded that "it could not very easily take up the question of the disposal of the property of other nations." As if to prove the point, when Stanley approached the Dutch the reaction was emphatically NO! "No part of the Dutch Empire is for sale."[33]

Although the issue of New Guinea was the most controversial proposal Stanley made in his tireless efforts to prevent war between the U.S. and Japan, it was not the only proposal in his attempt to bring peace. In spite of the October 15 fall of Prince Konoye's Japa-nese Government, replaced by Admiral Hideki Tojo (an outspoken militarist and member of the war party), Stanley was not discour-aged. In fact, he would redouble his efforts. When the Japanese gov-ernment sent Saburu Kurusu as a Special Envoy from Emperor Hirohito to Washington in a last minute effort to avoid war with the U.S., Stanley saw his chance.

THE LIFE AND MINISTRY OF E. STANLEY JONES

IN OUR TIME

According the *Washington Post* Stanley would shuttle with relative anonymity between FDR and the special envoys sent to Washington by the Japanese emperor in an effort to forestall war." He would then ask the Japanese in Washington whether they would participate in a peace conference with China under the auspices of the U.S if the U.S. would lift its oil embargo. The Japanese responded with an enthusiastic YES. Encouraged, Stanley forwarded this idea to the U.S. State Department, to FDR and to Lord Halifax, now the British Ambassador to the U.S. and Stanley's old acquaintance in India when he was the British Viceroy.

Unfortunately the U.S. response was to give the Japanese Ambassador Nomura and Special Envoy Kurusu a humiliating ultimatum — immediate capitulation to four American demands: "Get out of the Axis, get out of China, get out of Indo-China and equality of trade in the Far East." By the end of November the only hope for peace was for a spokesman for the Japanese peace party to serve as a personal emissary to FDR. FDR scheduled a personal audience with Nomura and Kurusu on November 28 at 2:30 pm.

Most Americans during and after the war assumed that a united Japan undertook world conquest, with no inhibitions and no internal opposition. During this time Stanley learned that it was more complicated. He was convinced that the diplomatic personnel at the Japanese Embassy in Washington were not playing games. They were a peace party and were trying desperately to find a basis for peace.

At about noon, Hidenari (Terry) Terasaki, the Counsel of the Japanese Embassy in Washington, whom Stanley had befriended earlier, implored Stanley to talk with FDR before the 2:30 meeting. In a letter by Terasaki's wife, Gwen Terasaki, we have this account:

> My husband went to Dr. E. Stanley Jones, the well-known Methodist leader who was using his prestige and friendship with the President to help the parties reach an amicable settlement of the crisis. He asked Dr. Jones if he could get in touch with the President and explain to him the Japanese situation psychologically so that he might be more receptive to their proposals. The Japanese were to see Mr. Roosevelt at 2:30 that afternoon

and it was 12:30 when Terry reached Dr. Jones. A call was placed to the White House and the President's secretary, Mr. McIntyre, read off the engagements already made for the intervening time before the Japanese delegation was scheduled to see the President. It was not possible for Dr. Jones to talk with Mr. Roosevelt but a message could be transmitted if Dr. Jones would dictate it to Mr. McIntyre over the telephone.

My husband and Dr. Jones then composed a letter, unmistakably in Terry's style of English: "We Japanese have been four years at war. When one is in a war mentality, he cannot think straight. The Allies were in a war mentality at the close of the last war and made a bad peace. *You help us from a war mentality to a peace mentality. Don't compel us to do things but make it possible for us to do them. If you treat us this way, we will meet you more than half way. If you stretch out one hand, we will stretch out two. And we cannot only be friends, we can be allies.*"

The entire message was to be delivered by Jones by word of mouth and nothing was to be in writing. Mr. Roosevelt was now at Warm Springs, Georgia, where he had gone for a few days' rest. Dr. Jones called the White House and spoke to Mr. McIntyre again, asking if he might take a plane and speak with the President in Georgia. Mr. McIntyre said he might, but he suggested that if the message could be written it could be brought to his office at the White House and sealed in his presence. It would then be put in a special bag and taken by plane with a courier to the President the following Monday morning. Mr. McIntyre would guarantee that no one would see the contents of the message until the President opened it himself. Terry agreed that most of the message could be delivered by that method, but he insisted that unless one part of it could be handled verbally it could not be sent at all. The message was written, except for this reserved portion and taken to the White House, but by this time the situation had worsened. The President had changed his plans and was returning to Washington by train to arrive on Monday morning.

The letter was given to the President at the railway station and he read it on the way to the White House. The suggestion contained in the message was, of course, that the President send a cable to Hirohito appealing for peace. The Emperor rarely took part in politics, but if he interfered, it was known that the Japanese leaders would comply — all of them — including the war ministry.

On December 3, Dr. Jones requested audience with Mr. Roosevelt to deliver the verbal message. It was arranged for him to talk with the President if he got there within twenty minutes, and he was instructed to go to the east gate where someone would meet him and take him in the back way in order to avoid newspapermen.

Mr. Roosevelt told Dr. Jones, "Two days before I got your letter I thought of sending the cable, but I've hesitated to do it, for I didn't want to hurt the Japanese here at Washington by going over their heads to the Emperor."

Dr. Jones replied, "Mr. President, that is the purpose of my visit. I have come to tell you that this suggestion of sending the cable did not come from me, but from the Japanese Embassy. They have asked me to ask you to send the cable. But obviously they could not let me write that, for there must be no written record, since they are going over the head of their government to the Emperor."

"Oh, then, that wipes my slate clean; I can send the cable." "But," Jones said, "the Japanese tell me that you must not send the cable as you sent the other cable to the Emperor over the sinking of the Panay. They tell me that the reason you got no reply from the Emperor was that it never got to him, but was held up in their Foreign Office. This time, they tell me, you must not send it through the Foreign Office, but direct to the Emperor himself. I don't know the mechanics of it, but that's what they suggest."

Mr. Roosevelt said, "Well, I'm just thinking out loud. I can't go down to the cable office and say I want to send a cable from the President of the United States to the Emperor of Japan, but I could send it to Grew, for Grew as an ambassador has the right of audience to the head of a state and he can give it to the Emperor direct, and if I do not hear within twenty-four hours — I have learned to do some things — I'll give it to the newspapers and force a reply!"

It was hoped that the cable would not be held up by the Japanese telegraphers who would handle it before it reached Ambassador Grew and that Grew could obtain immediate audience with Hirohito; this might have the same effect as the proposed meeting with Premier Konoye.

At the conclusion of the meeting Dr. Jones mentioned that the President must never refer to Mr. Terasaki in connection with the message. Mr. Roosevelt told him, "You tell that young Japanese he is a brave man. No one will ever learn of his part in this from me. His secret is safe."

The cable was long and was not sent until December 5-two days before our world had burst apart. What could have happened to it, I wondered. Oh, God, what could have happened to it?[34]

President Roosevelt had sent the requested telegram on December 5, 1941 but tragically records from the American Ambassador in Japan show that the cable did not get to the Emperor until after the attack on Pearl Harbor. Counsel Hidenari Terasaki, would later write that the Emperor told him that if he had received the cablegram from Roosevelt a day sooner he would have stopped the attack on Pearl Harbor.

Stanley would devote an entire chapter to this episode in his *Song*, "Guidance — An Adventure in Failure."[35]

On December 8, the day following the attack, Stanley is in Pittsburg. Just two weeks earlier he had written to Rob and Dar Robinson that on the train in route he had an overwhelming feeling that a way would be found to prevent war. He now writes to them again, "I do not know how to interpret my experience on the train to Dayton. Perhaps it was assurance of God's approval in what I was doing & I thought it an assurance of peace in [the] Pacific."

December 10, Stanley wrote to Terasaki a significant letter (as we will soon understand) stating that they had done all that they could do and that the rest was up to God. "Dear Mr. Terasaki: Words cannot express my sorrow that things have turned out the way they have. I am perfectly sure that your group at Washington sincerely and earnestly tried to avert this hour. It is not your fault that the war party won. You did your best.... You did your best... This is to pray that God's grace may be with you in the dark hours and days ahead. Please give my best regards to Mrs. Terasaki and say to her that I shall uphold you both with prayer." In a letter dated December 12, 1941, Stanley thanks Dr. Robinson for his kind response.[36]

Stephen Graham asks, "Did Stanley mistake his fervent personal goal of peace with Japan for the "inner voice" of God's Holy Spirit? Or, did God have a larger and more important goal for him, a goal which transcended the immediate and desperate need for peace in the Pacific?" In my opinion, a great question, but can we have it both ways? No question!

"The immediate cause of the war was Japan's need for land and resources. There was a deeper cause, however. There was the racially motivated exclusion from the distribution of the spoils of war by the Allies after WWI and the discriminatory immigration policies of the U.S. For this reason, Stanley was asking the U.S. to take the "moral high ground" by proposing a practical solution to Japan's obvious need."[37]

Again, throughout this time Stanley never abandoned his call as an evangelist. He became increasingly convinced that the Gospel was not only for the individual but for society as well.

On Christmas Day, 1941, Stanley prepared a Christmas message (probably broadcast by radio). Stephen Graham writes that, "Amid the crash of things, something solid, unshakable remained. His world of real value was intact—the center of his faith—Christ—was unscathed. Stanley would come to think of the Kingdom of God as a universal idea, as the foundation for Christian mediation of political disputes throughout the world."[38]

Although Stanley still had a valid visa at this time his *Circular Letter* of December 26, 1941 stated that the war "prevented" him [via

the Inner Voice] from returning to India and that "Mrs. Jones, his daughter Eunice and his son-in-law, James Mathews, would become 'interns' for the duration of the war." He goes on to write that "Christ still rules, and I was never so sure as now that His way is the way of complete realism." Stanley has a way of maintaining his focus![39]

Over the next 3 years Stanley would publish a book a year, *Abundant Living* (1942), the booklet, *How to Pray* (1943) and *The Christ of the American Road* (1944). Then in 1946 he would publish *The Way*. Several of his earlier devotionals were becoming immediate best sellers but *The Way* was a strong statement regarding faith and the Church that would impact the Church at large.

In January and February, 1942 Stanley resumed his preaching schedule with the National Christian Mission sponsored by the Federal Council of Churches. He spent a week in each of the following places — Paducah, KY, South Bend, IN, Wheeling, WVA, Johnstown, PA, San Angelo, TX, Hagerstown, MD, Canton, OH, and Duluth, MN.

On March 7, Stanley writes Miss Nellie that when the war began he had thought he would "have to hibernate & write books." In fact, however, he would have "fine meetings" throughout the U.S. "I've never had a better hearing & response." Stanley's use of the superlatives, some say hyperbole — oh ye of little faith — was evidence of his being continually amazed by what God could do through his ongoing ministry.

CUTTING EDGE ISSUES

Stanley was always on the cutting edge with regard to social issues. Increasingly racial injustice would draw his attention. In April he was in Columbia, SC for a series of meetings. On his last night (April 29) Stanley spoke at the First Presbyterian Church. This was the primary election day for the office of mayor. The week before, the city election board purged from the roll of eligible voters all African

Americans. Before he spoke Stanley read, "Obituary for Democracy." Carried the next day on the front page of the *State* newspaper Stanley is quoted: "Democracy died today in the city when suffrage was denied citizens of this state, the only reason being the color of their skin."[40]

George Green, the reporter for the newspaper, countered that, "Every injustice done to the Negro in America is picked up by the Japanese and exploited for all it is worth. Doctor Jones, who has spoken at Columbia churches and schools since Sunday, argued. "Everything that happens here on a racial issue goes through the bazaar of the East...."[41]

Stanley pointed out that all during the war, almost no one questions the glaring and monstrous hypocrisy of asking African Americans to sacrifice their very lives overseas for a nation that defiantly refuses to give them any meaningful form of equality at home."

In late May, 1942 Stanley "had two days in Jackson, Mississippi under the auspices of the Negroes." They had a public meeting at night with twenty-five hundred Whites and fifteen hundred Blacks in the municipal auditorium. There were two Bishop Greens presiding and neither one was green. One was White and the other Black. This Jackson, Mississippi meeting would cause a stir well into the fall.[42] All this would become grist for his *Christ of the American Road* to be published in just over a year.

Stanley then reported that at his Blue Ridge, NC Ashram, again, as in 1941, members of the "colored race made very distinct contributions."

Then another important issue surfaces. Stanley would continue to hold his own evangelistic meetings through the end of June, including a Pastor's School in Dallas and an address at the National Education Association in Denver. In July he began holding his ashrams returning to one at Occidental College in Los Angeles. While on the west coast he spoke at several "relocation" camps for Japanese Americans. These internment camps, set up by the U.S. military after

Pearl Harbor, were established by executive orders from President Roosevelt and acts of Congress. All Japanese Americans on the West Coast, regardless of citizenship or loyalty to the United States, were ordered to leave their homes and report to these camps.

Remarkably, in the late spring of 1942, Japanese American pastors on "The Sunday Before" the Japanese Americans were evacuated to Assembly Centers preached in their various churches words of encouragement and hope. Copies of many of these sermons were compiled in a book. Stanley wrote the "Preface." There he writes, "120,000 Japanese Americans are in Relocation Centers that in reality are detention camps. 80% are American citizens and 50% are Christians. If their faith in democracy and their faith in God survive this ordeal, they will have proved themselves great Americans and great Christians."[43]

Stanley, after speaking at internment camps at Santa Anita and Pomona, devised a plan for individual churches to sponsor one or more Japanese American families. That is, to adopt the families until they became self-sufficient, and to include them within their fellowships. In reference to these families, Stanley wrote, "I have never felt the breathless silence of a spiritual craving more deeply in any meeting anywhere in the world."

July 10 1942, while still at Occidental, Stanley writes to his friends the Robinsons that perhaps the American Friends Service Committee, a well-known and highly regarded Quaker social service agency, could carry out the Japanese American resettlement under the sponsorship of the Federal Council of Churches.

Mark A. Dawber (of the Home Missions Council of North America) stated that it would be difficult to create "a general public opinion favorable to the American Japanese." He asked Stanley if he would be willing to campaign across the country in the interest of creating such a public opinion. Stanley responded that certainly he would use his existing schedule to make attempts to create such public opinion but that he could not cancel the engagements he now had.

He would need help from churches across the country. The churches did not respond.

Unfortunately, after continuing to exchange letters with various individuals and organizations throughout July and August, Stanley was unsuccessful in his attempts to move Japanese Americans out of the internment camps and re-assimilate them into American society.[44] The end result was that not only did these Japanese Americans remain in these camps throughout the war, they would become targets of public resentment and hostility for many years after the war. In fact, it was not until 1988 that Congress finally appropriated money to compensate the survivors of these camps for the loss of property and liberty.[45]

During these days (the summer of 1942) more and more people were asking Stanley why he remained in the U.S. and did not return to India. Stanley reported that he had heard from several sources that the British Government would not give him the necessary visa for him to return. He would later (January 1943) ask Diffendorfer to explain that his furlough had been extended.[46]

Meanwhile Mabel was alone in India. In one of her *Newsletters* (September 1942) she wrote: "There seems to be no possibility of my husband getting back into India until the war is over. Eunice and her husband are still here but they are stationed a long, long ways from Sitapur. I often wish Eunice were in America."[47]

To complicate matters even more, the vital connection her letters served in asking for support back in the U.S. was constantly detoured and then censored. Food had to be rationed and costs were inflated. A lump of sugar was given only on Sundays and meat only twice a week (or less if they could save some money to help the poor instead). When asked by her admirers, "What is your hobby?" she answered thoughtfully, "Boys, just boys."[48]

Speaking of her boys, Mabel wrote at the time that of those who had been in her school since 1911, "Some are in very responsible positions in Government service, dozens are preachers or teachers; some serve in hospitals as nurses and compounders; many are in business; others are electricians, radio mechanics, farmers, tailors, all decent self –supporting Christian men helping to build up a self-supporting Christian church…".[49]

In the meantime, Jim Mathews had been commissioned as a First Lieutenant in the U.S. Army and assigned to the Supply and Quarter-master Corps in Karachi. The U.S. army did not need any more chaplains but they needed people who knew the language and the terrain. He was hired and served as a supply officer helping to get supplies over the "hump" (the Himalayas) into China. Eunice joins him there in a secretarial post at his headquarters. The word soon surfaced about her considerable secretarial skills. She was immediately assigned to the new Office of Strategic Services (OSS) — a forerunner of the CIA set up in Karachi. Perhaps remembering that her mother would never reveal the pen name she used to write books earlier in her life, Eunice, for the rest of her life, would never divulge the secured private information from the OSS.

When Jim was transferred to Chabua, Assam, Eunice obtained a transfer to Chabua and was again assigned to his headquarters. They were fortunate to find living quarters on a tea estate off base.

Jim's work overseeing shiploads of supplies arriving from the U.S. was demanding and challenging as these supplies were vital for the war effort. Although Jim was never an official chaplain, over the next four years he performed baptisms and burials, celebrated the Eucharist and counseled troops.

Back in Sitapur, Mabel is frustrated, "If only the India leaders would get together and draw up a constitution and the Mohammedans and the Hindus would stop bickering, India could have independence at once except for control of the army and that is promised as soon as the war is over. But no! Leaders demand independence first."[50]

WITH BROTHER STANLEY, SIGNIFICANT ISSUES CONTINUE TO SURFACE

On August 10, 1942, Stanley wrote to President Roosevelt claiming that "British imperialism is in danger of entangling the Indian situation into hopeless knots. The Tory mind still has hopes of being left with the possession of India. In this they are dreadfully mistaken. India will get freedom, with or without the consent of the British. It would be far better to give the consent than to have it wrung from her."

Related to this, Stanley further suggested a joint Pacific Charter with Britain declaring their aims in the Pacific. Stanley enclosed a copy of this Charter that he had modeled on the Atlantic Charter that FDR and Churchill had already drawn up in 1941 for postwar Europe. The Atlantic Charter would become the basis for NATO. Stanley's Charter proclaimed its belief in democracy defined — as always — as "equality of opportunity." Moreover, equality of opportunity should apply to "all areas of life," including institutions — political, social, economic, and religious.[51]

Predictably, this Pacific Charter proposed a "new world order" that would consist of several points with particular focus on the grossly unfair distribution of wealth and resources between the poor nations and the rich nations of the world. This too was a Kingdom of God principle that would lift equality of opportunity (more equitable distribution of opportunity), to the consciousness of the world — postwar.

Interestingly, the issue of Britain giving up India was to become the major sticking point. The wartime alliance with Britain was critical and the issue of India so clouded the Pacific Charter that although Stanley did receive an official response to his Pacific Charter proposal from the State Department, the message was basically, "Thanks but no thanks. "

Nonetheless, Stanley's letter might have had some effect. In September, 1941, when Churchill delivered his House of Commons speech that India was not to be included in the Atlantic Charter, FDR did manage to bring some pressure on Churchill to give India more freedom and responsibility so that it could have a more independent role in the war effort.

Some believe that FDR's reading of the Pacific Charter may have had an important role in motivating the President to give the Atlantic Charter a truly global significance. This would also expose British moral and spiritual hypocrisy in applying the Atlantic Charter to white, Western nations but excluding non-white, non-Western parts of its own empire.[52]

DO BLACK LIVES MATTER?

Throughout the fall of 1942 the issue of race, especially the interracial meetings, began to resurface. In late November a Methodist pastor in Texas wrote to the World Service Agencies of the Methodist Church in Chicago asking why Jones was sent into the deep South with his out-spoken bitter opposition to the Jim Crow laws. He added that "Jones' views are not sane and he is a liability to the cause of missions and world service. He tends dangerously toward Communism, Socialism and especially social equality between all races."[53] He then wrote further that, "The laymen to whom we look for money are asking serious questions... It is my humble judgment that the Socialists and Communists are using the negro as a means of advancing their cause in the south and Dr. E. Stanley Jones is one of the chief aids to this cause."

It should be noted that by the start of WWI, every southern state had passed Jim Crow laws. These became entrenched over the next few decades. These laws permeated nearly every aspect of public life, including railroads, hotels, hospitals, restaurants, neighborhoods, and even Cemeteries. Whites had their facilities; blacks had theirs. The white facilities were better built and equipped. In particular, white schools were almost uniformly better in every respect, from buildings to educational materials. States saw to it that their black citizens were essentially powerless to overturn these laws, using poll taxes and literacy tests to deny them the right to vote. Jim Crow even extended to the federal government. Early in the twentieth century, discriminatory policies were rife throughout federal departments, and not until the Korean War (1950–53) did the armed forces stop segregating personnel into black and white units.

Before responding to the charges published in the World Service Agencies of the Methodist Church, however, Stanley accepted more requests for his services as preacher and evangelist. He spoke in Williamsport, PA to all the public school teachers. He then spoke to the supervisors, executives, and heads of departments of all the industries in the city. Finally he spoke to all the luncheon clubs of the city.[54] Imagine!

Then, on December 12, a disgruntled Jones, after waiting for over two weeks to insure a reasoned response to the charges of his being a Communist and Socialist in his attitude toward the Jim Crow laws, gave this reply."

You ask why I should come to the South? I was born in the South and educated there — may I not visit my homeland? You say that I am guilty of an "outspoken advocacy of bitter opposition to the Jim Crow law here." If that is a crime then I plead guilty. If [asking] for equal rights for citizens of the American democracy is a crime, then I'm guilty. You say: "He tends dangerously — toward social equality between all races…." If this is a crime, then so be it. It is treason against Democracy and against the Christian faith to advocate inequality of treatment of races.

If I should be kept back from India permanently, which God forbid, then I should consider seriously giving the balance of my working days to help the Negroes of America to an equal status in our democracy and to their fullest development as a people. Notably, the color question has become a worldwide question….

You suggest that I "tend dangerously toward Communism." In

my book, *Christ Alternative to Communism*, I advocate neither Socialism, nor Communism, nor any other "ism" but I advocate the Kingdom of God on earth. If that is treason, make the most of it.[55]

This has been described as Stanley's "most providentially inspired, his most perceptive and most prophetic of all the letters written on the subject."[56] He insisted that, "Race prejudice is not inherent; it is socially imposed. A child knows nothing of it."[57]

If racial issues were only beginning to become the focus of public attention in the U.S. in 1942, they were already the focus of international attention because of WWII. Stanley had already named the racial dimensions of Japanese imperialism in the Pacific.

ECUMENISM IS BACK

Between December 1942 and June, 1943 Stanley published three articles on ecumenism, first in the *Christian Century*, a second in the *Christian Advocate* and another in the *Christian Century*. The common thread was to become a new focus (if not obsession) — Church Union. As he engaged issues relevant to the Pacific Charter, he had traced his thinking and praying about a new world order to early Methodist influences.

First, John Wesley's understanding of "the world is my parish," was consistent with Stanley's understanding of the Kingdom of God as a Methodist/Wesleyan emphasis on church union. Again, Wesley often quoted, "If your heart is as my heart then give me your hand." Stanley would begin to see this rubric as a "federal union." In his *Song*, Stanley saw three ways of uniting American Christians: amalgamation, federation and federal union. Interestingly, he would model his three forms of ecumenical polity on the history of the American states in their various efforts to create a United States of America. We will learn more about this argument for federal union in his *Christ of the American Road* to be published in 1944.[58]

AND THE INDIAN INDEPENDENCE

In January1943 Stanley wrote to Roosevelt again. Churchill's non-inclusion of India in the Atlantic Charter meant that the political battle of the East has already been lost. Stanley, the forever optimist, believed that the situation could yet be salvaged but that Roosevelt was the only one who could do it. Stanley suggested that FDR give clear and convincing support of his appreciation for "Britain of Democracy," but at the same time denounce the imperialism of the "Britain of Empire. Otherwise the U.S. must be prepared to go to war every 25 years to rescue that British Empire from the wars that imperialism arouses. This would include not only India but also all of the non-white majority populations of Asia, Africa and Latin America.[59]

Once again the ultimate source of all this for Stanley was his concept of a new world order as the Kingdom of God.

AND STANLEY'S FOREVER PRESSING ROUTINE

Still early in 1943 Stanley continues his seemingly impossible schedule. He speaks at a youth conference in Georgetown, Texas and held meetings in a Unitarian Church sponsored by the Ministerial Association of Quincy, Massachussetts.

Not surprisingly, by the end of February 1943, all of this was beginning to affect his health. He wrote to Diffendorfer from Eugene, Oregon that for "ten days I have been skirting pneumonia. The doctors begged me to give up and go to the hospital but I told them I had not missed an engagement in twenty-five years, so they allowed me to go on, on the condition that I would whisper into the microphone. I then carried on a whispering campaign. I have come through it and am well again.[60]

Then, unbelievably on February 29 (Sadie Hawkins Day) Stanley spoke to 3,000 students at Oregon State University in Corvallis, Oregon. In spite of the fun and frivolity, "two minutes after he began to speak, the students "were in pin drop silence and never moved for three quarters of an hour" as he presented Christ.[61]

From Oregon Stanley is back to Los Angeles for the Breakfast Club and then to a High School in Hollywood before moving on to Nevada to speak to the State Legislature there. Then in March, still on the West Coast Stanley gave a radio address from Los Angeles to the Japanese internment camps. He then spoke on India to the prestigious Commonwealth Club in San Francisco and then addressed 3,000 prisoners at San Quentin.

Next we find Stanley speaking to the students at the University of Tennessee in Knoxville. The entire student body attended his meeting and "nearly all of them" stayed "for an after meeting for personal decision. Stanley then held meetings at Berea College in KY. In several of these meetings he arranged for the Rev. Paul Turner, an African American lawyer and minister, to lead the music.[62]

In April 1943 Stanley wrote that he was excited about the success of *Abundant Living*. After only 4 and a half months in publication there were 150,000 copies in print. All the while he continues to collect material for *The Christ of the American Road*, once again in an attempt to "interpret the kind of Christianity emerging out of the American civilization."

In the summer of 1943 Stanley writes to Miss Nellie about a "great meeting" in Chicago with the Negroes. The African-Americans in that great meeting were deciding whether they would embark on civil disobedience of the Jim Crow Laws across the country. Wisely, they decided not to have it as a mass movement but to pick out a few places — Richmond, Washington, New York and Chicago — and have only trained disciplined volunteers who would disobey Jim Crow and then take the consequences. ... "I was the only white speaker and they took my message wonderfully. I hope I helped to turn them into non-violent channels."

Predictably, Stanley's outspoken advocacy of racial equality was rooted in his concept of the Kingdom of God. For Stanley the laws of the moral universe were the principles of the Kingdom of God applied to human behavior and the first law of the moral universe was equality. We are all created with equal moral dignity by God; therefore, we should all have equal moral dignity in the eyes of one another. God created human beings to live and interact in a world governed by these laws of the moral universe. When we obey these laws, we cooperate with God in the purposes of God's human creation and we reap the abundant fruit of living in harmony with both God and others. When, however, we knowingly disobey these laws, we resist God's purposes and reap the bitter fruit of living in tension and conflict with ourselves, with God and with those around us. This is why Stanley insisted on racial equality for all people around the world. Racial equality was a Kingdom principle.[63]

The month of June, 1943 Stanley was in Mexico, holding evangelistic meetings in Monterrey, Saltillo, Aguacalientes, Guadlajara, Mexico City and Chihuahua. In Mexico City about 1200 people attended each night. Toward the end of the tour (June 30) he wrote to his good friends the Robinsons that the churches were "packed out." About 1100 (according to local estimates) would stay after preaching for counseling.

Then, while still in Mexico, Stanley published a third article on federal union in the *Christian Century*, "Federal Church Union — A Reply" (June, 1943). The first had been in the *Christian Century*, a second in the *Christian Advocate*. Here Stanley responded to various criticisms of his proposal for federal union of Christian churches. At the beginning he insisted that this was not his proposal but "a proposal proposed to me" (no doubt his "inner voice"). "As I was walking across the veranda of a mission house in India about six years ago, not thinking about church union at all, suddenly there it was — the whole proposal, in full bloom. Again, it seemed to be 'given,' from a source outside of myself."[64]

Although Stanley was careful about any claims of a divine rev-

238

elation (not to mention his "inner voice"), he did believe that God was directing him to the relevance of federal union and that gave him "an inner poise and detachment about the whole matter." Since this was God's idea — not Stanley's — he knew that he was not ultimately responsible for its adoption and implementation, or even its rejection. *This general attitude was important.* It enabled him to endure scathing and sometimes slanderous criticism, the kind he had received over his decision to resign the episcopacy, the controversy over the economic withdrawal from Japan, his criticism of the Madras Conference, or even racial equality. This same detachment, believing that these issues were Kingdom of God related and therefore much larger than the man, remained a mainstay for Stanley for the rest of his life.[65]

Interestingly, before leaving Mexico, the ever curious Stanley took time to visit a new volcano.[66]

Throughout the next few years, at every opportunity, including his preaching missions, Stanley would speak out against the Jim Crow laws and argue for better treatment of the Japanese internments. As a case in point, Stanley was back in the U.S. in July but during the last three months of 1943 he spent two weeks in each of the Japanese internment camps in Rivers, Arizona, Poston, Arizona, Manzanar, California, and Topaz, Utah. He also managed to visit Canada and then made his first trip to Cuba. In Cuba he held meetings in Havana, Pinar del Rio, Cardenas, Matanzas, Santa Clara, Camaguey, Holquin, and Santiago de Cuba. He writes that he found Cubans most open and receptive.[67]

Now again, however, Stanley was apparently ready to return to India. He felt he had completed the task directed by his "inner voice" back in 1941.

On February 11, 1944, Stanley wrote to the British Passport Control Office in New York City, saying that he wanted to return to his "missionary work" in India. With assurances that he would take no part in politics, he would need freedom to express his deepest convictions. He promises loyalty to the missionary pledge. Furthermore, if allowed to return under these conditions he would endeavor to be a reconciling influence between Britain and India and between the Indians themselves. Several within the Methodist Mission Headquarters questioned the wisdom of his brutal honesty regarding "his need to express his deepest convictions" but Stanley found it difficult to return to India without clarifying his position.

Simultaneously, in February 1944, Stanley was visited by two FBI agents at the prompting of a confidential FBI informant, the FBI Director, J. Edgar Hoover, Harry Hopkins (special assistant to FDR), and FDR himself. In a letter to FDR (December 30, 1943) Stanley had written on behalf of a diverse but representative group of Christian ministers who had met in Washington D.C. "for a three days period of meditation and prayer." Their goal was to pray and then to face together the issues that were profoundly affecting all humanity in these days of crisis, but especially the starving millions in Europe.[68]

Even before President Roosevelt received Stanley's letter, the FBI was receiving information from the confidential source regarding Stanley's involvement in political activities. Hoover had written to Harry Hopkins (December 9, 1943) informing him about a mimeographed letter dated October 27, 1943 addressed, "Dear Comrades." It was written by John J. Handsaker, a minister of the Christian Church in Portland OR, to Rev. Archie Matson of Ketchikan, Alaska....Stanley is mentioned as he had written to Handsaker regarding a friend of Stanley's who had attended a dinner with President and Mrs. Roosevelt. His friend, perhaps prompted by Stanley who believed mistakenly that FDR and Churchill were at odds on this issue, had turned to Mrs. Roosevelt and asked, "Why is it we are not feeding the starving multitudes in Europe?" She then turned and asked her husband. Roosevelt would later deny the conversation as he did not want to give the impression that he and Churchill were at odds.[69]

After a letter written February 21, 1944, the matter was dropped and Stanley makes no more reference to these visits even though he would be revisited by the FBI at least one more time on May 27, 1944. Apparently a FBI employee complained about a speech Stanley had made on the previous day at the Daughters of the American Revolution Hall in Washington. Apparently Stanley mentioned the FBI investigation of all the Japanese Americans released from their various relocation centers. L.R. Pennington, an FBI agent, reassured Stanley that the intent of the investigations was not to relocate but simply to "check up on them." A few days later Stanley wrote the agent thanking him for clarifying the matter.[70]

In the meantime, in April, Diffendorfer attended the General Conference of the Methodist Church in Kansas City. There he discussed Stanley's application for a visa with Stanley's good friend and fellow missionary in India, Murray Titus (also at General Conference).

On April 29, 1944, Stanley wrote to Diffendorfer that the British Passport Office had denied his request for a visa "at this time." Diffendorfer wrote to Stanley that Titus felt that he should have simply applied for the visa without commentary (especially as related to Indian independence). Titus would write to Stanley mid-May saying that Stanley had made a "tactical mistake." Stanley's immediate response was to say that it was not a tactical mistake but that his honest response simply placed him in a morally advantageous position.

Then, Stanley, published a rather curious article in the *Christian Century*, "Gandhi and Christian Missions." In it he wrote that, "A prominent missionary is quoted as saying that Gandhi is 'Enemy Number One' of Indian Christians" (an apparent reference to his unnamed old friend J. Waskom Pickett from a comment published in the *South Carolina Advocate*). Apparently there had been some misunderstanding between Jones and Pickett as Pickett goes on to say that Stanley's comments regarding him [Pickett] as saying that Gandhi was the enemy of Christians was not accurate. What he did say was that "depressed class leaders in India called Gandhi the public enemy number one of their people." Pickett then added that Stanley was "not fully cognizant of the situation as it has unfolded in India since you were last there." Pickett then writes on May 18, 1944, that Stanley should try to get the decision on his visa reversed. "I am eager that this [decision] should not be permitted to cause new antagonism against Great Britain in the U.S.A."

Stanley responds with a three-page letter that he was grateful for Waskom's support of his desire to return to India. "I want to get back to India, Waskom…". He writes that his heart is there but he would have to be free to express his convictions. He then went on to reiterate the evils of British imperialism in India and on the perilous future of Christianity in an independent India. As usual, Stanley felt that he was being led in all of this by his inner voice. He concluded that he had no intention of a personal attack. "I am sorry, dear Waskom, to have to be at seeming odds with you on so vital a question. I love and admire you and have stood by you. But your attitude has troubled me… Forgive me if I've seemed over-blunt."[71]

June 1, 1944, Stanley writes to Lord Halifax explaining his position, especially with regard to his moral conviction regarding India's right to self-government, but also his willingness to stay out of politics as evidenced by his willingness to sign the "missionary pledge." Then Stanley wanted to know why he had been denied the visa. Halifax wrote that if he were to re-apply at the appropriate time (after the war) he would be permitted to return. Still the letters went back and forth. In the end, although other missionaries were permitted to return to India, the British refused Stanley's repeated requests and would not give him a reason for the denial.

No doubt, feeling as if he were being discriminated against, as was his custom this whole matter segued into Stanley's understanding of the Kingdom of God. All individuals are entitled to equal opportunity. The British system was fundamentally wrong; it was morally bankrupt, especially in its attitude toward India and more especially Churchill's refusal to allow India into the Atlantic Charter.

June 15, 1944, Stanley would publish his *The Christ of the American Road* where he would spell out more clearly his arguments for federal union, first mentioned in the three articles published in the *Christian Century* and *Christian Advocate* back in 1943/4. There he spoke of *amalgamation, federation and federal union* as possible solutions for church union, patterned after the formation of the American states.

Immediately, *amalgamation* was out. That was never seriously considered by the framers of the U.S. Constitution. After all, amalgamation is exactly the policy that King George III had tried to enforce when the states were British colonies, and amalgamation was precisely what Americans fought the Revolution to defeat.[72]

Secondly, *federation* was out as this was based on the Articles of Confederation that established a "league of friendship" among the sovereign and independent states. Just like the League of Nations that was created to maintain international peace after WWI, this did not work because "each constituent nation refused to surrender any sovereignty to the League," so that the Articles of Confederation lasted for less than a decade and ended by calling for another convention to establish a more viable national government. Stanley insisted that the Articles of Confederation failed for the same reason that the League of Nations failed. They both violated the "law of the Kingdom of God." He that saves his life shall lose it.[73]

Thirdly, a *federal union* form of unity was an outstanding political success in the U.S. It was a conscious (or unconscious) reliance on a law of the Kingdom of God. The U.S. was successfully created at the Constitutional Convention only because the individual states were willing to surrender some of their sovereignty to a new national government.[74]

Note, Stanley would apply this political history of the American states to the Christian churches in the U.S. He argued that amalgamation or federation would no more work among churches than it had among states. Amalgamation relied too heavily on "a desire for unity," while federation relied too heavily on "a desire for local autonomy and self-expression." Stanley strongly believed that Federal Union was the only way to combine these desires in proper balance.

Stanley called for the federal union of the various American denominations as "The Church of Christ in America." He further believed that this same principle of federal union could be applied to churches around the world as "The Church of Jesus Christ." Initially,

Stanley was encouraged that the World Council of Churches had been created just before WWII, even though it would not be able to function, even in an advisory capacity, until after the war."[75]

In light of all this, in the summer of 1944, two significant events were held, one in Columbus, OH and the other inBuffalo, NY. The Columbus meeting created an organization that became the Association for the Realization of a United Church in America. Stanley's leadership was the inspiration and his concept of federal union was the focus of the discussions. He volunteered to serve as the temporary president until "a leading layman" could be found. Then, the Buffalo meeting announced that "federal union" would be the basis of the organization's efforts to establish one united Christian church in the U.S. They unanimously adopted a "Statement of Purpose." It read in part, *"We commit ourselves to the general principle of Federal Union as offering the most promising plan for the realization of a United Church in America..."*[76]

As a follow-up to the Columbus/Buffalo events, Stanley realized, that in spite of the steadfast support of those who had attended those meetings, the idea did not ignite broad scale grassroots involvement until his August, 8, 1944 Northeast Ashram in Lake Winnipesaukee, N.H. There, Harvey Kazmier, an estate trustee from Boston, was in attendance. When Kazmier heard Brother Stanley talk about federal union he confessed that this became the defining moment in his life. From that point forward Kazmier's passion was to put Stanley's concept of *federal union* into practice among the Christian churches throughout America. This passion was so consuming that he convinced a small group of friends to join him. Together they approached Stanley saying that only with his personal leadership would their dream become a reality. For the moment, however, Stanley had to decline (until 1947).[77] Wait and see!

Although Stanley, by and large, stayed out of American domestic politics, after the Democratic National Convention in Chicago (July 19-21, 1944) he wrote to Vice President Henry A. Wallace from Lake Winnipesaukee on behalf of his Northeast Christian Ashram. Here, he expressed his dismay that Wallace, an outspoken liberal, had been replaced by Harry Truman. This was a fateful decision since FDR died shortly after his inauguration in 1945.

On September 4, 1944 Stanley wrote in his *Circular Letter*, "It has been the best year of my life, the very best." No doubt contributing to this elation was that two months after *The Christ of the American Road* was published all 50,000 copies of the first edition had sold out. Moreover the sales of *Abundant Living* had now passed 300,000. A Chinese bishop sent word that Generalissimo Chiang Kai-shek actually read a page from that book for his devotionals every day.

Stanley then writes that his heart was still in India; but, since the visa had been denied he would "try to be a missionary to my own people and shall continue to speak in behalf of India's freedom while here in America, where it counts more than if I were in India." Prophetically, he announced, "I shall get back to India for India is bound to get her freedom."[78]

In the meantime, Stanley remained active. During this period he was also busily collecting material ("itching to get at it") for a new devotional book to be entitled, *The Way to Power and Poise* (1946). Read it! It will bless you. Anne Mathews-Younes provides this capsule: "The Christian way is not only sanctity; it is sanity. Take it any way you will and pursue it and you will come out to one of two things: if it is not-the-way, you will come to a dead end: if it is the way, you will come to the Way. All the right ways lead to the Way."[79]

In this same September 1944 *Circular Letter*, Stanley, assuming that he would soon be able to return to India, outlined a proposed schedule of activities "for the next ten years" (1944-1954). (Pay attention here!)

For six months of each year (January until June), he would be in India. January to April, he would hold evangelistic meetings. May and June he would be at the Sat Tal Ashram.

Then, for the next six months of each year (July through December), he would be in the U.S., leading ashrams in July and August and then conducting evangelistic campaigns from September until the end of the year. Once the British permitted him to return to India, this "tentative" plan was, in fact, the schedule Stanley would follow for most of the rest of his life.

Stanley rarely made a public comment about his visa denial but he did express himself in a letter to Murray Titus (October 12), "The British are adept in the art of diplomacy and there is no beating them at this game…. But at least, they didn't dare say that the reason I put, was the reason for the refusal. They took refuge in secrecy."[80]

Surprisingly, Stanley's disillusionment with the Democratic Party after the Convention in Chicago led him to write to O.G. Robinson (November 2), "I am not voting for anybody because I did not register. Thomas [Norman Thomas, the Socialist candidate for president] would be the only man I could honestly vote for."[81]

Until the end of 1944 (November and December), Stanley is seemingly consumed with writing and conducting a series of evangelistic meetings, one in London, Ontario where there was such "splendid preparation… that twenty leading laymen called on the firms and factories of the City and asked the heads of these organizations to do 3 things: (1) Will your firm sponsor the Mission (allowing the use of their name as sponsor; (2) Will you send personal invitations; (3) Will you as head of the firm come to a luncheon? Of the two hundred and eight firms called on, one hundred and seventy-seven agreed."[82]

The other meetings were in St. Louis, MO. This mission was devoted exclusively to high school students (approx. 25,000 teenagers at 16 high schools—half under no real religious influence). To Miss Nellie he wrote on December 13, 1944 that he spoke on that day to 3,000 in two assemblies, "one colored and the other white." Then between speaking engagements he conducted interviews with students.

During this same time (while speaking to the youth) Stanley attended a meeting in St. Louis conducted by two officials from the U.S. State Department to acquaint the public in the midwest on a Dumbarton Oaks (a mansion in Georgetown, Washington D.C.) proposal for the United Nations. This was the first proposal of a world organization committed to maintaining peace after the war. Stanley wrote to his friend O.G. Robinson on December 15, that he applauded the purpose. He then writes further that, "This was the first time democracy of the State Department has come to the [people]. This argues well for the future."[83]

Several questions were raised at the meeting. The first question was, "Does this [proposed organization] go too far." Apparently not as Stanley responds, "No one agreed with this question." Then, "Are the proposals correct as they are?" Two hands went up. Then, "Does the Dumbarton Oaks proposal not go far enough?" The rest of the company (about 50 people) put up their hands. The State Department people must have had a jolt.

Stanley then wrote the Secretary of State, Edward R. Stettinius pointing out just one defect. "This thing seems to be a military alliance between five nations with a padding of democracy around it. That is not collective security — it is five nations (the U.S., the U.K., France, Russia and China) as the five permanent members of the UN Security Council telling the world what to do. No five nations are good enough or wise enough to boss the world." Stanley further suggested that they make these five nations temporary for the duration of the war and then transfer their power to a General Assembly. Stanley believed that ultimately they would need to lose their lives in order to gain them. In addition, Stanley was obviously concerned about the scores of nations (like India) that were subject to European imperialism. He then concluded the letter, "I trust, Mr. Stettinius, you will be courageous enough to insist upon this fundamental change. If so, you may completely change the complexion of the world situation. Now it is dark and foreboding."[84]

By the end of 1944 Stanley had so solidified his Kingdom of God principles that they clearly affected his attitudes toward all of his major issues. For example,

1. His opposition to British imperialism in India.
2. His proposal of a Pacific Charter as a guarantee of equity for all people everywhere,
3. His attempts to advocate church leadership in the resettlement of Japanese Americans.
4. His insistence on racial equality in his own meetings.
5. His Kingdom principles were also foundational for his ideas for federal union of Christian churches. His struggle with church unity had been building for half a decade.[85]

Self-surrender was, of course, the key to Jesus' expression and embodiment of the Kingdom of God in the New Testament. Reduce the words of Jesus to one sentence and it would probably look something like this: *To gain your life is to lose it, to be great is to be a servant, to be first is to be last.* While most Christians restricted the application of this kind of self-surrender to personal morality, Stanley was more holistic and expanded this Kingdom principle to corporate relationships between and among human institutions, especially the church at large. This prompted his vision of Federal Union as a way for Christians to speak as one. If they could resolve their theological and doctrinal differences, they could avoid the disunity that weakened her moral voice when speaking out on economic, social and political issues.

On January 2, 1945. Leo Pasvolsky, special assistant to Secretary of State, Stettinius, replied on the Secretary's behalf. He welcomed the opportunity to respond to Stanley's blunt criticism of the previous month that the proposed international organization (the U.N.) was really a military alliance disguised as a peace-keeping body. Pasvolsky's response was serious, thoughtful and reasoned. Obviously the two had different world views. Pasvolsky spoke from the "realistic" perspective of the purely secular mind. Stanley spoke from the perspective of the ultimate reality of the Kingdom of God. In classic Stanley Jones fashion, he argued that nations, like people, if they are to maintain international peace, must renounce sin and die to the slavery of selfishness — they must renounce self-interest by voluntarily giving up some of their sovereignty to an international organization whose ultimate allegiance is the Kingdom of God as revealed by Jesus Christ. This is important!

STANLEY IS IN LATIN AMERICA: APRIL TO EARLY AUGUST, 1945

After some hesitancy, due to considerable pressure from friends wanting him to attend the San Francisco Conference where the earlier Dumbarton Oaks proposals on the U.N. would be finalized, Stanley nonetheless decided to go ahead with his Latin American tour. Although he and others believed that he could have made a significant impact on that Conference, in the end he did not regret leaving for Latin America.[86] In the *Indian Witness* he wrote that he arrived " at just the right psychological moment."[87] The stage was set. First, the Roman Catholic Church, after what they interpreted as an uncertain peace following the global War, left a spiritual vacuum. Secondly, there was a religious and intellectual skepticism that was the result of the authoritarian control of the Roman Catholic Church. Stanley wrote that Latin American is just as religious as North America, except among the intellectuals. The Roman Catholic Church had, according to Stanley, weakened the character of the people. She had refused to allow the people to think or act independently — a mentality of spiritual and intellectual subservience."

Believing all this to be true, Stanley was in Santiago, Chile on April 29, 1945 where he mailed a handwritten note to Murray Titus. "I am having a grand time. There was enthusiasm among the 'Evangelicals.'" He had just spoken in the Municipal Theater, the first time ever it was given to Evangelical/Protestants, and with incredible results.

Stanley was in Argentina on VE day — May 8 — marking the unconditional surrender of Nazi Germany. Ironically, he writes to the

Christian Century, that his first day in Buenos Aires, just 15 minutes after reaching the hotel, two volleys of shots sounded in the street below. Some reported that as many as seventy were killed and many more wounded. The powers that be, the political—"a *fascist-minded* jittery government resting on bayonets," and the religious—"*a repressive Roman Catholic Church* who feared her lack of control over her people," left an opportunity for Protestant Christians. Suddenly, Protestant evangelical Christianity was no longer the religion of "Yankee" imperialism; it was the religion of personal freedom and political democracy. The door was open. Stanley was excited.[88]

Murray Titus (writing from Sao Paulo, Brazil, May 31, 1945) states that although it was unfortunate that Stanley had to miss the San Francisco meeting that his ministry in Latin America has born much fruit. Stanley maintained an incredibly hectic pace on this trip. Toward the end of July, he wrote, "I found they had me down for eight addresses for one day—I took six. In several other places I took seven! But I came out at the end of the series fresh and well" (shades of John Wesley). Stanley found that what sustained him through pressing and ceaseless demands was first of all *the inner resources of the Holy Spirit*. He also felt that Latin America was primed—psychologically and spiritually—for the greatest period of revival ever dreamed of—great enough and Christian enough and united enough to meet the hour of great opportunity."[89]

Following the surrender of Germany in May, Japan surrendered in August 1945 (the signing of the treaty would take place on September 2). Stanley is back to the U.S. in August as well.

Eunice (now pregnant) would arrive in New York on September 19. Jim would not join her for another ten months. Eunice stayed first with Jim's sister and her husband in Montclair, NJ and later with her cousins, Howard and Georgeanna Jones, both physicians in Baltimore. Stanley would join her for Christmas in Baltimore. Before the baby, Anne Treffry Mathews, was born, Eunice managed to find and buy an apartment in Manhattan.

The war is over. Stanley talks about the need for peace and the tragedies of war.

You just met Stanley and Mabel's first grandchild, Anne Mathews-Younes. She was kind enough to share with me a recent paper delivered in Japan entitled, "Japan Peace Talk." There she writes that

> E. Stanley Jones, as a fully surrendered person to Jesus, lived his life committed to peace and was vehemently opposed to war, knowing full well its tragic results on all of God's children. I want to share with you Jones' reasons for opposing war. Jones provides guidance for us today as we choose to become mediators of peace — peacemakers, who through words and deeds. introduce others to the Prince of Peace, Jesus Christ.

> War, according to Jones, is *a means* out of harmony with *the ends* it hopes to accomplish. War, therefore, is the vast illusion "the illusion that you can get to right ends by wrong means. It simply cannot be done. This is a fond and futile hope. Jones was opposed to war for many reasons, but first of all because war causes men [and women] to sin. Men [and women] caught in the act of war, do things they would never dream of otherwise.[90]

Anne Mathews-Younes lists her grandfather's various ways that war causes us to sin.

> First, it poisons the air with lies. The first casualty in war is Truth. War then poisons the air with hate. If the first casualty is Truth, the second casualty is Love.

> Then war causes us to sin economically. It creates waste and causes hunger. It exploits the helpless. War causes sin against persons. 40,000,000 lives were lost (either directly or indirectly) in WWII alone. War propagates the lie that war protects the innocent when in fact it protects the guilty. War exposes the innocent, both soldier and civilian alike, leading to insensate, useless slaughter.

> War also kills the consciences of persons. It lays hold of our finest virtues and prostitutes them. It lays hold on patriotism, hero-

ism, self-sacrifice, idealism, and turns them toward destruction. War stands against everything that Christ stands for. It sins against Christ. If war is right, Christ is wrong; and if Christ is right, war is wrong. Christ and war are irreconcilables. If I must make my choice, writes Jones, "I choose Jesus."

Our Muslim friends quote our Old Testament in justifying their attitudes toward war. Realize that the *Qur'an* is a re-interpretation of the Old Testament just as our New Testament is a re-interpretation of the Old Testament. Jesus says, "You have heard it said, but I say unto you." You can never make a case for war out of the mouth of Jesus, the prince of peace.

Dr. Mathews-Younes then concludes her address with Brother Stanley saying,

...that people don't want war. They hate it. They do want peace. But the political leaders of the nations do not seem to be able to orchestrate world peace. Here is a world hating war, afraid of war, and yet consistently drifting into war. Are we in the hands of a cruel fate, or is there something wrong with us and our attitudes? Perhaps the saying *is* true, most wars are the result of the male ego.

Stanley insisted that "we could 'stop' wars, by the use of the word *we*. If we said "we," then we would be free from war. The education of the human race is education in the use of one word, and only one word "we." When we learn that one word and live in our world as if that word matters, we would be living with our brothers and sisters, we would be mature as a race and free from war."

Brother Stanley, therefore, renounced war and was determined to give the balance of his days to finding a better way for himself and others to prevent it. He not only wrote about his deep opposition to war, he participated in our world as one who was always looking for ways to live in peace.[91]

STANLEY'S RETURN TO INDIA

Stanley was now more than ready to return to India. The British had stated that "after the war" he could re-apply. Sir Girga Shankar Bajpai was handling his request for the visa. Stanley also wrote to Lord Halifax on August 27 asking for his support. Stanley also met Mr. Rhys Davies, a member of Parliament in the Labour Government of Britain while lecturing across the country. Stanley wrote to Diffendorfer regarding Davies reaction. Davies said that Stanley's denial of a visa had been suppressed in England as it would have raised a great storm had it been known. He offered to raise the issue in Parliament if necessary.

Then on November 16, 1945 Stanley received permission to return to India. This time it was the Methodist Division of Foreign Missions, not the British Government that would hold Stanley accountable for his pledge. Again he said he would refrain from politics and endeavor to be a reconciling influence between Britain and India and between Indians and themselves. He did, however, insist that he be able to respond to issues when asked in public meetings. He eventually asked the Methodist Division of Foreign Missions to sign the pledge in his behalf.

After the war Stanley would find convincing evidence among both Americans and Japanese to support his earlier conclusion that there was a genuine Japanese peace party that was sincerely committed to finding a way to avoid war with the U.S. in the Pacific. Interestingly, General Douglas MacArthur told Stanley, "I agree with you; they [the Japanese] knew nothing of what was going to happen at Pearl Harbor." Admiral Nomura told him, "We had no notion of Pearl Harbor...."

Stanley would also continue to pursue the idea of giving New Guinea to Japan after the war. He even raised the question with General MacArthur during the American occupation of Japan. MacArthur's response was positive. "I've fought all over that country (New Guinea), and it is the most lush, underdeveloped country in the world…. The Japanese, being the best farmers of the world, could make a paradise out of it."[92] Stanley agreed but then expressed a word of caution to MacArthur, "If we continue to police as an overlord in that area of the Pacific there will be no lasting peace; and we shall be hated as few nations have been hated. Another war would be inevitable."

In light of Vietnam, Stanley's warning was both ominous and remarkably prophetic. Perhaps Stanley's inner voice led him to make his prophetic warnings about the disastrous consequences of an American policy of imperialism in the Far East.[93]

In Mabel's November 1945 *Newsletter* she writes that in January she would begin the eighth year of the hardest term she had ever had in India. "But I have repeatedly been glad that I was an old missionary and not a young girl in her first or second term. The war is over, but our anxieties are not. God has cared for us beyond what we had dared hoped, but sometimes there is not perfect peace."[94]

E. Stanley Jones, Eunice, Jim, Anne and Jan, 1949

Jim and Eunice, 2004 (Eunice's 90th Birthday Celebration)

Eunice and Stanley, 1916

CHAPTER EIGHT

THE ROAD TO INDIAN INDEPENDENCE

Stanley's Need to Reestablish his Ministry in India and Assist in India's Struggle for Independence; Mabel, Eunice and Jim are Now in the U.S.

Critical for the next five years (1946 to 1950), is that for Stanley, his single greatest passion involves the question, "Do you want to be different? Apart from self-surrender, all our surrenders to God are marginal and unimportant." The deepest conviction of Stanley's life is this: "Self-surrender is the way to self-expression. You realize yourself only as you renounce yourself. *You find God when you renounce yourself as God.* The self is trying to play God, trying to organize life around itself as God, and it simply does not work. The universe does not back it. You must lose your life to find it [the first principle of Christianity]. Lose your life to a higher will and then working out of that will, you will find your life again."[1]

Think on this.

In his *Circular Letter* for January 3, 1946, Stanley wrote that he had booked a passage to India and that he has no regrets for having spent this time in his native country. He had obeyed his inner voice to express God's kingdom reality and to apply it to the catastrophic "unreality" of WWII. He then wrote to Miss Nellie a handwritten postscript on January 7, that as he was preparing to sail he found a letter to her unsent. "So sorry. But it was Providence that I found it. I will send it off with the pilot. We are about to leave."[2]

STANLEY SAILS FOR INDIA, JANUARY 10, 1946

Stanley is back in Sitapur on February 8. He is delighted to be reunited with Mabel. The next day their son-in-law James Mathews paid them a surprise visit, but almost immediately Stanley is off again on an evangelistic tour around India and Mabel was on her own again.

Stanley now realizes, especially after the visit with Jim, that the India he had left six and half years earlier was not (much to his astonishment) the same India. It was rocked with strife and conflict and filled with bitterness and hate. What had happened? WAR was the most obvious answer but the larger question was, did the war help or hinder India's struggle for independence? Only time would tell.

The issue now was not Britain's intransigence, but the incessant violent conflicts between Hindus and Muslims. The leader of the Muslim League in India was Muhammad Ali Jinnah. Jinnah was originally an Indian nationalist who supported the Indian National Congress and its goal of Indian independence. In the late 1930s, however, he became "a bitter Muslim communalist" whose goal was the creation of a separate Muslim state independent of both Britain and Hindu India.

The primary task of the British Cabinet "Mission" negotiations in 1946 was to accommodate both Hindu and Muslim demands within the framework of self-government. The mission proposed a national government for British India, with limited powers, while insuring that the interests of both Hindu-majorities and Muslim-majorities would be protected. The Cabinet Mission attempted to set up an interim government but Muslims and Hindus could not agree on the composition.

Then on March 15, 1946, Clement Attlee, not known for his oratory skills, gave a rousing speech in the House of Commons. In it he stated that India would have independence (the word used for the first time); this independence would be within or without the commonwealth, and India would decide. If India decided to go out of the commonwealth, Britain would try to make the transition as smooth as possible. No minority would hold back the progress of the majority. It was said that this statement was so clear and so honest that it changed the emotional climate of a subcontinent overnight. A few days later Stanley was invited to a dinner party given by a Brahman so that he could meet the leading men of the city. Stanley remarked at the close: "For the first time in forty years I find myself in a mixed gathering of this kind, made up of men of the East and West, without any sense of tension."[3]

Such optimism was premature, however. There were still serious issues between Hindus and Muslims. Then there was Pakistan. Stanley could scarcely believe that Muslims would want to divide India. Pakistan for Muslims would hurt the 40 million Muslims in India more than it would hurt India as Muslims in India were unwilling to be a peaceful minority. They remembered how before British rule they were the proud inheritors of an Islamic destiny.

Stanley included a chapter on Pakistan in his *Gandhi* book saying that this was a chapter that he did not want to write but before his death Gandhi asked him to write about Stanley's correspondence with Jinnah. In that chapter he reminds us that Pakistan (from "Pak," meaning "holy," and "stan," meaning "place") symbolized a holy place of Islam. He concluded the chapter stating that Pakistan must abandon its attempts to set up a theocracy based on the Shariat and instead have a secular state with equal opportunities for all (with no special privileges for any). She must also abandon her separatist mentality and come back into a federal union with India, both for her own salvation and for the salvation of forty million Muslims in India.[4]

On April, 12, 1946 Stanley wrote to Jinnah, speaking as one who was detached both from the Indian and the British side of things. He proposed a possible way out of the impasse (similar to the British plan). First, that the Congress Party accept the "principle" of Pakistan. Second, an agreement between India and Pakistan to form a federal union with respect to defense, foreign affairs and other areas of mutual interest. Then he proposed two constituent assemblies with an Indian constitution and a Pakistani constitution. At the end he asked Jinnah if he would accept this in whole or in part. Jinnah's response (April 27, 1946) was noncommittal. He thanked Stanley but could not respond by means of correspondence; that is, he dare not put it in writing.

During Stanley's remaining time in India during 1946 he focused his efforts on evangelistic meetings and on his Sat Tal Ashram. He spoke in many of the places where he had spoken before the war, including Lucknow, Hyderabad, Travancore, at the Syrian Convention, Vellore and Madras. He comments, "No matter where I began, the theme was always Christ." He is the message that India so deeply needs.

Eventually, Mabel's poor health would not permit her to remain in India much longer. Stanley returned to Sitapur just for a couple of days in April to see how she was doing.

Their first grandchild, Anne, was born in Baltimore on April 17, 1946. Stanley loved his grandchildren and often wrote to them affectionately. Many of his letters to Mabel, Eunice and Jim were prefaced with the greeting, "Kisses for the kiddies." In one of his *Newsletters* for the year Stanley wrote that the grand-baby was indeed a grand baby.[5]

Mabel was now ready to leave India permanently. By her own

admission, she had a tired heart. In fact, just before leaving she spent some time in the Lee Memorial Hospital in Calcutta with another bout of angina. She was 68. All that was left was to find suitable leadership for the boys' school. Once back in the U.S. she would continue to support her boys through scholarship funds that she solicited (mostly by letter) and then administered.

STANLEY AND MABEL RETURN TO THE U.S.

Stanley would return to Sitapur just once more, for a couple of days in June, before leaving by plane for the U.S. The night before he left he asked Mahatma Gandhi for "a message to America from this new India that is coming into being." He replied: "I cannot speak of this new India until I see it in flesh and blood. I am like the disciple who said, 'I will not believe until I put my hand in His side and feel the wound prints. 'So I cannot speak of it or even believe in it until I see it."[6]

Mabel would depart from India by ship that same month leaving her heart behind after having served in India for 42 years. *She would never return*. She arrived back in the U.S. on August 24, 1946.[7]

By the time of Mabel's return Eunice had already been in the U.S. for nearly a year. Jim had returned just before Mabel and joined Eunice and baby Anne in New York City. For Jim, it was a time to embrace wife and daughter and to return to full time ministry. He could have served as a chaplain in the armed services during the war but chose to join the U.S. Army in India because he wanted to live under the same hardships that other American military personnel had to endure. Once in New York, James Kenneth Mathews became Secretary for India in the Methodist Division of Foreign Missions.

Mabel was now considered to be on furlough and her continued support was to be provided by missionary "appropriations" within the Mission Board of the Methodist Church.[8]

As for Stanley, once back in the U.S., from July to December 1946, Stanley spent much of the early summer at his Ashrams but then the rest of the summer and fall, he conducted his public meetings. He was first in South Bend, IN and then in Troy, OH. He wrote to Eunice and Jim that in Troy the mission planners "did something interesting and effective. They signed up 1200 people who would buy and read *Abundant Living* (published in 1942) as preparation for the Mission. Everyday the newspaper carried a reading from it and the pastors spoke on it once a month." He then concluded that the people were ready for a fresh encounter with the living God.[9]

In the midst of all this Stanley receives news from India that on August 16, the Muslim League withdrew from the Cabinet Mission negotiations. That same day Jinnah established August 16, 1946 as "Direct Action Day, when Muslims were to begin their struggle for Pakistan. The result in the words of one British historian was the "biggest and bloodiest outbreak of communal violence under the British regime up to that time."[10] Stanley was grieved.

In October, Stanley was in Mason City, Iowa (with no mention of Mabel in Clayton as she might have already been in route to Florida where she would buy a house and begin spending most her winters in warmer climes). During the rest of 1946 Stanley was in York, PA, Huntington, WV, the University of KY at Lexington, Indianapolis, IN, Mason City, IA, Philadelphia, PA, Toronto, Canada, Newark, NJ, El Paso, TX, Kansas City and St. Louis, MO and Redlands, CA. In some of these places he took along a visitation evangelism team that would go out in the city and make personal calls to win people to Christ. The success was anticipated. God was afoot!

By the end of November we find Stanley in Oklahoma City. The first night he spoke to 5,000 with a great after meeting. He wrote to Jim Mathews that "the last night was Youth Night; there were about 4,000 present…. These Oklahomans are marvelous people. For the first time in the history of the city the Negroes and Whites mingled freely in the auditorium and in the church…. Nearly one-half of those in the choir were colored—a sight for the gods to behold—and the

CHAPTER EIGHT

universe didn't seem to fall on us."[11] Racial equality was always an issue with Stanley Jones and being in such demand he could seemingly pull it off.

Speaking of being in demand, for several months Diffendorfer had been trying to persuade Stanley to attend the International Missionary Council set for the summer of 1947 where they were to consider a five-year plan for evangelism throughout the world. The committee wanted Stanley present. Stanley writes from Mason City, Iowa that he already had four ashrams scheduled for the next summer. Diffendorfer wrote one last time (December 5, 1946) in an attempt to persuade him suggesting that it would be a grave mistake for Stanley to miss this important meeting. Stephen Graham comments that "Perhaps Stanley did not fully understand the purpose and format of the committee meeting and one is tempted to ask if Stanley's decision to stick to his schedule of ashrams (both in the U.S. and India) was a mistake."[12] Somehow, I doubt it.

Stanley spent Christmas with Mabel in Florida, the first Christmas on the same continent for 6 and a half years. The time was short, however, as on December 30 he wrote from a retreat in Washington D.C. that he would soon be leaving for six months in India. In this last *Circular Letter* for 1946 Stanley writes to friends and patrons that when he returns to India he would begin construction at Lucknow of a sanatorium for the purpose of providing both for the spiritual and psychiatric needs of the people. He already had the money for the building as a memorial for E. V. Moorman who had financed his Ashrams in the U.S. This was the only psychiatric hospital in India at the time and continues to be a significant place of healing today.[13]

In the midst of all this, and before he leaves for India, Stanley managed to publish his devotional book, *The Way* (1946). There he gives us marvelous insight into emotions like resentment and the proper response to criticism. First, quoting from 1 *Thessalonians,* "Make sure that nobody pays back wrong for wrong, but always strive to do what is good for each other and for everyone else," he writes, "Remember that resentments have no part nor lot with a Christian. You cannot hold both Christ and resentments. One or the other must go. Do you want to go through life without Christ, chewing on resentments, a bitter, crabby, poisonous person? That's what you are headed for if you allow resentments to fester within you."

Then, once again he gives us this timely advice in response to criticism. "When criticism comes, I ask, Is it true? If it is true, I will change. I am only a Christian in the making, and I'll let this criticism make me. Therefore I owe much to my critics; they are the "the unpaid watchmen of my soul". Bless them! But suppose it isn't true. Suppose the criticism is unfair and unjust. I have determined that I would not change my attitudes toward the criticizer. I would not let his actions determined mine. As far as I know, I have no enemies because I have no enmity."[14] When someone goes low, Stanley always goes high.

INDIA WILL BE FREE!

On January 5, 1947, as Mabel's health was much improved, Stanley returned to India (January through June). He believes that he is returning to a "disturbed India," but in fact he was returning to an expectant and an awakened India, a glorious India in which to work. "I fairly tingle at the thought of it."[15] He flew TWA and even with stops arrived in 48 hours. The only disadvantage to air travel was the limited amount of luggage one could carry. He then concludes that "Your wealth is to be judged not by the abundance of your possessions but in the fewness of your wants!"

Stanley immediately writes to Gandhi that he has returned (the flight shortened the trip by weeks). Gandhi wrote back almost immediately (February 20, 1947), "Dear Dr. Stanley Jones, It almost appears as if you had never gone to America." He comments that air travel "effectively reduced the distances." He then moves quickly to the issues of communal violence, especially as related to the "Direct Action Day." He writes that he did all that he could do to stop it, traveling to some of the most troubled areas (Noakhali and Bihar) and applying his doctrine of *ahimsa,* the Hindu and Jainist concept of nonviolence. *Ahimsa* meant not just the rejection of physical violence but "actively returning good for evil." He writes further that in Noakhali (he had not yet been to Bihar), "Man became brute."

Even as Gandhi was writing to Stanley on February 20, the British Government in London announced that it would transfer power to an independent India no later than June 1948. Lord Mountbatten was appointed the new viceroy to supervise the transition.

Meanwhile, Stanley, like Gandhi, was in close touch with the violence that accompanied India's tumultuous and troubled road to independence. He wrote in a *Circular Letter* (April 1, 1947) that after he spoke in Lahore, the capital of Punjab, "the disturbances began which have resulted in over two thousand deaths and a great deal of arson and looting." Stanley also spoke of Calcutta where caste and communal loyalties brought the city to the brink of civil war. He spoke in a college founded by Dr. Ambedkar, the leader of the outcasts, where 55 of the 1300 students were outcasts. Stanley saw everything in light of the Kingdom of God, even the violence. Then, typical of Brother Stanley, he concluded that in spite of it all, "I find myself coming to the conclusion that I have had the greatest hearing and response I have had in the forty years I have been in India."[16]

Significantly, Stanley noted that the unmerited suffering that Gandhi and other Indian nationalists had experienced when they challenged the British Government with a campaign of nonviolent civil disobedience and fasting shocked the world and defeated the injustice and evil of British imperialism in India. Stanley had insisted that Gandhi's relationship with Britain (like his own relationship with Japan back in 1938) was one of redemptive friendship. The British would finally acknowledge (shades of Attlee) the immorality of their policies in that nation and withdraw from the Indian subcontinent.

IN THE MEANTIME, STANLEY IS OFF TO JAPAN

Briefly, in March, 1947, Stanley is in Tokyo visiting with Kagawa and others, promising to return for preaching missions every other year as long as he was able.

These Japanese missions set up in part by Kagawa would draw the attention of Emperor Hirohito who gave him a personal audience on several occasions. Stanley would also meet with Douglas MacArthur on a number of occasions and with such notables as John Foster Dulles.

On this first visit Stanley was also able to meet with the three Japanese diplomats (Norura, Jurusu and Teraski) whom he had met in Washington D.C. in 1941 but not seen since before the war. They were quick to say that they were just as devastated as Stanley when the Japanese attacked Pearl Harbor. Stanley made a valiant attempt to assure them that the work they had done in DC had still borne fruit. Nomura, after the meeting reiterated that if the cable FDR sent had arrived a week earlier "it might have changed the whole course of history."

Terasaki's American wife, Gwen, recalled Stanley's visit with her husband in March, 1947. As her husband came out of the Imperial Palace, He caught sign of an oddly familiar figure alighting from a taxi on the street below. The man was of medium build and carried himself with military erectness; as he turned from the cab he started briskly up the steps and his handsome head of snow white hair came into full view. It was Stanley Jones whom we had not seen since early December nearly six years before. The two men recognized each other at the same time. They fell into each other's arms and stood on the steps of the Palace weeping.

As soon as it could be arranged, Stanley and Hidenari (Terry) Terasaki met for a meal. With profound wistfulness they talked of the past, what could be done to help Japan recover, and how to prevent the recurrence of another war. It was at this luncheon with Terry that Stanley learned for the first time how nearly they had come to averting the tragedy in the Pacific. Terry informed Stanley that the Emperor had told him that if he had received the cablegram from Roosevelt a day sooner he would have stopped the attack. "What poignant memories my husband and his American comrade shared that night."

Terasaki's daughter, Mariko Miller, now living in the United States, also "recalls many pleasant visits between her father and Dr. E. Stanley Jones." She said that throughout his life, her father carried a letter of gratitude, comfort and reassurance from Dr. Jones, for his efforts on behalf of peace. Terasaki would show this letter to Stanley on the next visit.

"Dr. Jones not only tried to avert war but later tried to keep our Japanese Americans from being placed in internship camps in the United States. Jones specifically asked the Government that these persons be placed under the auspice and support of Christian churches. That was not to be...The Christian churches offered fellowship and support during this crisis, but Jones wanted to do much more."

During this time Stanley was given an Imperial audience with the Emperor by invitation of the Imperial Household. Terasaki met Stanley at the palace and served as the Emperor's interpreter for the conversation. They spoke for close to an hour and the Emperor, aware of Stanley's work in Japan and Washington, thanked him for both and invited him to come back!

After his return to India in early April, (and before leaving the Sat Tal Ashram for the U.S. the end of June), Stanley was consumed by efforts to affect a peaceful transition in India. He reports that he was greatly encouraged by the results of two missionary conventions — one in Kodaikanal in May and the other in Landour, Mussoories in June. These conventions discussed the role and status of Christian missionarie in an independent India. Both conventions, under Stanley's leadership, adopted "A Missionary Declaration" (called the

Landour Declaration) that welcomed the advent of a free and independent India and pledged missionary support for the new government.[17] Stanley also writes to Eunice in April that he had recently spent 10 days at Gandhi's Ashram in Sabarmati staying in the same room where he had stayed on previous occasions.

By late April and early May 1947 we find Stanley at the YMCA in New Delhi. Events were breaking rapidly. Stanley is still concerned about the status of Christian missions in India after independence. He works the system visiting with Chakravarti Rajagopalachari, a prominent Congress Party leader from Madras who succeeded Mountbatten as Governor-General of India after independence. Rajagopalachari assures him that missionaries would be "welcomed and with gratitude if they come in the spirit of humble service."

Stanley then reports meetings with Jawaharlal Nehru, who would soon be Prime Minister, and then with Jinnah. Nehru, like Rajagopalachari, assures Stanley that "We will welcome anyone who throws himself into India, identifies himself with us."

Not surprisingly, the meeting with Jinnah was not so cordial. First Stanley asks about Pakistan. If Congress concedes Pakistan would he be willing to enter union with India? After some banter back and forth suddenly Jinnah said that if Congress would concede Pakistan, "I will enter union with India and mean it." Stanley could scarce believe his ears. This was the very thing Congress had been offering and been turned down. Stanley goes immediately to Nehru and Mountbatten and writes to Gandhi and J.B. Kripalani, then President of the Congress Party. Kripalani thanks Stanley by return post.

However the meeting with Jinnah has an unfortunate sequel — a sad one. Within days Jinnah changed his mind. Stanley is embarrassed, no devastated, by the "moral hurt and disillusionment."

Stanley once again writes to Jinnah during the first week of the Sat Tal Ashram on May 12, 1947. This was to be a last ditch attempt to break the deadlock, first complaining of Jinnah's duplicity. He concluded the letter, "Since I had raised hopes, however dim, in the minds of those to whom I passed on your earlier word to me [of acceptance], I was bound to send them your second word [of rejection]."[18] Jinnah was unresponsive.

Stanley then writes another family letter on May 17, 1947 saying that "The crowd is slow in coming up [to the Ashram] but by the end of next week we will have more than we can accommodate." Along with swimming each day for exercise (he managed to lose five pounds) he begins writing another devotional book, *The Way to Power and Poise*.[19]

Then unbelievably, while Stanley is still in India, Mountbatten worked quickly to prepare for independence, dividing the sub-continent of India into three parts — India, West Pakistan (eventually Pakistan) and East Pakistan (eventually Bangladesh) — and set the dates for independence — August 14, 1947 for Pakistan and August 15, 1947 for India. This caught Stanley off guard along with the nationalist leadership and the British government back in London. He had assumed that India would gain independence in 1948. Stanley was suddenly deeply and intimately involved in negotiations with the top political leadership of the Congress Party and of the Muslim League, including both Nehru and Jinnah. Two issues were dominant — breaking the deadlock between Hindus and Muslims over Pakistan and the status of Christian missionaries in an independent India.

As the dates approached, however, violence erupted in a fury of ethnic cleansing along the borders of India and Pakistan. In Muslim majority districts Muslims attacked minority Hindus and Sikhs. In Hindu and Sikh majority districts Hindus and Sikhs attacked minority Muslims. The result was a holocaust with hundreds of thousands killed and an estimated 10 million refugees.

Gandhi and the leadership of the Congress Party only accepted the partition of Pakistan from India after years of continuing bloody communal violence led to despair. The fighting between Hindus, Sikhs and Muslims had made any other solution seem untenable as incessant communalism continued to thrive.[20]

Meanwhile, on May 10, 1947, Mabel writes to her "Friends" from Clayton, Iowa [Eunice was pregnant with their second child].

"How wonderful to watch spring come to America! It may be an old story to you but after eight years in the tropics it is a lovely experience.

Early in March I hurriedly left Florida for New York. Eunice was ill with pneumonia and baby Anne needed her grandmother. In April I reached Iowa, tired but feeling much better than when I left.

I am sorry so many letters are still unanswered. I have replied to nearly 200 of the most urgent ones since I returned. I am sorry that I cannot accept any speaking engagements. That is doctor's orders.

The letters from India are more and more distressing. Food is hard to get, high in price and poor in quality. Bitterness between Hindu and Mohammadan is increasing.

India will be given her freedom but if she uses that freedom to plunge her country into a religious war some other country will step in and that freedom will be lost.

A Brahman friend writes me, 'Both sides are now trying hard to win over the minorities.' My husband writes of a 'new attitude' toward Christians and I see by the papers that the Hindus dominated. Congress, in an attempt to win over the 60 million outcastes, have voted to abolish caste. …

Religions have certainly 'messed up' things in India. The Mohammadan despises the idol worshiping Hindu. The Hindu, remembering that during Mohammadan rule his idols were broken and temples desecrated, fears the Mohammadan. In neither religion is there any injunction to love one's neighbor."[21]

Mabel then concludes her letter by thanking her readers for their generosity as her boys are still in school. She had written to Dr. Sutherland the previous January that some of her money donated for her boys was going to Stanley. "Please make the Board understand that our marriage is a private one and does not extend to scholarships." She had lost two of her best givers because Stanley had mistakenly thanked them for the money that had been intended for the boys.[22]

At the same time Stanley was still in Sat Tal. He would leave India for the U.S. in late June.

Early July, 1947 Stanley is back in the U.S. He plunges into his summer Ashram schedule saying that they were the best in nine years.

Stanley then spends five days in July at Mabel's in Clayton, Iowa relaxing but resuming his writing of *The Way to Power and Poise*. Mabel writes that my daughter and her fifteen month old Anne were here for June and July and my husband has been home several times so we have more family life than usual." They all liked Clayton. It was a quaint little village, both peaceful and restful. Jim Mathews pops in for a few hours. Mabel was 69 and still eager to learn from the books she was reading.[23]

India becomes free and independent on August 15, 1947. In light of the continuing tension between Hindus and Muslim, the British did not transfer power, they simply abandoned it. Jawaharlal Nehru addressed the nation with a new Declaration of Independence and became the first prime minister of India. People were dancing in the streets.

India's independence did not come without a price, however. The riff with Pakistan and between Hindus, Sikhs and Muslims continued. At least 11 million Hindus, Sikhs and Muslims crossed borders (to this day one of the largest migrations in history). Flooding, violence (ethnic cleansing) and disease killed millions. Even in the midst of celebrations reports of violence in Calcutta with Muslim refugees fleeing what they now considered hostile territory toward what they considered to be the "Land of the Pure." In one day there were 4,700 dead, 15,000 injured and 150,000 homeless refugees.

Similarly, in equal numbers, Pakistani Hindus and Sikhs, whose ancestral homes were now in a foreign and hostile country, fled toward India. From Lahore hundreds were dead, buildings ablaze as smoke rose above hundreds of Panjabi villages. Ironically, back in

Calcutta, a bomb exploded near where Gandhi was fasting to end the killing. When Gandhi was asked what should a non-violent person do when confronting someone, he replied, "Attempt a gentle and affectionate persuasion. When it fails…one invites suffering in his own body to open the eyes of the person who is determined to see no light."[24] Gandhi then wrote eight conditions on which Muslims and Hindus must agree or he would fast to the death. Hindus believed that these conditions favored Muslims and in less than five months the tension would lead to his assassination.

As for the partition of Pakistan from India, Gandhi and the leadership of the Congress Party only accepted it after years of incessant and bloody communal violence between Hindus and Muslims.

Mabel writes to her "Friends" again on September 8 that "So many ask if I am going back [to India]. That is in God's hands. I have learned to walk a step at a time and not worry. When I asked my doctor he said, 'We will not talk about it now.' However, I am very much better, thanks to America's good food and climate."[25]

In her absence from India Mabel wrote letters (18,624 this year alone). Both James Mathews and Ralph Diffendorfer had been requesting that she write a statement that would be helpful for other missionaries in their cultivation of patrons. This was becoming even more important as they approached their Advance Campaign that was built on the hopes of raising special gifts and Mabel had "mastered the art" of writing "support letters" and raising money for special projects.

Her letters were brief, about one-and-a-half pages. In the open space below the duplicated portion she would add a personalized handwritten note. She never *asked* for money or for anything else for that matter; she merely stated an unmet need. The money poured in — enough to keep a thousand boys in school with scholarships. She did this for fifty years.[26]

In the fall of 1947, Stanley made good on his intensions from the summer of 1944 to supply leadership for the campaign for federal union. If you recall, Harvey Kazmier, at the Northeast Ashram in Winnipesaukee, NH, was ignited by Stanley's concept of federal union and had asked Stanley to be the personal catalysis. Stanley had demurred at that time but now was ready to participate. Kazmier convinced him to sacrifice 30 days to speak in thirty cities three times a day among American churches. Stanley was 64, Kazmier, who accompanied Stanley on the tour was 20 years younger. For Kazmier it was too much. An article in the *Saturday Evening Post* states that Stanley "breezed through the schedule without so much as pouches under his eyes. Midway, however, Kazmier began to break down and turned to Dr. Jones for help. That day Stanley had made three speeches and a radio address, had undertaken two newspaper interviews, had led two conferences and shaken 2,000 hands, all on a reserve of 4 hours' sleep. Kazmier asked, "How do you do it? Stanley replied, "Do what?" Kazmier said, "Keep going. I'm about dead." Stanley then added, "I feel fine, but you must [first] surrender yourself to [God] in this crusade. Then your strength will come from without, and your own stamina will not be sapped. If I leaned only on my own strength, I would be ten years dead." Self-reliance truly is one of the biggest sins in the Bible.

This crusade for a United Church was sponsored by the Association for a United Church of America that rented a $40 a month office in Brookline, MA and had a small volunteer staff supervised by Kazmier. The Association solicited pledge cards (membership of $1 per year and any additional support from those interested in church union). *The Saturday Evening Post* wrote that by early 1948 they were receiving between 3 and 4 thousand pledge cards a week with people promising personal prayer and commitment to federal union. At a meeting in Youngstown, OH Stanley said that "the purpose of the crusade was to saturate the soul of the church with the demand for unity." He prayed that this saturation would "precipitate into action." At first skeptical, Stanley soon became convinced that the crusade was a genuine movement of God in America.[27]

Between 1947 and 1954 Stanley would devote one month each fall to mass meetings in nearly 500 cities throughout the U.S. Over the 7 year period some 250,000 people sent in cards to the Association for a United Church in America pledging support for federal union.

Meanwhile, on Sunday morning, November 9, 1947, little redheaded Janice Virginia Mathews was born. Mabel joyously explained to her friends how her daughter and son-in-law had joined their names, James and Eunice in naming her Janice.

Stanley loved his grandchildren. Whenever possible they would meet in Clayton. According to Mabel's friend, Irene Frese, "Stanley liked to visit Clayton because no one was in awe of him there. Kids would see him walking down the street in his suit and yell out, 'Hi Stan!' Mabel would give readings from Stanley's books. She once spoke at Irene's Sunday school reunion, and told about Eleanor Roosevelt having one of Stanley's books at her bedside, which she read a little at a time. According to Irene, Mabel was very warm, friendly, lovable and *so* proud of her husband!"[28]

In January 1948, Stanley is back in India continuing to work on *The Way to Power and Poise*. This is interrupted on January 30, 1948 with the tragic assassination of Mahatma Gandhi. Since Chapter One dealt with the Gandhi assassination in some detail, here we give only a brief review of the issues, especially as related to India's independence.

You recall that Waskom Pickett visited with Nehru and Gandhi two days before the assassination. Pickett attempted to persuade Gandhi to move to safer lodging. Gandhi replied, "Why should I be afraid to die. All my hopes for a better India are being destroyed. Perhaps Gandhi dead will be more respected than Gandhi alive. A heavy hearted Pickett reported, "I failed completely."

Stanley expressed his reaction to the death of his friend in a letter written to "Ken" (Jim) Mathews and family on a plane leaving Delhi for Madras and Colombo, Ceylon (Sri Lanka). The universal comment was, "He came to a Christlike end."

Stanley's book, *Mahatma Gandhi: An Interpretation*, attempts to explain "The Meaning of His Death." Gandhi was on a fast to protest the disunity and dishonesty in Indian policy. "It was a great fast with great objectives. All of the objectives, however, were seemingly in favor of Muslims. He had laid down eight conditions, one of which was the restoration of the 117 mosques in Delhi which the Hindus and Sikhs had turned into dwellings or temples after the mass slayings. Stanley writes, "That some Hindus laid bare their feelings to me about the matter: 'Why didn't he fast against Pakistan, for Pakistan is the guilty party? Ours was retaliation. They began it all and are therefore responsible for what happened.'" Stanley's immediate reply was simple, "The Mahatma's strategy is correct. Suppose he had fasted against Pakistan. They would possibly have shrugged their shoulders and said: 'Let him die. What is that to us?'"[29]

Eventually, six days into the fast Gandhi became so weak that both sides signed an agreement conceding his points so the fast was called off. The fast wrought a miracle of the first order. People were parading the streets crying, "Save the Mahatma. Down with communal strife. Hindus and Moslems are brothers."

Immediately the Muslims saw Gandhi as their friend. The fast proved it. Their doubts were over.

Not all were relieved, however. The assassin was from Poona, the section of India from which Shivaji, the Hindu hero who was immortalized for conquering marauding Muslims, hailed. The expression went, "Shivaji makes the Maratha's blood flow faster as he thinks of Hindu ascendancy over the Moslem invaders."

Days before his death Gandhi said, "If I am to die by the bullet of a madman, I must do so smiling. There must be no anger within me. God must be in my heart and on my lips. And you promise me one thing. Should such a thing happen, you are not to shed one tear." Stanley writes, "Here was supreme poise awaiting calmly anything that might happen. He was never nobler than in this utterance."[30]

There were really two reasons back of the killing of the Mahatma:

his wanting an India for all, Muslims included, and his nonviolence. The group that Nathuram Godse (the assassin) represented felt that in advocating nonviolence the Mahatma was emasculating the Hindu. So Godse would attempt to stop nonviolence by violence. Result? The opposite of what he had hoped. He succeeded in losing the power of nonviolence.

Stanley believed that Gandhi was a "natural" rather than an orthodox Christian. "And yet how shall I defend that distinction? I don't. I leave it undefended. But it is the nearest statement of the facts I know." Gandhi's life seemingly manifested fruit that only faith in Christ could produce. Stanley then adds, that not one Hindu suggested that Gandhi's death was punishment for some sin in a former life. "His suffering was not punitive, but vicarious. He died for the nation and its sins. *But that points to the Cross rather than to karma.*"[31]

Jones concludes that had Gandhi (or Jesus for that matter) lived to a ripe old age the country would have lovingly put him on the shelf in his decaying years, and would have honored him, but would not have followed him. Now he dies at the height of his powers, and at the pinnacle of his influence, for he never stood higher and more triumphant that after his last two fasts, one in Calcutta and the other in Delhi. Gandhi was loved but almost as many were won to an allegiance to him by his death as by his life.

The delay on *The Way to Power and Poise* was not due exactly to the death of Gandhi, however, it was due to a telegram from Abingdon Press, his publisher. "How quickly can you produce a manuscript for Mahatma Gandhi…"? Stanley never wrote a book upon request and initially rejected the offer. After thinking and praying about it he decided that he could lay an honest tribute at the feet of the great little man and in two months he had finished the manuscript. He wrote to Jim Mathews, "I'm glad they asked me to write it."

Stanley's, *Mahatma Gandhi: An Interpretation* was published this same year (1948, Republished in January 2019 by Abingdon Press). Reminiscent of the letter written in December 1942 against the Jim Crow laws, this book was also geared toward the African-American struggle for equality in the U.S. Martin Luther King, Jr. would treasure this book. Years later (1964), at King's election for the Nobel Peace Prize (both King and Jones had been nominated for the honor), at a reception for King at Boston University before he traveled to Stockholm to accept the Nobel Peace Prize, Eunice was stopped by King and he asked to speak with her. He explained that her father's book on Gandhi clarified and mobilized his own understanding of non-violent civil disobedience. In fact, the book is now under glass in the Martin Luther King National Historical Site (Library) in Atlanta, GA, opened with a hand written note by King himself across one of the pages touting non-violence, "THIS IS IT!"[32]

STANLEY IS BACK IN THE U.S., JULY 1948

Mabel was busy as usual, averaging just over fifty letters every day for the whole of 1948. Imagine!

Stanley resumes his Ashram schedule for the rest of the summer. He then renewed his campaign for federal union. He writes in his September 30, 1948 *Circular Letter* that although they are presenting a controversial subject this movement of "the Spirit leaves behind no controversy or a split condition in any local situation." Only the Spirit could pull that off. Having said that, although the support of the laity was virtually unanimous the response of the clergy and church officials was decidedly mixed.

Articles in the *Christian Century* and *Christian Science Monitor* debated the issues at some length. Ultimately, Stanley writes that any chance of success was a union rooted in our fundamental spiritual nature. One critic, Dr. Truman Douglas, argued in the *Christian Century* that federal union does not go far enough. Stanley responded that the problem is that human (spiritual) nature is ambivalent—the desire for union with the whole on the one hand and the desire for local self-government, for self-expression, on the other. Douglas' proposal reflected only the desire for union.

Amazingly, the informal polls first conducted in 1948 showed that out of nearly 20,000 polled, only 28 voted against the proposed federal union. Still the clergy were not satisfied, supposedly concerned about apostolic succession and re-ordination. Predictably, there was Roman Catholic resistance as well, especially since only priests in the succession of St. Peter could serve the sacraments.

Stanley's zeal and enthusiasm for federal union sprang, of course, from the reality of the Kingdom of God in which he lived. Again, it had a solid Scriptural base in Ephesians 2:15-16.

Nevertheless, after another five years of traveling and speaking on behalf of federal union modeled on the Kingdom of God principles of self-surrender and of a new humanity out of both parties, woefully, nothing ever happened. Even Richard Raines, the United Methodist Bishop in Indiana, nearly 20 years later, would caution against such proposals.[33]

When Stanley returned to India in January 1949. He spent only two of the typical six months in his adopted homeland. The rest of the time was spent in Burma; Singapore; Kuala Lumpur, Malaya; Bangkok, Siam (Thailand); the Philippines; Japan; Korea; and China. He comments: "These were the most eventful four months of my not so uneventful life."

The crux of the trip was a month in Japan. Although he had been to Tokyo briefly in March of 1947, this would be his first visit as an evangelist. He wrote to the Methodist Division of Foreign Missions from the airport in Tokyo in February. "Photographers rushed up to me and said straight off: 'All Japan is talking about Christianity, what have you to say about it!' I replied that I favored it!...". Stanley was then rushed off to Yokohama where he addressed the military people and their dependents. He was then taken to Tokyo for the red carpet treatment given a room at the hotel for the General Headquarters — the Imperial. The next day he took the military train to Nagoya. There his first meeting was in a church that had been destroyed during the war and rebuilt by the Church World Service. Although the pastor was skeptical about Stanley passing out commitment cards (as the Japanese "would not write their names in public"), 150 out of the 450 people (half were non-Christian) signed their cards.

Stanley then speaks of a tour of Hiroshima where he held a prayer meeting on the exact spot where the atomic bomb exploded. Again, to the Division, he wrote that "It is nothing less than a miracle that in Hiroshima we could receive such love and response after what happened to that city." In three meetings 450 cards were signed stating a desire be a Christian. Over a thousand showed up for a meeting at a school hall. Unbelievably (perhaps miraculously is the better word), a pastor said to Stanley, "Sir, the fire of the Holy Spirit is burning in the hearts of the people. It is our new beginning." Stanley adds, "The fire of an atom had left this city a cinder but the fire of the Holy Spirit burning in the hearts of the people would rebuild that city on better foundations."[34]

Stanley would visit sixteen cities on the three main islands — Honshu, Kyushu, and Hokkaido. He reported that eight thousand non-Christians signed cards affirming their decisions to place their personal faith in Jesus Christ.

On March 18, 1949, Stanley met again with Emperor Hirohito, once more being given "an Imperial audience by invitation of the Imperial Household." Greeted by the Emperor's interpreter, his old friend, Terry Terasaki, Terry showed Stanley the letter that Stanley had written to him December 10, 1941 and said that the letter had "kept him alive spiritually during the war."

Stanley talked with Hirohito for three-quarters of an hour. Emboldened by their first visit two years earlier, Stanley suggested to the Emperor the possibility of his becoming a Christian. Graciously, Hirohito said that Jones had raised a very serious question and that he had great respect for Christianity; but since most of his people were Shinto, this reality had to be taken in to consideration.

Stanley then met again with General MacArthur, now the commander of the American occupation forces in Japan. As a follow-up to their conversation nearly four years earlier he and Stanley met for nearly an hour. Stanley talked about Christianity in Japan. He actually got up three times to leave but the General would not let him go. "I asked him what word would he send to America." Amazingly (Oh ye of little faith), MacArthur said, "Where you send one missionary, now send a hundred [again, shades of Marco Polo]. This is the greatest opportunity the Church in the world has faced in 500 years. How long the door may be open is uncertain, probably ten years." Oh my! Stanley, sensing still another opportunity, then broached the issue first raised with MacArthur at the end of 1945 of giving New Guinea to Japan. Again, MacArthur was sympathetic but unfortunately nothing would come of it.

Stanley admits that he had gone to Japan with "inner hesitation." Even though Kagawa had written to him that Japan was ripe for Christianity, Stanley was skeptical. Christians were a very small percentage of the population. After a short time, however, he wrote to the Methodist Division of Foreign Missions in NY, "As you see I'm here!" And how! Stanley was overwhelmed by the sincere and spontaneous warmth of his reception. Apparently the word had gotten out regarding his efforts to prevent the war in 1941. Stanley, however, sensed that it was something deeper. He wrote in the *Indian Witness* that the Japanese "belief" in the near divinity of the Emperor and of their superiority and destiny to rule (no doubt related to their belief that they had descended from the Sun Goddess) had created a spiritual collapse. The historian, Kenneth Scott Latourette writes that thousands were adrift emotionally and were searching for an answer to life's deepest questions. Super-nationalism had crumbled.

At the end of his time in Japan Stanley wrote to his good friend O. G. Robinson that although he was concerned about the lack of follow-up by the Japanese churches, "My month in Japan was the most fruitful I have ever spent in my life." There would be many other trips to Japan as he was now certain that he was being directed by the Inner Voice of the Holy Spirit to proclaim the good news of Jesus Christ to the Japanese people.[35]

Like so many other areas of interest and calling, Stanley was ahead of his time. Americans were not responsive to his plea for sending missionaries to Japan. Instead of constructing broad new spiritual foundations for the Japanese people, the Japanese would now focus their psychic and spiritual energy on rebuilding its devastated economy. Furthermore, Stanley was concerned about the political and military presence of the U.S. in Japan. He wrote in the *Indian Witness* that he prays that Americans would not stay too long.

On the night of March 18, shortly before Stanley left Japan, Michio Kozaki, the chairman of the National Christian Council of Japan (the official sponsor of Stanley's evangelistic tour) presented him with a statement of the council's sincere and deep appreciation for his work in that country. "It is really a marvelous thing that you could bring about such a wonderful result, even in such a brief span of time."[36] Kagawa was right, Stanley had come at an opportune time.

Before returning to India Stanley visited two other Asian countries — Korea and China. By April 1949 the communists under Mao Zedong already controlled large parts of the country, and before Stanley left China, they took over Nanking, the Nationalist capital of China, one of the last strongholds of Chiang Kai-shek. Stanley's host, the National Christian Council, in spite of the precarious situation, encouraged Stanley to venture inland. He was told that he would probably be the last one permitted into China before the bamboo curtain came down.

Stanley had evangelist meetings in Shanghai, Nanking, Chengtu, Amoy, and Canton. In each place "I was just a step or two in front of the Communist flood." He then adds that the reason for the communist victory was simple (verbalized in *The Way to Power and Poise*). The Kuomintang said that after the war they would put in land reforms. The Communists went one better. They redistributed the land as a part of their strategy. They won. Stanley was somewhat surprised that both Christians and non-Christians alike thought that the communist takeover was inevitable. There was simply no will to resist. The government had completely lost its hold on the people. There was not one defender! Why? The government began as a reactionary movement to sweep out feudalism with its social and economic abuses. Then it stalled — became conservative, then reactionary, then corrupt. It lost its moral drive and purpose. The Communists were the only driving force in the land. They stepped in when the Kuomintang abdicated and apparently God used the only broom at hand.

Stanley obviously disapproved of the ruthless tactics of the end justifies any-means. Moreover he could never agree with the outspoken atheism, nor would he sanction the idolatry of the communist party that was encouraged by its leadership to make an idol of Mao himself. Stanley then admits that God does use whatever means are available, including spiritually indifference and even evil means. In the *Indian Witness* Stanley says that Jesus took the worst thing that could happen to him and transformed it into the best thing that could happen. If Christianity was to survive in China it would have to re-examine it message and emphasis. Chinese Christianity, like Western Christianity was distorted by the philosophy of individualism. He then added that collectivism would probably drive Christianity to rediscover the Kingdom of God — its central message…. Christianity is not anti-capitalist or anti-communist, as such — it is anti-evil whether that evil be in capitalism or in communism. It must not be identified with either but with an unshakable Kingdom. Stanley's Inner Voice was whispering, pray for a new man out of the two (not unlike the Jews and Gentiles).

Stanley returned to India on May 4, 1949. In reflection, his deepest satisfaction came from the month in Japan. China's political future concerned him.

At the same time Mabel writes from Clayton regarding Stanley's travels, "Our family all had Christmas together with Eunice in New York. Christmas night, my husband left by air for Burma, Japan, Korea, China and India." Mabel then spent January in Miami. In late February, Eunice and family had moved from New York to Montclair, NJ, ten miles away, where they could have a yard and fresh air for the children. Mabel "went up in March to help with the 'grands' who are both adorable ages but very energetic!" Unfortunately Mabel was not well in Montclair so at the doctor's orders she had returned to Clayton, arriving April 1.

In the same letter Mabel writes a telling paragraph about her boys back in India. Read this carefully.

I was especially interested in reading of three of our old boys who are brothers. All are in Government service in Independent India. Godwill is Superintendent of Police in the Hazaribagh District; Bramwell is Superintendent of Police in the Katihar District and Roswell is a Doctor in the Indian Medical Service in Poona. These fine laymen are just as important to the work of the Kingdom as are pastors.... But I am especially thrilled when I read of sons or grandsons of a boy like the one brought me by the police in 1911. His mother, a low caste beggar, had died on the street. The boy was half blind, filthy in body and mind and hard to manage. After two years in school, I had him trained as a house helper and got him a job in a missionary home. He married and his son finished High School on one of your scholarships and became a foreman in a large mill at a good salary. Just before I left India, he brought me his little son and proudly announced that he could pay his entire support in school. The father also is a staunch supporter of his church. He told me that he hoped to be able to send the boy through college. I remember that when I took that boy from the street to the Brahman doctor to have his eyes treated he said, "Why do you bother with scum like this?" Well, we have taken many boys who might be considered as the scum of the earth and not all of them have made good but I could fill many pages with the record of those who have. I am very grateful that though I cannot be in Sitapur in person, through your help we can keep the school in existence. It has always been a venture of faith and God has blessed its work. May He bless you who help us.[37]

On May 15, 1949, Stanley wrote to Nehru. He mentions the apparent reason for the failure of the Nationalists and the success of the

Communists in China. Again, the Kuomintang stalled and turned corrupt. The Communists stepped in to complete the revolution. Stanley wonders if the Indian Congress would make the same mistake and turn a blind eye to the bribery and corruption among the lower ranks of officials. There is no record of an immediate response from Nehru (at least not for three years when Stanley would write him again).[38]

1949 clearly marks a genuine turning point in Stanley's long career as a missionary evangelist, both in America and abroad — he was becoming even more global. There were several reasons for this. The first relates to the fact that during his six years in the U.S. during the war he became more and more deeply involved in the religious and political affairs of the U.S. The second reason relates to his trips to Japan and China. The spiritual seed that Stanley had sown in D.C. in 1941 finally bore fruit when the Japanese people opened their arms to him and their hearts to the gospel.[39]

Post 1949, although Stanley's general goal of six months in the U.S. and six months in India remained the same, he was now willing to sacrifice some of that time for a more global influence to engage a genuinely universal spiritual need. One priority, however, remained constant, his commitment to the Christian Ashrams.

Incredibly, Stanley was still pursuing the idea of giving New Guinea to Japan. In the early 1950s John Foster Dulles (Secretary of State under Eisenhower) visited Japan to negotiate a peace treaty between Japan and the U.S. to end the war in the Pacific, both formally and officially. Stanley managed to meet with Dulles, "I saw him and presented to him the New Guinea proposal. His reaction: 'That is a very interesting proposal.' He called for a map of the Pacific to see where New Guinea was. He asked me to write a memorandum for Allison, who was an expert on Japan." Unfortunately, Stanley did not receive a favorable response.[40]

Mabel was now living in Orlando from November 1 to May 1 and in Clayton the rest of the year. In Clayton she spent most of her time alone in this quiet little refuge. Some years later she would write a little piece, "The Delight of Being Alone." There she reminisces, "I watch and am as a sparrow alone on the housetop (Psalms). Perhaps the sparrow or at least the psalmist, was unhappily alone. But not I! Even in this secluded village it is difficult to be alone long enough to get any task finished that calls for quiet application. How I delight in a rainy day, a day in which I can be reasonably sure that for that day at least I will be alone."

She concludes that piece saying that her door is always open. She would miss her friends if they did not come by. Yet, "How can one be lonely with books?" Kathryn Hendershot writes that according to her sources, "We would know less and less about Mabel's life after this time."[41] However, I learned from Mabel's family, that was not the case and Mabel would continue to engage actively with both family and friends through letters and visits as she continued living for nearly another 30 years and I have continued to include "happenings" about Mabel in this book.

Finally, Brother Stanley would publish *The Way to Power and Poise* (1949). Anne Mathews-Younes lifts up an application from Psalm 17:1-5, "To leave you concentrated on yourself is unhealthy and bad psychology. Any system that leaves you occupied with yourself is wrong, however learned it may be. This is the essential wrong with the cults of self-cultivation. Self-cultivation means self-concentration and self-concentration means self-deterioration—inevitably. It may bring an initial inner boost to begin to cultivate yourself, but it will mean an inevitable letdown. Gordon Allport, professor of psychology at Harvard, says: "Paradoxically 'self-expression' requires the capacity to transcend oneself in the pursuit of objectives not primarily referred to the self." Here psychology and Christian faith coincide: "He that finds his life shall lose it: and he that loses his life for my sake shall find it." Self-cultivation is all right and very necessary, provided the self has been surrendered to God. Then it can be cultivated, for it is God-centered and not self-centered.[42]

Thus, this chapter ends where it began with self-surrender. Stanley would enter the next decade riding the success of his seventeen books only to write thirteen more over his remaining years. As in his *Christ of the American Road* (1944) he would continue to embrace the issues raised there of self-surrender (especially for the American people). Related to that for Christians worldwide was the issue of equal rights for women (p. 70), for people of color (pp. 75-79), then liberty and justice for all (cf. pp. 95ff.), including people beyond our borders (pp. 82ff.). Politics would always be an issue (pp. 98ff), especially as related to war (pp. 100ff.) and nations working together for peace. His emphasis on unity would also address the modernists/fundamentalists split (p. 221). All of this would keep Brother Stanley on the cutting edge of a world in need of a saving knowledge of Jesus Christ.

Mary Webster, Anne Mathews and others, India, 1968

CHAPTER NINE

STANLEY' GLOBAL MINISTRY EXPANDS EVEN MORE WHILE MABEL, EUNICE AND JIM ARE IN THE U.S.

Meet Mary Webster, Stanley's Timothy

According to Douglas Ruffle's, *A Missionary Mindset*, Brother Stanley was in Argentina in the 1950s.[1] The following is a marvelous exchange between Ruffle and Carlos Gattinoni, a recently retired Argentinian Bishop. It was December 24, 1978. Ruffle, his wife and son had arrived in Argentina a few months earlier and were spending Christmas Eve with the Bishop and his extended family, including his district superintendent and his superintendent's wife, Anely Urcola, the Bishop's niece. Bishop Gattinoni had translated Stanley's book, *Christ's Alternative to Communism*. The book had received both praise and criticism. There was praise because of Stanley's objection to communism because of its lack of liberty and its materialistic atheism. Communism was a threat to much of Latin America at the time. There was criticism because Stanley respected communism's attempt to found a society on cooperation. In true Stanley fashion, he took communism seriously and made an honest attempt to describe it in objective terms.

At some point Ruffle asked the Bishop about his opinion of Stanley Jones as Stanley was well-respected in this part of the world. His books were very popular. "Did you know him personally?" The Bishop was exuberant. "Of course!" They had met in Buenos Aires several months after the Bishop had discovered Stanley's books. "He came to Argentina several times." Then the Bishop told Ruffle about a visit that Stanley had unexpectedly made one hot summer during the early 1950s.

Dr. Jones had been scheduled to lead a weeklong spiritual retreat in Uruguay. When his plane arrived in Montevideo, he found out that there had been a miscommunication along the way and the Uruguayans were not prepared for him.

He had come a long way and, of course, back then, it took months to exchange letters. It was a Saturday in January and he called me [the Bishop] from Uruguay to see if we might be able to arrange something in Buenos Aires on the spur of the moment.

I told him we would do what we could and yes we could arrange for him to preach in the evening at First Church in the city center. I said that many people were on vacation and that it was hot and we would not have time to advertise but we would try.

Jones boarded a ferry to cross the seventy-mile-wide *Rio de la Plata*, which separates Uruguay from Argentina. He arrived on Sunday morning.

I called several of our pastors and friends from other denominations. We announced in church on Sunday morning that E. Stanley Jones would be preaching at First Church beginning that evening. I urged them to spread the news and to pray for the event and to invite friends and to come. Quite frankly I was worried that we would get a very poor turnout.

Happily, the meetings increased in numbers nightly until we

had a proper revival on our hands as many were led into a right relationship with Jesus Christ.[2]

Ruffle's book, following Stanley's methodology, distills what he believes are the transferable principles that can inform a missionary mindset as today's Christian leaders and church planters reach out to their communities with the "untrammeled Jesus."[3] As we would surmise from the advice of his Hindu friend years earlier, this was all about "loving them the right way." Ruffle writes that "Just as Jones wrestled with the question of *the right way*, contemporary missionaries needed to discern what the right approach would be in our context." In the twenty-first century, Christians, both in the United States and Argentina, must relate to descendants from any number of religions, including Hindus and Muslims, "what recent demographers term 'nones,' that growing part of the population who do not identify with any religion at all."[4] Stanley related to these a century ago, proof again that Stanley Jones is just as relevant for today as he was for his own day.[5]

MARY WEBSTER

On March 19, 1950, Mary Webster,[6] a laywoman, who would often gave her Christian witness before Stanley spoke at ashrams, first heard him preach in Peoria, Illinois. She writes in her recently published biography about an announcement made in a church that "a very famous missionary from India, a Dr. E. Stanley Jones, would be speaking 35 miles from my home." Mary had married Roy Webster in 1945 and now lived on a farm with Roy and their two sons, Ted and Claude.

Interested in India, Mary had Roy drop her off at the church. She sat toward the front with empty pews ahead of her as she thought that Stanley might be showing slides. "However, the evangelist did not 'entertain' us, rather he explained God's 'Plan of Salvation.' I felt safe! I had 13 jobs in my small country church! However, he unnerved me when he said: 'Sitting in a church doesn't make you a Christian, any more than sitting in a hen house makes you a chicken!' You have to be born again! If you dropped your watch in the road and a car ran over it, you wouldn't pick up the broken pieces and take it to a jeweler and ask him to fix it! The jeweler would look at you in amazement and tell you that you needed a new watch! If we bring all the broken pieces of our lives to Jesus, He would give us a new life! But, we would have to bring God all the pieces!' I was stunned."

Many went forward for prayer. "I didn't believe that saying unspoken words to an invisible person could make any difference in my life, but what did I have to lose? If it didn't work, I could always go back to being 'normal!' So I gave God my will, but not my life!"[7]

Mary's husband picked her up from the meeting and both were silent on the drive home. Roy was absorbed with driving listening to music on the radio. Suddenly Nelson Eddy was singing her favorite song, *The Indian Love Call*. While she had not responded to the Altar Call at the church, "I was now listening to a call that I could neither hide nor run from. I was listening with my heart, not my brain and it was not Nelson Eddy, but Jesus singing to me!

> When I'm calling you, will you answer too?
> That means I offer my LOVE to you, to be your own.
> If you refuse Me, what will I do, loving you all alone?
> But, if when you hear My love call, ringing clear;
> And I hear your answering echo, so clear;
> Then I will know our Love will be true;
> You'll belong to Me;
> I'll belong to you!

At that moment, I loved Jesus and gave Him my heart and my life!"[8] Mary was suddenly different. Her relationship with Roy was so transformed that he went to church and was gloriously converted as well, as were her boys. Mary wrote to Brother Stanley about this experience and he invited her to attend the Texas Ashram later that year.

In April, 1950 Stanley leaves for India. Soon after he arrived he hoped to see Nehru and other government officials about the opening of Nur Manzil (Palace of Light), the Christian Psychiatric Center in Lucknow (the construction had begun three years earlier). Throughout the 1950s the relationship between Christian missionaries and the Republic of India was complicated by the government's delay in granting visas (and in some instances their denial of visas) to American missionaries. Stanley was forever seeking inroads to impress the Indians of his commitment to the people of India. The Nur Manzil hospital was the first hospital of its kind in all of India and still operates today.

Stanley would then speak in a series of evangelistic meetings in Shillong and Darjeeling before the beginning of the Sat Tal Ashram.[9]

In July, 1950 Stanley returned to the U.S. for the five summer Christian Ashrams. Recall that he had invited Mary Webster the previous March to attend the Ashram in Kerrville, Texas in August. Mary later wrote of the experience:

> I saw also the Lord, as Isaiah did, high and lifted up, and His Presence filled the Church, and my heart also. There were a thousand people present, but he [Brother Stanley] spoke as if I were the only one!... Later, I was privileged to serve as a part-time secretary to him in some of his overseas missions. Many people treated him as if he were a 'seven-day wonder,' a saint or a spiritual superman; but I noticed that God had given him a remarkable balance that kept him from forgetting that he was simply a man whom God had chosen to work through because of his willingness to be used. He possessed a 'spiritual transparency' that let you see not him, but Jesus through him!

Mary had never been to the south. There she became friends with a black woman. Before leaving the Ashram they all joined hands and repeated together, "Unreservedly given to God; unbreakably given to each other!" On the way home, Mary and her new friend even sat on the bus together (a thing forbidden in those days in the south). The driver gave her an extended look. Mary just looked back at him until he shrugged and continued on.[10]

From this moment on Mary would view both life and death differently.

Following the summer ashrams, Stanley, the forever pacifist, managed a trip to Washington, DC to see if he could do anything to head off another world war. Stanley feared that the Korean War might well escalate. India, acting on behalf of developing nations and nations that were not aligned with either the United States or the Soviet Union, had made a proposal for ending the war. Stanley thought the proposal might actually work. With this proposal in hand, in a period of two days he saw twenty-five members of Congress; he spent an hour with officials of the State Department and he testified for fifteen minutes before the House Foreign Affairs Committee. On September 1 he had a fifteen minute appointment with President Truman urging the president to go to the U.N. Assembly in person and make a serious appeal for peace around the Indian proposal. Unfortunately nothing came of this but one cannot help but admire the man for trying. This was a significant part of his passion.[11]

During the rest of September Brother Stanley was consumed by public meetings throughout the country on behalf of the Crusade for a United Church. Then, while working on a new book, *How to be a Transformed Person,* that he hoped to finish by the summer of the following year, from October through December he took on the normal schedule of evangelistic missions.

Meanwhile, let's not forget about Mabel. In her September 20 *Duplicate Letter* she writes that she is in Clayton happily writing letters and gardening. Although she would never ask for money—she simply stated a need—she is concerned that due to some dwindling support for her boys she has lost eighteen scholarships, meaning that they could take eighteen fewer boys at Sitapur. She plans on staying in Clayton until Christmas while Stanley is "still at work in America."

Early in 1951, Stanley, true to his resolve to visit Japan every other year, is back for his second evangelistic tour since the end of the war. In the three months during the first part of 1951 he visited forty-one cities, with an incredible 21,390 cards signed by Japanese who wanted to become Christians after they heard him speak. He called the trip (including another interview with Emperor Hirohito) "the event of the year — perhaps of my life." [Reader, please note that although Brother Stanley makes these kinds of superlative statements often, do not think that they were mere rhetoric. They were true to the moment because Stanley lived in the moment. Every day was a new beginning.]

Two years earlier Stanley had been concerned with the lack of follow-up among the Japanese converts so this year he took with him Dr. H. H. McConnell of the Department of Evangelism on the National Council of Churches (formerly the Federal Council of Churches in the U.S.) to instruct pastors and lay leaders in the techniques of visitation evangelism.

Once back in the U.S. Stanley again leads the summer Ashrams and Mary Webster shared her testimony at one of them in July. Jones notes at the time that although his personal witness was obviously communicating, sometimes his words would seemingly miss the mark. It became necessary for him to move over on occasion to allow others (primarily lay people) to share their witness as they could communicate at a wholly different level. Even though he could have perhaps done it better, his humble spirit (and no doubt his "inner voice") led him to train others in Lay Evangelism by asking them to bring a witness before he spoke. Mary Webster was the first.

Stanley writes, "We have tried to meet this need by bringing as a part of our team this year, Mary Webster, an untrained, but an effective lay witness. It was an eye-opener to many who have been brought up under the tradition that only the theologically trained could be used to win converts, to see an untrained farmer's wife used of God to win intellectuals and non-intellectuals by the simple power of witnessing, including some pastors themselves."[12] Stanley believed that each of us (including laity) has a sphere of influence where only we can minister most effectively and that the Holy Spirit is constantly preparing people for our ministry (1 Corinthians 12:14ff).

Then, three weeks after the July Ashram tragedy struck the Webster family. On August 11, 1951 Mary's husband Roy died instantly in a head-on automobile accident. Mary was sitting next to him and son Claude was in the back seat. Mary, though badly bruised, was not seriously injured but Claude, having been thrown forward into the dashboard, had a bad skull fracture along with injuries to both his legs. When Stanley heard, he immediately wrote to her, "half fatherly and half ministerial."

Mary wrote back immediately from her hospital bed (Stanley claimed that this was his "most unforgettable letter"). She described how victoriously Jesus was dealing with her (never dreaming that any eyes but his would ever see the letter later used in one of his books).

Ever since a year ago (that first Ashram experience at the silent Communion service), I've understood what death really is and have tried to tell others just how beautiful an experience it will really be. It seemed to me at the Communion service that I had a glimpse of eternity, and it was so beautiful my heart nearly broke with joy and rapture.

Well, it is one thing to tell someone something, and another thing to go through the experience. I wondered if when my time came to "taste death," if it would hit me as an evil thing, or if it would still seem to be as beautiful as it was at that communion service. Now I can tell you with all sincerity that my original opinion has been strengthened! I can truthfully say that, at least for me, death doesn't have any "sting." This may seem strange to you, as it certainly has to so many others, especially the doctors and nurses. Even when they told me Roy was killed, I didn't feel one bit like crying. I haven't shed a tear over it, nor do I feel like crying. God has been teaching me so much these past fifteen months, and He has so transformed my thinking that now I see this accident in its true light and not as an event that was designed to hurt me.

The truck that caused the accident was trying to pass another car when the truck driver saw us coming toward him.... The driver of the truck was utterly helpless, and it really was just an accident.... [Mary refused to press charges and forgave the man in court. He was so grateful that he gave his heart and life to Jesus]. I certainly do not believe that it was God's will that we be hurt or that Roy be killed. However, because the laws of the universe are truly dependable laws, they work no matter who obeys them or breaks them. How grateful I am that this is so! And God was right with us after the accident. I saw Him in the faces of those who out of the compassion of their hearts helped us.... Most of all I experienced God in that 'still, small Voice' that said over and over again to me, "Be not afraid Mary, for I am with you always, 'even unto the end of the world,' and 'I am the Resurrection and the Life, and whosoever lives and believes in me shall never die.' Do you Mary believe me?" I replied: "Yes, my precious Lord, I do believe that You are the one true God of the living!" And from then on my soul has been completely free of all things by His own precious holy love.

I read in the Bible these words: "Mary has chosen that good part that shall not be taken from her" (Luke 10:42). I have chosen that "good part" of my husband that no one can ever take away from me. He is 'one' with me now in the spirit of our Lord. It is as if he had just gone upstairs to rest, and I'll go too when I finish what I am doing, and we shall see each other again in the morning. So do not pity me. I find it impossible to pity myself.

The hardest part was telling Teddy about his daddy. It was like running a long sharp dagger into his little heart, but he will get over it, for he took it like a soldier. I have yet to tell Claudie about his father's death, but I will when he is well again.

Your happy sister,

Mary.[13]

In one of her Ashram talks Mary would describe an experience just before the accident. She had met the pastor of the largest church in the city at a retreat where the subject of death was discussed. When Mary asked him why, "if we Christians say we believe in the resurrection, do we cry and carry on so when friends and family members die?" The pastor asked if I had ever lost anyone I loved. I had to admit I had not. He told me to wait until I had, and I would know what grief causes people to do.

She was then surprised to see this pastor in the doorway of her hospital room after Roy's death. She invited him in but asked him to leave his sorrowful looking face behind for she had Good News for him. "He could no longer tell me I didn't know what I was talking about when it came to grief because now I had moved from believing in the resurrection, to knowing it (is real) from personal experience!

The pastor fell on his knees beside my bed and wept. He said he had dreaded coming to see me after my husband's death. He thought I had a 'Pollyanna' approach to death. He expected me to be broken in spirit, not radiant, and certainly not witnessing to the Resurrection! He then asked me to take his pulpit the following Easter Sunday [a thing he had never done before] because I knew the Resurrection was real, he only 'believed' in it." I "witnessed" from his pulpit the following Easter! What an incredible experience."[14]

Sister Mary was a remarkable woman, but she was not yet "completed." It is important to speak of Brother Stanley's challenge to her regarding the "infilling" of the Holy Spirit at an Ashram meeting, still in the early 1950s. Mary records the experience in her biography:

"At one of the Ashram meetings Brother Stanley spoke on the Holy Spirit. As I listened, I became more and more confused. I didn't understand what he was talking about and I felt sure there were others who were just as mixed up as I was—or so I thought."

After a swim the next afternoon Mary ran into Brother Stanley. "Young lady, I'd like to have a conference with you." All of a sudden Mary felt, "Now what have I done?"

She went to the meeting with Brother Stanley but inwardly she had her dukes up. Brother Stanley said, "I'd like to talk to you about the Holy Spirit." Impulsively she said, "Well if I don't have the Holy Spirit, who's spirit have I got?" He said "Well, don't make that mistake, Mary. You do have the Holy Spirit, for no one can say Jesus is Lord except by the Holy Spirit. The trouble is, the Holy Spirit doesn't have you. You have to surrender to him just like you did to Jesus." Mary had thought that the Holy Spirit was just related to the terminology of the Trinity, or was some sort of "influence." She did not understand at all what he was talking about. Brother Stanley said, "Well don't argue about it. Just kneel down here and ask God to tell you." She was afraid to ask God.

I didn't really know what Brother Stanley was talking about, and memories flashed from childhood where people acted strangely when talking about the Holy Spirit.... I had this deep fear about the Holy Spirit. Brother Stanley continued to try to help me. He said, "Mary, it's just wonderful for you to be on the level that you are. God is using you effectively. I want to help you to get from this current level to this new level, but I don't seem to be able to do it." He asked me to go to the chapel to pray so I did.

I knelt in prayer and said, "Now Jesus, I don't know what this is all about, but I'm not going to go backwards. I know that for four years a power that isn't my own has been working through me, giving me victory over so many things. This power has taken me through the death of Roy and made me happy and joyous and radiant and even victorious. This power has been available to me to help me to win people for you. I don't really understand what I need Lord, but I'm not going to lose what I already have."

I knew I didn't have what I needed. There was something missing and I lacked something. I know I did. However, because I couldn't understand it intellectually, I thought, "Well I'll let go of it. I'll just let God take care of this "problem." If his plan is salvation, let him worry about it."

Mary ran into Brother Stanley again that afternoon. She begged him to help her but he really did not know what to say to her. She said, "Well Brother Stanley, are you sure you know what you're talking about? Because it's so hard for you to explain all things to me. You're mixing me up." He said, "Well Mary, don't struggle with it. I'm sorry I even raised the question if it's going to upset you like this." Stanley then told Mary that Sister Selena, an African American friend of hers, (her same friend from the bus story) would understand and that she should go and talk to her.

Mary had gotten too comfortable. She realized that she was not growing. Just then, Sister Selena walked by. Selena had energy. She was full of graceful power. Mary sensed that she had none of this. The conversation went like this.

Now Selena, I love you very much and I trust your judgment. Brother Stanley told me this afternoon that I had a spiritual need. Do you think so? Selina's face lit up, "Honey, I've been praying for this day." That didn't make me feel too good either, and so I said, "Well Selena, he's telling me I need something. What do I need." She said, "Well Honey, let me put it this way. When I make baking powder biscuits I prepare the ingredients, roll them out, cut them out and put them in the oven. The recipe says, 'Bake for fifteen minutes.' If I open the oven door after ten minutes, those biscuits are all golden brown on the outside, but they are not baked in the middle. Honey, there is no question you are in the oven, but you are not baked yet."

I know now that she was talking about the message of Romans, but she explained it in a way that I could understand. I said, "Look, Selena, when this happens to me, when I am fully baked will you tell me? She said, "I won't need to. You'll tell me."

In the night Mary had a feeling of expectancy and a deep, urgent feeling came up within her. At the silent communion service the next evening Mary sat at the back of the auditorium because she did not want to disturb any of the other 300 people in the auditorium in case she began shouting or yelling. Then as she received the elements of bread and wine she said, "Well, I'm coming back to you tonight. Not as a sinner, but as a child of God. I'm yours." I came to God and said, "I want to belong to you, lock, stock and barrel. I don't want to think a thought that's not from you. I want to be totally and utterly dependent upon you because I choose you, not because I have to but because I want to be dependent upon you for everything." Then, with her eyes fully closed, for the first time in her life she saw a vision of a clear square glass vase that was slowly filling to the top. The moment I got empty enough of myself, he could fill me. He did and suddenly she was so full of the love of God she wanted to embrace the world. She thought, "My heart's going to break right here in front of these people. I can't contain this kind of love. He's just pouring his love through me." From that moment on Mary Webster was different.[15]

Brother Stanley was convinced that the revitalization of the church would come through the laity and so he consistently highlighted their significant contributions. He wrote, "If the church is pastor-centered then the output will be rhetoric, if it is lay-centered, the output will be action. It will be the Word become Flesh, not the word become word."[16]

From the early 1950s Stanley included lay witnesses in the Christian Ashrams. He wanted everyone to know the "how," the "powder biscuits" of living a life following Christ. He believed that we could each be transformed as we surrendered our lives to Jesus and could then draw on the power of His Holy Spirit as we moved through our lives.

Again, Stanley found Mary Webster to be a profound example of how an ordinary life transformed and redeemed by the Holy Spirit could become a force for sharing the love of Jesus Christ to all she encountered. "Mary feels that she is not the source of things but only the channel and that God speaks to her directly. And He does! 'A watch doesn't create time — it simply registers it. A violin doesn't create music — it simply registers the music in the violinist. So we don't create — we transmit.' She is the clearest channel of transmission I've ever seen. Let's read just a bit more about Mary's amazing story of transformation, written by Brother Stanley himself.

The very center of the Christian faith is the Incarnation, in which the Divine Word becomes flesh — the Idea becomes Fact. All other faiths are the word become word, the idea projected as an idea. In Jesus the Idea walked. It spoke in human life and manifested Itself in human relationships. Jesus transformed religion from idealism to realism. Where this faith is sincerely tried, it becomes incarnate as fact. It works in human relationships. And wherever it is tried, it produces something so exquisitely beautiful that we stand "lost in wonder, love, and praise.'"

From many outstanding examples of Christian growth I am picking one and for several reasons. One is that the person is an ordinary person, with ordinary education, with ordinary abilities. The second is that she was placed in a very common place situation — on a farm. And third, she wasn't always what she is now. (Her sister-in-law said: "Before her conversion Mary's attitudes were all wrong.") And because she was an average, I pick her out to let the average person see what can happen when average life is fully surrendered to God and responsive to His will. And I pick her out because in doing so I can easily look past her and beyond her and above her to the source of her life and power —Christ. One can so easily see that attached to Christ, she has everything, and apart from Him she has little. I wrote to her one day: "Sister Mary, I hope all this attention and adulation you are getting will not go to your head, but to your knees." She wrote back: "Brother Stanley, it doesn't go to my head or to my knees. It just hasn't got my name on it. It doesn't belong to me at all. So I lay it all at His feet as fast as it comes."[17]

Although the facts are slim, we can assume that for the rest of 1951 Stanley resumes his usual schedule of public meetings on behalf of the Crusade for a United Church and then his own evangelistic missions. Stanley would join Mabel in Montclair, NJ for Christmas with the entire family. Eunice was pregnant again, this time anticipating a boy (the name already chosen). Mabel would stay until the baby was born.

Apparently the Montclair house was a busy place, especially around Christmas, with guests in and out almost daily for tea or a meal with lots of fellowship. Many of these guests were from India. Jim had just returned from an extended visit to India two months earlier. He was basically optimistic although somewhat concerned about communism. Although the Indian Government was strongly anti-communist the conditions, especially toward the poorest, were none better now than before. "Such a condition is fertile soil for agitators."[18]

Stanley would leave by plane for India via Sweden on January 1.

Early 1952 finds Brother Stanley back in India. In the U.S., James Stanley (Stan) Mathews (joining his sisters Anne and Janice), was born to Eunice and Jim Mathews on February 17, 1952. According to Mabel's May 20, 1952 *Duplicate Letter* he is a "fine healthy eight pounder." She was there assisting the new mother and child for the first week after the birth.

As she writes this letter Mabel was back in Clayton in her "little old home nestled against a high Mississippi bluff" (but with no telephone or radio). It was a "vine-covered cottage adorned with Concord grapes, flowers, and berries galore."

During the spring, Stanley was conducting the annual Sat Tal Ashram and writing. While at Sat Tal he writes to Mabel confirming Jim Mathews' concerns regarding communism. Stanley is especially distressed over the growth of Communism among the educated classes who are being deluged with free, attractive literature from Russia.[19] For the rest of his time in India he conducted his usual preaching missions.

On May 20, 1952, Stanley wrote once again to Jawaharlal Nehru, perhaps to remind him of his support for and personal identification with the Indian nationalist movement and perhaps somewhat concerned about Jim Mathews' news the previous Christmas regarding the threat of communism. In the letter he enclosed an article to be published the next day in the *Christian Century*. Recall that Nehru was a lifelong socialist committed to the redistribution of land as well as to the elimination of corruption, the same goals that Stanley had mentioned in his earlier letter written on May 15, 1949. There Stanley was concerned about the possible expansion of communism. In the *Christian Century* article Stanley refers to that earlier letter, warning against apparent corruption, especially among some of the lower officials. He is remembering how the communists had seized on the nationalists corruption in China as the linchpin toward the revolution there.

On May 29, 1952 Nehru responded saying that he had "sent a quotation" from Stanley's letter "to all of his cabinet ministers and to all state governors." His primary concern was Stanley's assertion that there was still corruption among officials in India. He was amazed and no doubt disappointed as he had made many attempts to wipe out corruption. He could not imagine where Stanley got his facts. Nonetheless, Nehru had great respect for Stanley as a friendly critic of his government and readily accepted his warning.[20]

Once back in the U.S. Stanley returns to his usual routine of summer Ashrams, public meetings for a United Church and preaching missions.

Mabel's *Duplicate Letter* for October 20, 1952 states that she is still in Clayton. Over the summer she had "many guests, 113 of them from out of town — not bad for a town without a passenger train or a bus line."

Mabel's routine for the next several decades would be "to remain in Clayton until the first snow. Then she would leave for her home on E. Marks St. in Orlando, Florida until spring." Her plan was to spend the winters there (usually November 1 to May 1), except for the customary two weeks in Montclair around Christmas.

Mabel closes this letter with her usual concerns regarding funds for scholarships for her boys (apparently several of the elderly supporters had recently died). She was still remarkably hands-on as she mentions securing the help of the District Inspector of Schools to provide movies supplied by the U.S. Information Service twice a week, one for the younger school children and one for the older.

Early in 1953, Stanley was again in Japan, for three months (his third biennial evangelistic tour since the end of the war). He spoke in seventy-two cities and received approximately thirty-four thousand decision cards. Stanley actually wondered himself why he continued to be so successful as a Christian evangelist in Japan, even during the American military occupation. He finally concluded (in his June 11, 1953 *Indian Witness*) that his initial experience in India had taught him that indigenous peoples frequently "desire to please an occupying power," even to the point of "converting to their religion." Many such conversions, however, did not go deep. Then, just as he had learned to "disentangle" Christianity from Western imperialism in his early years in India, he had managed to dissociate Christianity from the postwar occupation in Japan. Although this was a brilliant achievement, nonetheless, after the occupation non-Christian attendance at Christian churches would decline due, in part, to the continued "moral and spiritual chaos" among the peoples of Japan.

As Stanley analyzed the significance of the thirty-four thousand "decisions for Christ" he had no illusions as to what that actually meant. After the 1951 crusades he realized that only about a fourth of those signing cards actually joined a Christian church. Now he was determined to find the reason. Where did the fault lie? Was his method too shallow? At one point he determined to deepen his message. Perhaps it was the fault of the Church. She was no longer a small sect on the borders of Japan's life as a nation. Had she, in the expectation of winning a nation to Christ, lost her focus.[21]

Stanley was quick to acknowledge that part of the problem was endemic to Christian evangelism itself. The evangelist was not in a position to disciple and nurture converts into a life of faith. The evangelist was called in to bring non-Christians to the feet of Jesus Christ as sinners in need of the salvation that only Christ could give. He realized that evangelism itself was nearly always inadequate. So, he was determined to do better and he wanted Japanese churches to do better. He was bold enough to tell Japanese Christians "that the Church of Japan was a pastor's church, organized around the pastor" and pastor's churches produced weak laity who contribute little or nothing to Christian evangelism. He found that somehow well-meaning missionaries had given the impression that all laity, especially women and young people, should be excluded from full participation. Women could not have a meeting without the pastor being present to pray, read the scripture and preach a sermon. Young people had to wait until they were forty before they could assume any responsibility. This needed to change.

In the meantime, this is not to say that Brother Stanley was ineffective for in the long run thousands saw him as a living example of what he preached. They told how the internal and external barriers in their lives had been broken and how their relationships with God, themselves and those around them had been changed forever.

Sabrow Yasumura served as his interpreter on this third tour. At the conclusion of his three months with Brother Stanley, Yasumura comments that, "when I think of good interpretation, I realize that it demands a depth of spiritual experience on the part of the interpreter in order to transmit the power of the speaker. This was not just about logical truth but spiritual power as well. To borrow a term from Dr. Jones, it requires a full surrender in order that God's own reality may be revealed." He then comments that "there is no long praying and no repetition of vain words. Just a quiet, unhurried hour of meditation over a passage in the Bible and communion with the living Christ in a most unpretentious manner, and yet almost everyday he talked about some new discovery in the Bible passage."[22] That was a powerful witness.

Then, while still in Japan Stanley read a newspaper article reporting on a parliamentary debate in India about the status of missionaries. It was so "painful" to read that Stanley responded with an "Open Letter" to the Government of India. He did not publish the letter but sent it to some of the national leaders. Apparently the Indian government suspected that Christian missionaries were agents of Western imperialism and that any religious conversions would upset the fragile political balance between a Hindu majority and the various minority religions in India. Ironically, Stanley, who had spoken out so forcefully on behalf of India was now suspected of the crime of neocolonialism. The "Open Letter" was a frank reflection of his dismay. For ten years the independent nation (the new Republic) had increasingly denied visas to Western Christian missionaries. India's concern was proselytism. Latourette writes that although India appreciated the establishment of Christian schools, hospitals, dispensaries, orphanages and institutions for the handicapped, it still objected vigorously to changing the religious orientation of Indians. They accused missionaries of dabbling in politics. Even the circulation of literature for religious propaganda would now not be permitted.[23]

Suddenly, as Stanley is planning his itinerary for the rest of the year in India and the U.S., he is wondering if the government of India would even permit him to return. Then, if permitted to return would he be able to lead the annual spring ashram at Sat Tal. For the first time in 46 years of connection he felt not wanted. India was his adopted homeland, where he had his second conversion experience (Lucknow), where he met and married his wife, Mabel, where their only child Eunice was born, where he had poured out his heart and soul for nearly half century to fulfill God's call to proclaim the good news of Jesus Christ.

Critical to all this was that Stanley had been insistent that genuine Christian conversion would so change human character that Christian converts would make positive contributions to the success of the world's largest democracies.

The responses (May, 1953) to his open letter were encouraging and reassuring. The consensus was that "if evangelistic missionaries would do evangelistic work in the spirit and outlook in which I was doing it there could be no objection." The Governor of Madras, Sri Prakasa, wrote offering his personal support and encouragement, "I am, therefore, sorry that any incident should have occurred which has resulted in your feelings of despondence for the future." Then, after reminding Stanley that the British *had* used "missionaries as their collaborators in the imperialism game" he suggested to Stanley that he might advise missionaries to have nothing more to do with politics. Stanley did just that at the Sat Tal Ashram.

In the summer of 1953 Stanley left India for the U.S. (he would not to return to India for just over a year). He immediately engaged his usual schedule of summer ashrams, his continuing Crusade for the United Church, followed by his one week preaching missions. Next, he spent a week with Mabel in Clayton, Iowa and began to toy with the idea of an autobiography. In December he apparently follows her to Orlando in time for Christmas.[24]

On January 3, 1954, Stanley was 70 (Mabel would be 76 on April 3). His friends held a birthday celebration that Stanley says, "It did not go to my head, but to my knees." By January 9 Stanley writes in a *Circular Letter* that he was now no longer toying but actually writing his autobiography. Then the "inner voice" stopped him to work instead on another devotional book, *Mastery, the Art of Mastering Life.* This would be published in 1955.

For the next few months Stanley maintained his usual schedule of preaching and writing. Then, on July 1, 1954, he and Mabel both officially "retired from the Methodist Board of Mission." Stanley comments, "You may retire me as an active missionary of the Board of Missions, but you cannot retire me as a missionary." Mabel concurred.[25]

There would be another celebration of Stanley's 70th at Sat Tal after his return to India in the late summer. Although he was officially retired he remained as busy as ever. Then, just when he seemed to be making some headway against the negative images of American missionaries, the U.S. sent military aid to Pakistan when Kashmir, a region lying between India and Pakistan — and claimed by both nations — was becoming a serious and volatile issue. Stanley was enraged — he believed it was a grave mistake. He wrote an outspoken article in the November 11, 1954 issue of the *Christian Century* stating "that to give military aid to Pakistan meant giving arms to a belligerent nation and was an unfriendly act to India."

Immediately, Stanley, with a group of Indians and missionaries at Sat Tal felt obliged to draw up a declaration "to clarify the position of Christian missions in India." This summarized and reaffirmed many of the basic principles that Stanley had articulated during his long missionary career in India. Basically it reaffirmed that "social services should not be used by missionaries as 'bait' for conversion to Christianity." The Christian gospel is not for "any particular nation," but for everybody." Proselytism should be rejected. Missionaries "*should have no political or financial connections with the government of the country from which they come.*" They should take no part in the politics of the country to which they go. No missionary should attack any person's religion and the property and institutions of foreign missions "should be transferred as quickly as possible to responsible bodies of indigenous Christians."

Stanley's objection to U.S. military aid to Pakistan and the Sat Tal Ashram's Declaration clarifying the position of Christian missionaries in India, were soon in the news.[26]

Apparently, Stanley is back in the U.S. toward the end of 1954 as he writes in his January 25, 1955 *Newsletter* that Mary Webster joined him in five of his week-long series. "She has taken more than her quota of speaking and a very large share of the personal counseling. She has grown amazingly in depth and in effectiveness and in divine wisdom in getting people into the Kingdom."[27]

Stanley makes his fourth biennial tour of Japan in the spring of 1955. The peace treaty formally ending WWII in the Pacific had been signed and American occupation had ended. There were still political tensions between the U.S. and Japan, however. The fear of communism (the so-called red menace in Asia), was rapidly polarizing almost all the nations of the world and giving birth to the decades long Cold War to follow. As a result some American troops remained in Japan, "not to supply personnel and provisions for the UN military forces during the Korean War, but to maintain 'internal security' in Japan."[28]

Against this background, as this fourth mission was launched Stanley's Japanese hosts were comfortable enough with his outspoken views on international politics not to allow the American government policies to stand in the way of another important evangelistic mission. By now, Stanley did not have to "disentangle" Christianity from American and Western imperialism. He could, instead, concentrate his efforts on the obstacles to evangelism within the Japanese churches. As recorded on his previous missions there was still a need for lay participation. We will see this being remedied in the future.

After Stanley's return to the U.S. for the summer ashrams of 1955, his *Mastery, the Art of Mastering Life,* is published. This was his twentieth book.

In January 1956, just before leaving the U.S. for six months in India and Southeast Asia, Stanley spoke in the Arena in Norfolk, VA to 4,000, one third of whom were African Americans. He writes that he was grateful for the meeting because he knew that the first thing they would ask me in the East would be: "What is America going to do about segregation?" His reply would be that under God these "two races were going to work this thing out together."[29]

In route to India, Stanley spent a week in Cairo where he held meetings in the large Presbyterian Evangelical Church in the city center. That church continues to have a strong inner-city witness today.

Back in India Stanley conducted a series of meetings for non-Christians in Gorakhpur, Belgaum and Madurai before speaking at the Mar Thoma Christian Convention in Maramon. This was followed by two more series of meetings in Punjab and Gujarat. He then went to Burma and Malaya.

In Burma Stanley held a number of meetings in Rangoon and an Ashram in the mountains of Kalaw. Here the "Karen rebels," who were Christians, were leading an insurgency against the government. In his 1956 *Circular Letter* Stanley writes that a Karen girl, who had been four years with the rebel forces in the jungles, came to the Ashram and was transformed. Stanley also wrote to the four Karen Christian leaders urging them to give up this useless and disastrous struggle, to come out and cooperate with the government.[30]

Finally, Stanley returns to India for his Sat Tal Ashram before leaving for his 1956 summer schedule of ashrams back in the U.S. In the midst of all this he manages to stop by Montclair to pick up granddaughter Janice, dropping her off in Clayton for the summer. He actually returns to Clayton twice during the busy summer to do some writing (*Christian Maturity*) and fishing. At the end of the summer Jim, Eunice, Stan and Anne dropped by for a wonderful family visit.

After the usual fall of preaching and writing, while still in the U.S., Stanley writes an important letter to President Eisenhower on December 26, 1956, "I believe that our national destiny is to take that last portion of the pledge of allegiance to the flag: '*with liberty and justice for all*' and apply it to all at home, to set our own house in order. And then go out into the world situation and apply it there... to all men everywhere..."

Stanley then continues, "The social revolution is on, especially in the East. Subject nations are throwing off imperialisms and colonialisms. Man is on the march. The Communists did not produce a social revolution — they betrayed it. They have turned it into channels of tyranny and compulsion. We must rescue it and turn it into channels of freedom and democracy." He would not be alone. Even Prime Minister Nehru embraces "with liberty and justice for all."

Stanley then speaks of emerging opportunities, primarily the Suez Canal with its access to the East."

Finally, Stanley concludes, "I believe, Mr. President, that God is matching you against this opportunity and armed with that simple phrase, 'with liberty and justice for all,' you can assume a moral leadership in this social revolution. If you do, Communism will not get a look in..."

Stanley had the pulse of the world. Who was more global at the time! He was the true renaissance man.

Jim and Eunice Mathews are gaining their own significant notoriety as Jim is elected Bishop in India in 1956. He declined the post suggesting that Indians should be ministered to by their own people.

On January 11, 1957, President Eisenhower responded to Stanley's letter written just a few weeks earlier thanking him very much and that he concurred. He especially appreciated, "with liberty and justice for all." "Frankly, it is a message I have been trying, though per-haps in an entirely inadequate way, to make the central theme of most of my speeches and documents that have to do with world af-fairs."[31] The correspondence with Ike continued for some years.

Almost immediately Stanley is on board a plane flying from Chi-cago to San Francisco headed for Japan. In route he outlines his sched-ule for the rest of the year. In his January 28, 1957 *Circular Letter* he wrote that he would spend three months in Japan followed by two weeks in Korea before leading the Sat Tal Ashram in India. He would then return to the U.S. for six Ashrams during July and August. In September he would once again speak on behalf of the Crusade for a United Church before completing the year with one-week evangelis-tic missions in fourteen different cities across the country.

So, Stanley is once again traveling throughout Asia. He is in Ja-pan with his growing team with him. Korea is next before returning to India. As a pacifist he seemed ever embroiled in wars and rumors of wars. This would only increase during the 1960s.

After Mabel's return to Clayton in May she completed a 356 page book (which will be published shortly by the E. Stanley Jones Foun-dation), "Educational Adventures in India." This book is not a per-sonal account of her time in India as it focuses almost exclusively on her school and her efforts to ensure top-notch educational experi-ences for her teachers and students. She does discuss the difficulties of living in India. It is, quite frankly, an amazing book replete with stories of her time in India. The pages are full of insights that mark her as loving, perceptive, disciplined, attentive and extremely hard working. For nearly half a century she had invested in boys from different castes, classes and races.

Most of all, Mabel was patient and wise. It seems that new mis-sionaries were forever seeing things done differently, and would au-tomatically think that they were done wrong and it was up to them to change them. Mabel kept saying, "Don't be in a hurry. Their ways may not be our ways but that does not mean that our ways are neces-sarily better. You may find that the Indian knows better than you what is best for him." Mabel and Stanley were on the same page in so many ways.[32]

Deservedly, on May 27, 1957, Mabel, while attending the commencement services at Upper Iowa University at Fayette (her alma mater where she graduated in 1903 with her Bachelors and in 1907 with her Masters), was presented a Golden Key, symbolic of having "survived fifty years since [her] graduation." Then, even more significantly, she was awarded an honorary Doctor of Humane Letters for her pioneering efforts in education. D. Elton Trueblood delivered the commencement address. In retirement, she continued to keep over 1,000 boys in school through scholarships she had personally cultivated from friends in the U.S.[33]

In July, Anne (now eleven) and Janice (now nine) joined grandfather Stanley at an Ashram at Keuka Lake, in NY. Their father reported that they both found it to be a meaningful experience.[34]

In September, Stanley's book of daily devotional meditations, *Christian Maturity* was published by Abingdon Press. He then adds in a *Circular Letter* that his next book would be on the topic of "Conversion." Such a book was needed as he surmised that only about a third of church members knew what conversion was by first-hand experience. He solicits instances of striking conversions that could be used (without names) for the book. Stanley then resumes his preaching missions for the fall.

Mabel writes twice in October, once to Eunice with news of Clayton and her plans to return to Florida the first of November. The second was a *Duplicate Letter* stating that Stanley had been to Clayton three times (briefly) since June but she would probably not see him again until late December.

Mabel then shares news of her boys. One who was an orphan had finished school and had a job. He wrote that "I am very happy in my work. There were no Christians in this village but now after five years of teaching, thirty-six families have been baptized. They have given a piece of land for a church and will give 600 rupees and free labor. I have given a month's salary ($15). A non-Christian man has given 3000 bricks and another has given three bags of cement."

Mabel concludes her letter by answering a question. "Is it true that the Sitapur School is the *first* boys school in India to be managed by a woman and to have all women teachers?" Mabel replies, "Yes, this is not only true but I believe it is still the *only* school where boys are taught by women." You might recall that Mabel was a bit of a feminist.

From the beginning her school had been highly praised by Inspectors. Mabel quoted from one, "I was much struck by the intelligent responses when I worked with the boys. They are far in advance of boys in parallel classes in other schools. What is especially interesting is the presence of the ladies in a boys school. It was a pleasure to visit the school. The boys have advanced far further than the boys of corresponding classes in any school that I have ever visited."[35]

Before moving on, it is significant that in 1957, in order to promote greater independence and greater local responsibility among the Ashrams (they were growing rapidly in many nations throughout the world), the Ashram Movement was incorporated in Texas as the American Christian Ashrams. They now had a board and greater accountability.

There is a handwritten letter from Mabel to Eunice, written from Orlando on January 12, 1958. Unfortunately Mabel had slipped on ice in her carport and had fallen (ice being a rare occurrence in Florida). Nothing was broken but ligaments were strained in her knee, hip and shoulder so that she was now in a wheelchair. She mentions that "daddy" was in Africa but she had not yet heard from him.

Then on February 22, Mabel writes in a *Duplicate Letter* that "my husband has been writing from the Belgian Congo in the interior of Africa. There were no roads to that Mission Station, so they flew in. He has now gone on to India and expects to be back in America on June 18."

Before moving on to speak of Brother Stanley there is a telling story recorded in this same letter. Mabel writes regarding one of her boys:

One of them nearly lost a chance for an education because I was in debt and felt I dared not take in another boy. I remember so well the young woman who came to me one morning with a five year old boy. Her husband had died and she had secured a scholarship in the Government Training School for midwives. This would give her a chance to become a decent, self-supporting woman. But she could not take her little boy with her and she had no one who could care for him. I shook my head but she was the "importunate widow" come to life.

"He is so little," she said. "He won't take up much room; and he eats such a little. Just keep him one year. He is a very bright boy and he will learn a lot in a year. I beg you. See I have brought his clothes." She held up two little cotton shirts and a pair of pajamas, old and patched but clean.

I again shook my head. She burst into tears. "I will work hard. I will learn quickly and when I earn, I will pay."

I said finally what you would have said. "Leave him." The next year, she provided his clothes. Then she began to pay something for his food. At first only 4 cents a month and then as much as 33 cents a month. Someone sent a scholarship and he finished High School. Then he entered one of our Theological Schools and is now a devoted Christian pastor. We never know what possibilities are wrapped up in a boy."

Early 1958 would mark yet another new and important phase of Brother Stanley's ministry. As mentioned by Mabel in her February *Duplicate Letter* he would begin holding evangelistic meetings in the Central African country of the Belgian Congo. At 74 years of age, Stanley was actually expanding his ministry into another continent adding to the already overload of the ashrams. He reminds the interested reader that Africa from the days at Asbury College was his first love (from early 1907). The Belgian Congo was just beginning to break the chains of European colonialism. Ghana, a British possession had become independent in 1957.

In spite of the anti-American and anti-Western attitudes, at no time was Stanley prevented from conducting evangelistic missions in Africa. It is interesting that the independent movements in Latin America during the last century were now sweeping Africa as well. Stanley writes that "you cannot suppress the demand for human freedom. It is innate. Wise colonialists will prepare for it and welcome it and further it."[36]

It is also significant that along with the political tide of nationalism in Africa was a rising spiritual tide. In Wembo Nyama in the Central Congo, Stanley held a five-day ashram primarily for the missionaries. In Lodja (also in Central Congo) Stanley encountered what he called a "very remarkable spiritual awakening" (*Circular Letter*, January 25, 1958). The Africans spend whole nights in confessing their sins publicly and the sins they confessed were "startling" including cannibalism, witchcraft, idolatry and adultery. Evangelists for centuries have known that the key to revival is the open confession of sin. Belgium officials commented that the Africans as Christians were now better citizens. One official actually asked that 50 Christian workers be sent to another tribe were there had been no Christian work. Government processes could never change the African. Ultimately, change must happen from within. In the final analysis, it was not the foreign missionaries that would lead the revival. In reality, the revival would being lead by Africans under the guidance of the Holy Spirit.[37]

Stanley then spent four days in Elisabethville, Belgian Congo, speaking sixteen times. Notably, in the 3,000 member Methodist Church the crowds responded in great numbers. Missionaries said that if you treat the African (not as children as was the habit of so many) but with respect, honoring their mentality, they would respond.

Alexander Reid, the District Superintendent in the Central Congo Conference of the Methodist Church, thanked Stanley for his visit. In a letter written on February 25, 1958, he wrote: "In behalf of the Central Congo Conference of the Methodist Church, I want to express to you our deep and lasting appreciation for your visit to us during the past month. Your messages and your life have so exalted Christ that our folks who were there for the week can never be the same." Reid then affirmed Stanley's use of the three-fingered salute, "Jesus is Lord!" When Reid traveled 150 miles north of Lodja he found natives greeting each other with the same three-fingered salute.[38]

Back in India the issue of delaying Indian visas to American missionaries surfaces again in April. Stanley and Rev. H. A. Townsley conducted interviews with three top government officials about this problem— Prime Minister Nehru, the home minister, Govind Ballabh Pant, and President Rajendra Prasad. Nehru agreed that, in general, relations between missionaries and the government were "better." Stanley wisely explained why, after the war, Christian missionaries increased from 2,500 to about 5,000. This increase came not from the "old line missions," like the Methodist, but from more "marginal groups," the independent groups. As for the Methodist, 93% of the Bishops, District Superintendents and the heads of almost of all Methodist institutions were Indians. He believed that these independents somewhat naively threatened the mainline churches that had been working for decades to present the gospel in an Indian way. Apparently, the independents (especially the Pentecostals) were not convinced that the "Indian way" was adequate and were proselytizing— in effect making Pentecostals out of Christians rather than making Christians out of non-Christians.

Stanley is back in the U.S. for his usual summer Ashram tour, followed by his normal fall schedule of preaching and writing. He anticipates joining Mabel for Christmas.

The following year (1959) Stanley is back conducting his sixth biennial tour of Japan.

He continues to be concerned about follow-up among new converts within the Japanese ashrams (John Wesley insisted that "to lead people to Christ without also providing adequate opportunity for growth and nurture was to beget children for the murderer."). Stanley takes several others with him on this tour. He not only took Dr. McConnell to continue his training for visitation evangelism, he included Melvin Evans, Tom Carruth and Mary Webster (later Tattersall) to be part of the team and to speak to these issues as well.

Evans (the head of Democracy in Action in the U.S.) attempted to help the Japanese improve human relations by changing the lives of management in the midst of their industrial boom. Evans attempted to help the Japanese change human relations by changing the lives of management. Because of Japan's rapidly growing "almost miraculous postwar industrialization" Stanley asked Evans to "come to Japan and put his movement into Japanese industrial relations." Stanley later writes (again in the *Indian Witness*) that Evan's movement has taken root and is proving very effective in Christianizing industrial relations. One Japanese head of a large business concern stated that his men were no longer mad at him. When Stanley asked why he replied, "Because I'm no longer mad at them."[39]

There was still another problem encountered in Japan, however — how to teach Christianity as a form of transformation instead of information. He writes in an article in his *Indian Witness*, that the Japanese were "taught to know about Christ, instead of to know Christ. In order to overcome this problem he took with him Dr. Thomas Carruth, the head of the Prayer Life Movement in the Methodist Church (Carruth would later become one of the primary leaders in the newly chartered United Christian Ashrams).

Stanley again also included Mary Webster. As a lay woman, she was especially effective in speaking ahead of Stanley at the six ashrams. Tom Carruth and Mary Webster were both powerful witnesses alongside Brother Stanley.

In the midst of his continuing busy schedule Stanley finds time to speak out against racism. Interestingly, while Stanley was still in Japan he learned that Asbury College had voted to segregate. Stanley wrote as a faithful alumnus and member of the Board of Trustees that it was with deep sorrow of heart that the trustees had voted to make the institution racially segregated. Stanley then wrote to Dr. Johnson, the president of Asbury, February 19, 1959 from Tokyo tendering his resignation from the Board.[40]

Amazingly, Stanley is still thinking about New Guinea. He had brought up the possibility of ceding New Guinea to Japan both before, and after the war. He writes again to Richard Gardiner Casey, the former Australian minister, on April 11 arguing that giving New Guinea to Japan, especially if the grant were made under the auspices of the United Nations, would strengthen the security of Australia. Casey, now in a role more directly under the Prime Minister, responded on May 31, 1959. The gist of his message was that since their first discussion "there have been too many changes in the world and in light of Japanese aggression it is not the policy of the Australian Government to acquiesce."[41]

At the end of the tour Stanley wrote to son-in-law Jim on July 8, 1959 that Tom Carruth and Mary Webster were with him in Japan and Korea. Carruth would only be able to remain with him in Japan and Korea this time, but would come to India the next trip in 1960. Stanley then adds for the sake of propriety that "obviously Mary Webster and I could not go on alone without him."[42]

Stanley is finally back in India for the Sat Tal Ashram, maintaining his brutal schedule there before returning to the U.S. for another brutal schedule until the end of the year.

Stanley concludes the year 1959 by insisting that this was the best year ever. How can he remain so optimistic in the face of everything going on around him? We allow Brother Stanley to speak for himself.

"Do not fight with yourself. The key is for you and yourself to be partners in a great cooperative enterprise of fulfilling an unfolding will of God."[43]

Stanley was accused of being disciplined but he never thought of himself as disciplined. His discipline simply became a way of life.

There is something in Jesus that is native to Stanley's blood, to his nerves, to his tissue, to his organs, to his relationships — to him as a total person. He is native to Jesus and Jesus is native to him. They were made for each other as the eye is made for light, the conscience for truth, the aesthetic nature for beauty. So discipline is functioning in the way we are made to function. Therefore, discipline is delight.

There is no use trying to discipline yourself until you surrender yourself. The central discipline is self-surrender [Stanley's forever passion]. To try to discipline yourself without a surrender of yourself means you are sitting on a lid. The discipline in that case means tension — trying to discipline a recalcitrant self that doesn't want to be disciplined. So the usual idea of discipline is tense nerves, a determined will asserting itself against all deviations from the discipline. That is far from Christian discipline and alien to it. Christian discipline is complete surrender to Jesus Christ as Lord, with no "ifs" and "buts" and no strings attached. He is Lord of me and everything that belongs to me and is related to me. Then around that new center the surrendered self is disciplined and cultivated — and expressed in freedom.[44]

The Apostle John wrote (I John 5:13), "For to love God is to keep his commands; and they are not burdensome." Why? — Because what he commands, his nature commends. God can only will our highest good for that is His nature. "God is love." It does not say that God loves but that God is love. Not to love would violate his nature. So, all Gods commands are love in action and therefore good in themselves and good for us.[45] Amen!

Eunice Mathews

Eunice and Mabel

Anne Mathews-Younes, Robert G. Tuttle (Author), Lillian Wallace, and
Jennifer Tyler in Sat Tal, India, Oct. 2017

CHAPTER TEN

THE 1960s: THE BEST IS YET TO COME:

Stanley is Much on the International Scene While Mabel Settles into Retirement

Throughout the 1960s Stanley was fond of saying (again his marvelous use of the superlative) that his most recent evangelistic mission or the events of the past year as a whole were "the best ever." Stanley, now an international celebrity, continued to schedule almost nonstop public meetings and ashrams, sometimes speaking four and five times a day.

It was only toward the end of the decade that his pace began slowing down. His informative *Circular Letters*, to this point written four times a year, would be reduced to twice a year. He would increasingly need help completing his heavy schedule, relying on friends like H.H. McConnell, Mary Webster and Melvin Evans to assist him. Nonetheless, in spite of approaching his 80th year he maintained his lifelong practice of traveling, speaking and writing on almost a perpetual basis. The only threat to his health was a mild form of diabetes that he controlled by diet.[1]

As Stanley's Ashrams continued to multiply worldwide, it became impossible to attend all of them personally. Yet, watch Brother Stanley go....

Early in January 1960 Brother Stanley is back in the Belgian Congo holding ashrams at Wembo Nyama (the central Province) and Katanga (the southern Province). Providentially (no pun intended), the Chief in Katanga Province (with 1,500,000 subjects) was converted at the ashram. He was baptized April 17, 1960.

In just over two months (June 30, 1960), Belgian Congo became independent. Stanley was praying that the Christian Ashram experience would help prepare both missionaries and Africans for the difficult period of adjustment.[2]

Soon afterwards, the newly converted Congolese Chief visited the U.S. State Department on a goodwill tour and was asked by an interviewer on TV, "What is your faith?" The Chief put up three fingers and said enthusiastically: "Jesus is Lord."[3]

On February 10, 1960, in her *Duplicate Letter,* Mabel wrote a to her longtime faithfuls. She was distressed to hear the news that Miss Pyari Phillips had died suddenly of a heart attack in India. Mabel's own sister, Carrie Lossing, had died just four days earlier (at 78).

Miss Phillips had taken over the school in Sitapur some years earlier and would be difficult to replace. She had just recently written to Mabel a cheerful letter that the boys had enjoyed a happy Christmas, thanks to the Christmas Fund. "I do love these boys. They are no more naughty than normal boys should be. The matron is a jewel and the teachers are very helpful. No one ever complains and we are all very happy together."[4]

Mabel then writes to her grandchildren just a week later mentioning upcoming birthdays and congratulating them on what she assumes will be good report cards.

322

Stanley writes to President Eisenhower again in early 1960 (during the last year of his second term). This time Frederic Fox, a special assistant to Eisenhower (who remembered Stanley's earlier letter from late 1956), writes, May 25, 1960 that the President has made the phrase, "'with liberty and justice for all,' the central theme of his life and work."[5] Stanley was grateful and pleased.

Also in 1960, Jim Mathews was elected to the episcopacy again. Jim and family had been living in Montclair, NJ for ten years. Although not a delegate to his own Methodist Northwestern Jurisdictional Conference (where Bishops for the area are elected), he was there as the Associate General Secretary of Global Mission meeting with a group planning to establish a university in the Belgian Congo. (Stanley had just returned from the Belgian Congo in January). Scheduled for yet another meeting at another Jurisdictional Conference, before he dashed off to the airport Mathews managed to address his own conference on a "delicate matter that related to a bishop already serving in Africa. His expertise in global perspective lent itself to speaking to the entire body for ten minutes."[6] Obviously, Providence was at work as most were impressed for in his absence, and much to his surprise, he was elected bishop himself.

When Jim returned to Montclair Eunice gave him the news but without much enthusiasm as Jan was crying and Stan refused to speak to him. Nonetheless, this time, he accepted the election. He was consecrated in Washington, D.C. at the National Methodist Church on June 19, 1960 and the family moved from Montclair, New Jersey (where they had deep roots) to Newtonville, Massachusetts. We are told that a family camping trip out West eased the transition a bit.

Jim Mathews, as Bishop, continued to be active in the Civil Rights struggles. As early as 1960, he met with Jackie Robinson and other prominent African-Americans to discuss growing racial tensions.[7]

Jim served as bishop of the New England Area for 12 years and then in the Washington (D.C.) area for eight more before retiring in 1980 — well, "sorta retiring." He would continue to serve as Bishop (filling in an occasional vacancy or for some special need) until 1996 — do the math — he would be the longest serving United Methodist Bishop.

In 1961, as Brother Stanley realized that the Ashram movement had continued to become so diverse in its locations, nationalities and languages, there was a need for a single organization to preserve the integrity of their spiritual focus. At the same time there was a need to accommodate the different national and cultural expressions of the common search for a deeper and more meaningful *koinonia* (community). Therefore, the Ashram movement once again changed its name, this time to the United Christian Ashrams, the name that the organization still bears today. By this time the ashrams were so successful that within a very few years (between 1968, when Stanley published his *A Song of Ascents,* until 1970) there were over 100 ashrams throughout the world, including Canada, Puerto Rico, Mexico, Spain, Uruguay, Peru, Bolivia, Brazil, Argentina, Chile, Israel, Japan, India, Burma, Korea, Taiwan, the Philippines, Indonesia, Malaysia, Singapore, Germany, the Netherlands, Norway, Sweden, Denmark, Finland, the Belgian Congo (Congo), Nigeria and Southern Rhodesia (Zimbabwe).[8]

Stanley saw the Ashram organization as a pyramid with numbers of people increasing from top to bottom. At the apex was the head of the ashram, Jesus Christ. Just below Christ were the Three (later the Four), followed by the Seven, the Twelve, the 120, the 150, the Church and finally the Kingdom of God. In terms of authority and responsibility the Seven — under Christ — were comparable to a board of directors with ultimate power over the policy, personnel and property of the United Christian Ashrams. The Three were an executive committee of the Seven.

Brother Stanley would remain actively involved in every aspect of the United Christian Ashrams throughout his life.

On August 24, 1961, the *Indian Witness* published a "request asking for letters of appreciation" from all those who knew how well

Mabel Jones had served India and her children and especially from those whose lives had been changed by her ongoing attention and care. These would be published in a book.

The article went on to say that, "The name 'Jones' is widely known, not only in India but all over the World. While Dr. Stanley Jones carried the good will of one country to another and has inspired the people in various countries by his personal life and devotion to his Lord and Master, and by his writing, *Mrs. Jones was, throughout her ministry, interested in building up the lives of children and young people.*"[9]

On January 26, 1962, the Stockholms-Tidningen Newspaper (actually the Stockholm Times in English) announced that "Dr. E. Stanley Jones, United States born missionary, has been nominated for the 1962 Nobel Peace Prize." This was for his reconciliation work in Asia, Africa, and between Japan and the United States before WWII.[10] Although not selected, this recognition was terribly significant.

Stanley spent part of the 1962 summer in Clayton writing and fishing but then, after leaving for his ashrams, Mabel's oven exploded and the house was ablaze. She writes in her next *Duplicate Letter* that "The town folk worked furiously to save the main part of the house but the roof over two rooms was destroyed and one wall." She concludes that the Insurance Company promised to have it all restored by the time she returns the following June (1963).

Stanley celebrated his 79th birthday on January 3, 1963, in Durham, NC. Significantly, the celebration took place in "a Negro church." He blew out 79 candles with a single puff. He writes from the Huntington Court Methodist Church in Roanoke, VA four days later, "So, I have some breath left."[11]

By the end of January 1963 Stanley is off to South America and then on to India before returning to the U.S. the end of June. He manages only one night in Boston with his daughter and family before flying off for his summer ashrams.

By the time Stanley returns from South America, Mabel is back in

Clayton with her helper/friend Dorothy Fisher. Dorothy is going over the repairs to the house as they recover from the fire the previous summer.

As Stanley resumes his schedule, Jim Mathews was again on the civil rights scene. Just four months before John Kennedy's assassination (November 22) Jim (as a United Methodist Bishop) was invited to join the President at the White House to discuss civil rights issues. Jim then participated in the "March on Washington for Jobs and Freedom" and was present at Dr. Martin Luther King's "I have a Dream" speech on August 28. HUGE!

In the midst of all this, Stanley is planning on spending time with Mabel. He did manage one short "vacation" in the late summer enjoying fishing down on the banks of the Mississippi while Mabel tended her garden. He was then planning a second visit following the Ashram in Missouri but on October 9 he received a letter from W. W. (Bill) Richardson, now general secretary of the United Christian Ashrams, stating that they had planned on allowing him time to be with Mabel after the Missouri Ashram but the Wyoming Ashram had changed the time of their meeting in order to make it possible to have Brother Stanley with them. The ashram folks in Wyoming felt they needed Brother Stanley present to keep their momentum moving forward. Not surprising, this reduced Stanley's second visit with Mabel to less than three days.[12]

On December 10, 1963 Mabel writes a *Duplicate Letter* from Orlando. "Two things have rejoiced my heart this summer. A generous friend gave $5000 to the Endowment Fund and two others have each left it $100 in their wills." She then adds that Stanley will arrive on December 17 and that Eunice and family hope to come in the spring. "All are well and busy. That seems to be always true of our family! But we like it that way."

Following Christmas, and anticipating Brother Stanley's 80th birthday, Bill Richardson organized eight American birthday dinners. These began on December 30, 1963 in Chicago and continued until

January 14, 1964 in San Francisco. Notables attending some of these celebrations included Luther W. Youngdahl, U.S. District Judge and former Governor of Minnesota and Methodist Bishop Gerald H. Kennedy.

From San Francisco Stanley left immediately for India where he had (by far) the greatest celebration of his 80th birthday. This took place at the Mar Thoma Syrian Church in south India. There, 75,000 gathered to acknowledge over a half century of missionary evangelism in India. He was given a beautiful ivory box, reportedly a "precious gift" to mark the occasion.

Even at the age of 80 Brother Stanley continued to enjoy an extraordinary international reputation. In fact, *Time* magazine reported in its January 24, 1964 issue that Stanley Jones's "fame overseas as an American evangelist is matched only by Billy Graham."[13]

The remaining part of this six month trek included more ashrams, not only in India but in Japan, Hong Kong, Thailand, the Philippines, Finland and Sweden. Writing from New York at the end of this tour Stanley happily reports that we are now realizing that most of these ashrams can carry on without us. They were self-sustaining, self-supporting and self-propagating.[14]

On Easter Sunday in 1964, Bishop James (Jim) Mathews and African-American Bishop Charles Golden were barred (on Easter Sunday) from entering an all-white Methodist church in Jackson, Mississippi.[15] Neither Jim nor Bishop Golden would be deterred as this simply became more grist for the holiness mill — especially as related to civil rights.

These were momentous days. Across the world Prime Minister Jawaharlal Nehru, the first Prime Minister of India, died on May 27. Mabel writes that "It will take a strong man to hold India together."[16]

Also indicative of the 1960s was Stanley's own continuing bold resistance to racism. He was back in the U.S. by the end of June in time to take note of the signing of the landmark Civil Rights Act by

President Lyndon B. Johnson on July 2, 1964. It should be noted that the American civil rights movement (begun in the mid-1950s) owes Stanley Jones an enormous debt. His *The Christ of the American Road* set the tone in 1944. In that book Stanley made an astounding prediction.

> Unless effective measures were taken to end racial discrimination in the U.S., Negroes, probably joined by whites, may have to resort to noncooperation, by picking out certain injustices and then, through volunteers trained in nonviolent methods, refuse to obey these specific injustices and take the consequences of that civil disobedience.

Think Rosa Parks and consider young Stanley (when just a boy) standing on a streetcar when a woman of color had no seat. Stanley stood to give her his seat and tipped his hat. The entire car murmured and Stanley's dear Miss Nellie was totally taken aback.[17]

So, how do we get equal rights for all? Here, Stanley notes in his *Song*, "There seem to be two choices. It is either violence or nonviolence." Almost unknown to most is that when Stanley met Martin Luther King, Jr., King said, "It was your book on Gandhi that gave me my first inkling of non-violent noncooperation." Stanley responded, "Then my book [on Gandhi] was not a failure." King replied, "No, if we can keep the movement nonviolent. That is the question which is now acute. The way for the Negro to achieve his freedom is to turn this whole movement from violence to nonviolence." Then, straight from the mouth of Gandhi, King quotes, "We will match our capacity to suffer against the other's capacity to inflict suffering, our soul force against his physical force; and we will wear our opponents down with goodwill."[18]

It is significant that King insisted that without exception, nonviolence in his own campaigns and demonstrations for racial equality was the rule, even when confronted with the most extreme and frightening provocations. With amazing consistency the marches and protests that he led were, in fact, nonviolent.[19]

Martin Luther King Jr. would receive the Nobel Peace Prize on October 14, 1964.

All of this obviously related to Stanley's understanding of the Kingdom of God that would remain a constant focus for the rest of his life.[20]

Throughout the fall of 1964 Stanley is conducting preaching missions. He was then with Mabel in Orlando December 16 for just over a week before flying on to Boston on Christmas Eve to be with his daughter and children. Mabel writes in her *Duplicate Letter* that "with so many friends and relatives down here [in Florida] the day is never a lonely one for me. I find the long trip to Boston in mid-winter too hard in many ways and I prefer to visit them as I go or come on my way to Clayton."

Mabel then adds that "The letters from India of late have not made pleasant reading. Once more there is famine — little food, high prices and people are starving. Life for most folks in India is a struggle to survive." Her Boarding Schools had been in great distress. The Manager wrote, "When I told the boys they could stay in the school they wept for gladness. They may be on short rations but at home there would probably be much less.... We still have 200 lovely boys."[21]

Stanley is back in India in early 1965. After a brief stay at Sat Tal he heads off to Africa and Asia.

By 1965, as European colonialism crumbled throughout Africa and Asia, social and spiritual upheavals accompanied the political transitions to independence. Stanley traversed these troubled continents for a very important reason. During one interview a radio reporter in Southern Rhodesia (Zimbabwe) was curious, "You are going to all the trouble spots of the world — Rhodesia, Congo, Nigeria, Indonesia, Malaysia, India — why? Stanley replied, "The Chinese have a word for 'crisis' made up of two characters — 'danger' and opportunity.' In every crisis there is opportunity, so I go to see if I can help in that opportunity." Admittedly, some of this may seem like foolhardy adventures, but I feel "the pressure of the Spirit, the call of God," so I go and it has been proven time and again that these adventures are of God.[22] Once again Stanley's "inner voice" kept nudging him into places where "God's voice was heard small."[23]

On April 27, 1965, Stanley wrote from Panang (a resort island off the coast of Malaysia), "The first stop on this four month tour was Southern Rhodesia, where a white civilization is trying to stem the tide of a rising black nationalism." Stanley wonders wisely, "Why not a 'new man' out of both parties where (in the case of Africa) a new continent could be composed of Western achievements in science and technology with African political leadership?"

Actually, while in Rhodesia, Stanley confronted the racism of the white minority by holding a healing service in a Christian ashram where "black men laid their hands on the heads of white people — never before done — and they were healed!"

Stanley's next stop was his third trip to Congo, a destination that "horrified" the whites of Rhodesia because for them the Congo was "the symbol of red ruin." As Stanley visited the Congo the outcome of the struggle between communists and non-communists was still unclear. Stanley prayed with Moise Tshombe, the troubled Prime Minister of Congo, that Congolese Christians would be the cement that holds the country together. Tshombe commented that apart from the Church he saw no solution for the problems of Congo. These words proved prophetic as he (a Christian) was dismissed from his position less than six months later by President Kasa-Vubu and Congo (Zaire after 1971) has struggled with internal unrest to the present.

Stanley would conclude the African leg of his 1965 tour in Nigeria. There he visited five different cities, held an ashram and because of the presence of a large proportion of Christians among the officials of the national government, concluded that Nigeria was the "most progressive and hopeful of African democracies. Unfortunately they had just discovered oil and the oil money would eventually lead to unheard of corruption. Less than 1% of the newly discovered wealth would reach the people. It is almost as if one cuts down those pagan totems (remember the Old Testament Asherah poles), buries them, and then leaves them in the ground long enough, they turn to oil.[24]

Next, Stanley stopped in Indonesia. Sukarno, a nationalist leader, was exploiting the anti-American and anti-Western ferment. While in Indonesia, Stanley was also troubled by Sukarno's attempt to unite his people in support of his territorial ambitions in neighboring Malaysia. Indonesia's Muslim population would soon become the largest in the world.

By April 1965 Stanley was in Malaysia, a paradise next to Indonesia. He described an Ashram at Port Dickson, the nearest port to Indonesia and the spot where Indonesian guerrillas were being sent over to invade Malaysia. True to Stanley's indomitable spirit, he went on with the Ashram as if nothing were happening. Most interesting! He then returned briefly to India.

After leaving India, the final destination of Stanley's far-flung series of trouble spots was perhaps the most troubled spot of all, Los Angeles. The riots in Watts, a section of the city, began on August 11. As the plane landed the pilot said that fires were ragging in Watts. He pointed out the billowing smoke where a racial conflagration was evidence of the pent up angers.[25]

Stanley is soon busy again. Between Ashrams, he is in Clayton (twice) fishing and writing. Mabel writes in October that after "Eunice had seen the children back in school (Stan in Groton, an Episcopal School, Janice in Wooster, a Presbyterian College, and Anne back for her second year at Earlham, a Quaker College) she [Eunice] then drove to Clayton for a few days before Jim arrived to drive back home with her." When they arrived, Jim found an invitation to meet with Pope Paul VI in New York. He would be the first Pope to visit the Americas.

Ironically, in the Fall 1965 Stanley was invited to speak at Emory University in Atlanta where Dr. Thomas J. J. Altizer, the leader of the God-is-dead movement, was a member of the faculty. In his address Stanley stated, "I hear there has been a death since I was last here. If the person who announced it will say, 'As far as I am concerned, God is dead,' I will accept it." The students roared. Stanley then met with Altizer for an hour in order to understand more fully the source and significance of his unique theology. After the interview Stanley wrote, "Altizer had simply "theologized his own emptiness of God." Stanley called the movement "the strangest movement I have ever come across in all my days..."

The point was that for Altizer, although God was dead, Christ is alive. Stanley responded that a Godless Christ is unthinkable. If you find Christ you find God, and He is very much alive the moment you find Christ. Stanley at 81 concluded that the God-is-dead philosophy "opens up a tremendous mission field to present a living God..."[26]

Following the experience at Emory, Stanley, with the recent memories of the Watts riots burned into his spirit, travels to the even deeper South. This time Decatur, Alabama, where blacks and whites together faced the harsh realities of racial discrimination from the standpoint of their common faith in Jesus Christ. Quite frankly, Stanley believed that he was "going into a caldron." Actually his meetings at an inter-racial dinner for pastors and their wives, and other civic and religious leaders were entirely peaceful and exhibited a commitment to resolve racial problems through patience and love.[27]

Stanley once again travels for the Crusade for a United Church, albeit with lesser enthusiasm as the movement seemingly is no longer striking fire. Then after Christmas, he is back in India.

During 1966 and 1967 Stanley, for the most part is back and forth between the U.S. and India with a focus on the ashrams.

On January 18, 1966, Stanley receives a letter from Richard Phillips, the acting Assistant Secretary for Public Affairs with the U.S. State Department. Phillips' letter is actually a reply to an earlier letter from Stanley to President Johnson about a proposal for peace in Vietnam that had been made by the President of India, Dr. Radhakrishnan. Phillips thanked Stanley for his interest and stated that the United States had "been in contact with the Indian Government" with respect to Radhakrishnan's proposal. "We find his suggestion interesting and believe there is much in it that might be acceptable." Unfortunately, Stanley's (nor Radhakrishnan's) boldness did not lead to the immediate end of the war.[28]

Then almost immediately Stanley flies from Delhi to the Galilee in Israel expecting to open a fruitful new mission field. Still reeling a bit from the God-is-dead movement among the "avant-garde thinkers" Stanley now looks to Israel to establish his next ashram. Traveling with Rev. Don Saylor, a Lutheran pastor from Columbus, OH (Saylor had taught pastoral counseling at the Sat Tal Ashram in years past and this book is dedicated to Don and Patricia Saylor) and sister Lila (a Greek Orthodox nun who was very active in the ashrams) Stanley is looking for a suitable location. He would return the next year, hopefully to make the purchase.

On May 12, 1966, predictably, Allister R. MacKay, the associate treasurer of the Crusade for a United Church, writes that Stanley's old friend, Harvey Kazmier, sensing that Stanley's passion for federal union was losing its grassroots support, was in the process of closing his office in Boston and moving it into his home in Newton, MA. They had given such a worthy cause a good run but had come up short. Nonetheless, Stanley would continue to hold his related concept of Federal Union as one of his major passions.

Now back in the U.S. for the rest of 1966, Stanley assumes his normal routine of Ashrams and preaching missions but without the Crusade for a United Church engagements. This did not slow his pace, however.

Let's follow Brother Stanley just for the next six months in some detail. From October 30 to November 3 he conducted a Spiritual Life Mission at the First Methodist Church in Garden City, Kansas. He spoke to the youth for an hour before the evening Festival of Faith service which included Protestants and Roman Catholics.

The next week Stanley spoke at a Religious Emphasis Week at Anderson College in Anderson, Indiana. Although speaking mainly to students it became a community-wide affair. The next week

(November 11-18) find him doing a weeklong mission at St. James African Methodist Episcopal Church in Cleveland, Ohio (this was preceded by a One Day Ashram at the same church). These services included Presbyterian, Baptist and C.M.E. churches as well. From November 20-22 he conducted an Ashram in Medina, New York. On Thanksgiving Day and following he was in Phoenix, Arizona at the Paradise Valley Methodist Church for a preaching mission followed by a Sunday morning service at the same. From November 27 to December1, find Stanley at the Casa de Paz y Bien Ashram in Scottsdale, Arizona.

During the rest of December Stanley preached a mission at the First Methodist Church in Omaha, Nebraska (attended by all other Methodist Churches in the area, including the Bishop), an Ashram in Columbus, Ohio, a Spiritual Life Mission at the First Methodist Church in Kane, Pennsylvania and a one day Puerto Rican Ashram at Riverside Methodist Church in New York City (sponsored by his old friend, Roberto Escamilla). There were over 100 pastors present marking the beginning of still further activity among the Puerto Ricans in the New York area.

Stanley was with Mabel from December 18-23 before spending Christmas and the few days following with Jim, Eunice and the grandchildren. On New Years Eve, from 10 am. to 3 pm, he held a retreat at the Fellowship House for International Christian Leadership in Washington, D.C. On New Year's Day he spoke at the Chicago Sunday Evening Club, a bit of his routine for over 20 years.

January 3-6, 1967, Brother Stanley preached a Spiritual Life Mission at the Vermont Street Methodist Church in Quincy, Illinois. From January 8-13 he preached a Mission and Ashram combined at the First Methodist Church in Pensacola, Florida with the "entire backing of the Board of Evangelism of the Alabama-West Florida Conference, the Ashram Committee in Pensacola and the Conference Board of Lay Activities (somehow including a Conference-wide "Spiritual Life Meeting" at Blue Lake, near Andalusia, Alabama). Back in Florida, on January 14 there was a Saturday meeting of the "Seven" (Ashram

Board) before a Sunday morning service at Northside Methodist Church in St. Petersburg. January 16-20 Brother Stanley led the Ashram in Avon Park, Florida, before leading a Spiritual Life Mission, in cooperation with the South Lake County Ministerial Association, the next week at the First Methodist Church in Clermont, Florida.

Stanley writes on January 28 that his spiritual autobiography, *A Song of Ascents* is finally complete. This culminated his third attempt to write an autobiography. His *Song* was published in 1968.

From Florida Stanley flies to Honolulu, Hawaii for an Ashram at the Central Union Church January 29-February 5. Those organizing the Ashram asked Mary Webster to come as well.

Japan is next, February 6-April 10. His expanding global routine had forced him to interrupt his somewhat normal biennial visits to Japan so this was important. The National Christian Council of Japan arranged the itinerary throughout the southern parts of Japan.

Korea is next, April 11-25. The itinerary here is arranged by Rev. Greenfield Kiel, General Secretary of the National Christian Council and Bishop Lee of the Methodist Church in Korea. There were Round Table talks with various small groups and home visiting during the days with open meetings in the evenings. Then there were mass meetings at cities outside of Seoul.

Stanley is next off to the Philippines, April 26-May 8. The first four nights were large outdoor mass meetings with loud speakers in one of the plazas in the heart of Manilla. Choirs from various churches throughout the city provided the music. This was followed by a weeklong Ashram arranged by the World Division of the Board of Missions of the Methodist Church in the Philippines.

In June Stanley is back to India for the Sat Tal Ashram. Mary Webster is still with him and granddaughter Anne has joined them as well. In route, he had intended to stop in Galilee to see about "the site the Israeli government was offering us on the bluff overlooking the Sea of Galilee." On June 1, however, he was awakened by the

Inner Voice saying, "Cancel." The Six Days War (June 5-10, 1967) broke out the day before he was to arrive in Tel Aviv.[29] The Galilee land purchase for the Ashram property would never happen.

Meanwhile Mabel is back in Clayton. She has no doubt been praying for her husband, especially while in Japan, Korea and the Philippines. Never far from humor, she quotes the Saturday Evening Post, "Children grow and go; husbands travel; dogs roam; only the cat and I stay home."

"Bishop Jim" was traveling as well. He was recently in London for a committee arranged by the Chaplain to the Queen and entertained at Windsor Castle where the Queen gave a reception for them. In August he would be in Greece.

With India forever on Mabel's heart she writes that news from Sitapur is again disturbing. She was not surprised at the reported riots. "I wonder how we would act if we were starving. I never cease to be amazed at what I see thrown away in our garbage cans. In India our old tin cans and waste paper were eagerly begged for and even paid for, and no food was wasted.

The school was "besieged by requests to take more boys.... Fortunately, we have 13 acres of ground and they can raise onions, potatoes, and many Indian vegetables, including pigweed, which we in America consider useless."[30] She concludes her *Duplicate Letter* with accolades for her former boys (some were with her when she took over the school in 1911). They have since risen in positions of trust by the Church and in Government Service and are now helping to support the school.[31]

Mabel was struggling with cataracts but the doctor wants to put off surgery for the present.

Once back in the U.S., no doubt after a difficult time in India (per Mabel's report of famine), for the rest of 1967, Stanley resumes his usual schedule of preaching missions and Ashrams. He would spend a couple of vacations with Mabel from September 11-23 and December 14-23(in Pensacola and Orlando), but not Christmas.[32]

1968 is the year that Stanley would publish his spiritual autobiography, *A Song of Ascents*. This book, perhaps more than any other, has affected my own sense of what it means to be a Christian.

Unfortunately most, if not all of the biographies of Stanley Jones tend to dwindle out at this point in his life, as if not much happened during the last five years of his ministry. Believe me, Stanley Jones' life would not begin with a bang and end with a whimper. His life began with a bang and ended with a resounding YES!

Mabel at 90 was still raising money to support her boys in India. It was mentioned earlier that she wrote letters expressing the needs by telling stories of her boys rather than just asking for money. The Board of Missions would continue to use her methods as a model for other missionaries for years to come.

Her eyesight was getting worse. While she can still see she hurriedly reads all of Shakespeare's plays within a two week period so that she could reflect on them if her eyesight failed completely.[33]

Stanley continued his traveling, speaking and writing. His last three books would be written with the same passion as *The Christ of the Indian Road*, published 43 years earlier. His, *The Reconstruction of the Church – On what Pattern?* (1970), *The Unshakable Kingdom and the Unchanging Person* (1972) and *The Divine Yes* (1975, posthumously) were some of his best yet. They demonstrate his commitment to the issues that affect the world. They are timeless, being just as relevant today as they were then.

They all remind us of the deepest conviction of Stanley's life: "Self-surrender is the way to self-expression." You must lose your life to find it (again, according to Jesus the first principle of Christianity).[34] Along with many of the ancient church fathers, Stanley believed that "Jesus is Lord" was the earliest Christian creed.

Tragically, on April 4, 1968, Martin Luther King was assassinated at the Lorraine Motel in Memphis, Tennessee.

Stanley and Mary Webster were in India. Mary writes a fascinating letter to granddaughter Anne at Earlham College on April 18. Among birthday greetings she writes that "This is just to report on "Granddaddy in the rice paddy" (Anne's term of endearment for her grandfather created when she traveled with him in India a few months before). We are getting on quite well and I try not to do anything to upset him." Stanley was so demanding of himself that he apparently found it difficult to comment on others (good or bad). He made an attempt never to allow someone else to hear something from him secondhand that was not positive. Mary writes that Stanley is saying such wonderful things to her about the rest of the family (he is so "very proud of Mabel;" Eunice "is really a brilliant woman in her own right;" he thrills to the possibility of Anne traveling with him again in the summer), Mary wishes he would speak these compliments to them personally. At 84 years of age, he is still insisting on carrying his own weight, sometimes to a fault (that would include carrying heavy suitcases).

Mary attends Stanley's every engagement. In spite of the heat, they are going along well and the meetings are wonderful. Mary is so helpful, serving as a virtual secretary, Stanley is eager for her to travel on to Europe with him but she is ready to get home where she hopes to see Anne. "You (Anne) really *are* fabulous! I loved every minute with you and we both wish you were with us now."[35]

Then, just two months after Martin Luther King's assassination in Memphis, Robert F. Kennedy was shot at the Ambassador Hotel in Los Angeles on June 5 and died the next day. He was a presidential candidate having just won the California primary in the 1968 election. Along with King, Kennedy was a champion of civil rights. This had to give Brother Stanley pause.

Mabel writes an interesting *Duplicate Letter* from Orlando in July. She regrets not venturing over to Clayton this year but her eyesight has deteriorated to the place where she cannot see well enough to travel safely. She anticipates surgery in the winter. She then states that Stanley has returned from India and Europe and is now filling his normal routine of engagements (no doubt meaning Ashrams throughout the summer and preaching missions in the fall). She expects him to visit her in Florida beginning August 28. "He will miss his fishing in the Mississippi River but there must be fish somewhere in Orlando's more than 35 lakes."

Mabel concludes her letter with the good news that "an Endowment Fund for our Boys' School in Sitapur [drawing only on the interest] will keep it in existence after I drop out." She thanks many of her "faithfuls" for keeping individual boys in school. "I wish I could tell you of the many who are now fine self-supporting members of the church in India."[36]

In October Brother Stanley wrote to Eunice, Jim and Anne after a short flight to Bethlehem, PA. He had just seen them briefly in Chevy Chase where he spoke at Wesley Theological Seminary, discussing the substance of his soon to be published book, *The Reconstruction of the Church – On what Pattern?* The whole student body gave him a standing ovation. He was told that this had never happened before. He was surprised as his presentation was rather conservative (perhaps the students were reacting against the new "avant-garde").

Stanley had then preached in Washington D.C. on Sunday morning to a packed house (twice). In the afternoon there were 500 out for the Youth meeting and 25 stood offering themselves for the ministry, 55 for the Mission Field, 85 for full-time work as laymen and 80 for personal surrender. The pastor told Stanley that he did not believe that that could happen. Stanley must have been thinking, "Oh ye of little faith."

In Bethlehem, PA, the Mayor gave him the key to the city (his third in a month including Charlotte, NC and Sandy Springs, GA). He closes his letter, "I'm looking forward to Christmas! Love to all. Lovingly, Daddy."[37]

We can finish out 1968 with another letter from Stanley to Eunice, Jim and Anne. This one is dated December 5 from California. He had some "interesting" days, especially at Lodi where he spoke six times a day. Held in a large Seventh Day Adventist Church, seventeen churches participated, including the Roman Catholics. There was a well-attended regular ashram (150 persons), followed by a "One Day" ashram (200 persons).

Stanley is then off to Sacramento for a brief TV interview before another series of meetings that were "not so strenuous." He concludes the letter by repeating his plans for Christmas in Orlando.

It should be mentioned that although Eunice was less than enthusiastic about Jim's appointment as Bishop to the Massachusetts area (actually the New England Conference of the United Methodist Church), she soon ingratiated herself into the community, not only in a supportive role for Jim, but also as a social activist. During the late 1960s, Matthew Dumont, M.D., assistant commissioner for drug rehabilitation for Massachusetts, asked Eunice to write a book for The North Conway Institute that would provide the Commonwealth a sense of purpose and direction in a critical and confused area. Dumont said that the Institute took a bold and creative step by commissioning "an intelligent, open-minded, sensitive and articulate layperson [Eunice] to find out what she could about the drug scene in Massachusetts and what is being done about it at the community level." The result was, *Drug Abuse: Summons to Community Action.*

First published in the *Boston Globe*, fifty thousand copies of the books were next distributed to schools, churches, state agencies, federal armed forces agencies, libraries, hospitals, YMCAs, the St. Paul Council on Alcohol Problems and Drug Abuse, the Massachusetts Council of Churches and Boston's Drug Seminars. Together, these stretched along the east coast from New England to Florida.

Eunice described six case histories of community responses to drug issues that she recognized as symptomatic. Dumont writes that while not de-emphasizing the dangers of widespread drug use, "Eunice Mathews manages to avoid the panic and rage that causes so many people to turn to hastily conceived panaceas or repressive police tactics as a way of controlling their anxiety."[38] Still relevant? Yes!

Then, on March 21, 1969, Mabel writes to Eunice from Orlando.

Husband Stanley and granddaughter Anne are off to Mozambique for a several week evangelistic trip to Africa. Stanley had written that if Mabel would go to Clayton he would take an engagement in Minneapolis so that he could plan a visit. That must have been good news but she wonders how he will get back and forth. Furthermore, although she is eager to get back to Clayton, there is no one to drive her. "All her 'dependables' are dead, or old, or gone."

Then on June 8, 1969 Mabel writes Jim a letter thanking him sincerely for "depositing" her in Clayton. She hopes that some son-in-law of his will be as good to him one day.

Stanley's ashrams were still the mainstay of his own sense of belonging. I mentioned in the Introduction that I attended several of these Ashrams with Brother Stanley back in the summer of 1969.

After writing Eunice from Idyllwild, CA on August 19, while conducting an Ashram with over 300 in attendance, Stanley is off to Hawaii and then on to American Samoa, Australia and New Zealand. He meets granddaughter Janice at the airport in Los Angeles. She will be with him through Hawaii, Samoa and parts of Australia. In Samoa Brother Stanley uncharacteristically questions some of the food they are being served while Jan bravely eats whatever is put before her without a question. He no doubt is proud of her. He and Jan are both well although Stanley is taking medication for some eye trouble. Thankfully his diabetes is under control.

The meetings went better than expected in Samoa, "a little better than Honolulu." The Samoans "are very lovable people and we are grateful to be here."[39]

From Samoa it is on to Australia and New Zealand.

Let's finish out the decade with some of Brother Stanley's thinking from late in his *Song*, especially as relates to his ongoing passion — out of two, one body.

Stanley is about to deliver his "soul" on church union as his book that embraces the subject, *The Reconstruction of the Church – On what*

Pattern? is soon to be released. This has been his passion for nearly three decades but apart from an article in the *Indian Witness* the following May, these would be his last words published on the subject.[40] Although he has moved beyond the Crusade for a United Church with the closing of the office in May of 1966 by his old friend, Harvey Kazmier, in his *Song* his passion still shines through.

When Stanley speaks about church union, he frequently calls it *ecumenicity*. That literally means "throughout the world." Ecumenism, however, needs a body to avoid becoming a ghost. Stanley still has a plan—the many becoming one.

At the time (the late 1960s), Stanley still believed that the tide of church union was accelerating. By way of explanation, he could not imagine the U.S. political system wiping out national and state boundaries (and identities) and merging them into one super state—"that would be unthinkable." He is grateful that the U.S. kept its states within a national government. This met the two basic urges in human nature—a desire for union with the whole and the desire for local government. He believed that union and freedom are the two basic urges *in all of human nature*. If we ever get together as a worldwide church it would need to be on the principle of federal union—but as a universal plan.

Stanley insists that *he envisions union, not merger*. He explains that the drawback to large church mergers is that the rate of progress is reduced to the slow pace of the whole. In Federal Union, however, you have union, but you have the freedom within that union to experiment and advance as one of the branches. In fact, the branches can enrich the whole. Federal Union provides for both while merger would not. Federal Union would NOT be one super church.[41]

Stanley then admits that there would be objections. For example: Why should Federal Union gets its pattern from the secular state. Stanley counters that Federal Union is not from the secular state. It is from the New Testament (Ephesians 2:15), "The new man out of both parties..." Marriage is a Federal Union. The United Kingdom is a

Federal Union. General Motors is a federal Union. He then illustrates with the story of a missionary in the Congo who struggled with her two selves. One wanted to be a missionary while the other was afraid. Stanley advises her to surrender both her selves to Christ so that a new person could emerge, different, but at peace.[42] One has to like that!

Another objection was that Federal Union in the U.S. is geographical. Stanley counters that Federal Union in the Church would not be geographical but theological and psychological. Even in the U.S. the real working force is not in the state but in her political parties—across state lines. Republicans and Democrats as working units are psychological and political. They must, however, work together toward a common goal. Is that relevant? Yes!

Some accused Stanley of wanting to be the head of the "serpent," a Protestant Pope. Stanley countered, NO! He had no church office and did not want one. He wanted only to be the bearer of good news. He simply prayed for a united voice for the sake of the Kingdom.

Stanley once talked with President Rhee of Korea about uniting the churches of Korea on the Federal Union plan. Rhee was excited. Stanley, while insisting that each denomination would need to decide on the plan and personnel themselves, Rhee made the mistake of mandating church union for the country as a whole and was eventually exiled (to Honolulu); he ended up a lonely man needing the fellowship of like-minded Christians.[43]

Stanley concluded that for Federal Union to work, there would have to be mutual recognition, the right hand of fellowship among all—Roman Catholic, Orthodox, and Protestant. Unfortunately, Stanley sang his "song" of Federal Union almost as a soloist. Someday, he prayed, it will break into a Hallelujah Chorus with one theme—Jesus Christ is Lord. He hoped to live to hear it. He did not and neither have we.[44]

As noted above, another prominent note in Brother Stanley's *Song* was also related to the two becoming one—racial justice. This came to a head in the late 1950s and early 1960s but stayed with him until he died.

Regarding the Civil Rights movement in the U.S. Brother Stanley was on the side of human rights. He was bound in every man's bondage and could only be free in every man's freedom. Remember that he tells the story of Columbia, SC back in April of 1942, where he announced the "death of Democracy in Columbia" because the blacks were denied the vote.

Then came Atlanta. Speaking to a symposium on democracy, please note Stanley's response to a woman who over the radio insisted that Ham's encounter with the naked body of his drunken father, Noah, set the stage for black slavery (Genesis 9:20-27). Stanley countered that he did not get his "racial attitudes" from Ham or Noah, but from Jesus Christ who was the Son of man, not the white man or black man or brown man, but the Son of Man. Paul writes, "In Jesus Christ there cannot be Greek and Jew [race distinction], barbarian and Sythian [cultural distinction], bond or free [social and economic distinction], male or female [sex distinction]." All persons are persons for whom Christ died. We are all equal before God and each other.[45]

As a case in point, Stanley speaks of children taking an examination at Cambridge University. 98% of black Africans passed, 80% of white Europeans passed, but only 30% of Asians from the subcontinent of India. Why? According to Jones, the Indians were from wealthy families with no incentives to achieve — no patriotic, economic or religious incentives. The Africans studied hard (you sometimes had to wrest the books from their hands). The teacher said that boys out of the bush have every bit as much intelligence as the European boys.

Stanley asked George Washington Carver how he ever got started with all of his discoveries. Carver said, "I put a peanut in my hand and I said, 'Mr. Creator, what's in that peanut?" the Creator answered, "You've got brains, go find out." He would not tell Stanley (when

Stanley asked), what universities turned him down when they found he was black. He held no resentment.[46] Stanley then said, "Dr. Carver, you and I are in the same business. You are discovering wonders in peanuts and I'm discovering wonders in people." As Stanley closed with prayer in Carver's home they kissed each other's hands. Stanley went away feeling he was in the presence of greatness — real greatness. "His (Carver's) presence lingers like a benediction."[47]

Again, the future of race relationships lies in the possibility of producing a new man out of both parties — like the black and white keys on a piano. Note, the white does not give equal rights to the black as if some kind of "Brother Bountiful." Civil rights are the basic rights of the blacks as well as whites. It is not a gift but the white responsibility to recognize a God given right to all — to man as man, to woman as woman.

When the white is reluctant to concede equal rights he reaps what he sows. To keep the black in bondage is bondage itself for all of us.

Black Power as soul power, as power of the ballot and power of nonviolent non-bending suffering will win. Physical power will mean vast bloodshed and worse — deeper hatred. Stanley quotes King's "A Letter from a Birmingham Jail" calling for nonviolence and Stanley saluted him and the future.

Add to this the words of Charles Spalding, a Negro businessman in Durham, NC. "Equality cannot be demanded; it must be earned by character and achievement. If the Negro wants equality, except the equality of opportunity, he must earn it by character and achievement. Although equality of opportunity is a basic right given by God, equality itself must be earned."[48]

Stanley left one other thing with Martin Luther King, Jr.. Treat a person like a person; he will react as any other, perhaps conservative or radical. Treat the Negro as a person and he will vote as any other, perhaps conservative or radical. The white man will do the same. Both races will vote together on both sides of the aisle.[49] King said, "This is important. I must emphasize it. It will allay many of the fears of the white man that the Negro will vote as a race, instead of conservative or radical."[50]

The next place to go with all of this is to the two types of social, economic and political structures. These normally line up between America (the U.S./West) and her allies on the one side and the Soviet Union (Russia/China) and her allies on the other — between individualism and collectivism. Is there any way for the two to get together? If they go to war no one will win. To coexist is one way but there is a better way — again, the one new man out of both parties.[51]

Individualism is a truth but it is a half-truth. Collectivism has a truth, but it too is a half-truth. Individualism forgets that life is social and collectivism forgets that life is individual and personal. Hegel says that life moves from thesis to antithesis to synthesis. Stanley believes that the synthesis — that third something — must be the Kingdom of God, a society where you love your neighbor — the truth in collectivism — as yourself — the truth in individualism. This is something beyond individualism and beyond collectivism — it gathers up the truth in each, and eliminates the wrong of each. It can emerge as that third something — the Kingdom of God society that is beyond each, but gathers up the truth in each, in a society where you love your neighbor as yourself. How do we keep from saying a hardy, Amen!

As we close this chapter it bears repeating that in Stanley's *Song*, the deepest conviction of his life was "Self-surrender is the way of self-expression. You realize yourself only as you renounce yourself (again, the first principle of Christianity). You find God when you renounce yourself as God. The self is trying to play God, trying to organize life around itself as God, and it simply doesn't work." Thus, perhaps the greatest sin in the Bible is self-reliance — trusting anything or anyone other than God to sustain you.

When Stanley applied this "truth" to the church he insisted that within herself she has the principle and power of redemption, Jesus Christ. When she gets stale and irrelevant, she can refresh herself by

His refreshing Presence; when she begins to get self-serving, He points with nail-pierced hands to the issues and leads the way; when she loses her power to change people and situations, He brings revival and passion and concern.[52]

Recently, a friend sent me an email with these verses from Meister Eckhart.

> Do you want to know
> What goes on in the core of the Trinity?
> I will tell you.
> In the core of the Trinity
> The Father laughs
> And gives birth to the Son.
> The Son laughs back at the Father
> And gives birth to the Spirit.
> The whole Trinity laughs
> And gives birth to us.

How is that for the Three becoming One! Stanley liked that.

E. Stanley Jones: "Jesus is Lord"

CHAPTER ELEVEN

THE LASTING LEGACY:
"JESUS IS LORD"

The Need to Remind us that it Really is
All About Jesus

For several years granddaughter Anne had become increasingly helpful to Brother Stanley. Like her mother before her, she had taken courses in stenography and typing so that she could join Mary Webster in assisting Stanley as his secretary. Her "granddaddy" says that she was particularly efficient in making travel arrangements and was showing real interest in "evangelical mission."[1]

Mabel, at 92, continued to struggle with her failing eyesight. Stanley, at 86, in spite of some increasing weaknesses, is ever on task. The man is as busy as ever. We left him in route to Australia and New Zealand in the fall of 1969. He eventually returned to California, via the Philippines, where he had excellent meetings. He even managed to see a diabetic specialist in Manilla. He concludes that he fell in love with the Filipino people. "They have a real destiny in the evangelization of the eastern world."[2]

THE 1970S

On February 6, 1970, Stanley writes to Eunice and family from Atlanta commenting on an excellent newspaper interview that he had seen about Eunice. "I learned a lot about my daughter that I didn't know before. You have a genius for giving details and it was very illuminating..."

Stanley had been attending lectures at Emory University, one by Hubert Humphrey. Humphrey gave us "a really great address.... When I got in line to shake hands with him, he came to me and said, 'Oh, Stanley Jones, I've been reading from your books for years and been praying for you, and to think I should see you at last!'" Stanley sent him a copy of his *Song.*

Stanley also attended classes taught by Professor Claude Thompson, "a Godly man who exuded grace and peace." Then, as an experiment, Stanley would gather with students in the evenings for a couple of hours of dialogue. That went extremely well as the interaction was "remarkably redemptive."

Next, Stanley is off for India. Mary Webster is with him, complete with dictating machine for transcribing his latest book, *The Unshakable Kingdom and the Unchanging Person* (1972). On March 30 he writes from Bombay, where he spent the previous day (Easter Sunday). He had just completed a wonderful series of meetings in Hyderabad with packed out houses every night. Three Indian Bishops (two retired) came to every meeting. One night when he called for those interested in physical and spiritual healing, 500 stood. Amazingly, Mary Webster had a parallel service in Secundabad, five miles away with similar results.

There was a good report from Rev. J. Cottelingam, the new manager of the Sat Tal Ashram. They were hoping to begin construction on a new building before long. There was a strike in the schools but some of the Christian schools had been left open. This gave Stanley some pause.

Stanley and Mary Webster were traveling mostly by plane but were anticipating a 32 hour trip by rail on the Grand Trunk Express from Agra to Vijayawada.

The communists were creating disturbances in Kerala and West Bengal. President V.V. Giri, the only person to be elected President as an independent candidate, had to invoke the "President's Rule" by appointing a man to take over the government in West Bengal. Right-wing and left-wing Marxists were fighting each other. Interestingly, Stanley concluded that "fortunately, the Communists have divided."

As stated earlier, Stanley was trying to arrange an appointment with President Giri in Delhi where he was soon to have a few hours over-night before leaving for the U.S. He had already been in touch with former President, Radhakrishnan while in Madras. Dr. Radhakrishnan was not well so they spoke only by phone regarding the possible revival of the peace plan for Vietnam that they had proposed to President Johnson some months earlier.[3]

On April 9 Stanley writes again to Eunice and Jim that he did indeed meet with President Giri (and Prime Minister Indira Gandhi) while waiting for the plane to the U.S. in Delhi. This conversation related to Stanley's missionary mindset regarding proselytizing and conversion. Stanley "accepted the latter while repudiating the former." The President responded, "I'm with you 100%." All of President Giri's children and grandchildren were in Christian schools.

Mrs. Gandhi was not so agreeable. Apparently the "Court Ministers" were against both proselytizing *and* conversion and were putting some pressure on her. Nonetheless, after Stanley clarified the differences she was a bit more cordial than the last time they had met.[4] He had his picture taken with both the President and the Prime Minister before he left.

Stanley and Mary Webster left India for the U.S., via Copenhagen, on June 22. Before leaving Bombay he writes another letter to Jim and Eunice regarding Mabel's appointment with an eye specialist. This was much to his relief. He then mentions something regarding

Ashram funds at Sat Tal but concludes by saying that "Mary Webster makes a tremendous impression on Christians and non-Christians by her witness." Stanley is bringing home great photos of Mary and Anne taken together the previous year.

After only two days with Eunice and family, Stanley is off to Lake Junaluska in North Carolina for an ashram.

Meanwhile, back in India, a small book by Violet Paranjoti entitled, *An Evangelist on the Indian Scene: Dr. E. Stanley Jones,* was published with mixed reviews. An August 1970 article in *The Bombay Tract and Book Society* stated that "To write about the great contributions to India by Dr. Jones as a missionary, social worker and reformer, founder of ashrams, and a writer of religious and devotional books is not an easy task. It must be said that the author has done her best." Alas, faint praise.

Then, Mabel writes from Orlando with questions about Anne's recent wedding saying that "Daddy" is due for a visit in September.

Stanley then writes from Orlando on October 15 to "Eunice, Jim and the Satellites." Mabel's vision seems to be improving but she is still reading with a magnifying glass. Stanley had been reading to her the hand-written letters. At the moment he was preparing to leave for the airport while listening to the World Series. He was a huge Baltimore Orioles fan. They won the 1970 Series in five games.

Stanley then comments that he anticipates that Jim will hopefully join him in Sat Tal the following summer. The manager, Cottelingam, is suddenly under attack and is "out with everybody now at Sat Tal." There seemed to be an issue with money.

Meanwhile, Stanley stays busy. On November 18 he writes about a meeting in College Park (Maryland) at the Methodist Church (where the altar was full), and then on to the Episcopal Church for a healing service. We know he was scheduled next for Tulsa, Oklahoma but the engagement had to be cancelled only to be replaced by another in Danville, Virginia. He then heads off to Marietta, Georgia ("great meetings") and then on to the Nazarene College in Kankakee, Illinois. He also spoke at the local Nazarene Church at nights (reportedly to 1000s). The young students who drove him to Chicago wanted to "kidnap" him and keep him in Kankakee. What fun!

Next, Brother Stanley flies to Philadelphia to be driven by Roberto Escamilla to the Methodist Retirement Home in Wilmington, Delaware. Perhaps Eunice visited the facility as well to look it over as her mother would be there briefly as a resident when she broke her hip in 1974.[5] Stanley concludes this letter stating that Roberto Escamilla will go with him to South America the following March and April (as interpreter and speaker). He is also planning on taking Mary Webster with him to Japan (as lay witness and secretary) the next October and November.

Stanley will then be with Mabel in just a few weeks in Orlando (December 18-21), before flying up to Boston (December 24-25). He will then leave for an Ashram in Mexico, December 26-30. What a life!

1971, THE PACE CONTINUES

Unfortunately Stanley's schedule did not allow him to join Roberto Escamilla for the anticipated tour of South America in March and April but Roberto made the trip on his own following the same schedule planned earlier by Brother Stanley.

Then, there is a lengthy letter from Mabel to Eunice on July 22. She is still in Orlando. She discusses everything from silverware to genealogies, but does not get to Stanley.

We do know from a Stanley *Circular Letter* (October 1971), that he has begun work on *The Divine Yes* (he confesses that this may be his last but that he will go out with a resounding yes!). This last book would be completed with the assistance of Eunice Mathews and Mary Webster and would be published after his death in 1975.[6]

As planned, Stanley in October and November, 1971 leads one more evangelistic campaign in Japan with Mary Webster and others (this would be his 10th). They traveled to more than 45 major cities (all four islands), and Stanley spoke 154 times. During those two months approximately 6,000 Japanese responded to Stanley's invitations. Many accepted Christ for the first time while others rededicated their lives to the Christian faith.

Mary Webster writes to Eunice and Jim on November 3 that Stanley is seemingly in excellent health and is taking the amazing schedule in his usual stride. "God has restored his speech and you ought to hear him preach! Wow! I know that 'wow' is a very inelegant word, but it really says what I mean. His sermons are so wonderful and it is just as if he goes off into another realm while he is preaching. People just sit there spellbound." She goes on to say that she has taken most of his sermons in shorthand, then transcribes them for the interpreters ahead of time. Both the evangelistic meetings and the Ashrams have been well attended. At the Osaka Ashram there were six ministers from Korea and six from Taiwan. The Taiwanese pastors want to double the Christian population in Taiwan and Mary believes that they will do it.

In a P.S. Mary says that she has bought "granddaddy" two suits of long underwear so he can keep warm. He does not like to be treated like an old man but was no doubt grateful for her thoughtfulness.

Stanley follows "suite" with a letter of his own to "Eunice, Jim and the Rest" on November 18. They are getting down to the end of the "road" in Japan. That road has been smooth for the most part with the best hotels and good food. Mary, however, watches what he eats.

The evangelistic response is not as large numerically as in the early days (the public meetings are now mostly in churches instead of halls), but, wherever, both are packed with perfect attention (especially among the students) and excellent response. His emphasis on the unshakable Kingdom and the unchanging Person (and this is important) brings together the "liberals and the conservatives." Much to his delight, apparently a healing took place among the clergy. The younger "radical" clergy "locked up" the older conservative clergy for a day and a half and would not let them out until they agreed to change. Then, the two sides agreed that they were both included in Brother Stanley's understanding of the unshakable Kingdom. You have to love this.

One more letter from Stanley to Eunice, Jim and the "Brood" is dated December 1 from the International House in Tokyo. The day before he had delivered his final messages. In the afternoon he spoke to 3,000 students. They clapped him "out of the hall" by way of ovation. In the evening the meeting was held in the Town Hall with 3,000 present and hundreds of decisions. "Altogether, it was the best series of the ten I've had in Japan. They asked me to come back. They thought I was a miracle to be going so strong at 87. Mary left that same day for Honolulu while Stanley would follow along the day after.

Stanley then returned to the U.S. He stopped in Oklahoma City for an Ashram at a Roman Catholic seminary. On December 8, shortly after midnight he suffered a stroke that severely impaired his speech, sight and physical mobility. "Everything was lovely and I went to bed in peace. But during the night I awoke to go to the bathroom and found I was paralyzed."

We now watch his recovery as he continues to write letters.

A few day later, granddaughter Anne, an occupational therapist, accompanied "Granddaddy" from Oklahoma City to Massachusetts General Hospital in Boston. As ill as he was they actually allowed her to bring him onto the plane with her. As soon as he was well enough to participate in rehabilitation, Stanley was transferred from Massachusetts General to a nearby rehabilitation facility and subsequently to D'Youville Hospital in Cambridge, Massachusetts.

On December 24, 1971, just two weeks after his stroke, Stanley wrote to Prime Minister Indira Gandhi. He was still concerned about the tense and difficult relationship between the U. S. and India that developed because of the conflict between India and Pakistan. There was still trouble between India and the two Pakistans. Pakistan had been divided in 1947 into Pakistan and East Pakistan. India and Pakistan were never one country. On December 3, 1971 Pakistan had made a preemptive air strike against India. India responded by invading both East Pakistan and Pakistan. Pakistan surrendered to India but then India withdrew from East Pakistan so that Sheikh Mujibur Rahman could establish a government in the new independent nation of Bangladesh.[7]

It would be good to remember that these were days of Henry Kissinger and Richard Nixon. In brief, Kissinger had said after his historic visit to China that "if China intervened on the side of Pakistan that the U.S. would *not* come to the aid of India."

1972, MIRACLE AFTER MIRACLE

Although Stanley was unable to attend the annual meeting of the United Christian Ashrams Board (the Seven), scheduled for Orlando, FL on January 3, 1972 (his 88th birthday), thanks to Mary Webster, he did manage to forward the contents of a memorandum.... .

Although Stanley would live for another year he dictated his "Last Will and Testament" (actually a memo to the Ashram Seven). His desire was for the

Ashram movement be kept open theologically, spiritually and practically...., to be and do: evangelical and evangelistic, in the sense of being responsive to and obedient to the whole Gospel, commending it to all mankind; ecumenical, transcending all denominational and sectarian division (from Roman Catholic to Pentecostal); inclusive, with equal participation of all without respect to race, nationality, class, age or sex; perpetually relevant to the times and the real needs of humankind, committed to Christ and his Kingdom, individually and corporately; guided by the Holy Spirit, together with the combined wisdom of the concerned and committed fellowship.[8]

For Stanley the ashrams were the consummate expression of the Kingdom of God.

Just as Stanley himself relied on the Inner Voice as the final authority for his personal decisions and actions, so the Holy Spirit would need to guide the decisions and actions of each Ashram as discerned by the collective wisdom of the community — the *koinonia*. This was critical if the Movement was to continue to manifest the mind and Spirit of Jesus.

Indira Gandhi responded to Stanley's Christmas Eve letter on January 5, 1972. "Thank you for your letter. A large number of American citizens have written to me. I am grateful for your support of India's action and for the sympathy you have shown for the democratic struggle of the people of Bangladesh. This is proof, if proof were needed, of the American people's love of liberty and justice. With every good wish for 1972."[9]

Then on January 15, 1972 Stanley wrote a follow-up to his previous memorandum to the Seven of the United Christian Ashrams, "I do not know what the future holds, but I know who holds the future. I am ready to be healed or not be healed. I belong to the Unshakable Kingdom and the Unchanging Person. I haven't had a blue hour since it happened. Victory, victory, victory."[10] READER, TAKE NOTE!

Although Stanley's dream in 1967 of establishing a permanent Christian Ashram in the Galilee did not come to pass, he did (in the last year of his life) lead a World Ashram Congress in Jerusalem. Bill Berg, one of the "Three" of the United Christian Ashrams, testified about the miracle of Stanley's participation in that World Ashram Congress. Actually, the "miracle" began several months before.

Berg writes, "I believe in miracles. In January of 1972, I stood with Jim and Eunice Mathews, Bill Richardson and Gordon Hunter at the bedside of Brother Stanley in the Boston Rehabilitation Hospital. He was paralyzed on one side and was suffering from gravely impaired speech and sight. Doctors had predicted that he would not walk or lecture again. I recall saying that day, 'Brother Stanley, you have often said that you were going to keep going until the boiler bursts. But I believe that there is still life and fire in the old boiler and that God is not through with you yet."

Then during the late spring, miraculously Stanley, along with Jim Mathews, Jim's daughter Anne and son Stan, left for India. A letter from Stanley describes the last leg of the trip back. After a day in Delhi they hired an air-conditioned car and drove toward Sat Tal. In route Stanley is taken to the Clara Swain Hospital in Bareilly where the doctor there familiarized himself with Stanley's condition and invited him back for treatment. Then they journeyed on to Sat Tal where he found things to be better than expected. The summer Ashram was already fully booked. Compared with the 117 degree heat in Delhi, the climate at Sat Tal was wonderful.

In Sat Tal Anne continued his therapy — vigorously and often painfully — but Stanley was grateful to have it. In fact, he was so encouraged that he asked son-in-law Jim to help him learn to walk again.

The first walking lesson began on the verandah. The effort was a miserable failure. The following morning the result was the same. Brother Stanley could barely stand up even with assistance. Left alone, he lost his balance immediately. It began to look as if the doctors were right."[11] He would never walk or preach again.

On the third day, however, a change began to manifest itself. Each morning the Ashram family studied the Scriptures and prayed and on this particular morning the text spoke of the lame man from the book of Acts. Peter says, "Silver and gold have I none but what I have I give to you, 'In the name of Jesus Christ of Nazareth, get up and walk.'" Beginning that day these were the words whispered into Brother Stanley's ear before each of his "walking" lessons. Not surprisingly, he began gaining strength. The Ashram family then began to pray around the clock, many fasted.

At first it was difficult for Stanley to stand up from his wheelchair. Each day, however, he rose from his wheelchair with greater ease. With the aid of his cane he began to take steps alone. After a week he could walk back and forth the length of a wooden track with rails made by the village carpenter. As his walking improved, so did his voice. This man who had preached 60,000 sermons was walking and preaching again.[12]

After a month or so Anne felt good enough about her grandfather's progress that she went trekking nearby with a second cousin, the son of Stanley's cousin, Mabel Wagner.[13] Anne then returned to the U.S.

Remarkably, in June, after preaching sermons on several occasions at Sat Tal, Brother Stanley, with long-time friends, Lillian Wallace and Eileen Richards, traveled to Jerusalem for the World Ashram Congress. He was strong enough to stand at the podium for the keynote address entitled, "Jesus Is Lord." As Lillian Wallace stood behind him holding his belt to steady him, Stanley preached rejoicing, "This is one of the happiest moments in my life, if not the happiest" (talk about superlatives)!" Sam Kamaleson sang "How Great Thou Art" at the close and "heaven came down."

Following the Jerusalem Congress Stanley returned to India.

On July 4, 1972 Stanley wrote once more to Mrs. Gandhi congratulating her on the agreement she had negotiated with Pakistan's Prime Minister, Zulfiqar Ali Bhutto just two days earlier. At the end of the war between India and Pakistan, Bhutto, had come to India to negotiate the release of Pakistani prisoners of war. At the same time the Prime Minister and Bhutto reached an agreement that neither country would resort to war to settle their dispute over Kashmir. This issue would be resolved bilaterally without the intervention of any third party.

Stanley writes that "nothing in recent days has given me so much real satisfaction and joy as your magnificent achievement in the treaty renouncing force in the settlement of questions between India and Pakistan. You have done a magnificent bit of statesmanship. We are very proud of you and your achievements. This puts India back into the leadership of the search for world peace..... I shall pray for you and thank God for you."[14] Stanley concludes the letter by referring to the excellent medical care he was receiving in the Indian hospital at Bareilly.

Indira Gandhi wrote back July 11, 1972 thanking him and wishing him a speedy and complete recovery.

At this point there is significant correspondence between Stanley and Mabel explaining their two perspectives on life and ministry.

Mabel had written first on August 17 summing up the essential difference between the two. She relied on her "sub-conscious mind" whereas her husband relied on his "inner voice."

In a rather long reply (August 30), to Mabel's letter of August. 17, Stanley attempts to clarify the issue, albeit somewhat bluntly.

To "My dear Mabel, when you say sub-conscious mind, I would try to add that the sub-conscious mind surrendered to the Holy Spirit IS THE INNER VOICE. The essential difference is that I do not belong to myself: I belong to the Spirit and the Spirit's voice is the final authority." Stanley then admits that he may be wrong in some of his attempts at interpreting that voice but if mistaken there is always Divine forgiveness.

Now here is the crunch for Stanley, "The essential difference is this: with you, you are the final authority in your sub-conscious mind. With me it is the Holy Spirit Who is the Final Authority. You are under your own guidance while I am under the guidance of the Holy Spirit. Again, if I misinterpret there is forgiveness."

So, they live in two different though related worlds. In one according to Jones she is the final authority according to her best judgment. In the other Stanley is under the authority of the Holy Spirit, the Inner Voice. We do not have further information about if Mabel actually viewed her sub conscious as distinct from the Holy Spirit. Conceivably the words that Stanley and Mabel used suggest more of a difference between these two dedicated followers of Jesus than is warranted.

No question, Stanley would always listen to and respect Mabel's advice unless he honestly believed that it was contrary to the Spirit. He insists that he is not giving up his mental processes; he is simply yielding to how he believes the Spirit is leading.

Interestingly, Stanley concludes with reference to their home in Florida. Stanley apparently paid for it out of his book royalties but he would yield to her final authority with regard to matters related to that home.

Some conclude that these two strong personalities in some sense thrived off each other. "He was what he was because she was what she was and she was what she was because he was what he was in terms of allowing each other the freedom to follow their own calling." Mabel and Stanley put up with a lot of hardship to allow the other be what they were.[15]

The fact remains that Stanley rarely speaks of Mabel in his writings and she rarely speaks of him in hers. [16] Yet they both stood in the shadows keeping watch — one over the other. Stanley writes Mabel again on September 12 and 20 (probably his last) discussing the possibility of seeing an eye doctor in Atlanta when he "returns to the U. S." He signed both, "With my love."

The return to the U.S. for Stanley never happened.In December he wrote to the entire family a corporate letter saying he was delighted to know that Mrs. Aspinwell would stay with Mabel during the winter.[17]

1973, AND THEY LAID HIM TO REST

The last international issue to concern Stanley in the last year of his life was Vietnam. Note his letter to President Nixon January 7,

1973, signed by 19 members of the Sat Tal Ashram. This would be his last public word on Vietnam (just two and a half weeks before his death). It was not a personal letter but a letter on behalf of the Sat Tal Ashram, deploring the "continued bombing of Vietnam" and calling on the President "to cease immediately the bombing and seek a peaceful and humane solution to this war."[18]

Then David Henderson, a close friend, recorded this account of the last weeks of Stanley's life in India. "The days were full of activity. Two hours every morning were devoted to corrections and additions to the rough draft of *The Divine Yes*. We read aloud, *The Christ of the Indian Road*. He took laps around the Ashram grounds. Newspapers were read to him daily but mostly he passed his last weeks in a deep poignant solitude.

"My last moments with Brother Stanley were as he was being removed to Bareilly hospital with a worsening lung infection. I want you to follow the doctor's orders," Henderson teased. Stanley answered, "You follow His," Stanley never ceased diverting attention from himself to his Lord."[19]

Premila Roy, the daughter of the Rev. Dr. Manni Dutt Patial and his wife Hira, has shared notes from her memoirs of these last days.[20] Manni and Hira were regular visitors to Brother Stanley in the hospital during this last stay and Premila remembers things that they shared about him. She listened carefully as she overheard them talking about Mabel Wagner and others.

Stanley died on January 25 shortly after his 89th birthday surrounded by close friends. This was almost exactly 25 years after the death of his friend Mahatma Gandhi. Prime Minister Indira Gandhi sent a telegram to Manni Patial that same day:

> Deeply grieved to know that Dr. Stanley Jones is no more. Through his earnestness and dedicated service he earned widespread respect. The people of India mourn a good friend.
>
> - Indira Gandhi

Again, David Henderson records the events at the time of Brother Stanley's death. When he died, wife Mabel was informed immediately.

We know that Mabel Wagner was one of the ones with him when he died and immediately wrote to Eunice of his 'quick and quiet release from the body no longer useful to him.'" A month later she wrote a four typewritten page letter to Mabel describing Stanley's last moments and the service held for him in the hospital chapel. In that letter Mabel Wagner writes that she remembered asking Stanley long ago about his absence from Mabel and Eunice and all he said was, "It hurts." Mabel perhaps managed her aloneness better than Stanley. "After years of aloneness Mabel came to a quiet, wholesome place of enjoying her own company." James Mathews quotes Mabel, "But a day to myself is cherished more than gold: time to discover lost values, to enjoy one's own company. If you can't endure this it is time to wonder why."[21]

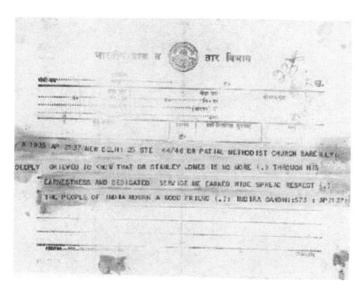

Indira Gandhi's telegram to Manni Patial

Following the memorial service in the Bareilly hospital chapel, Manni Dutt Patial took Brother Stanley's body to Delhi for cremation. He sat on the gurney with Stanley's head in his lap the entire way. Following the cremation Stanley's ashes were placed into two containers and turned over to Stanley's brother's son, Everett Jones, who had actually come to India to bring Stanley to Atlanta to visit with an eye surgeon.

Stephen Graham states that since India was Stanley's adopted homeland for most of his life his heart was buried in India (that no doubt was a metaphor since Stanley's heart was indeed in India for

over 60 years).[22] Half his ashes were buried on the hillside up from the main lodge at Sat Tal while the remaining ashes were interred in the Bishops' Lot at Mount Olivet Cemetery in Baltimore after a service of recognition and praise at Memorial United Methodist Church.

Stanley writes in his *Song* that "the half has not been told." Yet, he thrilled at the half that could be told.[23] Stephen Graham concludes his biography with a sampling of letters or testimonials from people across the years.[24] They are an interesting read.

1974 TO THE PRESENT

In 1974 Mabel fell and broke her hip but her hip replacement did not work so she was sent to the Methodist Retirement Home in Wilmington, Delaware until a room was available at the Asbury Methodist Village in Gaithersburg, MD, near Eunice and Jim.[25]

Mabel read continuously until her eyesight completely failed her. It is said that she never watched one single TV program yet she lived by the images of her two great love affairs, one with Stanley (and family) and one with India.

It is said that Mabel was not so much into her birthday gala on April 3, 1978. Dear Mabel died on June 23, 1978 at age 100. James Mathews died Sept. 8, 2010 at age 97. Eunice Mathews died Feb. 27, 2016. She was 101. May their tribe increase!

E. Stanley Jones, 1960s

CHAPTER TWELVE

Stanley Jones Looks to the Future

For a Time Such As This

E
Stanley Jones was such an eclectic that much of his ministry is just as relevant for today (and in some instances more so) as it was for his own day.

Here, we will first take slices from Brother Stanley's long life as a missionary/evangelist and summarize some of his most lasting contributions, especially as they relate to some of the important issues that continue to plague our world today. Then, in our Conclusion we will attempt to encapsulate the heart of Stanley's overall message taken from the final chapter of his *A Song of Ascents*. Much of this is taken verbatim from previous Chapters in order to capture the "moments."

Admittedly, Stanley and Mabel Jones experienced many "disappointments and near misses" throughout their lifetimes. Even more importantly, however, there were huge successes, many of which provided responses and solutions to issues relevant to the contemporary Church as well. The following headings attempt to capture some of those issues. With this in mind, let's begin:

First, let's ask Stanley Jones if black lives matter. Stanley was always on the cutting edge with regard to social issues. Increasingly racial injustice would draw his attention. Predictably, Stanley's outspoken advocacy of racial equality was rooted in his concept of the Kingdom of God. He keeps returning to the laws of the moral universe as the principles of the Kingdom of God are applied to human behavior. The first law of the moral universe is equality. We are all created with equal moral dignity by God; therefore, we should all have equal moral dignity in the eyes of one another. God created human beings to live and interact in a world governed by these laws of the moral universe. When we obey these laws, we cooperate with God in the purposes of human creation and we reap the abundant fruit of living in harmony with both God and one another. When we knowingly disobey these laws we resist God's purposes and reap the bitter fruit of living in tension and conflict with God, ourselves and those around us. This is why Stanley insisted on racial equality for all people around the world. Racial equality was a Kingdom principle.[1]

Let's go back over a couple of outstanding examples regarding this important issue. In April, 1942 Stanley was in Columbia, SC for a series of meetings. On his last night (April 29) Stanley spoke at the First Presbyterian Church. This was the primary election day for the office of mayor. The week before, the city election board purged from the roll of eligible voters all African Americans. Before he spoke Stanley read, "Obituary for Democracy." The next day the front page of the *State* newspaper quoted him: "Democracy died today in the city when suffrage was denied citizens of this state, the only reason being the color of their skin."[2]

In late May, 1942 Stanley "had two days in Jackson, Mississippi under the auspices of the Negroes. They had a public meeting at night with twenty-five hundred Whites and fifteen hundred Colored in the municipal auditorium. There were two Bishop Greens presiding and neither one was green. One was White and the other Black." This Jackson, Mississippi meeting would cause a stir well into the fall.[3] All this would become grist for his *The Christ of the American Road* to be published in just over a year.

368

Stanley then reported that at his Blue Ridge, NC Ashram, again, as in the previous year, members of the "colored race made very distinct contributions."

By the end of November, 1946, we find Stanley in Oklahoma City. The first night he spoke to 5,000 with a great after meeting. He wrote to Jim Mathews that "the last night was Youth Night; there were about 4,000 out.... These Oklahomans are marvelous people. For the first time in the history of the city the Negroes and Whites mingled freely in the auditorium and in the church.... Nearly one-half of those in the choir were colored—a sight for the gods to behold—and the universe didn't seem to fall on us."[4] Racial equality was always an issue with Stanley Jones and being in such demand he could seemingly make the point.

Another prominent note in Brother Stanley's *Song* was closely related to all this—the two becoming one. This came to a head in the late 1950s and early 1960s as racial justice related to civil rights. Civil rights was a passion of Stanley's until he died.

Regarding the Civil Rights movement in the U.S., obviously Brother Stanley was on the side of human rights for all. He was bound in every man's bondage and could only be free in every man's freedom. Paul writes, "In Jesus Christ there cannot be Greek and Jew [race distinction], barbarian and Sythian [cultural distinction], bond or free [social and economic distinction], male or female [sex distinction]." A person is a person for whom Christ died. We are all equal before God and each other.[5]

Again, the future of race relationships lies in the possibility of producing a new man out of both parties—like the black and white keys on a piano. Note, the white does not give equal rights to the black as if some kind of "Brother Bountiful." Civil rights are the basic rights of blacks as well as whites. It is not a gift but the white responsibility to recognize a God given right to all—to man as man, to woman as woman.

Stanley insisted that when the white is reluctant to concede equal rights he reaps what he sows. To keep the black in bondage is bondage itself for all of us.

Black Power as soul power, as power of the ballot and power of nonviolent, non-bending suffering will win. Physical power will mean vast bloodshed and worse—deeper hatred. Stanley quotes King's "A Letter from a Birmingham Jail" calling for nonviolence and Stanley saluted him.

Even greater understanding can be added to all this from the interesting perspective of Charles Spalding, a Negro businessman in Durham, NC. "Equality cannot be demanded; it must be earned by character and achievement. If the Negro wants equality, except the equality of opportunity, he must earn it by character and achievement. Although equality of opportunity is a basic right given by God, equality itself must be earned."[6]

Apart for the wisdom of non-violence civil disobedience, Stanley left one other thing with Martin Luther King, Jr. "Treat a person like a person; he will react as any other, perhaps conservative or radical. Treat the Negro as a person and he will vote as any other, perhaps conservative or radical. The white man will do the same. Both races will vote together on both sides of the aisle.[7] King said, "This is important. I must emphasize it. It will allay many of the fears of the white man that the Negro will vote as a race, instead of conservative or radical."[8]

Jesus struck one of his earliest blows for the Kingdom of God when he struck at racial prejudice. The pious Jew at the time thanked God he was not born as others. Jesus incurred the wrath of the nation by saying that the prophet was sent to the leper Naaman, the Syrian, and to the widow in Zarepath, a gentile. They led him to the brow of a hill.[9] The moment Stanley put his feet upon the Way of Jesus a new reverence for a person as a person came into his heart. Remember the streetcar in Baltimore with Miss Nellie. Stanley gave his seat to a black woman and tipped his hat. That was 64 years earlier (c. 1901). He had just committed himself as a new Christian to a reverence for people and their possibilities apart from race and color and status. Stanley then says (meaningfully) that there is not a spot on earth where he had been that he would not gladly stay and invest another life – if he had one. Throughout his life Stanley Jones despised attitudes that excluded anyone – worldwide – from the fellowship of the church. The issues of race and equality simply meant that he loved all people.[10]

Next, related to Stanley's advocacy of equality and his principles of inclusion are the issues confronting gays and lesbians. Although his attitudes toward gays and lesbians was not addressed specifically, Stanley's principles of inclusiveness surely apply. We tend to stop reading at Romans 1:27. E. Stanley Jones scholar, Steve Harper has written an excellent book, *For the Sake of the Bride* that addresses the argument poignantly.[11]

How does the church wrestle with issues where there are contradictory convictions? Could the church theologize its way through a contemporary issue with contradictory convictions based on a historical issue with contradictory convictions? How can the church arrive at a place where she is able to work through her theology without becoming completely polarized?

Brother Stanley insisted that all peoples tend to consider themselves superior – Romans, Greeks, Chinese, Persians, Japanese, Haitians, Irish, Americans, Australians, Danes, French, New Zealanders, Indian and on and on it goes. They all have special names and phrases that identify their innate superiority. Stanley's oft quoted phrase that "People who think they are always right are always wrong because they think they are always right," seems relevant. Surely his understanding of human rights and church unity could inform and advise the United Methodist Church as she wrestles with contradictory convictions, and if not keep us together, at least enable us to treat each other with love and respect.

Now, ask Brother Stanley about the devastation of war and how to prevent it.... (as you have read, Stanley Jones singlehandedly nearly prevented the bombing of Pearl Harbor, but even more importantly, his cognizant, consistent stand again all forms of war led various peoples on every continent toward peace and justice).

Again, Stanley talked incessantly about the need for peace and the tragedies of war. You've met Stanley and Mabel's first grandchild, Anne Mathews-Younes in Chapter 6. She was kind enough to share with me a recent paper delivered in Japan entitled, "Japan Peace Talk." There she states and I reiterate,

> E. Stanley Jones, as a fully surrendered person to Jesus, lived his life committed to peace and was vehemently opposed to war, knowing full well its tragic results on all of God's children. I want to share with you my grandfather's reasons for opposing war. Jones provides guidance for us today as we choose to become mediators of peace — peacemakers — who through words and deeds. introduce others to the Prince of Peace, Jesus Christ.

> War, according to Jones, is *a means* out of harmony with *the ends* it hopes to accomplish. War, therefore, is the vast illusion — the illusion that you can get to right ends by wrong means. It simply cannot be done. This is a fond and futile hope. Jones was opposed to war for many reasons, but first of all because war causes men [and women] to sin. Men [and women] caught in the act of war, do things they would never dream of doing otherwise.[12]

Dr. Mathews-Younes lists her grandfather's various ways that war causes us to sin. First, it poisons the air with lies. The first casualty in war is Truth. War then poisons the air with hate. If the first casualty is Truth, the second casualty is Love.

> Then war causes us to sin economically. It creates waste and causes hunger. It exploits the helpless. War causes sin against persons. 40,000,000 lives were lost (either directly or indirectly) in WWII alone [14,000,000 in China. Count the 6,000,000 Jews in the Holocaust, then millions of Germans, Japanese, Russians, Brits, Americans, and on and on it goes]. War propagates the lie that war protects the innocent when in fact it protects the guilty. War exposes the innocent, both soldier and civilian alike, leading to insensate, useless slaughter.

> War also kills the consciences of persons. It lays hold of our

finest virtues and prostitutes them. It lays hold on patriotism, heroism, self-sacrifice, idealism, and turns them toward destruction. War stands against everything that Christ stands for. It sins against Christ. If war is right, Christ is wrong; and if Christ is right, war is wrong. Christ and war are irreconcilables. If I must make my choice, writes Jones, "I choose Jesus."

Our Muslim friends quote our Old Testament in justifying their attitudes toward war. Realize that the *Qur'an* is a re-interpretation of the Old Testament just as our New Testament is a re-interpretation of the Old Testament. Jesus says, "You have heard it said, but I say unto you." You can never make a case for war out of the mouth of Jesus, the prince of peace.

Dr. Mathews-Younes then concludes with Stanley that people do not want war. They hate it. They want peace. But the political leaders of the nations do not seem to be able to orchestrate world peace. Here is a world hating war, afraid of war, and yet consistently drifting into war. Are we in the hands of a cruel fate, or is there something wrong with us and our attitudes? Perhaps the saying is true, most wars are the result of the male ego. Is there no way to hold our leaders accountable!

Stanley insisted that "we could 'stop' wars, by the use of the word *we*. If we said 'we,' then we would be free from war." That may seem a bit naive, but think about it. "When we learn that one word and live in our world as if that word matters, we would be living with our brothers and sisters, we would be mature as a race and free from war."

Stanley, therefore, renounced war and was determined to give the balance of his days to finding a better way for himself and others to live in peace. He not only wrote about his deep opposition to war, he participated in our world as one who was always looking for peaceful solutions.[13] These peaceful solutions usually spoke of Jesus.

So, the logical next step is to all of this is to ask Stanley about the related issues of peace and justice... Shivraj Mahendra reflects,

Jones defines *peace* as "joy grown quiet and assured." The promise of peace is found in Jesus Christ. It is in him that our joy is fulfilled. When joy increases, peace emerges. When we rejoice in the Lord, we are at peace. "Peace comes from adjustment – adjustment to reality – and there can be no adjustment to reality without adjustment to God." People today are trying to adjust to the demands of the workplace and to the demands of their cultures in which they live. People are in pursuit of peace in terms of happiness and material blessings. Materialism has never brought peace. It has only brought greed and unrest. Blind pursuit of worldly success and riches has consumed the peace of mind and heart. The heart longs for more than material. It longs for the spiritual. It will not be at peace with anything but God.[14] [I am reminded of the words of St. Augustine in his *Confessions*, "Thou hast made us for Thyself, and our heart is restless until it finds rest in Thee"].

Jesus said, "peace be with you," and breathed the Holy Spirit on his disciples (John 20:22-23). "The peace of the Holy Spirit—the peace of divine presence, adequacy and power"—affirms Stanley Jones. May this peace be ours today! *"The condition to gaining this peace is forgiveness [releasing all resentments."* Forgiving those who have hurt us is the foundation for gaining godly peace. And peace [gained through forgiving others] is the key to righteousness and justice.[15]

[Consequently] Jones understands *justice* in terms of righteousness (Matthew 6:33). Righteousness is right-relationship [— the fruit of forgiveness]. To him, the Kingdom of God meant justice and justice meant right relationship with people and with God. [So, as God forgives us in Jesus, so we forgive others. Frequently, in his own day], Stanley Jones envisioned liberty and justice within the context of racial equality between Black and White, and ultimately as the foundation of democracy.[16]

Incredibly relevant to all this is that, Shivraj Mahendra points out,

Today our world is being torn apart by resurgent racism, violence and terrorism, human rights violations, persecution of Christians, not to mention natural calamities. Peace seems to be disappearing from the world..." [If we are to learn from E. Stanley Jones], Shivraj Mahendra asserts, "It is high time for Christian principles for peace and justice to emanate from the far corners of our society. It is high time to become missionaries, like Stanley Jones, who toiled for peace, justice and reconciliation. It is high time to live like the light of Christ in the world going dark. It is high time to promote peace and justice in family, society, nations"[and most of all the Church].[17]

In the Spirit of E. Stanley Jones, Shivraj Mahendra concludes and exhorts us,

The only way to be a channel of peace and justice, was first to surrender ourselves to God. A surrendered self is an available self for the mission of God. Christ is the mediator between God and people. [Again, self-surrender really does lead to peace because it leads to forgiveness. God in] Jesus is the real peace and justice for the suffering world [because he set the stage for forgiveness.] Let us adjust ourselves with God. Let us come in right relationship with God. Let us receive the peace of Christ. Let us also help others to do the same. May the Lord help us![18]

OK, it is time now to talk about guns in our American culture. Unfortunately, in light of the recent tragedies in places like Charlottesville and Las Vegas, Florida, Texas and Pittsburgh (not to mention Syria, the Middle East, North Korea and many of the streets around us), Stanley is all too relevant. Stanley owned a rifle (for protection, not for himself but against tigers threatening local villagers). He would never advocate guns for the general populous. *Total surrender to God meant that we totally depend upon God for protection of life and limb.* Remember, the number one sin in the Bible is self-reliance. *To rely on anyone or anything else is idolatry.*

Ask Stanley about communicating with high school and college students. Let's take just a snippet.

On February 29, 1943 (Sadie Hawkins Day) Stanley spoke to 3,000 students at Oregon State University in Corvallis, Oregon. In spite of the initial restless fun and frivolity, "two minutes after he began to speak, the students "were in pin drop silence and never moved for three quarters of an hour" as he presented Christ.[19] Almost immediately he spoke at a High School in Hollywood, CA and then within days to the entire student body at the University of Tennessee, Knoxville. "Nearly all of them 'stayed' for an after meeting for personal decision. From Tennessee Stanley goes to Berea College in KY. In several of these meetings he arranged for the Rev. Paul Turner, a black African American lawyer and minister, to travel with him and lead the music.[20] The student reports were that Stanley's message was "electric."

So, what was his message?"Do not fight with yourself. The key is for you and yourself to be partners in a great cooperative enterprise of fulfilling an unfolding will of God."[21] Students understood this.

Students thought of Stanley as being disciplined but he never thought of himself as disciplined. He gave them this insight. "My 'discipline,' for me simply became a way of life. There is something in Jesus that is native to our blood, to our nerves, to our tissue, to our organs, to our relationships—to us as total persons." Stanley was native to Jesus and Jesus was native to him. They were made for each other as the eye is made for light, the conscience for truth, the aesthetic nature for beauty. So discipline is functioning in the way we are made to function. Therefore, discipline is delight and self surrender is still the key.

There is no use trying to discipline yourself until you surrender yourself. The central discipline is self-surrender [Stanley's forever passion]. To try to discipline yourself without a surrender of yourself means you are sitting on a lid. The discipline in that case means tension—trying to discipline a recalcitrant self that doesn't want to be disciplined. So the usual idea of discipline is tense nerves, a determined will asserting itself against all deviations from the discipline. That is far from Christian discipline and alien to it. Christian discipline is complete surrender to Jesus Christ as Lord, with no "ifs" and or "buts" and no strings attached. He is Lord of me and everything that belongs to me and is related to me. Then around that new center the surrendered self is disciplined and cultivated — and expressed in freedom.[22]

Interestingly, students found this perspective "freeing." It was beyond the burden of classroom, even home and Church. The apostle John wrote (I John 5:3), "For to love God is to keep his commands; and they are not burdensome." Why? — Because what he commands, his nature commends. God can only will our highest good for that is His nature. "God is love." It does not say that God loves but that God is love. Not to love would violate his nature. So, all God's commands are love in action and therefore good in themselves and good for us.[23] Students around the world were saying, Amen!

While we are at it, ask Stanley about how to live a Christian life in a Hindu or Muslim community. Basically, he took the advice of Gandhi — emphasize love, talk more about Jesus, learn about other religions more sympathetically (so that we can lift up the good that is consistent with the mind of Jesus), but never ever adulterate (water down) your own religion...".

In his, *The Christ of the Indian Road*, Stanley wrote, "While speaking to India, I was led along to a simplification of my task, my message and my faith — and I trust of my life."

At first Stanley's task was more complex. He was trying to hold a line from Genesis to Revelation consistent with the prevailing views of a western civilization and the western Christian Church. Yet he soon realized that the heart of the matter had been left out. Then he realized that he needed to shorten his line and take his stand at Christ and before the non-Christian world to know nothing but Jesus Christ and him crucified. Then he saw that that is where he should have been all along. The gospel lies in the person of Jesus, that Jesus himself is the Good News, and that Stanley's one task was to live and to present Him. His task was simplified and *vitalized*.[24] Less was more.

A young seminary student at one of his Ashrams asked this question, "Brother Stanley, isn't your philosophy of life too neat? Too Rosy?" Apparently he had a professor who attempted to reverse the words of the Apostle Paul to say, "Where sin abounded, grace did much more abound," into "Where grace abounded sin did much more abound." Stanley was singing his "song" against the grain of modern theological trends that were prevailingly pessimistic.

Stanley responded that Jesus pronounced the doom of all evil. "Every plant that my heavenly Father has not planted will be pulled up by the roots" (Matthew 15:13) – perhaps not today or tomorrow, but the "third day, YES!" Paul speaks about "dethroned powers..." (I Corinthians 2:6). It may take time but evil is doomed. Isaiah pronounced the doom of the gigantic Assyria army camped outside the gates to Jerusalem "by no human sword" (Isaiah 31:8). What was that "sword"? It was the Word of God proclaiming an inherent moral universe! That afternoon, an angel of the Lord went out and took out 185,000 of them so that Jerusalem was set free. Stanley would bet his life on the moral universe having the last word. There is Hope! Sin tries to assimilate what cannot be assimilated. Stanley is concerned about the direction the world seems to be taking – its moral decay – but NOT overly so. He knows that in the end, God prevails.[25]

Stanley then admits that there is, however, another side of evil – unmerited suffering. Stanley had his back to the wall on this issue for several years. Hindus and Buddhists simply say that suffering is not unmerited. It is the result of sin from a previous life. All suffering is just. Stanley was always suspect of a premise that came to that conclusion. What kind of a system of rewards and punishments has no memory (in this life) connecting the reward and the punishment? "So, when trouble comes, 'My karma is bad.' I deserve this." This may make for a patient people but it puts a brake on repentance and faith in Jesus. A Hindu once said to Stanley: "Jesus must have been a terrible sinner in a previous life."

Nor could Stanley accept the Muslim answer that insists that all suffering is the will of Allah. Where has God gone if everything that happens is his will? Similarly, Stanley could not accept the possible Old Testament solution — the righteous will be exempt from trouble (the premise behind Job's miserable comforters). Many of the prophets struggled with this as they saw the righteous suffer, sometimes because they were righteous. Society demands conformity to its predominant whims. If you fall beneath its standards it will punish you. If you rise above it, it will persecute you. "Woe unto you Jesus said, when all men speak well of you."[26]

The Old Testament does, on occasion, suggest another answer, "In spite of it all, I will rejoice in the Lord, I will find joy in the God of my salvation" (Habakkuk 3:17). Habakkuk calls God a wimp for two chapters for apparently not interceding on behalf of His people before he finally gets the point in Chapter Three and celebrates his new found freedom. In the end, God prevails.

Nor can Stanley accept the Stoic answer. "My head might be bloody, but it will be unbowed under the bludgeoning of chance." In shutting out suffering, however, the Stoic shuts out love and pity as well. It made him hard and uncaring. Stanley concludes that if the righteous were exempt there would be chaos. A righteous person would lean too far over a tall building and the law of gravity would be suspended while the bad person experienced its natural consequences. Increasingly Stanley knows that he must obey the laws of the moral universe as the purpose of those laws are to produce character. So, what is Stanley's key to relating to peoples of other religions.

It is the principle of the Round Table we will discuss in a moment. Let the non-Christians speak of their experience of what their religion does for them. Then Stanley would simply speak of Jesus and what Jesus does for him.

Ask Stanley about Round Table Conferences as an effective tool for sharing Jesus in an environment that is non-threatening, yet basically affirming — especially with peoples of other religions and strong differing opinions.[27]

It was during the 1920s (up until the Great Depression) that foreign missions reached its zenith. It might help to know that early in the 19th century there were less than 300 Catholic Priests in Missions and only 100 Protestant missionaries worldwide (no women). By the 1920s there were thousands. In 1928 alone $60 million were spent by Mission agencies, a staggering amount in that day. Although officially neutral towards British rule and Indian independence, things would begin to change. Many of the more traditional approaches to evangelism were no longer as effective in many countries of the world. Increasingly, Western missionaries, especially those in India would be facing this problem in light of rising Indian nationalism.

Perhaps understanding these issues more than any other person, in the 1920s Stanley began organizing his "Round Table Conferences" that for the rest of his life would become one of his most effective tools for influencing both Christians and non-Christians alike. At one point he felt that his style of lectures mentioned in the earlier chapters were "too public and professional and not sufficiently personal to be an authentic instrument of Christian evangelism." Then, using the same group of local Indian leaders and officials who organized and chaired his lectures, he asked them to invite about forty or so of the "leading men" of the city to participate in a Round Table Conference. At these Round Tables (usually 2/3 non-Christian) no one sat at the head. Each person was asked to share their own experience as to what their religion had done for them. *Stanley would go last and talk about Jesus.*

Stanley insisted, "know the Truth and the Truth will set you free from passing fads." At the Round Table he did not have to defend Jesus. Jesus was his own defense. People would argue with their images of Christianity, even dogma, but not with the person of Jesus. Stanley says: "You can fling mud at the sun but that sunshine is its defense. He had told students that Jesus appeals to the soul as light appeals to the eye, as love to the heart. Paul was not so successful in Athens as he spoke more of good views than good news. So he went on to Corinth determined to know nothing but Jesus Christ and him crucified." Stanley's aim as well would be to preach nothing but Jesus Christ and him crucified.[28]

The Round Table was never a place for idle chatter or even for plotting future strategy. It was a way of allowing different perspectives to find common ground, to know and appreciate each other. Many of the participants were then drawn to Stanley's larger meetings and were soundly converted.[29] This was even more evidence of Stanley's genius.

At one point Stanley wrote regarding one of his Round Table conferences, "Christ was upon us to the point of tears." He returned to his room thanking God for the way Christ is capturing the heart of India.[30]

As the years progressed, Stanley would hold more and more Round Table Conferences for his inter-religious discussion groups in conjunction with his evangelistic meetings. These were always the best venues for including the various religious leaders in the area.[31]

Now ask Stanley about issues relevant to immigration. I clearly recall in my research happening upon this exchange. Toward the end of 1933, Stanley met with President Roosevelt (FDR) to discuss two crucial issues on relations between the U.S. and the Far East, Japan in particular. First, after WWI Woodrow Wilson had a vision for a League of Nations that could possibly unite the Far East (much like the NATO Accord in the North Atlantic), but it failed miserably as the United States washed its hands of involvement in international affairs and retreated into a foreign policy of isolationism and xenophobia. This fear of foreigners (especially racial prejudice against Asians) was reflected in the restrictive immigration laws adopted by Congress in the 1920s.

Secondly, as a result, Japan was excluded from any discussions of the League of Nations and then the immigration quotas against Asians so offended (the Japanese in particular), that these two issues would become the main source of Japanese grievances against the West and were never resolved to Japan's satisfaction. Japan responded by turning to militarism and imperialism and this would set in motion the events that would lead to WW II. Surely we can see the relevance of all this on the contemporary scene.

Stanley believed that his sensitivity to matters such as this was a part of God's call on his life. He was one of the first to perceive Japan's feelings of being a victim of international prejudice, especially in light of its needs for land and natural resources. Japan was being primed to act independently.

After the visit with Stanley, Roosevelt promised to look into the matter but it is said that sometimes Roosevelt would promise to look into something and then do nothing. Unfortunately, he did nothing and the stage was set for war in less than eight years.

Ask Stanley about the full significance of the Kingdom of God as already and not yet. So that our Mother the Church could *act today and anticipate tomorrow,* Stanley embraced a routine for most of his life that would seek to expand and explain his Kingdom of God principles—"an unshakable Kingdom, an unchanging Person"—to impact the Church-at-large.[32] This involved extensive travel all over the world.

By the end of 1944 Stanley had so solidified his Kingdom of God principles that they clearly affected his attitudes toward all of his major passions. For example,

1. His opposition to British imperialism in India.
2. His proposal of a Pacific Charter as a guarantee of equity for all people everywhere,
3. His attempts to advocate church leadership in the resettlement of Japanese Americans.
4. His insistence on welcoming persons of all races and ethnic groups in his own meetings at home and abroad.
5. His Kingdom principles were also foundational for his ideas for federal union of Christian churches. His struggle with church disunity had been building for half a decade.[33]

Again, self-surrender was, of course, the key to Jesus' expression and embodiment of the Kingdom of God in the New Testament. Reduce the words of Jesus to one sentence and it would probably look something like this: *To gain your life is to lose it, to be great is to be a servant, to be first is to be last.* While most Christians restricted the application of this kind of self-surrender to personal morality, Stanley was more holistic and expanded these Kingdom principles to corporate relationships between and among human institutions, especially the church-at-large. *This prompted his vision of Federal Union as a way for Christians to speak as one.* If they could resolve their theological and doctrinal differences, they could avoid the disunity that weakened the moral voice of the church when speaking out on economic, social and political issues as well.[34]

Ask Stanley about a "moral universe" where we thrive only in a positive response to God's moral laws. We have already noted that in a moral universe, an orderly God so created the universe that if we live our lives according to the moral standards of basic morality and goodness, we could be healthy, vibrant instruments of grace. So, if we are to overcome the basic urges that tend to distract — self, sex and the herd — we must totally surrender to the Spirit of the living God if we are to avoid the kinds of extremes that alienate, divide and cause dissension? Stanley was totally convinced that the human heart is the same around the world. He found himself returning to his developing understanding of living in a *moral universe* where we cannot live outside the principles of God's intended purpose for his creation, especially as outlined in the Sermon on the Mount, without destroying ourselves. The theme of a moral universe would gain more and more momentum as his ministry continued to evolve.

What about global Church unity and ecumenism (federal union)? Is there any hope for uniting the global churches so that we can rise up against the evil in the world with a common voice? Can we stop cancelling each other out with needless duplication and dissension — that insecurity that needs to protect its own turf. Several children were asked recently, "Who started the American Civil War?" One child responded, "FOX News and MSNBC!

During the late 1930s, Stanley was months at Sat Tal continually struggling (as always) with *church unity*. As he prayed he sensed a spiritual malaise among Christians due to a lack of unity. In India obstacles to Christian unity came from two sources. *First,* was the social, economic, political, and racial differences between Western Christians and Indian Christians. *Second,* was the denominational differences among Christians within India. Across the years Stanley's ministry focused on both of these issues at one time or another (especially in the late 30s and early 40s). This problem had plagued him throughout his ministry. He would address it in some detail throughout his ministry.

During the latter part of 1940, Stanley's meditations at Sat Tal the previous year on the need for unity are now back with a rush. Perhaps with some memory of his reaction to the perceived over emphasis on ecumenism at Tambaram, Stanley now begins to focus on church union. This focus would give him fresh insight into ecumenism.

He now came to three conclusions about the church. *First,* "Christians are the most united body on earth — if they only knew it — united at the center but divided at the circumference." *Second,* "God does not prefer one Christian denomination over another." God delights in any of the saints, no matter the denomination, if they surrender to Him. *Third,* "the expressions and manifestations of the faith and life that are common to all Christians are varied and diverse."

Between December 1942 and June, 1943 Stanley published three articles, first in the *Christian Century,* a second in the *Christian Advocate* and a third in the *Christian Century*. The common thread was to become a new focus (if not obsession) — Church Union. As he engaged issues relevant to the Pacific Charter, he had traced his thinking and praying about a new world order to early Methodist influences.

First, John Wesley's understanding of "the world is my parish," was consistent with Stanley's understanding of the Kingdom of God as a Methodist/Wesleyan emphasis on church union. Wesley often quoted, "If your heart is as my heart then give me your hand." Stanley would begin to see this as a "federal union." In his *Song,* Stanley saw three ways of uniting American Christians: amalgamation, federation and federal union. Interestingly, he would model his three forms of ecumenical polity on the history of the American states in their various efforts to create a United States of America. We learned about this argument for federal union in his *The Christ of the American Road,* published in 1944.[35]

On the basis of these three conclusions Stanley proposed that all Christians in the U.S. drop their denominational labels and become members of a federal church—The Church of Christ in America. In an article in the *Christian Century,* written some years later he would conclude with words reminiscent of the *Communist Manifesto,* "We have nothing to lose except our dividing walls." He honestly believed that the Church united could speak with authority both to nations and societies. The Church failed because she did not speak with one voice. His idea of a federal church would never find traction but would eventually result in his *The Christ of the American Road* (1944).

Ask Stanley about the importance of time apart as embraced by the Worldwide Christian Ashram Movement. As Brother Stanley was awarded the Gandhi Peace Prize he was introduced as "a great missionary, evangelist to the intelligentsia, prolific writer, and promoter of peace and reconciliation. *He founded Christian Ashrams in north India and took them to the USA and across the globe."*

For Stanley, who was unable to visit Mabel as often as he might have wished, these ashrams both in India and the U.S. (and eventually worldwide) would become his virtual home for the rest of his life. Since establishing his first Christian Ashram at Sat Tal in 1930, until his death, nothing was closer to his heart than these spiritual retreats. On the basic principle of self-surrender, these ashrams continually transformed Brother Stanley and those who participated in them.

Although the format changed outside India, some say that these Ashrams were perhaps Stanley's most enduring contribution to the

Body of Christ. Certainly his books and articles inspired millions. His public evangelistic meetings led thousands into to a personal relationship with Jesus Christ. His interviews and counseling sessions reoriented the lives of thousands more. Yet, it was the Ashrams that had the greatest global impact.

Inspired by the steadying influence of these Ashrams, Stanley learned to sing in the midst of all that was going on around him. He writes: "With WWI and then WWII, needlessly destroying lives, how can you sing? You can sing by gazing at Jesus and glancing at evil. Never gaze at evil (pessimism) and glance at Jesus (optimism). Live spelled backward is evil. Good has everything behind it so evil is weak and good is strong. If life misses the mark, misses Jesus, it becomes iniquity. This is not a doctrine. This is a demonstration, demonstrated around us daily."[36]

Again, the central focus of the Christian Ashram is Jesus Christ — the living Word become flesh. The central problem of human kind is self-centeredness. We have established previously that the two biggest sins in the Bible are self-reliance and oppressing the poor. The essential response to this living Word of God is self-surrender. This movement, born in the heart of India and nurtured in the heart of Stanley, is universally congruent with the mission of God — to call His wayward children home. The Christian Ashram is a place where "home" is experienced here and now — the Kingdom of God in miniature — on earth as it is in heaven.[37]

Stanley writes, "Of all the notes that make up my *Song of Ascents*, one of the most important is the Ashram note. Without it I would have lacked a disciplined fellowship.... [where I could] live out my life in a close-knit fellowship of the Spirit — they responsible to me and I responsible to them, at a very deep level, the level of experimental living. . . . their transformations have been an invitation and a spur to further transformations in me. They have helped make me."[38]

It is important to note that all of the ashrams were called a complete success as most of the participants were spiritually transformed.

That is what the Christian Ashram is all about. Many participants in the Open Heart, when speaking candidly about their needs and expectations simply said, "I need more God; I need more of the Spirit of Jesus!" They returned to their work renewed and refreshed by Jesus, the Son of the living God. They were healed by the power of His Holy Spirit.

Now ask Brother Stanley about his use of Scripture — the Word of God? What about prayer? What about the importance of sharing one's faith in Jesus with others as the Holy Spirit empowers us to feed the hungry, clothe the naked and visit the sick and imprisoned as well?

As the Word become flesh, Jesus passed on to others what he had gained through his own time in the Word and prayer. Stanley writes that He modeled at least three things — time in the Word, prayer and then sharing with others what he had learned through time in the Word and prayer. This became ingrained in Stanley.[39]

The *Scriptures* are a record of God's self-revelation — "a letter from home." Stanley meets the Word — Jesus — in the word as the Word become flesh. Without the Word our well runs dry. Stanley was obviously a man of the word as his works are literally permeated with texts from both the Old and New Testaments.

Stanley's custom was to spend about an hour and a half each day in prayer. The first half hour was usually spent interceding for others, asking nothing for himself. Then he would spend an hour pacing (outside if possible between 5 to 6 in the evenings). Stanley frequently speaks of his listening post (listening to his inner voice) where he was open to God's suggestions that later became emphases recorded in his sermons, lectures, articles, and books.

Stanley speaks of praying without ceasing. We breathe without ceasing. Can we not pray without ceasing? To be in love is for that love to pervade all that we do, consciously and subconsciously. Stanley was subconsciously set to pray. Remember that the Spirit's main work is to empower through the subconscious, the Spirit prays with us and for us and in us when we are busy with many things. Prayer is not trying to bend God's will to my will but aligning my will to God's will. Stanley found himself praying less and less for things as he prayed for more and more of Him. To have Him is to have everything.

Sharing what he learned in absorbing the Word and absorbed in prayer is the third habit. It is important to share God — what Jesus does for him. That which is not expressed, dies as a law of the mind. Stanley supplied the willingness to share; God supplied the power.[40]

Surrender means partnership. Jesus said, "But your Advocate, the Holy Spirit whom the Father will send in my name, will teach you everything." And, "when he comes who is the Spirit of truth, he will guide you into all truth" (John 14:26; 16:13). The Holy Spirit will teach you everything — that is *illumination*. Then He guides you into possession of what he teaches — that is *illustration*. So, you see and seek; you become the illustration of what he illuminates — the Word become flesh — in you so that He launches you into incredible ministry among the least.[41]

Please know that redemption goes beyond Jesus dying upon the cross and rising again to demonstrate his victory. He now implements that redemption by coming into our hearts by the Holy Spirit to abide with us forever. "The Holy Spirit is the applied edge of redemption, applied where we need it most, down amidst the driving urges in the subconscious mind." Stanley reiterates that the work of the Holy Spirit is in the area of the subconscious mind. In conversion we surrender all that we know but in receiving the Holy Spirit we surrender all that we do not know as well — including the subconscious urges of self, sex and the herd. The Holy Spirit moves in and takes over these subconscious urges — not to wipe them out but to cleanse them. Self, he consecrates to surrender, sex, he consecrates to procreation and intimacy within marriage and herd, he inspires to creativity, to loyalty — beyond the herd — upon the highest social entity — *the Kingdom of God*. The Holy Spirit not only cleanses these urges but coordinates them!

We are not beyond temptation when filled with the Spirit. Self, sex and herd are still there. Temptation is not sin. The Holy Spirit simply empowers the three for a joint operation.[42] I like that.

Again, to find the gift of the Holy Spirit demands self-surrender — our all for His all. To surrender our all gives us the right to take His all — "Himself" — the gift of the Holy Spirit (Galatians 3:14). Surrendered to Christ and having the gift of the Holy Spirit we have a new center for disciplining our lives — Jesus Christ. Try and discipline your life around an un-surrendered self and you will fail. To surrender fully is to be fully reinforced — empowered — by the Holy Spirit.

What can Brother Stanley teach us about how to respond to criticism? When someone was critical (even unfairly) toward Stanley Jones he would either learn from the criticism if it had any merit whatsoever or in return, he would always go high. A church once cancelled an invitation to me simply because I asked if they would ask the sisters and brothers in the congregation, for the six months before the beginning of our mission, to make a conscious effort never to allow someone else to hear something from them secondhand that was not positive. They simply could not do it.

Stanley's absolute confidence in God led some to accuse him of being superficial, naïve, self-righteous and cocksure. May I say, there is not a whisper of any of that in Stanley Jones. Stanley lived all his life under opposition. He had a way of singing, frequently not on account of but in spite of...[43]

AND WHILE WE ARE AT IT, LET'S NOT FORGET ABOUT MABEL

Ask Mabel about educating children and the influence of Mahatma Gandhi. Considerable emphasis has been placed on Mabel's management of her school for boys in Sitapur. Hers was the first with women teachers. These women were, by and large, apparently more committed to the task than most men so that her boys excelled on every level.

Although Eunice speaks highly of Mabel as a strict, though fair, disciplinarian Robert Maves (in charge of the high school in Moradabad for 6 years during WWII) says that Mabel could be "stubborn, and she had a mind of her own, and ran a tight ship." She was undoubtedly inflexible at times and that could create emotional distances between herself and others but her weaknesses were also her strengths, strengths necessary to manage a school for boys that is still going today.[44]

In Chapter 4 we noted that in early 1923 Mabel heard Gandhi speak in Sitapur and was so impressed she wrote to him asking for a copy of his powerful address. He wrote back beginning a 25 year correspondence. Since Mabel's correspondence with Gandhi would focus on education and disciplinary matters, it is significant that Mabel's philosophy of education was far closer to Gandhi's Satyagraha (emphasizing the genius of non-violence) than it was to the West. Both Stanley and Mabel remained close friends with Gandhi. Once when Stanley was visiting Gandhi the Mahatma received a beautifully woven tea cloth from Kamala Nehru (the wife of Jawaharlal Nehru). Although Gandhi was grateful he had no need for the gift and gave it to Stanley saying, "Give it to Mrs. Jones with my love.[45] Someone once told Brother Stanley that "he was a good speaker but that Mabel was better."

Ask Mabel about women's issues. In spite of Mabel's occasional physical maladies, her schedule soon begins to rival (in some ways) Stanley's global schedule. Many believe that she is in touch with her own voice as a feminist. No question! Mabel fully understood women's issues but as a fully liberated woman she felt that most of the chatter about "liberation" was irrelevant to her. She writes in an open letter that she needed prayer warriors. "We cannot win India by might, nor by power, nor by money alone; it will be by His Spirit working in us—and in you."[46] This was the heart of Mabel Losing Jones.

E. Stanley Jones' Bronze Bust

Robert G. Tuttle, Jr. with a bronze bust of E. Stanley Jones
Lucknow, India, 2017

Conclusion

We stated previously that in our Conclusion we would attempt to encapsulate the heart of Stanley's overall message, especially as related to his demeanor and passion.

Bishop James Mathews wrote of Stanley after his death that, "I never saw him lose his temper; nor heard him speak ill of anyone, nor even a hint that he was discouraged or depressed...."

On the 100th anniversary of Stanley's birth in 1984, Roberto Escamilla, a Methodist pastor still deeply committed to the Ashram movement and who accompanied Stanley as interpreter while Stanley was leading ashrams in South America, commented, "Stanley, during the 'Open Heart' and 'Overflowing Heart' sessions, took copious notes (just as he did in all of the Ashrams). Everything people would say was important. Even if he could not understand the language, he would watch the faces and expressions in an attempt to penetrate into their emotional and spiritual conditions.[1]

Let me say this again: Stanley was far ahead of his time! Rather than simply winning people to Christianity, he was winning people to Jesus Christ, the universal "Man."

We now close our biography with some important thoughts from Stanley's *Song*, a final chapter entitled, "What Life Has Taught Me — So Far." Stay with this as I summarize. These thoughts could change your life forever.

In reality, what Life *in Christ* has taught Stanley so far is that "life" in general and Life in Christ specifically have been teaching him the same thing—"one faintly and the other fully." So Stanley sums up this "Life" in these brief paragraphs.[2]

1. Everything on earth from the lowest cell to the highest created order has within it an urge after the fuller, higher life. Tagore writes: "Everything lifts up strong hands after perfection." We want to live, not just more fully but better. The moment we say better we have a religion. We are incurably religious.

2. There is a moral universe that we do not produce through codes of religion but that we discover written into the nature of things. The universe is not indifferent to our virtue and vice—it takes sides—where we get results and consequences. Work with the moral universe and the results will sustain you. Work against it and consequences will haunt you. We are free to choose. You do not break these laws; we break ourselves upon them—and they are class-blind, color-blind, race-blind, religion-blind—break these laws and you get broken.[3]

3. Human response to the religious urge within and the pressure of the moral universe is to set up systems of religion, some crude as idol worship, some complex as philosophies. Religion is the human search for God.

4. There is a God. That there is only one God is obvious to many who realize that the same Law that is at work in tiny human cells is at work in the farthest gigantic star—the universe is not a multiverse; it is a universe—with the stamp of one creative Spirit upon it all.

5. The universe could not have happened by chance. The idea that atoms floating in space could chance upon universal law and order is absurd. All that is descriptive of earth points to order out of chaos. "The relationship of the Supreme Source to all of creation" is seen in the person of Jesus—the key to the whole. The Jesus revealed in the New Testament supplies the Law that governs us and our conduct.[4]

6. Again, that resident forces within nature could produce the universe without the hypothesis of an intelligent Being — God — is equally absurd. How could resident forces within nature move toward intelligent ends without themselves being intelligent? God apparently created something that created something that created something and on and on it moves toward a moral universe, beckoned by ideals, our evolution in our own hands to go up or down by choice. God could have created all at once but wouldn't it take more intelligence to produce the kind of a world with free agents of choice? If you cannot say no, your yes is meaningless.

7. Science by its very nature cannot give a complete answer to life. Science measures the quantitative aspects of life — the means. Religion weighs the moral and spiritual ends for which those means are to be used. Science cannot give a complete answer to the poetry of Longfellow. It takes "religion" to evaluate those imponderables. Science can build or destroy — it is constructive or destructive. The powers of science are morally neutral. What then do we need? Two things — the powers and techniques of science plus the spirit of real religion behind those techniques directing them to great moral and spiritual ends.[5]

8. While religions are our search for God, there is a Way — Jesus — that is not our search for God, but is God's search for us. There are many religions but one gospel — the good news of God's search for us through Jesus Christ. Some ask, "Is not Christianity simply one search — one religion among many? Note, Jesus never used the word "religion." He never intended to bring one religion to set alongside other religions. He came to set Himself over and against all human need — no religion has the answer to that need. Jesus is God's redemptive offer as God's answer for everyone.

9. If there is but one God, what is that God like in character for what God is like in character, we must be like. We cannot be at cross-purposes with Reality without getting hurt. So, how do we know what God is like? Some look at nature and see God's laws but we are not subjects asking for a law — we are sons and daughters asking for a loving Creator. Stanley looks to the prophets and teachers and is grateful for every inspired word but is not satisfied — for the medium through which the message comes is imperfect. God can be and is revealed through a book but not perfectly. The Book is impersonal but God is infinitely personal. The only way for God to be revealed perfectly is through a perfect Person. The Word had to become flesh. Now we know what God is like — God is Christ-like — Jesus Christ is God's self-revelation.[6]

10. The distinctive thing about Christianity that sets it apart is the Word become Flesh. All religions have the Word become word — a philosophy or moralism but the gospel, the good news of Jesus Christ, is the Word become flesh — the divine idea become fact.

11. That reality orients our definition of good and evil. To think of goodness is not to add virtue to virtue; it is to think of Jesus. He is goodness incarnate — so, our code is a character. Good is to be like him in character and bad is not to be like him in character. This definition may not be fixed — as our conceptions of him are ever improving; it is growth in conception and in character.

12. The New Testament is not the revelation of God — that would be the Word become printer's ink. [Do not worship the Bible — that is Bibliolatry — worship the God revealed in the Bible]. The New Testament is the inspired record of the revelation seen in the face of Jesus Christ — the Word become Flesh.

13. The Old Testament is a period of preparation for Christianity; it is pre-Christianity, perhaps sub-Christianity. Christianity is Christ. Revelation was progressive, culminating in Jesus Christ as God's perfect, ultimate, final self-disclosure. Jesus made his own word final: "You have heard that it was said by them of old... but I say to you...". The only way to think of God is to think of Jesus.

14. Jesus did not come merely to disclose God's character. He came to make it possible to be remade in the likeness of that character. He came to redeem us from what we are and to remake us in the likeness of what he is. He is not simply a teacher; he is a redeemer.[7]

15. Jesus came not simply to give us his word or example; he came to give himself. He became like us that we might become like him. He was baptized into our world for just over thirty years—into our temptations. He became sin for us at the cross—like us in every way! [Hebrews, 1-2]. Do not ask Stanley to explain it; he cannot. He simply bows in humility and repentance—at the wonder of the cross—that God should give His only Son for Stanley Jones. Stanley bows and is redeemed.

16. Sin and death are inextricably bound up. Jesus took our sin and our death to the cross. Then he rose from the dead. Everything *a-priori* says he *should*. Everything *a-posterori* says he *did*. Such an alive movement could not have come out of a dead Christ. He made people alive and still does. Stanley knows Him better than he knows anyone on the planet and He knows Stanley better than anyone else knows him on the planet. "This Jesus has made this man [Stanley] well and whole—saved! From what?—not from hell or to heaven but from himself—sins, conflicts, futility, emptiness *now*!

17. The deepest need of global humanity is to be converted, to be regenerated, to be made over again. With Jesus he repudiates proselytism (Matthew 23:15). [Stanley was weary of Christians "converting" Christians into a particular sect rather than converting non-Christians to Jesus Christ]. Stanley quotes Matthew 18:3, "Except you be converted and become as little children, you shall not enter the Kingdom of heaven." Jesus makes us different—as different from the ordinary as we are different from the animal. We need not remain the same; we can have new birth, another chance when we have failed miserably at the business of life—our inherent tendencies can be reversed—a new blood transfusion, a transplanted heart. Anyone who does not take that is a fool.[8]

18. Redemption goes beyond Jesus' dying upon the cross for us, and rising again to show his victory. *Jesus now implements that redemption by coming into our hearts in the Holy Spirit to abide with us forever.* The Holy Spirit is the applied edge of redemption, applied where we need it most, down amid the driving urges in the subconscious mind.

Stanley reiterates that the work of the Holy Spirit is in the area of the subconscious mind (perhaps exclusively). In conversion we surrender all that we know but in receiving the Holy Spirit we surrender all that we do not know as well—including the subconscious urges of self, sexuality and the herd. The Holy Spirit moves in and takes over these subconscious urges—not to wipe them out but to cleanse them. Then the Holy Spirit not only cleanses them but coordinates them!

19. To state this last point just a bit differently, we are not beyond temptation when filled with the Spirit. Self, sexuality and herd are still there. Temptation is not sin. The Holy Spirit simply empowers us for a joint operation.[9]

20. To be filled with the Holy Spirit demands self-surrender—our all for the Spirit's all. To surrender our all gives us the right to take the Spirit's all, to be baptized or filled by the Holy Spirit (Acts 2:4; Galatians 3:14). Faith welcomes what we believe in—our birthright as children of God (John 7:39). We consent to the Spirit's initiation.

21. Surrendered to Christ and having the gift of the Holy Spirit we have a new center for disciplining our lives—Christ. Try and discipline your life around an un-surrendered self and you will fail. To surrender fully is to be fully reinforced by the Holy Spirit.

22. The Christian way is not an alien way; it is an affinity—the natural way to live. Stanley's conviction is that we are made in our inner structure and in our outer relationships by Christ; and to find him is to find ourselves, our brothers and sisters and how to live as a member of society. We are made for Christ as the eye is made for light (John 1:3; Hebrews 1:3; Colossians 1:16; 1 Corinthians 8:6). Stanley quotes three important Christian writers—John, Paul and the author of Hebrews—all saying the same thing—all things visible and invisible have been made by Christ and for Christ. We are made for him—it is a part of our DNA.

Stanley recalls the words of Augustine, "O God, thou hast made us for thyself and we are restless until we rest in thee." The Scriptures just quoted are even more specific than Augustine. We were made by Jesus Christ for Jesus Christ and to live any other way is to go to pieces. Is this too dogmatic? No, proven fact — apart from him we are orphaned, estranged, out of harmony with ourselves and the universe. On the other hand, to live in His Way is to be universalized — we are in harmony with ourselves and the universe. This is the best proven fact of Stanley's life.

Some object, "Jesus did not say — 'I am the way, truth and the life.' This was the product of later years." Stanley responds, "Who made John, Paul and the writer of Hebrews say this? — the Holy Spirit within and the facts of life without. To work from Christ down and then the facts of life up, we come out at the same place — the feet of Jesus.[10]

23. The Christian way is the natural way to live — "My burden is easy, my yoke is light." Those who believe that sin is the natural way and that the Christian Way is the unnatural way are a paralysis upon the Christian movement. God made us good. We make ourselves bad by living against the grain of the universe. 1 John 5:3, "God's commandments are not burdensome." Even our burdens become wings and sails and love. Stanley argues that to tell people to go to lunch when they are hungry is not a burden — our stomachs tell us the same thing. The way of the transgressor is hard. The Way of Christ is supernaturally natural.[11]

24. Prayer does not try to bend the will of God — it surrenders to the will of God and is in cooperation with the will of God. Throwing out a boat hook to the shore and pulling yourself in is not pulling the shore to you but pulling yourself to the shore.

25. Stanley was forever working out a life plan — God's life plan for him. He has the sense of being sent. John 15:16, "You have not chosen me, but I have chosen you to bear fruit…." 1 Corinthians 9:17, "Woe is me if I preach not the gospel," i.e. "I cannot help myself; it would be misery to me not to preach the gospel." It is a lifelong privilege. Stanley turned over all the money gained back into the ministry as a free expression of his joy and privilege.[12]

26. Stanley turned the business of preaching the gospel over to God without worrying about strength and health so he could concentrate on the ends.

27. Stanley believed he should work within the Church—not one church but all churches. He was a Methodist but believed in the Christian Church. With all her faults the church is the greatest serving institution on earth. She has many critics but no rivals in the work of human redemption. In all her places of ministry around the world she has always taken schools, hospitals, blind and leper asylums, churches, the gospel—everything to lift the body, mind and spirit of the human race.

Yet, Stanley has no illusions. Although the Church contains the best life of the Kingdom she is not the Kingdom. Never put your full weight down on the church for she will let you down. Put your full weight down on Jesus Christ. He will never let you down. Never gaze at the Church and only glance at Jesus—that leads to doubts. Stanley believes that $^2/_3$ of people in churches need conversion and are a field for evangelism.[13]

28. Humankind's greatest need is conversion, inside the church and outside the church. If the church has lost her ability to produce conversion she has lost her right to be called Christian. Even the central thing in biological psychology is conversion—a change of momentous scientific importance and interest. Like much of what Stanley says or quotes this was said some years ago but is as up-to-date as tomorrow morning's news. There are no substitutes for conversion. If we hold our peace the very stones will cry out. He loved the old African-American Spiritual, "Ain't no rock gonna take my place!" Stanley mentions in his book, *Conversion* (1959) that conversion can never be reduced to mere conversation—that would be verbal, not vital.

29. Conversion is the framework of the Kingdom of God. We convert to Christ, the person, and to the Kingdom, the order. Conversion is, therefore, both personal and social.[14] There can be individual conversions and corporate conversions. Corporate conversions mean that entities such as businesses or even states can be changed from a self-centered basis and attitude to Kingdom-centered basis and attitude.

If conversion is only to a denomination it is less than Christian conversion. Conversion must be Kingdom of God related if it is to be a head-on, total answer to our total need. Stanley relates this to a Kingdom totalitarianism that leads to freedom. Self-totalitarianism is inane and tame and leads to total bondage. Again, revolt against the Kingdom you revolt against yourself.

30. When Stanley takes stock and sums up what Jesus Christ has brought to him as a person he finds the following things:

a. Jesus has brought him God. The more he knows of Jesus the more he knows of God.[15]

b. Jesus brought him God and equally important, God brought him Jesus. Stanley does not know where God ends and Jesus begins.

c. Jesus brings him the Holy Spirit as experience—the applied edge of redemption. Moreover, the Holy Spirit illuminates the Redeemer.

d. Jesus brings a Trinity in unity—not a bare, monolithic God, but a God who is a society within God's own nature, teaching us how to live as a person and a person in society.

e. Jesus brings Stanley himself. Stanley was a nobody until Jesus found him. Now he is a somebody—no more self-loathing, self-hate, self-rejection—how can Stanley reject what Jesus loves? In himself—No. In Jesus—Yes!

f. Jesus awakened his mind. Before he was at the bottom of his class—no place for a Christian. So, he moved up toward the top. After college he always felt uneducated so he developed a hunger for knowledge. He picked people's brains and made everyone and everything teach him something that he kept in a black notebook—his treasure house. Stanley planned to die learning.

g. Jesus reconciled Stanley with his body—Stanley and his body are a team. 1 Corinthians 6:13. Jesus made it and is remaking it. To the degree that Stanley is surrendered to Jesus he has nothing but peace and healing.[16]

h. In doing all these things Jesus has saved him from self-preoccupation. He has saved Stanley from himself — the biggest salvation of all. In meeting Jesus Stanley wanted to put his arms around the world and the years never dimmed that impulse. The year following his publication of the *Song*, Stanley would travel to Hawaii, Japan, Korea, Philippines, India, Israel, Finland, Sweden, Norway, Denmark, Wales and then back to the U.S. to spend 6 months among the heterogeneous peoples who make up this country — blacks, whites and ethnics all.[17]

i. When Stanley found Jesus Christ he found the world in which he lives. "All things belong to you…". The world of sunrises and sunsets that God made full of beauty and art and the faces of children — a symphony of love. That world belongs to Stanley so he is in harmony with harmony and in love with love. God made it and saw that it was good and gave it to Stanley and all those who surrender to his Son Jesus Christ. "Lo, I am with you always, even to the ends of the earth."

j. When Stanley found Jesus Christ he fell in love with life. Stanley did not know what it was like to have a blue hour — not for 40 years after his healing in the Lucknow church. Some told him that he had made sacrifices. Stanley quickly denied that. "I have never made a sacrifice for Jesus Christ. Stanley flung at the feet of Jesus a tangled up and worthless life and Jesus gave him back a life of freedom and worth. Jesus had enabled him to turn every sorrow into a song, every hurt into a hallelujah. Stanley saw himself as a miracle of grace.[18]

Now, Brother Stanley sums it all up again. This is his story, this is his song — a "Song of Ascents" and the end is but the beginning. Thus far… He has written as a witness and author, now he writes as an evangelist. He wants to tell us HOW we can move from a doubtful "how" to a triumphant "that." Stanley has used a verse over the years for this purpose: "And we all, with unveiled face, beholding the glory of the Lord, are being changed into his likeness from one degree of glory to another; for this comes from the Lord who is the Spirit" (2 Corinthians 3:18). Note the steps:

1. Be completeley honest with yourself and God—put away all halfway measures—ask yourself, "Do I really want this 'changed' life—enough to pay the price?" Are you willing to surrender yourself to the Way—that is the important first step.

2. Then get the center of your attention fastened at the right center—"beholding the glory of the Lord." Your center is NOT your own failures and shortcomings. They have oppressed and discouraged you long enough. Know yourself but do not look too intently—what has your attention has you—not too much introspection. Similarly, do not look too long at the failures of others. Again, to place your attention on the negatives is to become a negative.

By the same token, do not gaze too long on good people for they are not good enough. Glance at them and gaze at Jesus—only gaze on Jesus. Again, behold the glory of the Lord—as teacher, Yes; as doer, Yes; as dying on the cross, Yes; as rising from the dead, Yes; but, primarily and continuously gazing on the "glory of the Lord." He is now at the right hand of full authority holding eternity and time in his hands—the Omega—the last word in human affairs. He is available to anyone in need. Get your attention on Jesus. Then all that is in him is transferred to you—forgiveness, grace, love, power compassion, health, everything. You are being "changed into his likeness." We become that at which we habitually gaze.[19]

Behold the glory of the Lord and become filled with his "glory"—from "one degree to another." Conversion can be like a ship in the locks of a canal where you surrender to the lock and are lifted up. The effect is usually in two degrees—the first is the conscious mind coming under the saving control of Christ, but in the next "degree" the subconscious mind comes under the control of the Holy Spirit. Now all of our urges are not suppressed but under the control of the Holy Spirit.[20]

You are no longer a suppressed personality but an expressed personality. Note again, Peter says of Pentecost and the coming of the Holy Spirit, that "*this* comes from the Lord." The "this-ness" of Christian experience is unique and verifiable—it brings its own witness. The Spirit bears witness with our spirits that we are children of God (Romans 8:16). John Wesley preached more from that text than any other text in the Bible.

Furthermore, "*this* comes from the Lord" — the "this-ness" is a gift. The only qualification is to be humble enough to receive it. "How blest are they who are poor, for theirs is the Kingdom of heaven" — with all of its resources, power, adequacy, freedom, joy—its everything. This is not self-realization but Christ-realization that leads to self-realization—to save your life is to lose it—realizing yourself as a child of God.[21]

Once more, "*this* comes from the Lord" — the "this-ness" is not to try harder; it is to receive. You are the recipient and Jesus is the giver of grace. You cannot produce it. Surrender so that your surrendered ego is poor enough to receive.

Stanley finishes his *Song* with an all encompassing thought — All of this comes from the Lord who is the Spirit." Who is this Spirit? The Spirit is the Lord whom you behold; Jesus is the pattern. The Spirit did not come to compensate for the absence of Jesus but to guarantee His presence. You were made into the likeness of Jesus, into his image—a Christ-like person. This turns idealism into realism—a realism *from within* for the Lord is not only the pattern, he is the power. Cooperate with the creative Spirit within and the Spirit does the rest.

Some complained to Stanley that they were not even good enough to begin. Stanley would counter, "You do not have to be good enough, you simply need to be willing." 1 Corinthians 6:9-11 reads, "Do not be deceived (by sin). You were washed, sanctified, justified in the name of the Lord Jesus Christ and in the Spirit of God." Stanley illustrates this with the story of a Japanese Admiral who lost everything after the War but in his emptiness met Christ and was filled with joy and peace.

After observing the world's emptiness for many long years Stanley is convinced that there is no way out except through Jesus—the Way now present and available. Jesus offers in his own person, a person who embodies the Kingdom of God that cannot be shaken and is himself that unchanging person, the same yesterday, today and to-morrow.[22]

As a concluding word, I remember reading the The Divine Yes when it was first released after Stanley had died in India. As usual, the impact was profound. Suddenly my preaching changed to more Biblical, and actually more theological as well. He reminded me that bad theology puts the people in bondage whereas good theology sets the prisoner free. I wanted to set people free....

Dan Long, a student just recovering from a heart attack and open heart surgery wrote in a letter that "I'm struck by these specific words/thoughts from Jones in A Song of Ascents."

> Then the dawning came—and what a dawning! I saw that everything the other faiths brought up was the Word become word and what the Gospel presented was the Word become flesh. ...All other faiths are philosophies or moralisms—man's search upward.... The Gospel is God's search downward.... All of the ideas of the Christian faith are guaranteed by the fact of Christ. They have taken shoes and walked.... I challenge anyone, anywhere, to expose his or her inner life to Jesus Christ in repentance and faith and obedience ... Such persons will be changed, profoundly changed, in character and life; and they will know it in every fiber of their being."[1]

Reader, take this to heart. Do it now! It really is all about Jesus for Jesus is Lord!

NOTES

INTRODUCTION

1 E. Stanley Jones, *Gandhi*, p. 1.

2 E. Stanley Jones, *A Song of Ascents*, p. 17 [subsequent references to The Song of Ascents will simply be, *Song*].

3 *Song*, p. 19.

4 *Song*, p. 20.

5 *Song*, p. 16.

6 *Song*, pp. 8f.

CHAPTER ONE

1 This letter and the one following from Gandhi are previously unpublished and sent to me by Stanley's granddaughter, Anne Mathews-Younes.

2 Stephen Graham, *Ordinary Man, Extraordinary Mission*, Abingdon, p. 325.

3 The first attempt on Gandhi's life was in 1934.

4 Martha Chamberlain, *A Love Affair with India*, pp. 133ff.

5 *Christian Century*, February 6, 1948 as a letter to the editor, "Gandhi's Death — the Indian Reaction," p. 209.

6 *Love Affair with India*, p. 133f.

7 *Christian Century*, February 6, 1948, as a letter to the editor, "Gandhi's Death — the Indian Reaction," p. 209.

8 Jones, *Gandhi*, pp. 36ff.

9 Jones, *Gandhi*, p. 37.

10 Jones, *Gandhi*, p. 37.

11 Jones, *Gandhi*, p. 38.

12 Jones, *Gandhi*, pp. 40f.

13 Jones, *Gandhi*, the "Foreword," pp. 5ff.

14 Jones, *Song*, pp. 260ff.

15 Stanley's *Mahatma Gandhi: An Interpretation*, although written some time after his Dec. 1942 letter against the Jim Crow laws, this book was geared toward the African-American struggle for equality in the U.S. Martin Luther King would learn from this book his own principle of nonviolent civil disobedience. p. 283.

16 This personal letter was given to Stanley's granddaughter, Anne Mathews-Younes.

17 Chamberlain, *Love Affair with India,* p. 133.

CHAPTER TWO

1 Mabel Jones, *Educational Adventures in India* (unpublished memoirs).

2 Anne Mathews-Younes has a copy of Mabel's ancestral chart.

3 Florence Clark, "Secluded Clayton Cottage is Hub of the World," *Dubuque Telegraph Herald,* 1949.

4 *Women's Missionary Friend,* 1904. Kathryn Hendershot, E. Stanley Jones Had a Wife, p. 4ff, tells us that Mabel's early exposure to Quakerism and Methodism aroused in her the Quaker "hunger for a deeper, more serious walk with God," along with the Methodist "plain, simple and self-giving lifestyles in cluding deeds of humanitarianism and benevolence but with an emphasis on the 'inner Light.'"

5 Mabel Jones, letter to St. Luke's Record, Sept. 1904.

6 Hendershot, E. *Stanley Jones Had a Wife,* p. 11.

7 Jones' letter to Rev. Thomas Long in the Asbury Seminary archives.

8 Jones, *Song,* p. 26.

9 Jones, *Song,* p. 27. Sixty years later, Stanley would publish a book entitled, "Conversion," that speaks to these issues in some detail (Abingdon Press, 1959).

10 During the late 1920s this sense of "home-ness" would extend to the entire "moral universe." In order to live as God intended we must obey the moral, physical and spiritual laws of the universe.

11 Jones, *Song,* p. 35

12 Jones, *Song,* p. 37.

13 Jones, *Song,* p. 64.

14 Jones, *Song,* p. 46.

15 Jones, *Song,* p. 48.

16 Interestingly, this on going dialogue with God (related to an "inner voice") would become for Stanley a guiding principle throughout his life.

17 Jones, *Song,* p. 44.

18 Jones, *Song,* p. 67.

19 Jones, *Song,* pp. 68-69.

20 Jones, *Song,* p. 69.

21 Jones, *Song,* p. 70. It should be mentioned that during his time in India Stanley became averse to the experience of speaking in tongues. I suspect that he became weary of Pentecostals, with their emphasis on tongues, attempting to make Pentecostals out of Christians rather than making Christians out of non-Christians. Stanley despised proselyting.

22 Jones, *Song,* p. 72.

23 Jones, *Song,* p. 72.

24 Jones, *Song,* p. 72.

25 Jones, *Song,* pp. 74-78.

26 Mabel Jones, letter to St. Luke's Record, Feb. 1905.

27 Mabel Jones, letter to St. Luke's Record, Feb. 1905.

28 Hendershot, *E. Stanley Jones Had a Wife,* p. 14.

29 Graham, *Ordinary Man Extraordinary Mission,* pp. 48, 49.

30 Hendershot, *E. Stanley Jones Had a Wife,* p. 18

31 Chamberlain, *Love Affair with India,* pp. 18-19.

32 Hendershot, *E. Stanley Jones Had a Wife,* p. 20.

33 Hendershot, *E. Stanley Jones Had a Wife,* p. 28f.

34 Jones, Circular Letter, October 3, 1911, Asbury Archives. After retirement, Mabel would write a substantial book on the subject c. 1957 (unpublished).

35 From her obituary.

36 The number 330 million comes from the Upanishads, this would have been the approximate population at the time when the Upanishads were written, thus in-line with the philosophy that every individual is counted as distinct.

37 Jones, Letter to Miss Nellie, October 24, 1912. Asbury Archives. Cf. Graham, p. 61.

38 Hendershot, *E. Stanley Jones Had a Wife,* p. 30.

CHAPTER THREE

1 *Song,* p. 79

2 *Song,* p. 82.

3 Chamberlain, *Love Affair with India,* p. 29.

4 *Song.* p. 80.

5 *Song.* p. 39f.

6 *Song,* p. 41.

7 *Song,* pp. 43f.

8 *Song,* p. 38. It is interesting that the Qur'an also reinterprets the Old Testament just as Jesus in our New Testament reinterprets the Old Testament but the New Testament reinterpretation is far different than the Qur'an's. Whereas the Qur'an underscores the Law and attempts to reinforce it without grace and the constant need for revenge and the call to war, Jesus and the New Testament reinforces the appeal to love and forgive. You could never make a case for war out of the mouth of Jesus.

9 *Song,* p. 81.

10 *Song,* p. 81.

11 *Song,* p. 42.

12 Hendershot, p. 34.

13 *Song,* p. 84.

14 *Song,* p. 82.

15 Chamberlain, *Love Affair with India,* p. 28.

16 "Today we might term Jones' psychological reaction to his considerable spiritual and physical distress, a Generalized Anxiety Disorder rather than nervous collapse. Anxiety and worry over both his health and his ministry began to interfere significantly with his psychosocial functioning and were no doubt pronounced and upsetting. Anxiety and disruption in functioning can occur with or without precipitants. In Stanley's instance he was stressed by Tetanus (lockjaw), a ruptured appendix, fatigue, and the call to preach Jesus to the intelligentsia of India. The impact of these stressors was likely to be increasing symptoms of restlessness, being on edge, and easily fatigued, with difficulties concentrating and considerable distress and impairment in his ministerial functioning. Jones would write that he could not "feed himself" spiritually on his own preaching and that he was preaching beyond his experience and hit a wall of spiritual crisis which contributed to his 'spiritual sag.'" Personal note from Anne Mathews-Younes. *Cf. A Song of Ascents,* p. 86.

17 Hendershot, p. 33.

18 Hendershot, pp. 33f.

19 Hendershot, p. 35., cf. *Song,* p. 86.

20 *Song,* p. 87.

21 Graham, p. 108.

22 *Song* p. 88.

23 *Hendershot,* p. 36. Mabel Jones, *Junior Missionary Friend* (Jan. 1916). pp. 5-6.

24 Bundy, an address at the ESJ School of Evangelism and World Mission, Feb. 1 1983.

25 *Wife,* p. 39. Cf. Graham, p. 123ff.

26 *Song,* p. 90.

27 I mentioned in the Introduction that as I have read the entire Bible yearly over the last 50 years it occurs to me that two sins are recorded time and again. The first sin is self-reliance. Some of my brightest students burned out in 2 to 5 years attempting to rely on their own resources. The second sin is oppressing the poor—you really do not want to do that!

28 *Song,* p. 91.

29 *Song,* p. 93. Cf. Jones, *Christ of the Indian Road,* pp. 8f.

30 *Song,* p. 94

31 *Song,* p. 95.

32 *Song,* p. 105.

33 *Song, p. 97.*

34*Song, p. 99.*

35 *Song, p. 101.*

36 *Song,* p. 102.

37 *Song,* p. 103.

38 *Song,* p. 104.

39 *Song,* p. 106f.

40 *The Indian Witness,* Nov. 4, 1918.

41 *The Indian Witness,* Dec. 1, 1917.

42 *Song,* p. 110. Graham, pp. 124-128.

43 *Song,* p. 112.

CHAPTER FOUR

1 *Song,* p. 114.

2 Graham, pp. 116f.

3 *Song,* p. 115.

4 *Song,* p. 115.

5 *Song,* p. 74.

6 *Song,* p. 74.

7 *Song,* p. 67.

8 Jones, *The Christ of the Indian Road,* p. 21; Cf. *Song,* pp. 109.

9 *Song,* pp. 118ff.

10 Jones, *Gandhi,* p. 19.

11 Ranbir Vohra, *The Making of India,* p. 143.

12 Graham, p. 144.

13 *Cf. Song, pp. 110ff.*

14 Jones, *Duplicate Letter, August 6, 1919,* Asbury Archives.

15 It should be noted that revenge is a basic tenet of Islam. A Muslim is bound by Sharia Law to exact revenge in perpetuity.

16 Graham, p. 129. Cf. *Song,* p. 110 for the reference to Dr. Frank North.

17 Jones, *Gandhi,* pp. 51ff

18 Jones, *Gandhi,* pp. 52ff.

19 Speaking of light, about this time a stellar and planetary harbinger was observed. There was a triple conjunction of the planets Jupiter (the star of kings), Saturn (the star of the Jews) and Mars (the star of warriors).

20 John 1:3-4,10.

21 *Song,* p. 110.

22 Jones, *Gandhi,* p. 61.

23 Jones, *Gandhi,* pp. 56f.

24 Jones, *Gandhi,* pp. 60f.

25 *Song,* p. 108.

26 *Christ at the Round Table,* would be the second book Stanley published (1928).

27 *Circular Letter,* April 20, 1926.

28 Stanley's first mention of the Round Table conferences was in his 1923 Circular Letter.

29 Hendershot, *Wife,* p. 71.

30 Taken from Mabel's book, *On Education,* p. 76. Cf. Hendershot, *Wife.* p. 44.

31 Anne Mathews-Younes writes, "I believe that what was called "nervous collapse" apparently by a physician in Mabel's case could have been an acute stress disorder. In light of the many traumatic circumstances she experienced such as her school children dying of cholera and her fears that Eunice might die as well, brought this on. I understand that she may have carried that "trauma" with her throughout her life as 'feelings' but which did not ultimately impair her capacity to contribute and function at a very high level." Personal note.

32 Imagine this! Susanna Wesley carried *The Imitation of Christ"* (by Thomas a Kempis) with her wherever she went for many years.

33 Letter from the family of Mabel and Stanley Jones.

34 There is a traditional burial site for St. Thomas today just above Chennai.

35 Kenneth Scott Latourette claims that the Syrian Church had in effect become a caste (Latourette, *Mission Tomorrow,* p. 181.).

36 Jones, *Duplicate Letter,* May 15, 1920.

37 Jones, *Duplicate Letter,* May 15, 1920. Cf. Graham, p.134.

38 One of Gandhi's own spinning wheels is still on display at his Ashram in Ahmedabad, Gujarat. There is also one of his walking sticks that he used for his "long walk" from his Ahmedabad Ashram to the sea (protesting the British control of the salt market). Gandhi vowed not to return to his favorite Ashram until India was free and independent. He was scheduling his return at the time of his assassination.

39 Jones, *Indian Witness*, October 26, 1921. Asbury Archives.

40 Jones, *Indian Witness,* October 26, 1921.

41 Graham, p. 157.

42 It is interesting that the Nestorians emphasized the humanity of Christ as much as his deity. Some have suggested that Muhammad was influenced by them but a more likely story is that Muhammad was influenced by the Arians in Spain. There are Nestorians in Baghdad today.

43 Jones, *Indian Witness,* "Evangelizing in the Land of King Feisul." Pp. 241f. Asbury Archives

44 Tuttle, *Story of Evangelism.* p. 317

45 Brian Moynahan, *The Faith,* p. 632.

46 J. Tremayne Copplestone, *History of Methodist Missions. Vol. 4.* NY Board of Global Ministries, 1973. Cf. Graham, p. 200.

47 *Song,* p. 221.

48 *Love Affair,* p. 137. Jones' daughter Eunice later returned the shawl to Nehru's grandson Rajiv Gandhi, who received it with gratitude on behalf of his family.

49 *Love Affair,* p. 35.

50 *Wife*, p.45f.

51 Jones, *Christ of the Indian Road*, p. 1.

52 Graham, p. 158.

53 *Indian Road, pp. 27f.*

CHAPTER FIVE

1 *Wife*, p. 54.

2 *The Christian Advocate*, January 28, 1926, "Evangelizing in the Land of the Pharaohs," p. 105.

3 Theologically speaking, it was not until the early 1940s, with the translation of Karl Barth's *Church Dogmatics*, that both sides would again be reading the same perspective with any great interest.

4 Graham, p. 183.

5 *Wife*, pp. 55, 154

6 *Wife*, pp. 60f.

7 Jones, *Along the Indian Road* (Abingdon, 1939), p. 189.

8 This was basically the format for the Round Table Conferences.

9 *Gandhi,* p. 61.

10 *Song*, pp. 134f. Stanley at one point states that a good bit of Gandhi's objection was that he believed that Christians do not "reject" Christ, they "reduce Christianity to a creed to be believed, an emotion to be felt, an institution to which [they] belong… a rite to be undergone—anything but a life to be lived." Gandhi concluded, "Christians have inoculated the world with a mild form of Christianity so that it is now proof against the real thing."

11 Graham, p. 172.

12 March 22, 1927 *Circular Letter*, quoted in Graham, p. 184.

13 Remarkably, during 1928 Stanley would find the time to complete and publish the book, *Christ at the Roundtable.*

14 *Indian Witness*, article, "Malay: Where Opportunity Beckons," November 23, 1927, p. 751.

15 *Wife*, p. 61. Cf. Graham. pp. 94ff.

16 Graham, p. 200.

17 *Wife*, pp. 63ff., Cf. Graham, p. 186.

18 Jones, a letter dated June 6, 1928 describes the experience. Asbury Archives

19 *Wife*, p. 154.

20 Graham, p. 192.

21 *Wife*, p. 63.

22 Mabel letter dated April 30, 1929.

23 Jones, *Circular Letter,* May 8, 1929. Asbury Archives.

24 Graham, *p. 241.*

25 These are personal notes regarding the civil disobedience during the 1930s from a Eunice Jones Mathews' paper on Mabel' life as a missionary/educator. p. 11.

26 *Wife,* pp. 64, 67 & 154. Cf. *Love Affair with India,* p. 101.

27 *Song,* p. 215.

28 Jones, *Circular Letter,* December 7, 1929. Asbury Archives. Cf. Graham, *p. 348.*

29 Jones, *Song.* pp. 220ff..

30 Jones, *Song,* pp. 220f.

31 Albin, a chapter on the Christian Ashram, *E. Stanley Jones and Sharing the Good News in a Pluralistic Society,* pp. 2ff.

32 *Song,* pp. 222f.

33 We will see the Ashram transferred to America in 1940 as a part-time Ashram. As a part-time Ashram the movement would spread throughout the world until "there are now over one hundred of them growing so rapidly that it is difficult to keep up with them" [in 1968]. *Song,* p. 222. Cf. Graham, p. 352.

34 In recent years, the summer Ashram in Sat Tal takes place over two weeks, May 15-29 in English; followed by a second two-weeks, June 1-4, in Hindi. In North America, Japan, Korea, and Scandinavia, a typical Christian Ashram is three to six days. Albin, Chapter, p. 5. Cf.*Song,* p. 215.

35 The Rev. Charles Kinder, in a personal interview with Tom Albin, described a conversation with Brother Stanley as Stanley helped him see the importance of allowing others to serve as the evangelist for the Christian Ashram and allow the movement to grow beyond his own physical ability and life expectancy. Albin, p. 3, Cf. *Song.* pp. 215ff.& p. 220.

36 Albin, p. 3. Cf. *Song.* p. 222.

37 *Song,* pp. 216f.

38 *Song,* p. 217.

39 Graham, p. 178.

40 *Circular Letter,* March 20, 1930.

41 *Song,* p. 137.

42 It is significant that of the 10 existing so-called high religions (those with transcultural impact) Hinduism is the oldest (c.3,000 BC). Judaism would follow but during the 70 years of the Babylonian exile five more surfaced. Two of these were Indian — Buddhism and Jainism — and both split from Hinduism over the caste system and the Hindu obsession with so many different gods.

43 Stanley quotes 2 *Corinthians* 5:15 that speaks of reconciliation. Graham, pp. 138f.

44 *Song,* p. 139.

45 *Song,* p. 140.

46 *Song,* pp. 140ff.

47 *Song,* pp. 141ff.

48 *Song,* p. 284.

49 Jones, *Circular Letter,* July 3, 1930. Asbury Archives.

50 For interesting parallels to this book, Cf.: http://urantiabooksources.com/pdf/194.pdf. © 2014 Matthew Block.

51 Albin, pp. 5f.

52 *Song,* pp. 222-233. Quoted in Albin, p. 6.

53 Albin, p. 6.

54 *Song,* p. 233.

55 *Wife.* p. 66.

56 *Wife.* p. 68.

57 Mabel Jones, *Newsletter,* January 14, 1931.

58 Mabel Jones, *Newsletter,* October 6, 1931.

59 *Love Affair,* p. 43.

60 *Circular Letter,* October 1, 1930.

61 *Circular Letter,* December 22, 1930.

62 Jones, *Indian Witness,* June 18, 1931. Cf. Letter to Miss Nellie, July 9, 1931, Asbury Archives.

63 *Wife.* pp. 70f.

64 Graham. p. 198. Cf. p. 213 on the Great Depression. Cf. *Wife.* p. 71.

65 *Wife.* p. 71.

66 Graham, pp. 207ff. More of the story of the remarkable Ambedkar will emerge in 1936 when Ambedkar would attempt to abolish the caste system or (much to Gandhi's dismay) take the depressed classes out of Hinduism.

67 Jones, *Indian Witness,* April 14, 1932. Asbury Archives.

68 Graham, p. 233.

69 Copplestone, p. 1136.

70 The October 3,1932 *Circular Letter,* and the December 15, 1932, *Indian Witness.*

71 Asbury Seminary Archives.

72 Jones, Letter to Diffendorfer, December 19, 1932.

73 These figures were reported in a letter to Diffendorfer, December 19, 1932.

74 *Harijan,* February 11, 1933.

75 Graham, pp. 210ff.

CHAPTER SIX

1 Mabel, *Newsletter,* Nov. 6, 1933.

2 *Wife,* p. 72/79. Cf. p. 154.

3 *Wife,* pp. 80ff.

4 Mabel Jones, *Duplicate Letter*, March 25, 1935, Asbury Archives.

5 *Wife,* pp. 151, 154.

6 Jones, *Circular Letter,* February 3, 1934.

7 Jones, *Indian Witness,* April 5, 1934. Reprinted from the British newspaper, *The Methodist Times and Leader.*

8 Bunhill Fields is a non-conformist graveyard. Among other notables Isaac Watts, John Bunyan and Daniel DeFoe are also buried there.

9 Baroness von Boetselaer letter to Diffendorfer, March 22 1934, Asbury Archives.

10 Bishop Raymond Wade letter to Dr. John R. Edwards, Asbury Archives.

11 *Circular Letter,* dated July 5, 1934.

12 In Stanley's day the term "kingdom" had no gender awareness. It was not intended, especially with Stanley as with Jesus, to suggest a male dominated realm. Today he might have preferred, the "Realm of God" but to do so here would seem a bit artificial. Thank you for understanding.

13 *Song.* p. 160.

14 *Song,* p. 162.

15 *Song,* p. 164.

16 *Song,* pp. 166f.

17 *Song,* pp. 166f.

18 *Song,* p. 171.

19 *Song,* pp. 173f

20 Jones, *Indian Witness,* December 6, 1934. Asbury Archives.

21 *Song,* p. 146.

22 *Song,*p. 147.

23 Jones, *Circular Letter,* December 20, 1934. Asbury Archives.

24 The ISIS will not be defeated on the ground or by endless attacks from the air. Those battle lines were drawn, not in desert sands but in the heavens. We fight against principalities and powers. Ultimately our weapons are not of this world!

25 *Song,* p. 151. Islam (and ISIS for that matter) may be meeting this need better than we are right now.

26 *Wife,* pp. 81ff.

27 Jones, Mabel, *Duplicate Letter,* November 7, 1935. Asbury Archives. Cf. Graham, p. 99.

28 Jones, Letter to Diffendorfer, November 25, 1935. Asbury Archives.

29 Diffendorfer, Letter to Stanley, February 28, 1936. Asbury Archives.

30 Jones, *Circular Letter.* December 18, 1936.

31 *Wife,* p. 88. Cf. Graham, pp. 248f.

32 Jones, *Indian Witness* for February 13, 1936.

33 Graham, p. 226.

34 Mabel Jones, *Newsletter,* January 25, 1937.

35 Graham, p. 230.

36 *Love Affair with India*, p.112.

37 Jones, letter to Diffendorfer, July 26, 1937. Asbury Archives. Cf. Graham, pp. 252ff.

38 Jones, *Circular Letter*, August 18, 1937. Asbury Archives.

39 Jones, a note to Mabel typed at the bottom of her copy of his *Circular Letter*, August 18, 1937.

40 Jorgensen, letter to Stanley, September 22, 1937. Asbury Archives. Cf. Graham, pp. 256ff.

41 Frederick Libby's letter commenting on Stanley's article published in both the *Indian Witness* and the *Christian Century* , is in the Asbury Archives.

42 Graham, p. 257.

43 Graham, p. 261.

44 Frank M. Toothaker, chairman of the Los Angeles Conference of the Emergency Peace Campaign (an organization whose goal was to keep the U.S. out of war), was highly critical as well. Graham, pp. 260f.

45 Jones, "Apply Gandhi's Method to Japan," *Christian Century*, January 19, 1938.

46 Jones', letter to Lord Halifax, February 3, 1938, marked "Private and Confidential," is in the Methodist Archives.

47 Stanley does not relate his impression of Newbigin. We do know that Newbigin would speak at the 1988 event fifty years later.

48 Craig Clarkson, Ph.D., Clarkson's dissertation (on Tambaram) is excellent. Although I have some question about his pitting Stanley against the church when Stanley was simply looking for alternative ways for talking about reaching the upper castes for Christ, Clarkson knows the material (and understands history and theology).

49 Jones, "What I Missed At Madras" *Christian Century*, May 31, 1939.

50 Post-war Germany (including Martin Niemoller) realized that Germany had turned to Nazism and Fascism looking for something to bring life into coherence, a goal with meaning and purpose. They chose the totalitarianism—Nazism. It let them down. The same could be said for ISIS. We now see that what we all should be seeking is God's totalitarianism—the Kingdom of God.

51 *Song*, p. 157.

52 *Song* p. 158. ,

53 *Song*, p. 159.

54 Graham, p. 263.

55 *Wife*. p. 91.

56 *Wife*, p. 96.

57 *Song*. p. 180.

58 Note the reaction of the church in Charleston, S.C. after the young man murdered the very people who had just welcomed him into their fellowship. They forgave!— Cf. *Song,*p. 181.

59 Note: *Christ's Alternative to Communism* (1935).

60 *Song,* p. 183.

61 *Song,* p. 184.

62 Notes from a talk on Stanley Jones by Anne Mathews-Younes, Cf. *Song,* p. 187.

63 *Song.* p. 189.

64 *Song,* pp. 191ff.

65 *Love Affair,* pp. 107-114. Bowen Memorial was named after a beloved American missionary who after arriving in India never left it. Stanley and Mabel had been married in that church twenty-eight years earlier.

66 *Love Affair,* p. 111.

67 *Love Affair,* p. 113.

68 Graham, pp. 208f.

69 *Song,* pp. 220ff. Graham gives a fairly detailed description of these events. pp. . 236-240.

70 Jones, *Indian Witness,* April 18, 1940.

71 Notes from the *North India Conference,* 1939, p. 254.

72 *Wife,* p. 99.

CHAPTER SEVEN

1 *Song,* p. 192.

2 Asbury Seminary Archives

3 *Wife,* p. 154.

4 *The Christ of the American Road,* pp. 12f.

5 Clarence Hill, "An American Gandhi Leads Christian Campers in Religious Revival on Michigan's Sands," Asbury Seminary Archives.

6 Albin, pp. 3f.

7 *Song,* p. 224.

8 Albin, p. 4.

9 *Song,* p. 226.

10 *Song,* pp. 226f.

11 *Song,* p. 229.

12 *Song,* p. 227.

13 *Song,* p. 227.

14 *Song,* p. 226.

15 *Song,* p. 175. Cf. p. 391.

16 *Song,* p. 176.

17 *Song,* p. 177.

18 *Christian Century,* Mar. 19,1941. Cf., *The Christ of the American Road,* p. 67.

19 *Song,* p. 196. Cf. Graham, p. 266.

20 Undated *Circular Letter,* Cf. Graham, p. 266.

21 Jones, *Letter to Miss Nellie,* March 8, 1941.

22 Jones, *Letter to Brother Parr.* April 2, 1941

23 Jones, *Letter to Miss Nellie,* March 22, 1941.

24 Jones, *Letter to Brother Parr,* April 3, 1941.

25 Mabel Jones, *Newsletter,* August 4, 1941.

26 *Song,* pp.194f.

27 Graham, p. 280.

28 Jones *Letter to Brother Parr,* April 3, 1941

29 Jones, *Letter to Mrs. Robinson,* Asbury Seminary Archives.

30 Jones, *Letter to Brother Parr,* April 3, 1941.

31 Mabel Jones, *Newsletter,* August 4, 1941.

32 Anne Mathews-Younes article, "Japan Peace Talks." Cf. Graham, pp. 268, 269.

33 Jones, "An Adventure in Failure: Behind the Scenes Before Pearl Harbor," *Asia and the Americas,* December 1945, p. 611.

34 An unpublished letter from Gwen Terasaki provided by her daughter Mariko Terasaki, Cf. *Song,* p. 197.

35 Stanley would eventually publish two accounts of his activities in D.C. between September and December 1941. The first in December 1945 just after the end of the war in a periodical, *Asia and the Americas,* the second, 23 years later in his spiritual autobiography, *A Song of Ascents.* pp. 188ff.

36 *Indian Witness,* July 7, 1949, "The Greatest Christian Opportunity on Our Planet," pp. 508f.

37 Jones, "What Is America's Role in This Crisis," *The Christian Century,* p.388.

38 Graham, p. 275. Graham's book, *The Totalitarian Kingdom of God,* is an excellent study of these issues. Cf. pp. 99-109.

39 Graham, pp. 275f.

40 *The Christ of the American Road,* pp. 76f.

41 *Song,* p. 2.

42 Jones, *Circular Letter,* August 29, 1942.

43 *The Sunday Before.* ("Sermons by Pacific Coast Pastors of the Japanese race on the Sunday before Evacuation to Assembly centers in the late spring of 1942"). ed. Allan Hunter and Gurney Binford.

44 Jones, *Letter to Miss Nellie,* March 7, 1942.

45 *Graham,* p. 282.

46 Jones, *Letter to Miss Nellie,* March 7, 1942.

47 *Newsletter,* September, 1942. *Wife,* p. 104.

48 *Love Affair with India,* pp. 117f.

49 Mabel Jones, *Newsletter.* August 4. 1941.

50 Mabel Jones, *Newsletter,* July 12, 1943.

51 Jones' *Letter to to Roosevelt,* August 10, 1942, Asbury Seminary Archives.

52 Jones' Letter to Roosevelt, January 5, 1943, Asbury Seminary Archives.

53 The letter from this Methodist pastor in Texas and Jones' reply are in the Methodist Archives.

54 Jones, Letter to Ralph Diffendorfer, January 22, 1943, Asbury Seminary Archives.

55 Jones, Letter to the Methodist World Service Agencies, December 12, 1942. See, the Methodist Archives. Cf. *The Christ of the American Road.* pp. 75-79.

56 Graham, p. 283.

57 Jones, *The Christ of the American Road,* p. 169.

58 Jones, *The Christ of the American Road.* p. 191.

59 Jones, Letter to Roosevelt, January 5, 1943, in the Asbury Seminary Archives.

60 Jones, Letter to Diffendorfer, February 26, 1943,

61 Jones, *The Christ of the American Road.* pp. 152f.

62 Jones, *Circular Letter,* August 30, 1943. Asbury Archives.

63 *Song,* p. 222.

64 Jones, *Christian Century,* June, 1943.

65 Graham, p. 289.

66 Jones, *Indian Witness.* August 12, 1943.

67 Jones, *Circular Letter,* January 16, 1944.

68 Jones, Letter to FDR, December 30, 1943. Asbury Archives, Cf. Graham, pp. 302, 305.

69 For an excellent discussion of this Cf. Graham, pp. 302-305.

70 Jones, Letter to L. R. Pennington, June 19, 1944. Asbury Archives

71 Jones, Letter to Pickett on May 31, 1944. Cf. Graham, p. 300.

72 Jones, *The Christ of the American Road.* p. 191.

73 Jones, *The Christ of the American Road..* pp. 191f.

74 Jones, *The Christ of the American Road,* pp. 192-200. Graham has a detailed account of these issues in his discussion of *The Christ of the American Road,* pp. 374ff.

75 Jones, *The Christ of the American Road,* pp. 193ff.

76 Jones, Letter to the Columbus and Buffalo meetings, December 18, 1944. Asbury Archive.

77 Graham, p. 301.

78 Jones, *Circular Letter.* September 4, 1944.

79 Anne Mathews-Younes, a term paper at Wesley Theological Seminary.

80 Jones, Letter to Murray Titus, October 12, 1944.

81 Jones, Letter to O. G. Robinson, November 2, 1944. Perhaps we can understand why Stanley did not vote but I add, "Sometime it is the lesser of two evils. May I

say, please vote! No matter what!"

82 Jones, *Circular Letter,* December 30, 1944.

83 Jones, *Circular Letter,* December 30, 1944.

84 Jones, Letter to Edward R. Stettinius, December 18, 1944. Asbury Archives. Cf. Graham. p. 308.

85 Jones, *CircularLetter,* December 30, 1944.

86 It is significant that in spite of Stanley's absence in San Francisco, a group of Protestant churches "did influence the final wording of the UN Charter." See December 18, 1944. Jones, Letter to E. R. Stettinius, Asbury Archives.

87 Jones, *Indian Witness,* "Report on Latin American Evangelistic Tour," October 25, 1945.

88 Jones, *The Christian Century,* "What I Found in Latin America." The article is in both the July 18 and the July 25, 1945 editions. Cf. Graham, pp. 310f.

89 Jones, *The Indian Witness,* "Report on Latin American Evangelistic Tour," October 25, 1945.

90 Anne Mathews-Younes paper, "Japan Peace Talk." September 29, 2016.

91 Anne Mathews-Younes paper, "Japan Peace Talk."

92 *Song,* p. 207. Cf. Graham, p. 269.

93 Jones, "An Adventure in Failure: Behind the Scenes Before Pearl Harbor," p. 616.

94 Mabel Jones, Letter to Dr. Sutherland, June 8, 1945.

CHAPTER EIGHT

1 *Song,* p. 231. Cf. p. 297.

2 Jones, Letter to Miss Nellie, January 7, 1946. Asbury Archives.

3 *Gandhi,* p. 19.

4 *Gandhi,* pp. 42ff.

5 *Wife.* p. 118.

6 Jones, *The Christian Century,* July 17, 1946.

7 *Wife,* p. 112f.

8 "Cross Reference Sheet for the Administrative Committee of the Mission Board of the Methodist Church," November 14, 1946.

9 Jones, Letter to Eunice and James Mathews, September 29, 1946.

10 Vohra, Ranbir, *The Making of India, A Historical Survey (1997).* p. 183.

11 Jones, Letter to James Mathews, November 22, 1946.

12 Graham, p. 318.

13 Jones, *Circular Letter,* December 30, 1946, Asbury Archives.

14 Anne Mathews-Younes, "Mental Health/Psychology."

15 Jones, *Circular Letter*, January 5, 1947.

16 Jones, *Circular Letter*, April 1, 1947. Asbury Archives.

17 Jones, Family letter, June 5, 1947, Methodist Archives.

18 Jones, Letter to Jinnah, May 12, 1947. Asbury Archives.

19 Jones, Family Letter, May 17, 1947. Asbury Archives.

20 Vorah, *The Making of India*, p. 183.

21 Mabel Jones, Letter to her friends, May 10, 1947, on loan from Anne Mathews-Younes.

22 *Wife*, p. 118.

23 *Wife*, p. 119.

24 *Love Affair*, p. 130.

25 Mabel Jones, Letter to her friends, September 8, 1947, on loan from Anne Mathews-Younes.

26 On February 20, 1949 Mabel would write a handout for missionaries on "Writing Effective *Circular Letters*." Cf. Wife, pp. 121-124.

27 Graham, p. 328.

28 *Wife*, p. 120. Hendershot interview with Irene Frese, March 27, 2004.

29 *Gandhi*, pp. 36ff.

30 *Gandhi, p. 38.*

31 *Gandhi*, pp. 38, Cf. p. 59.

32 *Song*, pp. 260ff. Cf. *Love Affair with India*, p. 145.

33 Bishop Raines, February 17, 1967, letter to Harvey Kazmier, Asbury Archives.

34 Jones, *Indian Witness*, "The Greatest Christian Opportunity," July 7, 1949. p. 508.

35 Graham, p. 337.

36 Michio Kozaki, Letter to Stanley Jones. Asbury Archives.

37 Mabel Jones, Letter, May 2, 1949, on loan by the family.

38 See below correspondence between Stanley and Nehru (Stanley would write on May 20, 1952 and Nehru would reply, May 29, 1952).

39 Graham, p. 344.

40 *Song*, p. 200. Letter from Dulles to Jones, February 9, 1951. Asbury Archives

41 *Wife*, p.125f.

42 Anne Mathews-Younes, "Mental Health/Psychology."

CHAPTER NINE

1 Ruffle, pp. 34ff.

2 Ruffle, p. 35.

3 Stanley uses the term, "disentangled Jesus." "Untrammeled Jesus" is perhaps the

better term in translation.

4 Ruffle, p. 40.

5 Stanley Jones was more than a man of influence; he was a man of faith who completely surrendered his life to an unchanging Savior, Jesus Christ, in order to enter that unshakable Kingdom of God.

Dr. Ruffle writes with passion and balance about the whole gospel for the whole world. The insights shared here should be studied and understood by missionaries (oberro fraternals), both at home and abroad.

6 Anne Mathews-Younes has compiled an excellent book taken from Mary Webster's unpublished autobiography and sermons, recently published by the E. Stanley Jones Foundation, *The Life and Ministry of Mary Webster, A Witness in the Evangelistic Ministry of E. Stanley Jones.*

7 *The Life of Mary Webster*, p. 33f.

8 *Mary Webster*, pp. 34f.

9 Jones, *Circular Letter*, April 30, 1950.

10 *Mary Webster*, p.57.

11 *Graham*, p, 362.

12 Jones, *Indian Witness*, June 18, 1959.

13 *Mary Webster*, pp. 41-44.

14 *Mary Webster*, pp. 45f.

15 *Mary Webster*, pp. 102-108 (excerpts).

16 Jones, *Christ at the Round Table*, p. 109.

17 This "conversation," compiled by Anne Mathews-Younes, is constructed using Mary's unpublished autobiography interspersed with Brother Stanley's writing about Mary, drawn from his book, *Growing Spiritually*, 1953.

18 MabelJones,"*Duplicate Letter*," January 22, 1952.

19 Mabel Jones, "*Duplicate Letter*," May 20, 1952.

20 Jones, *The Christian Century*, "India at the Polls," May 21, 1952, p. 616.

21 Jones, *Indian Witness*, June 11, 1953.

22 Sabrow Yasumura, "Three Months' Tour with E. Stanley Jones," p. 222. Asbury Archives.

23 Latourette, *Christianity in a Revolutionary Age,* Vol. V, p. 302.

24 *Wife.* p. 155.

25 *Wife.* p. 125.

26 Jones, *Circular Letter, June 26, 1954.* Cf. Graham, pp. 360, 366.

27 *Wife*, p. 151

28 Jones, *Indian Witness*, "Evangelism in Japan after the Occupation," pp. 189f.

29 Jones, "*Circular Letter*," January, 1956, Asbury Archives.

30 Jones, *Circular Letter, 1956,* Asbury Archives.

31 Jones, Letter to Eisenhower, January 11, 1957, Asbury Archives.

32 Mabel Jones, *Educational Adventures in India,* pp. 41f.

33 *Wife.* p. 127.

34 Jim Mathews Letter to ESJ, August, 1957.

35 Mabel Jones, "Duplicate Letter," October 18, 1957.

36 Jones, *Circular Letter,* April 30, 1950, Asbury Archives.

37 Jones, *Circular Letter,* January 25, 1958. Asbury Archives.

38 Letter from Alexander Reid, February 25, 1958, Asbury Archives.

39 Jones, "The Seven Main Needs of the Christian Movement in Japan," *Indian Witness,* June,16, 1959, p. 196.

40 This letter of resignation to the President of Asbury College can be found in the Asbury College Archives.

41 Jones, Letter to R. G. Casey, April 11, 1959, Asbury Archives.

42 *Wife,* p. 151.

43 *Song,* p. 298.

44 *Song,* p. 298.

45 *Song,* p. 299.

CHAPTER TEN

1 *Song,* pp. 335f.

2 *Graham,* p. 371.

3 *Song,* p. 353.

4 Mabel Jones, *Circular Letter,* February 10, 1960.

5 Frederic Fox, "Letter," May 25, 1960(Asbury Archives).

6 *Love Affair,* pp. 139f.

7 *Wife,* p. 127.

8 See a five page "Introduction" to the records of the United Christian Ashrams, Special Collections Department, Asbury Seminary. See also a book compiled and edited by Anne Mathews-Younes, *A History of the Christian Ashram in North America.*

9 Jones, *Indian Witness,* August 24, 1961.

10 *The Stockholms-Tidningen* was a Swedish language morning newspaper published in Stockholm, Sweden, between 1889 and 1984.

11 Jones, *Circular Letter,* January 7, 1963. United Christian Ashram Archives, Asbury Seminary.

12 *Wife.* pp.127f.

13 *Time Magazine,* January 24, 1964. p. 34.

14 Jones, *Circular Letter,* 1964 . Asbury Archives.

15 Expanding on this, in 1978, Bishop Mathews would join Mohammad Ali, Vice

President Walter Mondale, Dick Gregory, Buffy St. Marie, Stevie Wonder, and Marlon Brando in "The Longest Walk" in Washington, D. C., which drew national attention to the plight of Native Americans.

16 Mabel Jones, *Duplicate Letter*, June, 1964 (family personal collection).

17 *Song*, p.256. Cf. Graham, pp. 374, 376.

18 *Song*, p. 260.

19 Graham, p. 374.

20 *Song*, pp. 259f.

21 Mabel Jones, "*Duplicate Letter*," January 20, 1965 (private collection).

22 Jones, *Circular Letter*, April 27, 1965 (Ashram Archives, Asbury). Recall a similar statement from 1957.

23 "God's voice is heard small" is an expression frequently used by Oral Roberts when referring to places where the witness for Jesus was seldom if ever heard.

24 An Asherah pole is a sacred tree or pole that stood near Canaanite religious locations to honor the Ugaritic mother-goddess Asherah, consort of El.

25 Jones, *Circular Letter*, December 2, 1965, Asbury Archives.

26 Jones, notes on a private conversation with Altizer, Asbury Archives.

27 Graham, p. 373.

28 Richard Phillips Letter, January 18, 1966, Asbury Archives.

29 Jones, *Circular Letter*, July 1967, Asbury Archives.

30 Pigweed, for those who are interested, is called Amaranth.

31 Mabel Jones, *Duplicate Letter*, March 27, 1967.

32 *Wife*, p. 128.

33 *Love Affair with India*, p.135.

34 It should be noted that the "first principle" of Christianity mentioned several times throughout comes from the words of Jesus. If you had to reduce them to one sentence it would probably read something like this: "The only way to gain your life is to lose it; the only way to be first is to be last; and the only way to be great is to be servant of all."

35 Mary Webster letter to Anne Mathews, April 18, 1968. Private collection.

36 Mabel Jones, *Duplicate Letter*, July, 1968.

37 Jones, Letter to Eunice, Jim and Anne, October, 1968.

38 *Love Affair*, pp. 141f.

39 Stanley letter from Pago Pago, American Samoa, to Eunice, Jim and the rest, August 28, 1969.

40 Jones, *The Indian Witness*, May 21, 1970.

41 *Song*, p. 286.

42 *Song*, p. 298.

43 *Song*, p. 287.

44 *Song*, p. 288.

45 *Song*, p. 257. Cf. *Colossians* 3:9-11.

46 *Song*, p. 258.

47 *Song*, p. 259.

48 *Song*, p. 260.

49 *Song*, p. 261.

50 *Song*, p. 261

51 *Song*, p. 262.

52 *Song*, p. 272, Cf. p. 297.

CHAPTER ELEVEN

1 *Wife*, p. 128.

2 Undated private letter from Stanley to Eunice and Jim.

3 Family letter from a private collection.

4 Indira Gandhi served as her father Jawaharlal Nehru's personal assistant and hostess during his tenure as prime minister between 1947 and 1964. She was elected Congress President in 1959. Upon her father's death in 1964 she was appointed as a member of the Rajya Sabha (upper house) and became a member of Lal Bahadur Shastri's cabinet as Minister of Information and Broadcasting. She served as Prime Minister 1966-1977.

5 During a personal phone conversation with Dr. Escamilla he remembers meeting Stanley at the airport and the drive but does not recall with certainty that Mabel was there.

6 Jones, *Circular Letter*, October 1971. Asbury Archives.

7 The Provisional Government of the People's Republic of Bangladesh was established following the declaration of independence of East Pakistan on April 10, 1971. Cf. Graham, pp. 381, 384.

8 Jones, *"Memo to the Seven,"* January 3, 1772, Asbury Archives

9 Indira Gandhi Letter, January 5, 1972, Asbury Archives.

10 Jones, Letter, January 15, 1972, to the Board of the United Christian Ashram, Asbury Archives.

11 *A History of the Christian Ashrams in North America,* compiled and edited by Anne Mathews-Younes, pp. 196 ff.

12 It is interesting to note that John Wesley, who lived into his 89th year, is also said to have preached 60,000 sermons.

13 Mabel Wagner, who grew up in India was a cousin of Stanley through his brother - a cousin-in-law actually. Her husband, Paul Wagner, was involved in the Christian Ashram movement and there is information on both of them in the Ashram History book compiled by Mathews-Younes throughout, but specifically under the General Secretary appendix.

14 The Simla Agreement (or Shimla Agreement) was signed between India and

Pakistan on July 2, 1972 in Simla, the capital city of the Indian state of Himachal Pradesh. Graham, p. 382.

15 *Wife,* pp.150f. p.155.

16 *Wife,* . p. 156.

17 *Wife,* p. 128.

18 Jones, this "Collective Letter," January 7, 1973, from the Sat Tal Ashram, is in the Asbury Archives.

19 David Henderson's account of Stanley's last weeks is dated December 17, 1973. This is probably a transcription of an audio tape made by David Henderson. Asbury Archives.

20 Premila's husband was the Manager of the Sat Ashram and Estate until Lillian Wallace turned the charge over to him when she left. Premila's father, Manni Dutt Patial, had a very interesting history as well. He was an orphan out of a Hindu background. Lillian Wallace says that "He was the Lords helper and spokesman in his own right." Manni was a member of the same Bareilly Methodist Conference as Stanley. Private correspondence.

21 *Wife,* pp. 129, 146.

22 Graham, p. 385.

23 *Song,* p. 16.

24 Graham, pp. 385ff.

25 *Wife,* pp. 128ff.

CHAPTER TWELVE

1 *Song,* p. 284.

2 Jones, *The Christ of the American Road.* pp. 76f.

3 Jones, *Circular Letter.* August 29, 1942.

4 Jones, Letter to James Mathews, November. 22, 1946.

5 *Song,* p. 257. Cf. *Colossians* 3:9-11.

6 *Song,* p. 260.

7 *Song,* p. 261

8 *Song,* p. 261

9 *Song,* p. 255.

10 *Song,* p. 256.

11 Harper, Steve, *For the Sake of the Bride,* Abingdon Press, 2014.

12 Anne Mathews-Younes paper, "Japan Peace Talk." September 29, 2016.

13 Anne Mathews-Younes paper, "Japan Peace Talk."

14 Shivraj K. Mahendra, "Stanley Jones on Peace and Justice," Unpublished article, 2017. Jones' quotes from *Growing Spiritually,* pp. 148-149. This article was a talk given at the 14th Peace and Justice Conference in Kobe, Japan, Sep. 2017.

15 Shivraj K. Mahendra, "Stanley Jones on Peace and Justice," Unpublished article, 2017. Jones' quotes from *Growing Spiritually*, p. 154, *The Way to Power and Pois*, p. 240. Emphasis mine.

16 Shivraj K. Mahendra, "Stanley Jones on Peace and Justice," Unpublished article, 2017. Jones' thoughts from *The Choice Before Us*, (p. 173) and *The Christ of the American Road*, (p. 76).

17 Shivraj K. Mahendra, "Stanley Jones on Peace and Justice," Unpublished article, 2017. Notes in parenthesis are mine.

18 Shivraj K. Mahendra, "Stanley Jones on Peace and Justice," Unpublished article, 2017. Notes in parenthesis are mine.

19 Jones, *The Christ of the American Road*. pp. 152f.

20 Jones, *Circular Letter*, April 16, 1943. Asbury Archives.

21 *Song*, p. 298.

22 *Song*, p. 298.

23 *Song*, p. 299.

24 Jones, *The Christ of the Indian Road*, p. 7.

25 *Song*, p. 176.

26 *Song*, p. 177.

27 See Chapter 3 above.

28 *Song*, p. 108.

29 *Christ at the Round Table* would be the second book Stanley published (1928).

30 Jones, "*Circular Letter*," April 20, 1926.

31 Stanley's first mention of the Round Table conferences was in his *Circular Letter*, 1923.

32 Henry Knight, Professor of Wesleyan Studies at St. Paul's School of Theology, has written a book, *Anticipating Heaven Below*. Knight takes seriously Christian aspirations while grounding them in the realities of our present life. Stanley Jones would applaud.

33 Jones, *CircularLetter*, December 30, 1944.

34 Graham, pp. 297f.

35 Jones, *The Christ of the American Road*. p. 191.

36 *Song*, p. 175. Cf. p. 391.

37 Albin, p. 6.

38 *Song*, p. 233.

39 *Song*, p. 305.

40 *Song*, p. 306.

41 *Song*, p. 307. I once wrote a MA thesis, "An Evangelical Approach to Social Action Involving the Work of the Holy Spirit as Found in the Farewell Discourse of Jesus" — John 13:31-16:33.

42 *Song*, p. 380.

43 *Song,*p. 20.

44 *Wife,* p. 143.

45 *Love Affair,* p. 137. See above, Chapter 3, p. 96.

46 *Wife,* p. 72, 79. Cf. p. 154. See above, Chapter 5, p. 127.

CONCLUSION

1 Graham, pp. 349, 351.

2 *Song,* p. 373

3 *Song,* p. 374.

4 *Song,* p. 375.

5 *Song,* p. 376.

6 *Song,* p. 377

7 *Song,* p. 378

8 *Song,* p. 379.

9 *Song,* p. 380.

10 *Song,* p. 381.

11 *Song,* pp. 382, 383.

12 *Song,* p. 384.

13 *Song,* p. 385.

14 *Song,* p. 386.

15 *Song,* p. 387.

16 *Song,* p. 388.

17 *Song,* p. 389.

18 *Song,* p. 390.

19 *Song, pp. 391, 392.*

20 *Song,* p. 393.

21 *Song,* p. 394.

22 *Song,* p. 395.

23 *Song,* p. 97. Emphasis mine.

Bibliography

Adeney, Miriam. "Esther Across Cultures: Indigenous Leadership Roles for Women." *Missiology* 15 no. 3 (July 1987): pp. 323-335.

Albin, Tom, a chapter in an edited book, *E. Stanley Jones and Sharing the Good News in a Pluralistic Society.* 2017.

Bowie, Fiona, Deborah Kirkland, and Shirley Ardener. *Women and Missions: Past and Present.* Ann Arbor, MI: Edwards Brothers, 1993.

Chamberlain, Martha. *A Love Affair with India: The Story of the Wife and Daughter of E. Stanley Jones,* 2009.

Clarkson, Craig R. *Who Says Mission, Says Church: The Church-Mission Affirmation of Tambaram, 1938,* Ph.D. dissertation, Baylor University, 2015.

Collins, Kenneth. *A Real Christian Life.* Abingdon Press, 1999

Copplestone, J. Tremayne, *History of Methodist missions, Vol. 4: Twentieth Century Perspectives,* NY: Board of Global Ministries of the United Methodist Church, 1973.

Graham, Stephen. *Ordinary Man, Extraordinary Mission,* Abingdon, 2005.

Hardin, Joyce. "Missionary Women." *Institute for Mission and Evangelism* 3 (31ff.).

Harijan Magazine.

Harmon, Nolan, ed. *The Encyclopedia of World Methodism,* United Methodist Publishing House, 1974.

Harper, Steve. *For the Sake of the Bride,* Abingdon Press, 2014.

Hendershot, Kathryn. *E. Stanley Jones Had a Wife,* Scarecrow Press, 2007.

Henry Knight, III. *Anticipating Heaven Below,* Cascade Books, 2014.

Hollister, John. *The Century of the Methodist Church in S.E. Asia:* Lucknow Publishing House, 1956.

James, Edward, Janet Wilson James, and Paul S. Boyer, eds. *Notable American Women* Vol. II Cambridge MA: Harvard Press, 1971.

Jones, E. Stanley. *A Song of Ascents* (1968, his spiritual autobiography).

Jones, E. Stanley. *Abundant Living* (1942, devotional).

Jones, E. Stanley. *Along the Indian Road* (1939).

Jones, E. Stanley. *Christ and Human Suffering* (1933).

Jones, E. Stanley. *Christ and Present World Issues* (1937).

Jones, E. Stanley. *Christ at the Round Table* (1928).

Jones, E. Stanley. *Christ's Alternative to Communism* (1935, US title). *Christ and Communism* (1935, UK title).

Jones, E. Stanley. *Christian Maturity* (1957, devotional).

Jones, E. Stanley. *Circular Letters,* various issues.

Jones, E. Stanley. *Conversion* (1959)

Jones, E. Stanley. *Growing Spiritually* (1953, devotional).

Jones, E. Stanley. *How to be a Transformed Person* (1951, devotional).

Jones, E. Stanley. *How to Pray* (1943), booklet

Jones, E. Stanley. *In Christ* (1961, devotional)

Jones, E. Stanley. *Is the Kingdom of God Realism?* (1940).

Jones, E. Stanley. *Mahatma Gandhi: An Interpretation* (1948).

Jones, E. Stanley. *Mastery* (1955, devotional).

Jones, E. Stanley. *The Choice Before Us* (1937).

Jones, E. Stanley. *The Christ of Every Road – A study in Pentecost* (1930).

Jones, E. Stanley. *The Christ of the American Road* (1944)

Jones, E. Stanley. *The Christ of the Indian Road* (1925).

Jones, E. Stanley. *The Christ of the Mount – A Working Philosophy of Life* (1931).

Jones, E. Stanley. *The Divine Yes* (1975, posthumously).

Jones, E. Stanley. *The Indian Witness,* various issues.

Jones, E. Stanley. *The Reconstruction of the Church – On what Pattern?* (1970).

Jones, E. Stanley. *The Unshakable Kingdom and the Unchanging Person* (1972).

Jones, E. Stanley. *The Way* (1946, devotional).

Jones, E. Stanley. *The Way to Power and Poise* (1949, devotional).

Jones, E. Stanley. *The Word Became Flesh* (1963, devotional)

Jones, E. Stanley. *Victorious Living* (1936, devotional).

Jones, E. Stanley. *Victory Through Surrender* (1966).

Jones, Mabel. *Duplicate Letters,* various issues.

Jones, Mabel. *Educational Adventures in India,* unpublished memoirs.

Latourette, Kenneth Scott. *Christianity in a Revolutionary Age,* Harper 1962.

Latourette, Kenneth Scott. *Mission Tomorrow,* Harper, 1936.

Liddle, Joanna, and Rama Joshi. *Daughters of Independence: Gender, Caste and Class in India.* Rutgers University. 1986.

Mahendra, Shivraj K. "E. Stanley Jones on Peace and Justice" (Unpublished paper, Asbury Theological Seminary) 2017.

Mathews, Eunice and James. "My Father, E. Stanley Jones," *United Methodist Today,* June 1975.

Mathews, Eunice and James. "Stanley Jones — as Father (and Father-in-Law), *Transformation,* Winter 1983.

Mathews, Eunice and James. *Selections from E. Stanley Jones,* Abingdon, 1968.

Mathews, James. *A Global Odyssey,* Abingdon, 2000.

Mathews-Younes, Anne. *History of the Christian in North America,* ESJF, 2017.

Mathews-Younes, Anne. *Life and Ministry of Mary Webster,* ESJF, 2017.

Mathews-Younes, Anne. *Living Upon the Way,* ESJF, 2018.

McClendon, James, Jr. *Biography as Theology.* Trinity Press, 1974.

McPhee, Arthur. "Pickett's Fire: The life, Contribution, Thought and Legacy of J. Waskom Pickett, Methodist Missionary to India." Ph.D. dissertation, Asbury E.S.J. School of World Mission and Evangelism, 2001.

Moynahan, Brian, *The Faith,* Doubleday, 2002.

Norwood, Frederick. *The Story of Methodism in America.* Abingdon Press, 1973.

Pickett, J. Waskom. "The Promising Young Stanley," *The Indian Witness,* March 15, 1973.

Pickett, J. Waskom. *My Twentieth Century Odyssey.* Bombay, India: Gospel Literature Service, 1980.

Robert, Dana. "Revisioning the Women's Missionary Movement." In *The Good News of the Kingdom.* Dean S. Gilliland, Charles Van Engen and Paul Piersen, Eds. Orbis Books, 1993.

Robert, Dana. *American Women in Mission:* Mercer University Press. 1997.

Ruffle, Douglas, *The Missionary Mindset,* Discipleship Resources, 2016.

Seamands, John T., *Pioneers of the Younger Churches.* Wipf and Stock Publishers, 1967 (2002).

Snyder, Howard. "Missions, North American." pp. 1279-1286, *Encylopedia of Protestanism,* Vol. 3. edited by Hans Hillerbrand. Routledge Publishing Co., 2004.

The Indian Witness.

Tucker, Ruth. "Biography as Missiology: Mining the Lives of Missionaries for Cross-Cultural Effectiveness." *Missiology* 27 (April 1999): pp. 429-440.

Tucker, Ruth. "Female Mission Strategists." *Missiology* 15 (January 1987): pp. 73-88.

Tuttle, Robert. *On Giant Shoulders,* Discipleship Resources, 1984.

Tuttle, Robert. *The Story of Evangelism,* Abingdon, 2005.

Vohra, Ranbir. *The Making of India: A Historical Survey.* Armonk, N.Y. and London. 1997.

Webster, Mary (Tattersall). "In Loving Remembrance of Brother Stanley," *Transformation,* Winter 1983, pp. 14f.

Winter, Ralph and Steven Hawthorne. *Perspectives on the World Christian Movment* 3rd. edition. Pasadena, CA: William Carey Library, 1998.

Yasumura, Sabrow. "Three Months' Tour with E. Stanley Jones," *The Japan Christian Quarterly,* Summer 1953.

ABOUT THE AUTHOR

ROBERT G. TUTTLE, JR. is the Emeritus Professor of World Christianity at Asbury Theological Seminary. He lives with his wife, Dianne, in Cashiers, NC and Vero Beach, FL.

ABOUT THE E. STANLEY JONES FOUNDATION

The E. Stanley Jones Foundation is dedicated to bold and fruitful evangelism which shares the life-changing message of Jesus Christ to persons of all ages, backgrounds, life asituations and locations. The Foundation is also dedicated to preserving and extending the legacy of the late E. Stanley Jones who blessed millions of people around the world with his preaching, teaching and prolific written words proclaiming Jesus is Lord! Our vision is to reach every generation with the message of Jesus Christ; enlighten spiritual growth through education and inspiration; prepare both Christian leaders and laity to be followers of Jesus Christ, and make known the Kingdom of God today.

For more information and our current
programs, kindly visit us at:

www.estanleyjonesfoundation.com

Follow us on YouTube.

OTHER PUBLICATIONS
OF THE E. STANLEY JONES FOUNDATION

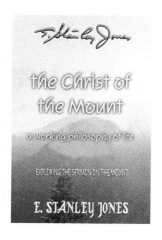

The Christ of the Mount:
A Working Philosophy of Life
Authored by E. Stanley Jones
List Price: $15.99
6" x 9" (15.24 x 22.86 cm)
312 pages
ISBN-13: 978-1542896030
(CreateSpace-Assigned)
ISBN-10: 1542896037
BISAC: Religion / Biblical Meditations /
New Testament

The Life and Ministry of Mary
Webster: A Witness in the Evangelistic
Ministry of E. Stanley Jones *Authored by*
Anne Mathews-Younes
List Price: $14.99
6" x 9" (15.24 x 22.86 cm)
286 pages
ISBN-13: 978-1544191799 (CreateSpace-
Assigned)
ISBN-10: 1544191790
BISAC: Religion / Christian Life / Spiritual
Growth

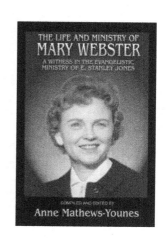

435

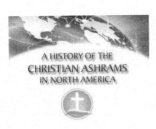

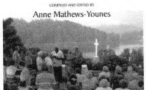

A History of the Christian Ashrams in North America
Compiled and Edited by Anne Mathews-Younes
List Price: $34.99
6" x 9" (15.24 x 22.86 cm)
528 pages
ISBN-13: 978-547229017
(CreateSpace-Assigned)
ISBN-10: 1547229012
BISAC: Religion / Christianity / History / General

Is The Kingdom of God Realism?
Authored by E. Stanley Jones, Foreword by Leonard Sweet, Afterword by Howard Snyder
List Price: $19.99
6" x 9" (15.24 x 22.86 cm)
428 pages
ISBN-13: 978-1976151514 (CreateSpace-Assigned)
ISBN-10: 1976151511
BISAC: Religion / Christianity / General

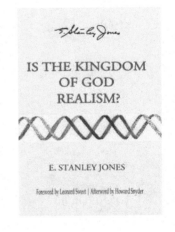

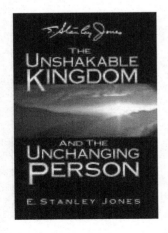

The Unshakable Kingdom and the Unchanging Person
Authored by E. Stanley Jones
List Price: $18.99
6" x 9" (15.24 x 22.86 cm)
408 pages
ISBN-13: 978-1974132935
(CreateSpace-Assigned)
ISBN-10: 1974132935
BISAC: Religion / Spirituality / General

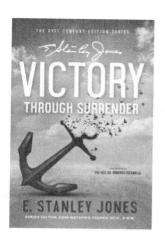

Victory Through Surrender
Authored by E. Stanley Jones, Preface by Anne Mathews-Younes
List Price: $12.99
6" x 9" (15.24 x 22.86 cm)
166 pages
ISBN-13: 978-1717548474
(CreateSpace-Assigned)
ISBN-10: 1717548474
BISAC: Religion / Christian Life / Professional Growth

A Love Affair With India: The Story of the Wife and Daughter of E. Stanley Jones
Authored by Martha Gunsalus Chamberlain, Preface by Anne Mathews-Younes
List Price: $14.99
6" x 9" (15.24 x 22.86 cm)
250 pages
ISBN-13: 978-1984960276
(CreateSpace-Assigned)
ISBN-10: 198496027X
BISAC: Biography & Autobiography

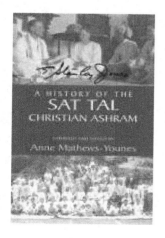

A History of the Sat Tal Christian Ashram (USA Edition)
Authored by Anne Mathews-Younes
List Price: $15.99
6" x 9" (15.24 x 22.86 cm)
238 pages
ISBN-13: 978-1722847524
(CreateSpace-Assigned)
ISBN-10: 1722847522
BISAC: Religion / Christianity / History /General

Living Upon the Way: Selected Sermons of E. Stanley Jones
Authored by Anne Mathews-Younes
List Price: $24.99
6" x 9" (15.24 x 22.86 cm)
454 pages
ISBN-13: 978-1724745736
(CreateSpace-Assigned)
ISBN-10: 1724745735
BISAC: Religion / Christianity / Sermons

Conversion
Authored by E. Stanley Jones
List Price: $15.99
6" x 9" (15.24 x 22.86 cm)
284 pages
ISBN-13: 978-1726458702
(CreateSpace-Assigned)
ISBN-10: 1726458709
BISAC: Religion / Christian living / Personal growth

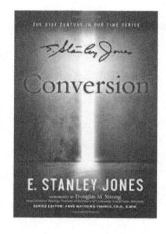

ALL PUBLICATIONS OF

The E. Stanley Jones Foundation

are available for purchase from:

www.estanleyjonesfoundation.com

and

www.amazon.com

Order your copies today!

Made in the
USA
Columbia, SC